Violence and Peace in Sacred Texts

Maria Power • Helen Paynter
Editors

Violence and Peace in Sacred Texts

Interreligious Perspectives

Editors
Maria Power
Las Casas Institute for Social Justice
University of Oxford
Oxford, UK

Helen Paynter
Centre for the Study of Bible
and Violence
Bristol Baptist College
Bristol, UK

ISBN 978-3-031-17803-0 ISBN 978-3-031-17804-7 (eBook)
https://doi.org/10.1007/978-3-031-17804-7

This Palgrave Macmillan imprint is published by the registered company Springer Nature Switzerland AG.
The registered company address is: Gewerbestrasse 11, 6330 Cham, Switzerland

Contents

1 **Introduction to the Volume** 1
Maria Power and Helen Paynter

2 **Violence and Peace in the *Mahābhārata* and *Rāmāyaṇa*** 9
Simon Brodbeck

3 **Spectres of Violence and Landscapes of Peace: Imagining the Religious Other in Patterns of Hindu Modernity** 29
Ankur Barua

4 **Jewish Interpretations of Biblical Violence** 53
Alan Mittleman

5 **A Hermeneutic of Violence in Jewish Legal Sources: The Case of the Kippah** 73
Laliv Clenman

6 **Buddhism and the Dilemma of Whether to Use Violence in Defence of a Way of Peace** 95
Peter Harvey

7 **Apologists and Appropriators: Protestant Christian Reckoning with Biblical Violence** 119
Helen Paynter

8 **Roman Catholic Teachings on Violence and Peace: The Credible Re-enactment of the Kingdom** 143
Maria Power

9 **Interpretations of Qurʾānic Violence in Shīʿī Islam** 165
Ali Hammoud

10 **Sacralized Violence in Sufism** 187
Minlib Dallh O. P.

11 **The Predicament of the *Sant-Sipahi* (Saint-Soldier): Sanctioned Violence and Martyrdom in the Sikh Tradition** 209
James M. Hegarty

12 **Experiences with Violence: Studying Sacred Text in Interreligious Dialogue** 237
Alisha Pomazon

Index 265

Notes on Contributors

Ankur Barua is university Senior Lecturer in Hindu Studies at the University of Cambridge. After a BSc in Physics from the University of Delhi, he read Theology and Religious Studies at the Faculty of Divinity, Cambridge, completing a PhD on the symbolism of time and embodiment in St Augustine and Rāmānuja. His primary research interests are Hindu Studies and the comparative philosophy of religion.

Simon Brodbeck was educated at the universities of Cambridge and London. He has worked at Cardiff University since 2008 and is a Reader in Religious Studies in the School of History, Archaeology and Religion. His research focuses most particularly on the Sanskrit *Mahābhārata*. His books include *The Mahābhārata Patriline* (2009), *Krishna's Lineage: the Harivamsha of Vyāsa's Mahābhārata* (2019), and *Divine Descent and the Four World-Ages in the Mahābhārata* (2022).

Laliv Clenman is Senior Lecturer in Rabbinic Literature at Leo Baeck College, London. She is also Visiting Senior Lecturer at King's College London. She teaches and supervises MA and PhD research in Rabbinic Literature and Jewish Studies. Her research explores challenging problems in Jewish law in antiquity, with a particular focus on issues of identity, gender, violence, and the construction of rabbinic authority.

Minlib Dallh O. P. is a Dominican friar and a visiting assistant professor at Candler School of Theology at Emory University in Atlanta GA (USA). His main field of research focuses on Islamic mystical tradition and he has a keen interest in comparative mysticism, with a special focus on love-mysticism in Judaism, Christianity, and Islam.

Ali Hammoud is a PhD candidate at Western Sydney University. He is broadly interested in Shīʿīsm, Islamic intellectual history, and the relationship between literature and philosophy. His thesis seeks to examine the history of Shīʿī philosophical commentaries on Rumi's magnum opus, the Masnavi.

Peter Harvey who holds his doctorate in Buddhist Studies at Lancaster University, under Ninian Smart, is Emeritus Professor of Buddhist Studies at the University of Sunderland, UK. His research focuses on early Buddhist thought and practices, and Buddhist ethics. He was editor of *Buddhist Studies Review* (2006–2020), journal of the UK Association for Buddhist Studies, having founded the Association in 1995 with Ian Harris, and from 2002 to 2011 ran an online MA Buddhist Studies program. He is author of *An Introduction to Buddhism: Teachings, History and Practices* (1990, 2nd edn. 2013), *The Selfless Mind: Personality, Consciousness and Nirvana in Early Buddhism* (1995), and *An Introduction to Buddhist Ethics: Foundations, Values and Practices* (2000).

James M. Hegarty is Professor of Sanskrit and Indian Religions at Cardiff University. His MA and PhD studies were undertaken at Manchester University under the supervision of Jacqueline Suthren Hirst. He studied Sanskrit with Valerie Roebuck. He has an abiding interest in the role of narrative in the transmission and adaptation of religious knowledge in early, medieval, and modern South Asia. He is the author of numerous works on the role of narrative in, and between, Hindu, Buddhist, Jain, and Sikh tradition, which span from the Pre-common Era to the Twentieth Century.

Alan Mittleman holds a chair in Jewish Philosophy at The Jewish Theological Seminary in New York City, where he has taught since 2004. He is the author of seven books, most recently *Does Judaism Condone Violence? Holiness and Ethics in the Jewish Tradition* (2018).

Helen Paynter is a Baptist minister accredited with the Baptist Union of Great Britain. She is tutor in biblical studies at Bristol Baptist College and director of the Centre for the Study of Bible and Violence. She is the author of a number of books on the relationship between the Bible and violence, including *God of Violence Yesterday, God of Love Today? Wrestling*

Honestly with the Old Testament (2019), and *Telling Terror in Judges 19: Rape and Reparation for the Levite's Wife* (2020).

Alisha Pomazon is Assistant Professor in the Department of Religion and Culture at St. Thomas More College at the University of Saskatchewan. Her work focuses on the history of Jewish-Christian Relations and Dialogue, textual hermeneutics, and the practices of social justice in Judaism and Catholicism.

Maria Power is Senior Research Fellow in Human Dignity at the Las Casas Institute for Social Justice, Blackfriars Hall, University of Oxford. She has written widely on the conflict in Northern Ireland and the role that religion can play in peacebuilding, her most recent book, *Catholic Social Teaching and Theologies of Peace: Cardinal Cahal Daly and the Pursuit of the Peaceable Kingdom*, was published in 2020.

CHAPTER 1

Introduction to the Volume

Maria Power and Helen Paynter

A so-called social experiment posted on the video channel YouTube a few years ago[1] sought to explore people's attitudes to violence in the Bible and the Q'ran. Random people walking around New York City were presented with a Bible wrapped in a Q'ran dust jacket and directed toward some texts appearing to call for violence and the subjugation of women. Most were quick to condemn the texts and distance themselves from them. Some explicitly compared them unfavourably with 'what the Bible teaches'. There was almost universal shock when the experimenter removed the

[1] https://www.youtube.com/watch?v=riDlxCvFZWw Accessed 16 May 2022.

M. Power (✉)
Las Casas Institute for Social Justice, University of Oxford, Oxford, UK
e-mail: Maria.power@bfriars.ox.ac.uk

H. Paynter
Centre for the Study of Bible and Violence, Bristol Baptist College, Bristol, UK
e-mail: paynterh@bristol-baptist.ac.uk

M. Power, H. Paynter (eds.), *Violence and Peace in Sacred Texts*,
https://doi.org/10.1007/978-3-031-17804-7_1

dust jacket and revealed the true identity of the text they had been sampling.

This experiment demonstrates a number of things, arguably none of them intended by the experimenter. It highlights the situation that in many parts of the world, popular opinion considers Islam to be a religion of violence. It exemplifies the fact that all the sacred texts of the world faiths contain some violence. And it shows the danger of evaluating anyone's faith based on an uninterpreted and selective reading of proof-texts.

Globally, the use of sacred texts to promote violence is one of the pressing issues of our time. In recent years, many societies and cultures have entered a new era of polarisation, in which appeals to sacred texts are made in the pursuit of political and economic gain. Further, current global events, such as the rise of groups like ISIS, and Christian fundamentalism in the United States and in Eastern Europe, place religion – and in particular attitudes to violence and peace – at the centre of global political discourse. In such instances, sacred texts may be deployed in a reductionist manner, with tropes taken out of context to enhance their popular appeal.

But alongside this, the *perception* of other people's faiths as violent and other faith's texts as deplorable, furthers suspicion, polarisation, and violence within and across communities and nations. But in actual fact, the interpretation of sacred texts by adherents of each faith is far more subtle than the popular imagination allows. Each of the major faiths has its own interpretive practices which seek to grapple with the complexities of what are generally very ancient texts. These interpretive practices may be developed in the academy or in the community; they are generally part of long traditions of interpretation within faith communities.

But just as each sacred text contains violent myths, narratives, laws, prayers and more, so they all, in various ways, call for peace. How are these apparently contradictory perspectives reconciled by interpretive communities? Is one text abrogated by the other? Does one text have interpretive control over another? Are divergent texts held in tension with one another? Is appeal made to diachronic development within the texts?

The conception for this volume arose from the editors' own grappling with these problems. Maria is a Catholic social ethicist and peace advocate, and Helen is a UK Baptist minister and biblical scholar with an interest in violent biblical texts. Positioned as we both are within the Christian faith (though within very different traditions), we are far more aware of the Church's perspectives on violence and peace than we are of the approaches taken in other faith traditions. How do those of other faiths grapple with these matters within their own sacred texts? We wanted to learn *of* the issues and their interpretations within other faith traditions, but we also wanted to learn *from* other faith traditions about the hermeneutical approaches taken in the academy and the believing community.

We, therefore, set out to commission a range of essays which would attempt to identify some of the issues raised by the texts of the major world faith traditions and to plot something of the diversity of responses to these challenges offered by scholars and adherents. It is not possible to offer an exhaustive study of the range of approaches taken by any of the faiths here covered, but by offering two chapters for the majority of the traditions, we attempt to sketch something of the range of approaches taken.

Too often, hermeneutical work like that which is showcased here takes place within academic or confessional communities which are siloed from one another. Concern for orthodoxy (correctness of belief) or orthopraxy (correctness of practice), and perhaps for apologetics (defence of the faith) tends to drive the conversation inwards. Here, by bringing together in a single volume voices from a diverse range of faith traditions who are willing to air some of the internal struggle on these issues, we seek to break the conversation out from these siloes and to open up spaces for generative and generous dialogue. This is further facilitated by a concluding chapter which draws together some common threads and offers some ways forward.

Our first chapter on Hinduism is written by the confessionally unaffiliated Indologist Simon Brodbeck. Brodbeck examines the two foundational narrative texts of Hinduism, the *Mahābhārata* and *Rāmāyaṇa*, which form the basis for interpretation and reinterpretations in many subsequent Hindu writings. The causes and mitigations of violence in these early post-Vedic texts are complex and layered, and Brodbeck explores the ways in which 'mythic' and 'realistic elements' interact with one another. This is followed by a chapter written by the Hindu-Catholic scholar, Ankur Barua. Barua explores some of the ideological and contextual factors which have contributed to Hindu expressions of violence and peace from the mid-nineteenth century onwards. In particular, he draws out the role of interactions between the Indian-Hindu community with Indian Muslims, and the construction of 'self' and 'other' in that colonial and post-colonial milieu.

Our first chapter on Judaism is by the Jewish philosophical theologian Alan Mittleman. Mittleman briefly outlines the scope of the violence within the Bible,[2] noting that it does not minimise the human problem of violence, but perhaps even amplifies it. Contrary to some contemporary imaginations, the embarrassment that this violence presents to faithful readers of the text is not a new issue. Mittleman therefore sketches out some ancient, medieval, and modern Jewish interpretations, with particular reference to a variety of rabbinic interpretive strategies which variously diminish, sideline, or justify violent norms. Building upon this, rabbinic scholar Laliv Clenman explores a contrastive problem: a rabbinic innovation of violence where there is no biblical precedent. This is the *kippah*, found in two early rabbinic legal works (Mishna Sanhedrin and Tosefta Sanhedrin), which was a particularly violent form of imprisonment and execution. The *kippah* was employed against the recidivist, the murderer without witnesses, and the refuser of warnings, categories of criminals for whom the normally correct disciplinary procedure proved legally impossible. It thus functioned, Clenman argues, as a solution to these hard legal cases, motivated by the desire to protect the law from destruction. Later rabbinic writings, however, tended to mitigate the human violence in these circumstances, casting it as a redundancy in the light of the inevitable divine judgment which would follow.

Our chapter on Buddhism was written by the Buddhist scholar Peter Harvey. Harvey surveys early Buddhist texts to draw out the diversity of their positions; while largely (and perhaps normatively) promoting peace, they also at times accept a limited form of violence, especially in pursuit of the *dharma* of reciprocity. He then goes on to examine the ways in which these values have been practiced in a range of historic settings, particularly the Tamil separatists in the Sri Lankan civil war. In his essay, Harvey draws out the role that religious nationalism can sometimes play in the promotion of violence, in spite of the teachings of the Buddha; and the practical irony of the perceived need to defend a peaceful religion with force.

This is followed by the two chapters on Christianity, written by the editors of this volume. First, Helen Paynter surveys themes of violence and peace within the Christian Bible. She briefly sketches some historic approaches to, and instrumentalisation of, biblical violence, before turning to the apologetic question of how the violence of the text might be reconciled with the conventional Christian view of God as all-loving.

[2] A terminological note is in order. Prof Mittleman and Rabbi Dr Clenman are, of course, referring to the Tanakh when they use the term 'Bible'. Dr Maria Power and Revd Dr Helen Paynter are referring to the Christian Bible when they use the same term.

Considering contemporary approaches to this question, Paynter highlights four broad lines of reasoning taken by Christian apologists, offering brief case studies for each one. None of them has proven wholly convincing to the Christian community, which continues to have diverse opinions upon the matter. This chapter's focus on mainly Protestant thoughts is followed by one from Maria Power. Power considers the development of Catholic social teaching in the twentieth and twenty-first centuries, which focuses on New Testament texts, particularly the Sermon on the mount, to develop a theology of human dignity, solidarity, subsidiarity, and the preferential option for the poor. When considered together, these form the basis of a Just Peace theology, which is offered as a valid – and preferential – option to Just War theory. In her study of papal documents, catechisms, and writings by prominent Catholic theologians, Power demonstrates the positively reinforcing roles played by Scripture, tradition, clergy and laity in developing a teaching which is then developed contextually in a variety of settings.

Our first chapter on Islam is written by the Shīʿī Muslim and scholar of Islamic intellectual history, Ali Hammoud. Hammoud considers the ways that Shīʿī scholars have interpreted *jihad*, with an exploration of historical and textual factors which influence the argument. A significant historical moment was the martyrdom of Ḥusayn, the third Imam, in 680 CE, which served to both legitimise and delegitimise certain forms of violence in subsequent Shīʿī thought. Hammoud shows how a variety of hermeneutical techniques have been applied to the Q'ranic texts by scholars within the emerging tradition, resulting in a rich diversity of interpretations within the historic and current believing community. Our second chapter on Islam is written by the Catholic scholar of mysticism in the Abrahamic religions, Minlib Dallh. Dallh examines the ambivalent relationship that Sufism has with the use of force and violence, with attention to Sufi interpretations of *jihad*. As an extended case study, he considers Ousman dan Fodio's spiritual and armed *jihad*, which led to the establishment of the Sokoto Caliphate in 1808 in Sub-Saharan Africa. Strikingly, following the use of armed *jihad* to establish the Caliphate, dan Fodio withdrew from political leadership to remain as spiritual leader only. Hammoud draws out the complexity of the internal and external factors which contributed to this historical movement.

We then have a single chapter on Sikhism, written by James Hegarty, who is a philologist and historian of Indian religious traditions. Hegarty surveys Sikh understandings of martyrdom and religiously sanctioned violence. He begins with an exploration of these themes in the canonical *Guru Granth Sāhib* and the *Dasam Granth*, demonstrating both continuity and discontinuity between these texts. He then turns to post-canonical writings, providing a wide-ranging survey of these themes in writings and other art forms from the eighteenth century to the present day. Through this exploration, Hegarty shows that the experience of violence (as martyrdom or religiously sanctioned action) and the theorisation of martyrdom and Sikh self-understanding are in a historic and ongoing dialectic.

The final chapter is offered by Alisha Pomazon, who brings her extensive experience in inter-religious dialogue, particularly Scriptural Reasoning, to the conversation. Pomazon ably sketches out many of the connections and distinctives of the various contributions in the book and makes a number of helpful points more generally. In particular, she highlights the power dynamics that are at work in the process of Scriptural interpretation and the role of both present community and inter-generational (i.e. historical) conversations in shaping contemporary interpretations. She points to the common theme of what might be termed the "hermeneutical spiral". This is a term used to describe the role of sacred text in shaping praxis and the converse role of sociological, ideological and historical context in shaping the interpretation of sacred text. Like most, perhaps all, of our contributors, Pomazon sees a plenitude of interpretive options as a virtue.

And this brings us back to the case study we began with. The more that we can appreciate not only the diversity of witness within a sacred text but also the plenitude of interpretive possibilities held by adherents to that faith tradition, the less we will be inclined towards reductionist understandings of other people's faiths. We hope that the contributions presented in this volume will aid towards that and help people both with and without the major faith traditions to appreciate the richness of the wrestling with issues of violence and peace that has gone before and continues today.

Finally, we would like to thank all our contributors for rising to the challenge of rendering complex and nuanced discussions, some of which have been ongoing for thousands of years, into a cogent and lucid précis of a few thousand words. We are grateful for their good humour and tolerance with the editing process. We would also like to express our gratitude to the editorial team at Palgrave Macmillan, for believing in this project and their help in bringing it to fruition. We dedicate this book to all those we have ever worked with who do not share our faith perspective, but who have been willing nonetheless to share their thoughts with us and to listen to ours. May understanding grow and – to use an image from the sacred text we share with our Jewish sisters and brothers – may all swords soon be beaten into ploughshares.

Pentecost, 2022

CHAPTER 2

Violence and Peace in the *Mahābhārata* and *Rāmāyaṇa*

Simon Brodbeck

The Two Texts

This chapter – which I write as a devotionally unaffiliated scholar of Indology – examines presentations of violence and peace in the Sanskrit *Mahābhārata* and *Rāmāyaṇa*, the two foundational narrative texts of Hinduism, both of which include wars as integral plot episodes.[1] These

[1] The *Bhagavadgītā* constitutes *Mahābhārata* 6.23–40. For the Sanskrit texts, see R. N. Dandekar, gen. ed., *The Mahābhārata Text as Constituted in its Critical Edition*, 5 vols, including the *Harivaṃśa* (Poona: Bhandarkar Oriental Research Institute, 1971–76); R. T. Vyas, gen. ed., *Vālmīki Rāmāyaṇa: Text as Constituted in its Critical Edition* (Vadodara: Oriental Institute, 1992). For translations, see the 'further reading' list at the end of this chapter. For juxtaposition and structural comparison of the two stories, see Sheldon Pollock, *The Rāmāyaṇa of Vālmīki* vol. 2 (Princeton: Princeton University Press, 1986), 9–10, 38–42; Madeleine Biardeau, 'Some Remarks on the Links between the Epics, the Purāṇas and their Vedic Sources', in Gerhard Oberhammer, ed., *Studies in Hinduism: Vedism and Hinduism* (Vienna: Austrian Academy of Sciences, 1997), 89; John Brockington, *The*

S. Brodbeck (✉)
Religious Studies, Cardiff University, Cardiff, UK
e-mail: BrodbeckSP@cardiff.ac.uk

M. Power, H. Paynter (eds.), *Violence and Peace in Sacred Texts*,
https://doi.org/10.1007/978-3-031-17804-7_2

two Sanskrit texts are usually dated to roughly the same period: the last few centuries BCE and the first few centuries CE. The earliest recoverable documents of these stories may have developed out of pre-existing texts and narrative traditions. Thereafter, they form a constant point of reference for Hindu thought. They are referred to and commented upon by all manner of subsequent texts. They are represented and reinterpreted in other narrative versions – other Mahābhāratas and other Rāmāyaṇas – in Sanskrit and in many other languages (now including English), and also in diverse other narrative media, for example as sculptured friezes in temples, or in ritual form as theatrical or dance performances, burgeoning in new forms in new media in different periods, but always in use as two basic cultural lenses through which to interpret the world. The two Sanskrit texts – the *Mahābhārata* credited to Vyāsa and the *Rāmāyaṇa* credited to Vālmīki – are not the primary access points to these stories for South Asians, most of whom do not know Sanskrit; and South Asians who learn Sanskrit and study these texts do so after coming to know the stories in other forms already. But the authority of the Sanskrit versions is tied up with their antiquity and allows them to stand as an orthodox paradigm, embodying a normative vision of monarchical society divided into two genders and four hereditary classes of men (brahmins, *kṣatriyas*, *vaiśyas*, and *śūdras*), classed approximately by occupation, but also by access to the *brahman*, the absolute, the sacred power behind sacred utterance. Brahmins, the teachers, scholars, and priests, through whom the gods are known and kept in favour, are presented as the highest class. Vyāsa and Vālmīki are brahmins. The brahmins help the *kṣatriya* kings and everybody else.

Sanskrit Epics (Leiden: Brill, 1998), 1–4, 28–40; Alf Hiltebeitel, 'Not without Subtales: Telling Laws and Truths in the Sanskrit Epics', *Journal of Indian Philosophy* 33.4 (2005), 460–61; Alf Hiltebeitel, 'The Archetypal Design of the Two Sanskrit Epics', in Vishwa Adluri and Joydeep Bagchee, eds, *Reading the Fifth Veda: Studies on the Mahābhārata. Essays by Alf Hiltebeitel, Volume 1* (Leiden: Brill, 2011); Simon Brodbeck, 'Sanskrit Epics: The Rāmāyaṇa, Mahābhārata and Harivaṃśa', in Jessica Frazier, ed., *The Continuum Companion to Hindu Studies* (London: Continuum, 2011), 97–98. Brockington says 'It is ... worth asking from the start whether designation of the *Mahābhārata* and the *Rāmāyaṇa* as "epics" affects our understanding of them' (*Sanskrit Epics*, 1); I eschew that designation here.

Literary Background

The *Mahābhārata* and *Rāmāyaṇa* are the first post-Vedic Sanskrit texts. Preceding them is the Veda, or the four Vedas, a large collection of texts that were the property of specific brahmin families and were used by them in and for their work, as they arranged, managed, and officiated at the ritual events whereby the gods are properly hosted. In the Veda, the ritual is an animal sacrifice, with a fire, guests, singing, and other entertainment. Ritual offerings are made into the fire, with the correct liturgy correctly pronounced. There is feasting, and the event is paid for by the host, paradigmatically a king, who gains specific personal rewards as a result of his generosity, particularly his generosity to brahmins. 'The Kshatriyas acquired legitimacy from the Brahmins by giving *dana* (gifts) to the latter.'[2]

The Vedic texts contain details of the ritual, speculations about its meaning and power, and a treasure trove of spells and charms. The later Vedic texts contain the beginnings of much Indian philosophy, some mythological narratives, and materials on society and government, with brahmins presented as operating in partnership not just with kings but with lords of economic units down to the individual household. The same ritual function exists at all structural levels, from the household upwards. Among later Vedic texts are the Dharmasūtras and Dharmaśāstras, 'Codes of Law', texts on normative pious behaviour, some of which are contemporary with the *Mahābhārata* and *Rāmāyaṇa*; indeed, the *Mahābhārata* includes sections of Dharmaśāstra within itself, and is particularly closely allied with the Dharmaśāstra credited to Manu.[3] The *Mahābhārata* and *Rāmāyaṇa* are in a simpler form of Sanskrit than most of the Veda; the *Mahābhārata* calls itself the fifth Veda, and it is aimed explicitly (as the

[2] Kaushik Roy, *Hinduism and the Ethics of Warfare in South Asia: from Antiquity to the Present* (Cambridge: Cambridge University Press, 2012), 18.

[3] Patrick Olivelle, ed. (with Suman Olivelle) and trans., *Manu's Code of Law: a Critical Edition and Translation of the Mānava-Dharmaśāstra* (Delhi: Oxford University Press, 2006); for shared verses, see 1009–34.

Rāmāyaṇa is implicity) at an audience of both genders and all classes, rather than at a brahmin male audience as the Vedic texts are.[4]

The Vedic texts are, among other things, a meditation on the violence done to the sacrificial animal. This aspect of Vedic texts is significant with regard to violence and peace in the *Mahābhārata* and *Rāmāyaṇa*. It recurs in philosophical discourse, and it has been studied at some length in various publications.[5] The violence of the sacrificial operation is explained away in various ways, by the deification of the victim, and/or by the making of an exception. *Manu's Code of Law* states that 'Within the sacrifice ... killing is not killing',[6] and in the *Mahābhārata* this exception is compared with the exception to the general rule of chastity:

> Revelation reveals that the fires are hungry for meat, and at sacrifices brahmins always kill animals, which, being sacramentalized by the incantations, then go to heaven, as we hear. Now, brahmin, if the old fires had not been so hungry for meat, no one would eat it now. Even now the hermits rule in the matter of eating meat: 'He who always eats only after having offered to deities and ancestors according to the Ordinance and with faith does not incur guilt by eating the remainder.' Revelation reveals that one thus equals a meat abstainer: a scholar of the Veda who goes to his wife at her season remains a brahmin.[7]

[4] Brahmins are not to teach *śūdras* the Veda: *Manu's Code of Law* 3.156; 4.80–81, 99; 8.272.

[5] Ludwig Alsdorf, *The History of Vegetarianism and Cow-Veneration in India* (ed. Willem Bollée, London: Routledge, 2010 [1962]); Jan E. M. Houben and Karel R. van Kooij, eds, *Violence Denied: Violence, Non-Violence and the Rationalization of Violence in South Asian Cultural History* (Leiden: Brill, 1999), 1–183; Francis X. Clooney, 'Pain but not Harm: some Classical Resources towards a Hindu Just War Theory', in Paul Robinson, ed., *Just War in Comparative Perspective* (Aldershot: Ashgate, 2003), 110–14; Laurie L. Patton, 'Telling Stories about Harm: an Overview of Early Indian Narratives', in John R. Hinnells and Richard King, eds, *Religion and Violence in South Asia: Theory and Practice* (London: Routledge, 2007), 13–21.

[6] *Manu's Code of Law* 5.39.

[7] *Mahābhārata* 3.199.9–12, trans. J. A. B. van Buitenen, *The Mahābhārata* vol. 2 (Chicago: University of Chicago Press, 1975), 623–24, adjusted. See also Alf Hiltebeitel, *Rethinking the Mahābhārata: a Reader's Guide to the Education of the Dharma King* (Chicago: University of Chicago Press, 2001), 202–9; Simon Brodbeck, 'Daśaratha's Horse Sacrifice in the Rāmāyaṇa', *Orientalia Suecana* 69 (2020), 6–7, 19–20.

This analogical shift, from violence against an animal to violence against a rule of chastity, seems to bypass the context of armed violence – the military contest – which for present-day readers, after two world wars and with continuing armed violence in various parts of the world (aided by a profitable international arms-supply industry), is probably a more natural kind of context for a book on violence and peace. This chapter discusses armed violence in the *Mahābhārata* and *Rāmāyaṇa*, but there is a long Sanskrit poetic pedigree for the presentation of violence as a sacrificial ritual, and since the host of the rite and his priest and the sacrificial animal are all males, this links directly to the matter of masculinity, which comes to the fore in our two royal stories.[8] The Vedic sacrifice exists within a social context where gender relations and symbols operate, and the discussion of male violence implicates the female.

Kingship and Violence

The Vedic texts contain clues as to what was happening, historically, before the *Mahābhārata* and *Rāmāyaṇa* were composed. In the *Ṛgveda*, the oldest part of the Veda, there is evidence of violence between chieftains and their warrior bands, for example over cattle, and between types of people, with some enemies described in a dehumanising fashion as *dāsa*s (fiends, savages, infidels).[9] Indra, leader of the gods, is celebrated as a victor in violent conquest, in the hope of winning his support for human perpetrators. The *Ṛgveda* mentions a 'battle of ten kings', wherein a certain chieftain's fortunes were reversed after he changed his priest.[10]

[8] Smita Sahgal, 'Situating Kingship within an Embryonic Frame of Masculinity in Early India', *Social Scientist* 43.11–12 (2015).

[9] Michael Witzel, 'Ṛgvedic History: Poets, Chieftains and Polities', in George Erdosy, ed., *The Indo-Aryans of Ancient South Asia: Language, Material Culture and Ethnicity* (Berlin: Walter de Gruyter, 1995), 324–26; see also Jarrod L. Whitaker, *Strong Arms and Drinking Strength: Masculinity, Violence, and the Body in Ancient India* (Oxford: Oxford University Press, 2011).

[10] *Ṛgveda* 7.18–19; Stephanie W. Jamison and Joel P. Brereton, trans., *The Rigveda: the Earliest Religious Poetry of India* vol. 2 (New York: Oxford University Press, 2014), 902–6; Witzel, 'Ṛgvedic History', 333–37; cf. Michael Witzel, 'The Vedas and the Epics: Some Comparative Notes on Persons, Lineages, Geography, and Grammar', in Petteri Koskikallio, ed., *Epics, Khilas, and Purāṇas: Continuities and Ruptures. Proceedings of the Third Dubrovnik International Conference on the Sanskrit Epics and Purāṇas* (Zagreb: Croatian Academy of Sciences and Arts, 2005), 22–25.

The *Mahābhārata* and *Rāmāyaṇa* present a social vision where the *kṣatriya* class has a monopoly on the use of force. The king is a *kṣatriya*, and by right he uses the *daṇḍa* or rod of punishment to enforce law and order within his own realm, as well as to conquer his enemies abroad. The king's use of violence is a service to his people. It is his basic tool, the badge of his office, the pillar of his masculinity, the phallic instrument whereby he releases the fecundity of his realm by stopping the big fish from eating the little ones.[11] It is said that war should be a last resort, after negotiation, the giving of gifts, and the sowing of dissention.[12] But Bakker speaks of 'the right, nay the duty of the king to wage war', and says that in pre-modern times 'This right, and hence the right to stage organized killing in the interest of the state, has, to the best of my knowledge, never been questioned in the brahmanical tradition'; 'War thus seemed to some extent to be a natural phenomenon and needed no justification'.[13] This certainly seems to be the case in the *Arthaśāstra* of Kauṭilya (if Dharmaśāstra

[11] On the king and violence, see *Mahābhārata* 12.67–71, 93–107, 121–22; *Arthaśāstra* 1.4.3–16; *Manu's Code of Law* 7.14–31, 87–113; Clooney, 'Pain but not Harm', 114–21. For the *Arthaśāstra* see R. P. Kangle, ed., *The Kauṭilīya Arthaśāstra, Part I: a Critical Edition with a Glossary* (Delhi: Motilal Banarsidass, 1986 [1960]). On the *kṣatriya* and violence, see *Bhagavadgītā* 2.31–32; K. N. Upadhyaya, 'The Bhagavad Gītā on War and Peace', *Philosophy East and West* 19.2 (1969), 163–66; Anantanand Rambachan, 'The Co-Existence of Violence and Non-Violence in Hinduism', *Ecumenical Review* 55.2 (2003), 116–17. For the phallic masculinity of the king, see Ariel Glucklich, 'The Royal Scepter (*Daṇḍa*) as Legal Punishment and Sacred Symbol', *History of Religions* 28.2 (1988); Sahgal, 'Situating Kingship', 9–15; Simon Brodbeck, 'Mapping Masculinities in the Sanskrit *Mahābhārata* and *Rāmāyaṇa*', in Ilona Zsolnay, ed., *Being a Man: Negotiating Ancient Constructs of Masculinity* (London: Routledge, 2017), 128–32. For the heroes' heaven, see Minoru Hara, 'Apsaras and Hero', *Journal of Indian Philosophy* 29.1–2 (2001); Danielle Feller, *The Sanskrit Epics' Representation of Vedic Myths* (Delhi: Motilal Banarsidass, 2004), 288; Wu Juan, 'Comparing Buddhist and Jaina Attitudes towards Warfare: some Notes on Stories of King Ajātaśatru's/Kūṇika's War against the Vṛjis and Related Material', *Annual Report of the International Research Institute for Advanced Buddhology* 18 (2015), 97–107; Jarrod Whitaker, 'Heroism, Military Violence and the State in Ancient India', in Garret G. Fagan, Linda Fibiger, Mark Hudson, and Matthew Trundle, eds, *The Cambridge World History of Violence, Volume 1: the Prehistoric and Ancient Worlds* (Cambridge: Cambridge University Press, 2020), 689–91. Though the king saves small fish from being eaten by bigger ones (*Mahābhārata* 3.185.7–9), he does this by eating fish smaller than himself.

[12] *Mahābhārata* 12.103.22; *Harivaṃśa* 15.48–55; *Manu's Code of Law* 7.198–200; *Rāmāyaṇa* 3.61.16.

[13] Hans Bakker, 'The Hindu Religion and War', in Anna S. King, ed., *Indian Religions: Renaissance and Renewal. The Spalding Papers in Indic Studies: Collected Papers Presented at the Annual Spalding Symposium on Indian Religions* (London: Equinox, 2006), 30, 33.

is a Code of Law, then Arthaśāstra is a Code for Profit), where the king is to employ violence freely as a means to achieve his ends.[14] But open war is a precarious business, and the king who wishes to prevail may resolve matters to his advantage by alternative means. He should seek to prevail by any means necessary. 'When the occasion was ripe, the king should expand his territory and fill his treasury through war', but 'war should be fought only when there is an opportunity to gain something without risking too much'.[15] For Kauṭilya, peace and war are two sides of one coin: 'Peace and activity constitute the source of acquisition and security. Activity is that which brings about the accomplishment of works undertaken. Peace is that which brings about security of enjoyment of the fruits of works.'[16] The *Arthaśāstra*'s assessment of violence depends only on the immediate consequences, for the king, of employing it. But elsewhere, attempts were made to associate the *kṣatriya* class with responsibilities as well as rights, and with specific rules of conduct, and of conduct in battle. Even if some of the rules are honoured in the breach,[17] the *Mahābhārata* and *Rāmāyaṇa* are conscious that their great battles should be righteous wars, in terms of both the justification for the war in the first place and the conduct of combatants during it. Messengers are not to be killed.[18] Rules of combat are detailed such that, for example, chariot-warriors should fight chariot-warriors, elephant-warriors elephant-warriors, cavalrymen cavalrymen,

[14] Torkel Brekke, 'Wielding the Rod of Punishment: War and Violence in the Political Science of Kautilya', *Journal of Military Ethics* 3.1 (2004), partially reproduced in Torkel Brekke, 'Between Prudence and Heroism: Ethics of War in the Hindu Tradition', in Torkel Brekke, ed., *The Ethics of War in Asian Civilizations: a Comparative Perspective* (London: Routledge, 2006); Patton, 'Telling Stories about Harm', 22–23; Kaushik Roy, 'Norms of War in Hinduism', in Vesselin Popovsky, Gregory Reichberg, and Nicholas Turner, eds, *World Religions and Norms of War* (Tokyo: United Nations University Press, 2009), 35–37.

[15] Brekke, 'Wielding the Rod of Punishment', 44, 49.

[16] *Arthaśāstra* 6.2.1–3, trans. R. P. Kangle, *The Kauṭilīya Arthaśāstra, Part II: an English Translation with Critical and Explanatory Notes* (Delhi: Motilal Banarsidass, 1986 [1972]), 317; cf. Brekke, 'Wielding the Rod of Punishment', 48; Patrick Olivelle, trans., *King, Governance, and Law in Ancient India: Kauṭilya's Arthaśāstra* (New York: Oxford University Press, 2013), 273, with 'rest' rather than 'peace'.

[17] M. A. Mehendale, *Reflections on the Mahābhārata War* (Shimla: Indian Institute of Advanced Study, 1995); Roy, *Hinduism and the Ethics of Warfare*, 35–38; Alf Hiltebeitel, *The Ritual of Battle: Krishna in the Mahābhārata* (Ithaca: Cornell University Press, 1976), 244–79.

[18] *Rāmāyaṇa* 1.5.20; 5.50.5–6, 11; 6.67.38.

and infantrymen infantrymen.[19] The duel between chariot-warriors is the standard set-piece.

More generally the king's activities are for development:

> Everything must be good for cows and brahmins; one should make war for their sake. But grain should not be trampled down, nor should anyone erect any obstacles to the plowing of the fields, nor where the Gods are paid honor, the ancestors, or guests.
>
> ... He who lives here looks to the benefits of doing so. Our army will attack any who will not remit to us as they are able.[20]

The king is frighteningly, violently powerful. Hence the necessity for his taking good counsel. Rāvaṇa, king of the monsters, is given good counsel and rejects it.[21]

Summary of *Mahābhārata*

The *Mahābhārata* tells of King Janamejaya, whose father was killed by snakebite, and who set out on a ritual to kill all snakes. While the ritual was occurring, he heard the full story of the war that was fought at Kurukṣetra between the one hundred Kauravas, who lost the war, and their cousins, the five Pāṇḍavas, who won it. The victors included Arjuna Pāṇḍava, Janamejaya's great-grandfather – a great friend of Kṛṣṇa, as shown particularly in the *Bhagavadgītā,* which occurred just before the war. Janamejaya, having heard the story of the Kurukṣetra war, called off his snake massacre uncompleted, and made peace with the snakes.

Most of the *Mahābhārata* is the story told to Janamejaya. It tells of the background and causes of the Kurukṣetra war; it gives an extended

[19] *Mahābhārata* 6.1.29; *Rāmāyaṇa* 6.90.4; Mehendale, *Reflections on the Mahābhārata War*, 5–8; see also *Mahābhārata* 12.96–97; Surya P. Subedi, 'The Concept in Hinduism of "Just War"', *Journal of Conflict and Security Law* 8.2 (2003), 352–57; Feller, *The Sanskrit Epics' Representation of Vedic Myths*, 263–66; Brekke, 'Wielding the Rod of Punishment', 48; Roy, *Hinduism and the Ethics of Warfare*, 26–38. Armies may not have consisted entirely of *kṣatriyas*: see *Arthaśāstra* 6.1.11; Whitaker, 'Heroism, Military Violence and the State', 685 n. 2, noting the general terms *yodha* and *yodhin* for 'soldier'.

[20] *Mahābhārata* 12.133.14c–15, 19, trans. James L. Fitzgerald, *The Mahābhārata* vol. 7 (Chicago: University of Chicago Press, 2004), 509–10.

[21] Raj Balkaran and A. Walter Dorn, 'Violence in the *Vālmīki Rāmāyaṇa*: Just War Criteria in an Ancient Indian Epic', *Journal of the American Academy of Religion* 80.3 (2012), 677–81; Clooney, 'Pain but not Harm', 18–19.

account of the battlefield action (books 6–10 of 18); and then it shows how the survivors coped with it afterwards. In narrating the history of the Pāṇḍavas and Kauravas before the war – the two sets of cousins always quarrelled, the kingdom was divided, the Kauravas beat the Pāṇḍavas at dice, molested their wife, sent them into exile for 13 years, and then would not give them their kingdom back – the text includes (especially in books 1 and 3) long sections consisting of stories that the Pāṇḍavas heard, including among them the story of Rāma;[22] and in narrating what happened after the war, the text includes (especially in books 12 and 13) extensive teachings from the dying patriarch Bhīṣma to Yudhiṣṭhira Pāṇḍava, the new king of the reunited ancestral kingdom. Janamejaya also hears, told in the *Harivaṃśa* after the story of the Pāṇḍavas has finished, the parallel story of Kṛṣṇa, and what he got up to when he was not with the Pāṇḍavas.[23]

What Janamejaya hears turns him from violence to peace. For the Pāṇḍavas, it was not so easy; they fought their war to its bitter end, after which more than a billion had been killed, and they did not live happily ever after, as Janamejaya does. Yudhiṣṭhira never got over the trauma of it. But it is made clear to Janamejaya, before and then again after the story of the Kurukṣetra war, that that war was required for the good of the Earth, who was overburdened, and that it was effected by the gods in descended form as humans.[24] Janamejaya's great-grandfather Arjuna was the god Indra, Yudhiṣṭhira was the god Dharma, and so forth. Before descending, the gods formed the plan of effecting a huge massacre of *kṣatriyas* for the good of the suffering Earth; but having descended they were in their human forms largely unaware of their plan as gods – apart from Kṛṣṇa, who, being Viṣṇu, knew it all, even in his human form, and made sure it was achieved.

Summary of *Rāmāyaṇa*

King Rāma's sons were born and raised at Vālmīki's hermitage after Rāma had abandoned their pregnant mother Sītā. They learned the story of Rāma from Vālmīki, and they performed it to Rāma at his horse sacrifice.[25]

[22] *Mahābhārata* 3.257–75; *Harivaṃśa* 31.110–42.
[23] *Harivaṃśa* 1–113.
[24] *Mahābhārata* 1.58–61; *Harivaṃśa* 40–45.
[25] *Rāmāyaṇa* 1.4; 7.84–85.

It is the story of how Rāma was exiled from his rightful kingdom for 14 years due to the machinations of his father's junior wife, and how, while Rāma was in exile, his own wife Sītā was kidnapped by the demon Rāvaṇa, and with the aid of friendly monkeys Rāma fought and won a great war against Rāvaṇa, and brought Sītā back to be his queen in the ancestral kingdom, where after his exile he ruled so very gloriously, but abandoned her due to mutterings among the people about what might have happened to her while apart from him.[26]

Whereas the *Mahābhārata* is commonly termed an *itihāsa* or 'history', the *Rāmāyaṇa* is said to be the first *kāvya* or 'poem'. It is inspired by Vālmīki witnessing a crane crying after the killing of its mate.[27] Balkaran and Dorn say 'It is telling ... that poetry itself is derived from grief, and grief born of violence'.[28] Like Yudhiṣṭhira, Rāma does not get to live happily ever after. These two do not get peace of mind. They suffer the pains of kingship in full. But they are the best kings.

The *Rāmāyaṇa* is more streamlined than the *Mahābhārata*; it includes fewer narratives incidental to the main story and fewer passages of extended teaching. But like the *Mahābhārata,* it contextualises its events, and the sufferings of its great king and his wife, within the framework of gods and goddesses doing an errand in the human world. For Rāma, like Kṛṣṇa, is Viṣṇu incarnate – these are two of the famous *avatāra*s of Viṣṇu. Viṣṇu's appearance as Rāma is due to a boon that Rāvaṇa secured long ago, that he (Rāvaṇa) would be invulnerable to all manner of beings but not to human ones, and so Viṣṇu must be in human form in order to kill him. Unlike Kṛṣṇa in the *Mahābhārata*, in the *Rāmāyaṇa* Rāma spends most of the story unaware that he is Viṣṇu, this being part of the artifice whereby he can be human enough to kill Rāvaṇa.

[26] *Rāmāyaṇa* 7.42–51; Robert P. Goldman, 'Ādyantaḥ: the Uttarakāṇḍa's Challenges for its Authors and Readers', in Simon Brodbeck, Adam Bowles, and Alf Hiltebeitel, eds, *The Churning of the Epics and Purāṇas: Proceedings of the Epics and Purāṇas Section at the 15th World Sanskrit Conference* (Delhi: Dev, 2018), 291–93.

[27] *Rāmāyaṇa* 1.2; Simon Brodbeck, 'Who Was it Was Cursed by the First *Śloka* Verse?', *Religions of South Asia* 16.2–3 (in press).

[28] Balkaran and Dorn, 'Violence in the *Vālmīki Rāmāyaṇa*', 661.

Justifications for Violence

Both texts provide a divine justification for the specific wars that they depict. It is clearly presented, but it operates at a theological and mythological level that contrasts with the otherwise ostensibly realistic level of the narrative and the motivations of its human characters. The business of the gods is presented in two different forms – as the treatment of a demonic problem, and as the rescue of the Earth from overpopulation – but it is also presented as something that the humans involved would not understand. As soon as they are humans, the main characters who effect the wars – with the exception of Kṛṣṇa – do not know what they are doing. Thus, in the *Bhagavadgītā*, Kṛṣṇa does not try to remind Arjuna that Arjuna is Indra and that he must fight as part of the divine plan previously agreed upon. After the Kurukṣetra war, Vyāsa reveals something of the divine plan in order to try to help the survivors come to terms with what has happened,[29] but without much success.

The Kurukṣetra war is far more devastating and problematic than Rāma's war against Rāvaṇa, and the gradual realisation that Kṛṣṇa is Viṣṇu may tend to lead not to acceptance of the war, but to criticism of Kṛṣṇa for having facilitated it. Such criticism is voiced by several characters.[30] The commentators explain Kṛṣṇa's apparent indifference to human suffering in terms of the divine plan,[31] but opinions may differ over whether or not this explanation is satisfactory. As Allen puts it, 'there is more to *dharma* than humans and human institutions can comprehend'.[32]

In both texts, there is also a human level at which a justification for violence is offered. The general justification is the abuse of a precious woman, a damsel in distress, Draupadī in the *Mahābhārata* and Sītā in the *Rāmāyaṇa*; and the woman is glossed as the realm by the *Mahābhārata*'s frame story of the overburdened Earth, by the *Rāmāyaṇa* detail that Sītā is born from and named after the 'Furrow',[33] and by the standard

[29] *Mahābhārata* 11.8.

[30] *Mahābhārata* 11.25.34–46 (Gāndhārī); 14.52–54 (Uttaṅka); cf. *Harivaṃśa* 115.14–25 (Janamejaya).

[31] Vishal Sharma, 'The Problem of Indifference to Suffering in the *Mahābhārata* Tradition', *International Journal of Hindu Studies* 24.2 (2020), 188–96; see also Phyllis Granoff, 'The *Mausalaparvan* between Story and Theology', *Asiatische Studien / Études asiatiques* 62.2 (2008).

[32] Nick Allen, 'Just War in the *Mahābhārata*', in Richard Sorabji and David Rodin, eds, *The Ethics of War: Shared Problems in Different Traditions* (Aldershot: Ashgate, 2006), 140.

[33] *Rāmāyaṇa* 1.65.14–16; 2.110.27–28; 5.14.16; 7.17.30–31.

mythology which depicts the king as the husband of the Earth.[34] This general human-level justification is the king's duty of protection, albeit in both stories it is actually a vain attempt to get back and re-protect what has been lost through a momentary lapse in protection (at the dicing match in the *Mahābhārata*, and when Sītā is kidnapped in the *Rāmāyaṇa*). The gendering of the kingdom is what makes the attempt vain, because although land might be held, lost, and then won back and re-held, it is not so simple with women. The stain of her having been lost at all makes it impossible to take her back properly. Draupadī's sons are all killed, and Sītā is rejected by Rāma. The violence meted out against the perpetrators of the indignities against Draupadī and Sītā is justified in human terms, but occurs too late to be effective in human terms. In human terms, those indignities needed to have been stopped before they happened, but the interference of the gods allowed them to go ahead in order to provoke the subsequent violence. In this sense, the gods sacrificed Draupadī and Sītā.

In both texts, there is also more specific human-level justification. In the *Mahābhārata*, after their exile, the Pāṇḍavas ostensibly attempt all the prescribed preliminary methods of resolving the dispute, including the sending of a special envoy, but they are driven to war by Duryodhana's refusal to return any land to them at all.[35] Balkaran and Dorn say that 'Vālmīki's *Rāmāyaṇa* functions to contrast proper and improper uses of force'; 'The *Vālmīki Rāmāyaṇa* asserts that protection and punishment, when alloyed with reason, represent sanctioned and necessary expressions of violence.'[36] Rāma's killings of Tāṭakā and Vālin are carefully justified by the royal code.[37] The killing of the monster (*rākṣasa*) Rāvaṇa is also justified by Hanumat because

> Conciliation does not yield good results in the case of the *rākṣasas*, nor are gifts appropriate in the case of those who have amassed great wealth. Dissension can have no effect on people who are proud of their strength ...

[34] J. Duncan R. Derrett, '*Bhū-Bharaṇa, Bhū-Pālana, Bhū-Bhojana*: an Indian Conundrum', *Bulletin of the School of Oriental and African Studies* 22.1 (1959); Minoru Hara, 'The King as a Husband of the Earth (*Mahī-Pati*)', *Asiatische Studien / Études asiatiques* 27.2 (1973).

[35] For Kṛṣṇa's report of his embassy to the Kaurava court, see *Mahābhārata* 5.148.7–19; Allen, 'Just War in the *Mahābhārata*', 140.

[36] Balkaran and Dorn, 'Violence in the *Vālmīki Rāmāyaṇa*', 661, 667.

[37] On Tāṭakā and Vālin see Balkaran and Dorn, 'Violence in the *Vālmīki Rāmāyaṇa*', 666–67, 675–76; on Vālin see Patton, 'Telling Stories about Harm', 26–28; cf. Pāṇḍu and the deer, *Mahābhārata* 1.109.12–17.

> Indeed, no resolution other than physical force will be possible in this matter.[38]

In the *Rāmāyaṇa*, Rāma only kills one human.[39] Pollock says that 'For Vālmīki violence becomes, quite literally, the strategy of the inhuman.'[40] So the issue of justifying violence between humans is hardly addressed. In the *Mahābhārata*, Arjuna raises this issue at the start of the *Bhagavadgītā*, when he asks how he can fight against his own relatives.[41] Kṛṣṇa's answer is that fighting is Arjuna's class duty and that he should do it without attachment, for Kṛṣṇa's sake. Violence is justified as a professional and religious duty, and the ethical aspect is defused, transferable only to the system as a whole. Kṛṣṇa says that everyone should do their class duty as a ritual sacrifice.[42] Because Arjuna is a *kṣatriya*, fighting for him is a 'ritual of battle'; the Kurukṣetra war is a 'ritual of battle', and the *Mahābhārata* identifies ritual homologies for its various aspects.[43]

Suffering Sovereigns

In their post-war sections, both texts feature the suffering of the victorious king, Yudhiṣṭhira in the *Mahābhārata* and Rāma in the *Rāmāyaṇa*, while he presides over long periods of peace and prosperity. Violent victory has been achieved at considerable personal cost that contrasts with the peace of the kingdom.

[38] *Rāmāyaṇa* 5.39.3–4, trans. Robert P. Goldman and Sally J. Sutherland Goldman, *The Rāmāyaṇa of Vālmīki* vol. 5 (Princeton: Princeton University Press, 1996), 226. See also *Rāmāyaṇa* 5.2.27; Balkaran and Dorn, 'Violence in the *Vālmīki Rāmāyaṇa*', 673.

[39] Goldman, 'The Uttarakāṇḍa's Challenges', 290–91.

[40] Pollock, *Rāmāyaṇa of Vālmīki* vol. 2, 15.

[41] *Bhagavadgītā* 1.28c–46; 2.4–9.

[42] *Bhagavadgītā* 3.9–16; 4.23; cf. *Chāndogya Upaniṣad* 3.16–17; Valerie J. Roebuck, trans., *The Upaniṣads* (London: Penguin Classics, 2003), 141–42; Patrick Olivelle, *The Early Upaniṣads: Annotated Text and Translation* (Delhi: Munshiram Manoharlal, 1998), 210–13.

[43] Feller, *The Sanskrit Epics' Representation of Vedic Myths*, 253–93; Whitaker, 'Heroism, Military Violence and the State', 691–94; *Mahābhārata* 12.99. For the compound *raṇayajña*, see *Mahābhārata* 2.20.15; 5.57.12; 5.154.4; 9.59.25; for the compound *yuddhayajña*, see *Mahābhārata* 12.99.3.

At various points, Yudhiṣṭhira rails against the duties of the *kṣatriya* class he was born into.[44] In the *Mahābhārata*'s 'Book of Peace', Yudhiṣṭhira is only with difficulty persuaded to assume kingship of the reunited kingdom in the wake of the Kurukṣetra war,[45] just as in the *Bhagavadgītā* his brother Arjuna was only with difficulty persuaded to fight that war in the first place. Yudhiṣṭhira is particularly unlucky in discovering that Duryodhana's great friend and champion Karṇa, who was killed by Arjuna, was in fact the Pāṇḍavas' eldest brother, given away by his mother at birth. Yudhiṣṭhira's critique of the violent *kṣatriya* role must be viewed in the context of the notion of *ahiṃsā* (non-harm), which was a feature of other religions (principally Jainism and, to a lesser extent, Buddhism) against which the Hindu *Mahābhārata* was positioning itself. Yudhiṣṭhira's critique must also be seen in the context of the extraordinary edicts of the historical King Aśoka.[46]

Aśoka, sometime supporter of Buddhism, claimed in his thirteenth rock edict to have been responsible for the deportation and/or death of hundreds of thousands of people during his Kaliṅga campaign. He said that these losses pained him, that he was now devoted to morality (*dharma*), and that he desired 'towards all beings abstention from hurting (*akṣati*),

[44] For criticism of *kṣatriyadharma* (Brodbeck, 'Mapping Masculinities', 144 n. 8), see *Mahābhārata* 5.137.5; 5.180.36–38; 6.48.37; 6.92.9; 6.103.49; 7.122.16; 7.164.23; 7.169.4; 12.7.5; 12.98.1; 12.192.110; 15.46.8 (cf. 8.64.20; 11.26.5); *Rāmāyaṇa* 2.18.36; 2.93.35; 2.101.20.

[45] *Mahābhārata* 12.7–38; James L. Fitzgerald, 'Making Yudhiṣṭhira the King: the Dialectics and the Politics of Violence in the *Mahābhārata*', *Rocznik Orientalistyczny* 54.1 (2001); Fitzgerald, *Mahābhārata* vol. 7, 81–142. The 'peace' in the title of *Mahābhārata* book 12 is not just the peace after the cessation of war, but also the ruler's peace of mind following the 'ritual of battle'; see Alf Hiltebeitel, *Nonviolence in the Mahābhārata: Śiva's Summa on Ṛṣidharma and the Gleaners of Kurukṣetra* (New York: Routledge, 2016), 21–25.

[46] Nick Sutton, 'Aśoka and Yudhiṣṭhira: a Historical Setting for the Ideological Tensions of the *Mahābhārata*?', *Religion* 27.4 (1997); Fitzgerald, *Mahābhārata* vol. 7, 100, 114–23; see also Israel Selvanayagam, 'Aśoka and Arjuna as Counterfigures Standing on the Field of *Dharma*: a Historical-Hermeneutical Perspective', *History of Religions* 32.1 (1992); Paloma Muñoz Gomez, 'Yudhiṣṭhira and the Blending of *Mokṣa* into the *Puruṣārthas*: a Way of Thinking about the Dialogue of the Ṣaḍgītā', *Journal of Hindu Studies* 12.1 (2019); Kanad Sinha, 'Redefining Dharma in a Time of Transition: *Ānṛśaṃsya* in the *Mahābhārata* as an Alternative End of Human Life', *Studies in History* 35.2 (2019).

self-control, (and) impartiality in (case of) violence'.[47] He also discouraged the sacrifice of animals.[48] *Ahiṃsā* is championed by some characters in the *Mahābhārata*, but royal violence is nonetheless defended against this critique.[49] As discussed above, an exception is made for *kṣatriya* violence: the Kurukṣetra war was a 'ritual of battle', and killing in a ritual is not killing, just as dutifully attempting to impregnate one's wife is not breaking one's chastity.

In both of our texts, the suffering of the victorious king during his post-war reign is premised on the divine context within which those particular wars were necessary. In Rāma's case, his suffering is a result of having banished his wife, which he did because she had to be abducted in order for him to defeat Rāvaṇa, an abduction which he (Rāma) unknowingly prompted for this purpose;[50] and then she was tainted and not a suitable queen. Bhīma Pāṇḍava says something similar about Draupadī at the dicing match, where she has been sacrificed for the sake of the divine plan: 'One of our lights has been put out, because our wife has been tainted: how can offspring be born from a tainted woman?'[51] And in the *Mahābhārata* Janamejaya does not descend from Draupadī, but from Arjuna's wife Subhadrā, Kṛṣṇa's sister.

The political peace during Yudhiṣṭhira and Rāma's reigns contrasts with the king's lack of peace of mind. Yudhiṣṭhira is troubled by having presided over such extensive and close bloodshed, and presumably by having staked Draupadī in the game of dice. Rāma is troubled by his treatment of Sītā. After the Kurukṣetra war, Bhīma tells Yudhiṣṭhira:

47 Trans. Bakker, 'The Hindu Religion and War', 29; cf. Romila Thapar, *Aśoka and the Decline of the Mauryas* (Oxford: Oxford University Press, 1961), 256: 'all beings should be unharmed, self-controlled, calm in mind, and gentle'. On Aśoka see also Patrick Olivelle, Janice Leoshko, and Himanshu Prabha Ray, eds, *Reimagining Aśoka: Memory and History* (Delhi: Oxford University Press, 2012).

48 See Aśoka's rock edicts 1, 3, 4, 8, and 11; Thapar, *Aśoka and the Decline of the Mauryas*, 250–55.

49 Hiltebeitel, *Nonviolence in the Mahābhārata*, 25–31; Tamar C. Reich, 'Sacrificial Violence and Textual Battles: Inner Textual Interpretation in the Sanskrit Mahābhārata', *History of Religions* 42.1 (2001).

50 Rāma prompts the abduction of Sītā by mutilating Śūrpaṇakhā; see *Harivaṃśa* 31.118; *Rāmāyaṇa* 3.16–18.

51 *Mahābhārata* 2.64.7, trans. John D. Smith, *The Mahābhārata: an Abridged Translation* (Delhi: Penguin Classics, 2009), 154, adapted.

> Now a terrible battle with your mind alone awaits you. A battle in which there is no need for arrows, nor allies, nor kinsmen; a battle you must fight by yourself – that is the battle that awaits you. And if you lose your life before the battle is won, you will arrive at another body and you will fight with it [your mind] again. So you must enter that battle now, Bharata bull. And after you have won it, great king, you will have done what you had to do.[52]

The yogic aspect implied here is not evident in the *Rāmāyaṇa*. Rāma's kingship is not so accessible in these terms.

Janamejaya and the Snakes

As mentioned, the story of Yudhiṣṭhira and his war against Duryodhana is told, several generations later, in the context of the violent feud between Yudhiṣṭhira's successor-but-one, King Janamejaya, and the snakes. This feud with the snakes actually originated in the time of Yudhiṣṭhira. When the ancestral kingdom was first divided and the Pāṇḍavas were given the wilder half, Arjuna and Kṛṣṇa together cleared a lot of land, by burning down the Khāṇḍava Forest and killing its inhabitants. Takṣaka the snake was away at the time, but Takṣaka's wife was killed, and Takṣaka's son only just escaped.[53] That son, Aśvasena, tried to get their own back on Arjuna in the form of one of Karṇa's arrows in the Kurukṣetra war, but he missed his target and was killed by Arjuna.[54] So when, years later, Takṣaka killed Janamejaya's father Parikṣit by snakebite, that act was motivated as vengeance. Janamejaya's attempt to kill all snakes is motivated in turn as vengeance for the death of his father Parikṣit. But as a result of his hearing the story of the Kurukṣetra war (the story of Yudhiṣṭhira and Arjuna), Janamejaya's genocidal project against the snakes is abandoned in favour of a peaceful solution. The story of Yudhiṣṭhira's suffering thus guides Janamejaya to break a multigenerational cycle of violence.[55] Insofar as the *Mahābhārata* is the story of Janamejaya being changed by the story of Kurukṣetra, both it and the story of Kurukṣetra that it contains are framed

[52] *Mahābhārata* 12.16.21–23, trans. Fitzgerald, *Mahābhārata* vol. 7, 199; cf. Ronald Inden, 'Ritual, Authority, and Cyclic Time in Hindu Kingship', in John F. Richards, ed., *Kingship and Authority in South Asia* (Delhi: Oxford University Press, 1998 [1978]), 51.

[53] *Mahābhārata* 1.218.4–11.

[54] *Mahābhārata* 8.66.1–24; Christopher Minkowski, 'Snakes, *Sattras* and the *Mahābhārata*', in Arvind Sharma, ed., *Essays on the Mahābhārata* (Leiden: Brill, 1991), 397.

[55] Hiltebeitel, *Rethinking the Mahābhārata*, 113–18; Tamar C. Reich, 'Ends and Closures in the *Mahābhārata*', *International Journal of Hindu Studies* 15.1 (2011), 42–43.

together as a didactic text on the subject of royal violence and peace. Janamejaya achieves peace in response to a story of violence.

Janamejaya and his Wife

At the edge of the frame, in the *Mahābhārata*'s final chapter, Janamejaya performs a horse sacrifice.[56] Just as the gods took form at Kurukṣetra to put such a violent scar in his ancestry, and just as Viṣṇu took form as Rāma in order to kill Rāvaṇa, who unfortunately compromised Sītā, Indra takes the form of the suffocated horse and, while Janamejaya's wife dutifully copulates with it as per the ritual injunctions,[57] Indra copulates with Janamejaya's wife. When Janamejaya discovers that his wife has been violated, he dismisses her and his priests, but after listening to advice he reconsiders and takes her back, and they live happily ever after.

The story of his ancestors does not instruct Janamejaya to call off the snake massacre. His calling it off is presented as a favour that he grants for Āstīka, a skilful singer who comes to the ritual;[58] and so the question of why Janamejaya should forgive the snakes is not directly addressed. But he is told why he should forgive his wife, Vapuṣṭamā ('Most Beautiful'):

> You're a man who has performed three hundred rites, and Vāsava [Indra] will not put up with it. But this wife of yours has not done anything wrong. Vapuṣṭamā has been bestowed upon you ... She is a precious woman, your majesty, a real gem, and you should embrace her ...
>
> Do not lay the blame on Vāsava, on your guru, on yourself, or on Vapuṣṭamā, for [the power of] time cannot be overcome in the slightest ...
>
> ... This woman is without sin, and she's a real gem. So leave your sorrow behind and enjoy her. If women who are without sin are abandoned, they too can cast curses. But women are not villains, your majesty ... The light of the sun, the flame of the fire, and the offering upon the sacrificial altar remain untainted even after they have been touched by someone else, and it is the same with women: they remain uncorrupted. Wise men should always

[56] *Harivaṃśa* 118.

[57] Stephanie W. Jamison, *Sacrificed Wife / Sacrificer's Wife: Women, Ritual, and Hospitality in Ancient India* (New York: Oxford University Press, 1996), 65–72.

[58] *Mahābhārata* 1.11.12–13.45; 1.49–53; for Āstīka's song of praise, see 1.50.1–16.

> honour women of good character – they should accept, caress, and revere them. Women should be revered like goddesses of fortune.[59]

The last act in Janamejaya's story must be read in the context of the rest of his story. Janamejaya's quarrel with his wife recapitulates his quarrel with the snakes: he gets violently angry and resolves upon an extreme course of action, but then he receives a text – in one instance, the story of his ancestors; in the other, the passage quoted immediately above – in the wake of which he subdues his anger and finds a peaceful solution. But here I would also understand the brief story of Janamejaya and Vapuṣṭamā in juxtaposition with the story of Rāma and Sītā, because I think it deliberately invites this. In pursuing such an analysis, we consider violence and peace not in terms of physical violence between men (or men and snakes), but in terms of procedural violence towards women.

The quoted passage is a rebuke to Janamejaya, but it can also be read as a rebuke to Rāma. Rāma's rejection of Sītā was prompted by his discovery that his subjects were muttering about his taking Sītā back after she had been in the possession of another. The subjects said:

> What sort of pleasure could be produced in his heart through the enjoyment of Sītā, since earlier Rāvaṇa, clutching her to his side, had forcibly carried her off to Laṅkā? And how can Rāma not despise her who was taken to Laṅkā and, what is more, placed in the *aśoka* grove under the control of the *rākṣasas*? Now we shall have to put up with this from our own wives as well. For people always follow what the king does.[60]

This public angle, unless it is merely implicit, is not present in the story of Janamejaya and Vapuṣṭamā. There is no mention of what the subjects might have said about Janamejaya taking his wife back after she had been violated by Indra. It is not clear that they would know it had happened. The two situations also differ in that Vapuṣṭamā has seemingly been violated, but Rāma knows that Sītā has not been, since she proved it to him by walking through fire at their reunion,[61] and we also know it because, in

[59] *Harivaṃśa* 118.24, 25cd, 33, 35c–36c, 37–38, trans. Simon Brodbeck, *Krishna's Lineage: the Harivamsha of Vyāsa's Mahābhārata* (New York: Oxford University Press, 2019), 360–61, adapted.

[60] *Rāmāyaṇa* 7.42.17–19, trans. Robert P. Goldman and Sally J. Sutherland Goldman, *The Rāmāyaṇa of Vālmīki* vol. 7 (Princeton: Princeton University Press, 2017), 334.

[61] *Rāmāyaṇa* 6.102–6.

accordance with the curse cast upon Rāvaṇa after he raped Rambhā,[62] Rāvaṇa's head would have exploded had he raped Sītā. But in matters of royal reputation, suspicion is damaging enough.[63] In abandoning Sītā, Rāma's concern is for his and his family's reputation.[64]

But Janamejaya listens to advice about his plan of action, in this matter as also in that of the snakes, and this is the larger part of his story: the story of his ancestors dominates the story of his snake sacrifice, and the words of advice quoted above dominate the story of his horse sacrifice. In the matter of abandoning his wife, Rāma by contrast consults only with his brothers, and as their elder he silences their advice or opposition in advance.[65] It is to Janamejaya's benefit that, at a similar juncture in his own story, he receives and heeds good advice. The story of Janamejaya's horse sacrifice thus responds to the story of Rāma and proposes – as the *Rāmāyaṇa* itself implicitly does – a new kind of masculinity for the king, and by implication also for his male subjects. By shifting their final terms of reference onto the relationship between man and woman, both texts comment on their contents in an interesting and significant way, using gender to frame the discourse of violence and peace just as they use it to frame other related discourses not discussed here – such as discourses of yoga, and of God and the cosmos.

Violence and the Gods

In closing, we return to the divine context of the wars in both texts. God repeatedly acts in the world in order to destroy, for reasons that are presented mythologically but that consequently remain slightly opaque. In the *Mahābhārata*, the war was between human males, and the death count was unconscionably high, as Yudhiṣṭhira knows, and so something significant and alarming obviously happened there, as the story goes. Coming to peaceful terms with such history is made easier for Janamejaya by the theological aspect of the Kurukṣetra war. In the end, for all the mythological

[62] *Rāmāyaṇa* 7.26.

[63] Simon Brodbeck, 'The Rejection of Śakuntalā in the *Mahābhārata*: Dynastic Considerations', in Saswati Sengupta and Deepika Tandon, eds, *Revisiting Abhijñānaśākuntalam: Love, Lineage and Language in Kālidāsa's Nāṭaka* (Delhi: Orient Blackswan, 2011), 222–27.

[64] *Rāmāyaṇa* 7.44.11–13.

[65] *Rāmāyaṇa* 7.44.18–20.

detail, it is a holy mystery why all those men died there, and that helps Janamejaya put the violence away into the past. And so the story of Janamejaya, as the *Mahābhārata* presents it, can help its audience to do the same. In both cases, as also for the *Rāmāyaṇa* and its audience, the centre of the holy mystery is the god Viṣṇu. He (and by all accounts it is a he) is to be known through the devotional discipline that Kṛṣṇa prescribes for Arjuna in the *Bhagavadgītā*; he is to be known, at least in part, as Arjuna suddenly knew him, as time grown old to devour everyone. Insofar as the mythology of the Earth's problem being solved by the gods (the damsel in distress being rescued) necessarily replicates the tropes found in stories about male humans, these texts implicitly critique the very theology that they present, at least as regards its approach to the problem of evil. But Janamejaya can learn from all that he has heard, and can be a great king while fighting the good fight against his mind, with all that he knows from Vyāsa about Viṣṇu, and without the trauma of having been used as the tool of the gods.

Further Reading

Simon Brodbeck, trans., *Krishna's Lineage: the Harivamsha of Vyāsa's Mahābhārata*. New York: Oxford University Press, 2019.

J. A. B. van Buitenen and James L. Fitzgerald, trans., *The Mahābhārata*, vols 1–3 and 7. Chicago: University of Chicago Press, 1973–2004.

Kisari Mohan Ganguli, trans., *The Mahabharata of Krishna-Dwaipayana Vyasa*. Delhi: Munshiram Manoharlal, 2000 [1883–96]. The chapter numbers in this translation usually differ from those of the critical edition. https://www.sacred-texts.com/hin/maha/, accessed 8 June 2022.

Robert P. Goldman et al., trans., *The Rāmāyaṇa of Vālmīki: an Epic of Ancient India*, 7 vols. Princeton: Princeton University Press, 1984–2017.

W. J. Johnson, trans., *The Bhagavad Gita*. Oxford: Oxford University Press, 1994.

W. J. Johnson, trans., *The Sauptikaparvan of the Mahābhārata: the Massacre at Night*. Oxford: Oxford University Press, 1998.

CHAPTER 3

Spectres of Violence and Landscapes of Peace: Imagining the Religious Other in Patterns of Hindu Modernity

Ankur Barua

One of the most vexed problems in the scholarship on the nexus of 'religion' and 'violence' is the proper way in which the relationship should be understood. While certain Hindu, Muslim, and Christian worldviews have become implicated in, or have been host to, forms of brutality, the crucial debate is centred on how we should understand such enmeshments. Are they to be seen in terms primarily of concepts relating to God and the world *or* of the material factors that shape the sociocultural spaces in which these concepts exist? We can also ask, of course, whether such a 'concept versus world' distinction can be meaningfully drawn in the first place. Such questions will frame our exploration of some modes of antagonism and amicability in the Hindu worlds *vis-à-vis* Indian Muslims. We adopt this

Postitionality: I write as a scholar of Indian Religions and a Hindu-Catholic.

A. Barua (✉)
Faculty of Divinity, University of Cambridge, Cambridge, UK
e-mail: ab309@cam.ac.uk

M. Power, H. Paynter (eds.), *Violence and Peace in Sacred Texts*,
https://doi.org/10.1007/978-3-031-17804-7_3

comparative perspective to highlight the point that contemporary configurations of violence structured by Hindu idioms are not generated in scriptural spaces quarantined from historical inflections. Rather, they belong to the *longue durée* of Hindu projects of cultural revitalisation, which emerged from the middle of the nineteenth century. The contours of these community-based identities are dialectically shaped by self-other intersections – idyllic invocations of primordially 'peaceful' Hindus are raised against lurid depictions of irredeemably 'violent' Muslims. These polarised projections constitute the burden of history for individuals who are engaged in peace-making processes in post-colonial India.

This essay is divided into three sections, which are related to each other. It will sketch some of the socio-political landscapes on which modernist Hindu forms of belligerence and benevolence have been constructed from around the 1850s. It will outline some premodern contexts where conceptual archetypes from Sanskrit texts were instrumentalised to configure antagonistic attitudes towards socio-religious outsiders. Our discussion will demonstrate the dense interrelations, across Hindu lifeforms, between those strands which legitimise or endorse violence and those strands which unequivocally denounce violence. On the one hand, a toughminded realism acknowledges some forms of violence as foundational to the quotidian jurisdiction of a king or a judge. On the other hand, there is a repeated insistence that all such enactments of violence should be ultimately transcended on vistas of perpetual peace. With the gradual institutionalisation of colonial modernity in British India (1858–1947), the fine balance between these two somewhat opposing pulls – worldly conflict or transcendental concord – becomes destabilised. This becomes an existential inheritance for Hindus in social milieus which are being increasingly restructured through western education, racialised hierarchies, the railways, the census reports, and so on.

Therefore, as we will see, the motif of 'Hindu violence' is an intricate tapestry of *ideational* and *institutional* threads. To name a few: the construction of Hindu*ism* as a unified body of 'religious' beliefs and doctrines; the mobilisations of anti-colonial movements through Hindu cosmological imaginations; the membership of a 'religious community' as the political identifier of an individual; the postcolonial imperatives of nation-building on landscapes structured by the category of a minority; the demographic anxieties relating to the dissipation of the Hindu 'community' through the conversion to Islam of some subaltern groups; and so on.

As prominent Hindu figures begin to configure projects of political autonomy and cultural sovereignty, they find themselves on dynamic landscapes shaped both by 'extrinsic' differences *vis-à-vis* Muslims of non-Indic origins and by 'intrinsic' differences *vis-à-vis* Indic subalterns. On these landscapes, we witness styles of both retaliatory violence and cordial benevolence. As we will see, there are Hindu ways of inhabiting domains of religious diversity which discern, in modes of hospitality, the spiritual self (*ātman*, *jīva*) in the seemingly distant other, and there are also Hindu ways of projecting, in modes of hostility, this worldly alterity as demoniacally alien.

The Persistence of Premodern Pasts

In the 'long' century between 1850 and 1950, the geopolitical terrains of South Asia witnessed some volatile combinations of cultural resurgence and anticolonial nationalism. These were often tinged with or structured by Sanskrit-shaped symbolisms. Some influential Hindu intellectuals, socio-religious reformers, and political leaders played a pivotal role in these processes. They creatively reconfigured the foundational concept of socio-cosmic order (*dharma*). First announced in the Ṛg Veda (*c.*1500 BCE), *dharma* becomes a leitmotif running through vast bodies of Hindu scriptural theologies, ethical treatises, and soteriological disciplines. In this Vedic cosmo-religious vision, the harmonious interrelations and the symbiotic synergies across the universe are viewed as dynamic expressions of the primordial order-instituting ritual sacrifice (*yajña*) of a cosmic person (*puruṣa*). It is this cosmogonic oblation that has generated structure-constituting and structure-sustaining *dharma* across ritual, ethical, and social domains. This Vedic understanding of *dharma* is reworked across the multiple *Upaniṣads* (*c.*800–400 BCE), the *Manusmṛti* (*c.*200 CE), the *Bhagavad-gītā* (*c.*200 BCE), the *Rāmāyaṇa* (*c.*400 CE), the *Mahābhārata* (*c.*400 CE), the encyclopaedic *Purāṇas* (*c.*300–1000 CE), and so on.

The centrality of *dharma* – with its reverberating resonances of coherence, stability, and harmony – to these religious imaginations is reflected by its occurrence in the very first verse of the *Bhagavad-gītā* ('on the battlefield of *dharma*') and the frequent citations of a phrase from the *Manusmṛti* which states that '*dharma*, when preserved, preserves'.[1] The

[1] 8.15.

male Brahmin composers of *dharma* treatises such as the *Manusmṛti* lay down some codifications of *dharma* which reflect their socio-elitist and androcentric presuppositions. The worldly duties of individuals are refracted through the hierarchically granulated prisms of gender and caste or social grouping (*varṇa*). For instance, the socio-moral duties of women, a man who belongs to the priestly (*brāhmaṇa*) or the servant (*śūdra*) caste, or a priest in the stage of life (*āśrama*) of a householder, and so on are precisely delineated in this vision of an ideal *dharmic* polity. This 'organic' ecosystem of *varṇa-āśrama-dharma* is embossed in the foundation of reality. Thus, the socio-moral *dharma* reflects, as well as reinforces, the cosmological *dharma*, and vice versa.

Vedic Cosmologies and Mundane Realities

Two aspects of this 'myth of origin' are especially significant for our discussion of the entanglements between self-affirmations of Hindu magnanimity and other projections of Muslim malevolence. Firstly, according to this socio-cosmic mapping, by properly discharging their intra-mundane *dharma*-shaped obligations, individuals contribute to the maintenance of the supra-mundane *dharma*. Therefore, the *dharmic* universe has a fractal-shaped structure, where all the worldly parts sustain the cosmic whole, which itself sustains them. Thus, in the *Bhagavad-gītā*, when Arjuna initially refuses to engage in a fratricidal conflict, Kṛṣṇa advises Arjuna that he is a warrior (*kṣatriya*), and there is for him no *dharma* higher than fighting in a righteous battle.[2] The implication is that if Arjuna – *qua* warrior – were not to fulfil his micro-*dharmic* responsibilities of restoring macro-*dharmic* order, the fabrics of reality would unravel. Secondly, this motif raises the momentous question of whether non-Vedic peoples, such as Muslims and Christians, can be located on *dharmic* domains. The compilations of *dharma*, which appear from around the turn of the first millennium, begin to crystallise the boundaries of an ethno-cultural group with Brahmin priests as the speakers of the perfected (*samskṛta*) language (that is, Sanskrit), the interpreters of Vedic truth, and the enunciators of the cosmos-ordering mantras. Thus, *dharma* becomes the ethno-linguistic marker of the way of life of a specific group of people, who are descended from the primordial person and whose sociocultural forms are to be defended against the barbarian 'outsiders' (*mleccha*). Their dwelling is

[2] 2.31.

Āryāvarta, the land of Ārya ('noble') people, and it roughly corresponds to present-day northern and north-western India. This is the hallowed ground where *dharma* is to be cultivated with their sacred language, Sanskrit. Moreover, they must avoid transactions with *mlecchas*.[3] As we will see, around 1800 years later, this nexus of Vedic origin and sacred geography would be reactivated in British India to represent Muslims as the paradigmatic *mlecchas*.

Such imageries of self-construction and other projections also run through the narratives of the *Purāṇas* where the gods (*devas*), symbolising *dharma*, are often overrun by the demons (*asuras*), symbolising *adharma*. The universe becomes an antagonistic site where 'good' *dharma* struggles with, and eventually (just about) overcomes, 'evil' *adharma*. This mythic paradigm is historicised by premodern Hindu poets who identify real-world enemies with demonic aliens. Thus, human kings are often presented as divine incarnations (*avatāra*) who have appeared to overcome the demonic powers which are threatening the privileges of Brahmin priests. For instance, the *Vikramānkābhyudaya*, which is set against the backdrop of clashes between the Chalukya and the Rashtrakuta dynasties (*c.*1100 CE), applies the *cosmological* template to these *historical* kingdoms. The text describes the God Viṣṇu's promise, in the style of the *Purāṇas*, that Viṣṇu will be born on earth to rid it of the demonic Rashtrakutas and restore Vedic order.[4]

Some contemporaneous texts apply to Muslim rulers the *Purāṇic* descriptors of 'Yavana' ('Ionian' for Indo-Greeks) and 'Śaka' (Indo-Scythians), which refer to two groups who had invaded from the north-west from around the second century BCE. They otherize Muslims as the demons of *Purāṇic* cosmology. Sanskrit and Telugu inscriptions from southern India, between 1323 and 1650 CE, concretize the cosmic war by rearticulating the stylised predictions in the *Purāṇas* relating to the 'dark age' (*kali-yuga*). For instance, the Vilasa grant states that with the defeat of the righteous king Prataparudra by Sultan Muhammad bin Tughluq, the 'pitch darkness of the Turks enveloped the world'. Brahmin priests were forced to abandon ritual activities, villages were confiscated,

[3] *Manusmṛti* 1.31; 1,87; 2:17–24; 10:44–45; *Vasiṣṭha Dharmasūtra* 6.41.

[4] Phyllis Granoff, 'Holy Warriors: A Preliminary Study of Some Biographies of Saints and Kings in the Classical Indian Tradition', *Journal of Indian Philosophy*, 1984, vol. 12, pp. 291–303, 294–95.

temples were desecrated, and so on. The grant also notes that the Muslim advance was halted by Prolaya Nayaka, who was an incarnation of Viṣṇu and who restored *dharmic* order by reinstalling Vedic sacrifices.[5]

The Essential Tension

However, these emphases on a world-*grounding* solidity have co-existed in a somewhat uneasy tension with the pursuit of a world-*transcending* dissolution of all finitude associated with suffering (*duḥkha*). While the scriptural texts noted above – from the *Upaniṣads* to the *Purāṇas* – are generally received as 'Veda-rooted', they can diverge significantly in their conceptualisations of the relation between the this-worldly *dharma* and the quest for liberation (*mokṣa*) from the cycles of rebirth (*saṃsāra*). This soteriological transformation involves the overcoming of spiritual ignorance and the realisation of the imperishable self. In Vedantic patterns of exegetical theology, we find distinctive articulations of a dialectic between concretisations of *dharma* in hierarchical milieus and pilgrimages towards the spiritual summit beyond all hierarchies. Therefore, a crucial motif that Vedantic commentators such as Śaṃkara (*c.*800 CE), Rāmānuja (*c.*1100 CE), Madhva (*c.*1300 CE), and others sought to explicate was the relation between the spiritual self (*ātman*) that is embedded in finite *dharmic* structures and the divine reality (*Brahman*) beyond all finitude.

Keeping in mind that our primary focus is not the doctrinal motifs of these Vedantic visions but their 'translations' into the hurly-burly of socio-political existence, we highlight below the central dialectic.

On the one hand, the embodied self is subject to the hierarchy of *varṇa-āśrama-dharma* in socio-ritual spaces. For instance, the *dharmic* obligation of the *śūdra* lower castes is to serve others, and the *strī-dharma* of women is to be dependent on their menfolk. Call this a 'vision of austerity' (VAU) – in these cosmologies configured by male priests, structure is to be sustained in a spatiotemporal world, which is precariously poised between the opposing forces of *dharma* and *adharma*. On these terrains of violence, the Brahmins are the guardians of divinity, and it is through their rituals that *dharma* is cosmologically regimented and *adharma*, enacted by *mlecchas*, is restrained.

[5] Cynthia Talbot, 'Inscribing the Other, Inscribing the Self: Hindu-Muslim Identities in Pre-Colonial India', *Comparative Studies in Society and History*, 1995, vol. 37, pp. 692–722, 696–703.

On the other hand, the true self is boundlessly free in non-hierarchical spaces, so in this state of liberation there are no *dharma*-structured differentiations. Call this a 'vision of abundance' (VAB) – in these eschatological vistas, the world is rooted in the spiritual egalitarianism of a limitless ontology of peace (*śānti*). By cultivating the *dharma* of liberation (*mokṣa-dharma*) laid down by a particular Vedantic tradition, the embodied self attains or recovers its spiritual nature, which is not modulated by *dharma* relating to gender and caste. In other words, *sub specie aeternitatis*, the universal *dharma* cannot be refracted differentially *vis-à-vis* Indic subalterns such as *śūdras* or circumscribed ethno-culturally *vis-à-vis* non-Indic aliens such as Indo-Greeks, Muslims, or Christians.

More tersely: if *dharma*-structured styles of VAU can motivate xenophobic antagonism in a world of scarce resources, styles of VAB, also *dharma*-structured, envision humanity as spiritually enfolded into primordial plenitude. The VAU-plane itself embodies an ethical tension between the particularised *dharma* that applies to a specific *varṇa* and the generalised *dharma* that applies to every *varṇa* – in one list, the latter comprises the virtues of nonviolence (*ahiṃsā*), truthfulness, non-stealing, purity, and mastery of the senses.[6] Reinforcing the VAB-motif, figures such as Mahatma Gandhi (1869–1948) would completely 'de-territorialise', in conditions of colonial modernity, the VAU-*dharma* so that it applies not only to the Hindu ethnos under Vedic canopies but to all humanity in non-antagonistic relationality.

Already some Vedic texts seek to deny the violence of the sacrifice – the animal victim in the *aśvamedha* sacrifice is told that it does not really die nor is it truly harmed but goes on to the gods.[7] This deep ambivalence towards violence appears in the *Upaniṣads*, where the individual's inner self (*ātman*) becomes the true sacrificial site, into which are offered mental functions homologised with material elements. This anti-ritualism provides the context for substitutionary vegetable offerings and the emergence of the ethic of nonviolence (*ahiṃsā*). Texts from the Sāṃkhya and the Yoga traditions are critical of violence to animals, while figures such as Kumārila (*c.*700 CE) and Śaṃkara develop the exegetical response that Vedic rituals cannot be regarded as impure on account of inflicting injury

[6] *Manusmṛti* 10.63.

[7] Brian K. Pennington, 'Striking the Delicate Balance: Teaching Violence and Hinduism' in Brian K. Pennington (ed.), *Teaching Religion and Violence* (Oxford: Oxford University Press, 2012), 19–46, 23.

on animals because such rituals are scripturally authorised.[8] This transcendental legitimisation or domestication of violence also structures the *Bhagavad-gītā*. Even as Arjuna surveys the 'austere' landscape of imminent fratricidal violence, he is advised by Kṛṣṇa, the supreme divinity, that it is only through the densities of his *dharma*-structured duty of fighting *adharma* that he can attain 'abundant' liberation. Thus, inhabiting a VAU-shaped socio-ritual milieu and fulfilling one's *dharmic* duties – which may include inflicting *dharmically* channelized violence – is a preparatory practice towards a VAB-shaped liberation.

Precisely by working through and moving beyond the violence of this-worldly *dharmic* domains, an ascetic can gain other-worldly *dharmic* power to intervene in the world. Through the cultivation of nonviolence, the world renouncer embodies a spiritual sovereignty to oppose or ally with kings.[9] In appealing to the *ātman*-centred power of *ahiṃsā* as a moral force that would prevail over Empire-instituted armies, and traditional Hindu antipathies towards the lower castes and Muslims, Gandhi was not the first – though he was the most prominent in our times – of such Hindu ascetic figures.

To summarise our discussion so far: human history repeats consecrated cosmology. The world-preservative dimensions of the *Purāṇic* paradigm are rearticulated in British India throughout Hindu anxieties regarding the degeneration of *dharma* in the body politic. This degradation is manifested in the incursions of Muslim marauders, the British socio-legal interventions in Hindu ritual spaces, and the conversions of Hindus to various British Christian denominations. If the cosmological *dharma* is the transcendental template for the social fields destabilised by *adharmic* antagonisms in colonial contexts, the clarion call for restructuring a Hindu 'home' vis-à-vis the attacks of 'foreigners' must also be issued with *dharmic* idioms. In these contexts, *dharma* becomes the social glue that would hold together the *communitas* of the Hindus in their socio-cosmic clashes with the Muslims.Therefore, the VAU–VAB dialectic repeatedly turns up in apprehensions relating to Muslims as the paradigmatic 'external others'

[8] Jan E.M. Houben, 'To Kill or Not to Kill the Sacrificial Animal (yajña-paśu)? Arguments and Perspectives in Brahmanical Ethical Philosophy' in Jan E. M. Houben and Karel R. van Kooij (ed.), *Violence Denied: Violence, Non-violence and the Rationalization of Violence in South Asian Cultural History* (Leiden: Brill, 1999), 105–183.

[9] Denis Vidal, Gilles Tarabout, and Eric Meyer, 'On the Concepts of Violence and Non-Violence in Hinduism and Indian Society', in Denis Vidal, Gilles Tarabout, and Eric Meyer (ed.), *Violence/Non-Violence: Some Hindu Perspectives* (Delhi: Manohar, 2003), pp. 11–26, 17.

in correlation with the lower castes on Hindu social spectra as the 'internal others'. Concurrently, however, other imaginations gesture towards a spiritual harmony that would transcend all oppositional antagonisms.

The Dynamics of Dharmic Domains

Several conflicting notions of nationhood were configured, imagined and enacted on the landscapes of British India. Some of these narrations were pivoted on the projections of the Muslim as the prototypical embodiment of *adharma* who was descended from medieval bloodthirsty invaders and was fanatically intent on desecrating Vedic Hindu cultures. The configuration of *dharmic* boundaries and the establishment of *dharmic* solidarity become two interrelated processes in constructions of Hindu identity on volatile terrains crisscrossed by colonial hierarchies, racialised projections, and competitions for limited socioeconomic resources.

The imagination of two distinct communities of 'the Hindus' and 'the Muslims' was implicated in colonial policies and Orientalist scholarship. Under the Judicial Plan of 1772, Governor-General Warren Hastings decreed that all disputes concerning matters such as inheritance, marriage, and so on would be settled by the East India Company in accordance with the Qur'ān for Muslims and the socio-religious compendia in Sanskrit (*śāstras*) for Hindus. This declaration was followed by the Government's sponsorship of N.B. Halhed's *A Code of Gentoo Laws* (1776). One presupposition of this Plan was that it was possible to distil a singular Hindu code out of the diverse *śāstras*, ignoring the traditions of contested interpretations. Another pre-supposition was that the natives could be placed under two clearly discernible legal jurisdictions, namely, *the* Hindus and *the* Muslims. In this reification of religion, the self-understanding of Brahmin scholars as the custodians of sacred *dharma* was endorsed, while a specific category called 'Anglo-Mohammedan law' was constructed with some Central Asian texts such al-Marghīnānī's *al-Hidaya*.[10]

Crucially, Halhed presented Hastings as the restorer of the moral system of the Vedas and the deliverer of the Hindus from their Muslim

[10] Barbara Metcalfe, 'Introduction' in Barbara Metcalfe (ed.), *Islam in South Asia in Practice* (Princeton: Princeton University Press, 2010), pp. 265–70, 266–67.

oppressors.[11] Such British self-congratulatory inventions of a Muslim darkness from which they had heroically delivered the Hindus into the 'enlightenment' of modernity were related to their historical memories of the Crusades and to their anxieties about the 'Muslim' Mughal rulers whom they had recently displaced. Their Eurocentric projections of Islam would have a long survival through uncritical re-articulations by some Hindu scholars – with cataclysmic consequences across South Asia to this day. Thus, Tarinicharan Chatterjee's widely read Bengali textbook, *History of India* (1858), punctuates the narrative into the 'Hindu' phase of ancient glory, followed by the tyranny unleashed by the 'Muslim' invaders, and the present epoch of degradation. These invocations were partly shaped by the writings of some British Orientalists who believed that by turning to foundational texts such as the Vedas, they were recovering the pristine elements of Hindu*ism*. This sense of a rupture between a primordial Vedic vision and its later accretions was appropriated by various figures who believed that through a recovery of the ancient worldview, they could bring about a Hindu renaissance. For some, the deterioration could be traced to the time of the *Mahābhārata* and for others, to the 'dark ages' of the Mughal emperors, but they were in agreement that a resurgent Hindu*ism* must drink again from the fonts of a Vedic 'golden age'.

These *Purāṇic* figurations of the Muslims – as one militarised phalanx which pushed a unified bloc of peaceful Hindus into (nearly) terminal decline – began to develop against the backdrop of a colonial obsession with numbers, which was manifested in a mass of data about land, caste, religious grouping, and so on. The taxonomic classifications such as the decennial all-India census from 1870 produced a social landscape dotted with enumerated groups of Hindus and Muslims. As Peter van der Veer points out, while distinctions across Hindus and Muslims were not generated by the British *ex nihilo*, 'to count these communities and to have leaders represent them was a colonial novelty, and it was fundamental to the emergence of religious nationalism'.[12] Thus, the notion of a 'religious community' began to play an increasingly more significant role on Indic terrains, where the question of the political affiliations of Muslims and

[11] Rosane Rocher, 'British Orientalism in the Eighteenth Century: The Dialectics of Knowledge and Government' in Carol Breckenridge and Peter van der Veer (ed.), *Orientalism and the Postcolonial Predicament: Perspectives on South Asia* (Philadelphia: University of Pennsylvania Press, 1993), pp. 215–49, 222.

[12] Peter Van der Veer, *Religious Nationalism: Hindus and Muslims in India*, (Berkeley: University of California Press, 1994), pp.19–20.

subaltern Hindu groups came to the fore. Some prominent members of the Muslim intelligentsia began to articulate their conviction that the Muslim 'community' had fallen behind the Hindu 'community' in the race for advancement through English education and government employment.

Around the time of the Morley-Minto Reforms in 1909, which granted separate electorates to Muslims, political presence thus became a field of quantitative contestation. These Reforms stipulated a reserved number of 'minority' seats for Muslims in Municipal and District Boards. Electoral representation was now a crucial variable shaping the access of a particular 'community' to socioeconomic resources. This colonial configuration of socio-political space on the 'communal' basis of numbers was concurrent with vigorous projects to construct Hindu*ism*, Islam, and Sikh*ism* as unified communities out of various classes, castes, and regional groups. Thus, in the 1930s, the question of which Indians were to be classified as 'Hindu' or 'Muslim' was not simply (if it ever was) a matter of an individual's spiritual dispositions. This question had wide-ranging ramifications for the material careers of the members of each 'community'.

Projections of Solidarity

These 'communal' dynamics provided the backdrop for the quasi-apocalyptic claim that Hindus, because they were divided into numerous castes, were a weakened body which could not resist the onslaughts of the well-organised Muslims. From the 1880s, several pamphlets presented Islam as a fanatical religion driven by bloodthirsty intruders who were intent on killing peace-loving Hindus in the name of a holy war.[13] These VAU-modulated anxieties were fuelled by the publication of U.N. Mukerji's *Hindus–A Dying Race* (1909). On the basis of the 1901 census, Mukerji claimed that Hindus would disappear within 400 years because of the relative rise in Christian and Muslim populations. As preparations for a Hindu Conference in the Punjab in October 1909 gained momentum, the organisers received the writings of Mukerji: Muslims had multiplied by 33 per cent between 1872 and 1901, and Hindus only by around 17 per cent. This speedy multiplication of Muslims was attributed to their aspiration for solidarity, material welfare, and strength, and the decline of Hindus to

[13] Prabhu Bapu, *Hindu Mahasabha in Colonial North India, 1915–1930* (London: Routledge, 2013), 86.

their lack of political organisation. Therefore, the delegates highlighted the need to strengthen the consciousness of Hindu unity by popularising Hindu scriptures, celebrating Hindu festivals, producing a distinctive Hindu history, and so on. They emphasised the formation of consensus across the Hindu 'community', which had to be organised to defend itself against the All-India Muslim League (established in 1906) and the British government. Criticising the Indian National Congress (established in 1885) for not supporting 'Hindu interests', the Conference called for a 'Hindu-centred politics'.[14]

These oppositional constructions of Hindu*ism vis-à-vis* Muslims are vividly crystallised in a contemporary text (1910) whose authors seek to refute the charge that the Arya Samaj, established in 1875, was a 'political' organisation which was fomenting seditious revolution against the British. The text states that before the arrival of its founder, Swami Dayananda (1824–1883), the Hindus had forgotten the pure wisdom of the Vedic scriptures. Swami Dayananda valiantly fought against the forces of unrighteousness, superstition, and servile reverence for clerical authority. Emphasising that his mission was purely 'religious', the authors describe his titanic struggle: 'Citadel after citadel was captured by frontal attacks … The battle thickened. He bore the brunt all alone'.[15] They present the 'Vedic church' as a universal religion for humanity and Swami Dayananda himself as an exemplar of forbearance: 'He always met taunts, curses, anathemas and imprecations, with blessings, benedictions, good wishes and loving thoughts, and frowns by sweet smiles. Such was the man whom the followers of Mohomed … charge with intolerance'.[16] Around this time in Bengal, in the wake of anti-Partition agitations (1905), volunteer brigades, gymnasiums, and nationalist societies were organised which were directed at *svadeśī* ('indigenous') enterprises. The novelist Bankim Chandra Chatterjee (1838–1894) had invoked the Goddess Kālī as a symbol of the motherland and – reflecting our VAU-VAB dialectic – oriented the Hindu tradition of monasticism towards a selfless this-worldly dedication to the nation. The fearsome aspect of Kālī symbolised the regenerative violence necessary for political independence, and the revolutionaries

[14] Ibid., p.18.

[15] Munshi Rama and Rama Deva, *The Arya Samaj and its Detractors: A Vindication* (Dayanandadabad: Rachna Book Center, 1910), p. 6.

[16] Ibid., pp. 97–98.

would work as agents in the divine manifestation of the Mother.[17] The Sanskrit-shaped invocation *Vande Mātaram* ('I revere the Mother'),[18] which was the rallying cry during these anti-colonial protests, remains a divisive slogan in Hindu–Muslim conflicts on postcolonial terrains.

In short, for the Arya Samaj and several other organisations, such as the All-India Hindu Mahasabha (established in 1915), the need of the hour was Hindu organisation (*saṅgathan*) against the perceived threats of the Muslim other. The communitarian identity that they sought to mobilise involved the promotion of Hindi instead of Urdu (which was viewed as a 'Muslim' language) and the protection of the cow. B.S. Moonje, the president of the Mahasabha (1927–1933), articulated the unease in these terms: 'In India ... the Moslem heads and the Christian heads are yearly increasing in numbers and are hopefully aspiring to swallow up the majority community of the Hindus or to reduce it to a minority community'.[19] While Hindus were divided into the 'water-tight compartments' of numerous castes, Muslims were well-organised and flourishing members of an organic community. Lamenting that pacific and cowardly Hindus had been overrun by violent Muslims, Moonje called for the reinstallation of Vedic animal sacrifices so that Hindus would become hardened to the sight of blood and killing.[20] Claiming that violence to defend one's rights should not be condemned, Moonje declared that he rather liked 'the Muslims for the virile vigilance with which they protect their racial interests ... which, alas, is visibly lacking in the present-day Hindu race'.[21]

[17] Barbara Southard, 'The Political Strategy of Aurobindo Ghosh: The Utilization of Hindu Religious Symbolism and the Problem of Political Mobilization in Bengal', *Modern Asian Studies*, 1980, vol. 14, pp. 353–76.

[18] Julius Lipner, "Icon' and 'Mother': An Inquiry into India's National Song', *Journal of Hindu Studies*, 2008, vol. 1, pp. 26–48.

[19] Prabhu Bapu, *Hindu Mahasabha in Colonial North India, 1915–1930* (London: Routledge, 2013), p. 52.

[20] Ibid., p. 85.

[21] Christophe Jaffrelot, 'Opposing Gandhi: Hindu Nationalism and Political Violence' in Denis Vidal, Gilles Tarabot, and Eric Meyer (ed.), *Violence/Non-Violence: Some Hindu Perspectives* (Delhi: Manohar, 2003), pp. 299–34, 306.

The Historical Hierarchies of Hindustan

Under the leadership of V.D. Savarkar (1883–1966), the Mahasabha began to pursue even more vigorously a (hyper-)masculinist programme of establishing the undivided Hindu nation (*rāṣṭra*). For Savarkar, the Hindus are a people who dwell in their fatherland (*pitṛbhū*) of Hindustan and are bound together by the ties of common blood because they are descended from their Vedic fathers.[22] Savarkar admits that these characteristics apply to the majority of Indian Muslims who, if they are 'free from the prejudices born of ignorance', are able to love Hindustan as their fatherland, and who, because they have been recently converted to Islam, have inherited Hindu blood. Crucially, however, Indian Muslims cannot be called true members of the Hindu nation because they do not pay homage to the common culture, which is inherited from Vedic times and preserved through Sanskrit. In a modern-day recapitulation of the *Manusmṛti*'s VAU-projections of *mlecchas*, Savarkar declares that Muslims are a people with extra-territorial allegiances to Arabia. Their 'love is divided' since they do not view Hindustan as a holy land (*puṇyabhū*). In contrast, centuries of conflicts with Pathans, Turks, Mughals, and others have united Hindus into a singular nation, for they 'all suffered as Hindus and triumphed as Hindus', and were thus 'individualised into a single Being'.[23] The crucial moment in this Manichean reconstruction of history was the invasion of Hindustan, a land of peace and plenty, by Mahmud of Ghazni (*c.*1000 CE). Savarkar's apocalyptic delineations of this catastrophic day are suffused with VAU-inflected idioms: 'the conflict of life and death began [on that day]. Nothing makes Self conscious of itself so much as a conflict with non-self… Hatred separates as well as unites'.[24]

Reworking Vedic Visions for the Present

The premodern *Purāṇic* paradigm of a *dharmic* world teetering on the brink of *adharma* because of the onslaught of aliens – here, Mahmud lurking at the gates of Hindustan – is also reflected in some contemporary texts and movements. From 1911, the Rām-līlā procession during the

[22] Vinayak Damodar Savarkar, *Hindutva* (Delhi: Hindi Sahitya Sadan, 2003 [1928]), pp. 84–85.

[23] Vinayak Damodar Savarkar, Hindutva (Delhi: Hindi Sahitya Sadan, 2003 [1928]), pp. 43–45.

[24] Ibid., pp. 42–43.

festival of Dusshera in Benaras and Mathura historicised the mythic depictions in the *Rāmāyaṇa* of the God Rāma slaying the demon Rāvaṇa. These narratives were correlated with political tussles such as the Queen of Jhansi's battle with the British during the massacres of the 'Mutiny' of 1857. The provincial administration was alarmed by the report that in a procession the Queen rode 'on horseback with a British soldier transfixed on her spear'.[25] Reworking such militant imageries, Savarkar denounced Gandhi's call to nonviolence as a promotion of Hindu passivity in the face of the aggressive Muslims who were a powerful minority, with their numbers increasing at every census. He declares to his audiences that if the British were defeated in a world war, Indian Muslims could call upon neighbouring Muslim powers and re-establish Muslim rule.[26] He laments that because of the Gandhian claim that the true spiritual warrior is the spinner of homemade cloth, Hindus had largely refused to join the Army so that the percentage of Muslims in it had risen to 62 per cent. However, after the British Government opened up the armed forces to Hindus, the Mahasabha sent thousands of Hindus there, so that this figure has come down to 32 per cent.[27]

Thus, Hindu (hyper-)masculinity would become the vitalised site for the bio-cultural regeneration of a unified Hindu nation which would avenge the racial humiliations it had suffered under the British masters. Several leaders of the Mahasabha called for the establishment of wrestling gymnasiums, where the manliness of Hindus would be cultivated to counter the British racial stereotype that the Hindus were an effeminate people. For instance, at the 1923 session of the Mahasabha, M.M. Malviya called for the construction of a temple to the deity Hanumān and a gymnasium in every village and urban quarter of the country.[28] Such mobilisations were concurrent with 'communal' riots during the 1920s whose major flashpoints were the synchronisation of Hindu festivals such as Rām-līlā with the sacrifice of cows during Eid and the playing of music by Hindus in front of mosques. From the 1930s, the Mahasabha pursued several militarisation drives to mobilise Hindus in the event of an Islamic invasion.

[25] Sandra B. Freitag, *Collective Action and Community: Public Arenas and the Emergence of Communalism in North India* (Berkeley: University of California Press, 1989), 199–205.

[26] Vinayak Damodar Savarkar, *Hindu Rashtra Darshan* (Poona: Maharashtra Prantik Hindusabha, 1992 [1949]), p. 86.

[27] Ibid., p. 125.

[28] Prabhu Bapu, *Hindu Mahasabha in Colonial North India, 1915–1930* (London: Routledge, 2013), p. 83.

Medieval 'Hindu' kings such as Maharana Pratap (1540–1597), Shivaji (1627–1680), and others, who had valiantly fought against the 'Muslim' Mughals, were reclaimed as exemplars of Hindu self-rule (*svarāj*).

Some of the Mahasabha's themes are reflected in the cultural imaginations of the Rashtriya Svayamsevak Sangh (RSS; established in 1925), which portrays the embattled Hindu nation as the Mother who should be heroically revered and selflessly served by her courageous sons. In an appropriation of mythic motifs, Dusshera – symbolising the victory of *dharma* over *adharma* – is given a martial tone and weapons associated with Shivaji are venerated. The formal hierarchy includes charismatic leaders such as K.B. Hedgewar (1925–40) and M.S. Golwalkar (1940–73), and a network of organisers who are usually young unmarried men. These organisers have an ascetic lifestyle, and they supervise the functioning of the branches (*śākhās*) at the grassroots and coordinate the activities at regional and national levels. The members of these branches meet once a day for an hour of games and training in martial arts, and they finish with a prayer to the Motherland. Crucially, echoing our VAU–VAB dialectic, these mobilisations are referred to as forms of spiritual training and are often said to generate a strong sense of solidarity among the participants.[29]

Gandhi's Struggles with Nonviolence

On the other side of these idioms and institutions of competitive antagonism stood Gandhi, with his somewhat tragic attempts to foster modes of Hindu–Muslim amity. These were often read by his opponents as 'favouritism' towards Muslims. The common representation of Hindu lifeforms as intrinsically 'peaceful' is partly a result of viewing a conceptual monolith called Hindu*ism* through the life and teachings of Gandhi. However, Gandhi himself had a far more realistically grounded awareness of the violent potentialities of certain patterns of Hindu hermeneutics. He presented the *Bhagavad-gītā*, which was invoked by some contemporaries in their 'revolutionary terrorism', as an allegory of an ongoing conflict within every human soul. According to him, *ahiṃsā* ('not-violence') was not simply the avoidance of harm to others but was 'a positive state of love, of

[29] Daniel Gold, 'Organized Hinduisms: From Vedic Truth to Hindu Nation' in Martin E. Marty and R. Scott Appleby (ed.), *Fundamentalisms Observed* (Chicago: University of Chicago Press, 1991), pp. 531–93, 568.

doing good even to the evil-doer. But it does not mean helping the evil-doer to continue the wrong or tolerating it by passive acquiescence ...'.[30] Gandhi believed that we instinctively respond to violence with brute-force because we have not cultivated what he called soul-force (*ātma-śakti*). While we think that retributive violence is the proper way to redress the balance, we overlook the fact that retaliatory viciousness only adds another loop to a feedback spiral in which both we, the oppressed, and they, the oppressors, become deeply intertwined. People who have acquired a taste for violence can progressively become desensitised to its destructive power. Instead, we must train ourselves towards the ideal of the *sthita-prajña* in the *Bhagavad-gītā* (2.54) – the individual who has overcome all enmity, greed, and fear through the spiritual surgery of negating the acquisitive ego. Like an enlightened Arjuna who might rise above hatred precisely on a battlefield, Gandhi's 'soldier of the spirit' (*satyāgrahī*) has effected the (higher) violence on the ego, which would end all (lower) violence directed at the world.

However, since the sense of humanity has become eclipsed in the violent oppressors, it is the oppressed – as the *sthita-prajña* – who must vicariously undertake the strenuous task of awakening their moral sensibilities. The oppressed would accomplish this recovery through suffering love expressed in the form of fasts, long marches, and civil disobedience. Since we are, in Gandhi's VAB-vision, interconnected units of a spiritual whole, the *satyāgrahī* would attempt to bring about this transformation by appealing to the moral core (*ātman*). Therefore, in Gandhi's 'moral utopianism', *svarāj* ('self-rule') meant not simply the end of British rule but also the moral regeneration of humanity across all binaries. When in September 1947, Gandhi began a fast in a Calcutta torn apart by Hindu–Muslim conflict, many people laid down their weapons and wept at his bedside. Lord Mountbatten, the last Viceroy of British India, claimed that Gandhi had succeeded where 55,000 soldiers had failed in Punjab. Gandhi saw in this 'heart-transformation' a confirmation of his conviction that soul-force is more powerful than brutal retaliation. Gandhi's 'this-worldly asceticism' would have resonated with a motif shaping Indian Sufi lineages – by renouncing the structures of violence in one's self, the holy

[30] Mahatma Gandhi, *The Collected Works of Mahatma Gandhi*, volume 18 (Delhi: The Publications Division, 1965), p. 195.

individual becomes a radiating heart whose spiritual strength is more transformative than any temporal power.[31]

At the same time, Gandhi's attitude to violence was responsive to context. For instance, he held violent resistance to be superior to cowardice in extreme situations and, again, he supported the British in the first world war on the grounds that it would be immoral not to assist a government that had provided domestic order during peacetime. These nuances were usually lost on his opponents such as his assassin N.V. Godse who claimed that Gandhian non-violence had led the nation to enslavement, for Hindus had lost the strength to fight back: 'I firmly believed that the teaching of absolute Ahimsa, as advocated by Gandhiji, would result in the emasculation of the Hindu community …'.[32] Instead, invoking an explosive scriptural archetype, Godse declared: 'I will consider it a religious and moral duty to resist and if possible overpower [the aggressor] by the use of force … In the *Mahabharat*, Arjun had to fight and slay quite a number of his friends and relations …'.[33]

Anxieties of Identity

These volatile interconnections between militarised masculinity and national narration are highlighted in Savarkar's pithy summary of *Hindutva* ('Hinduness'): 'We are Indians because we are Hindus and vice versa'.[34] The Muslims have 'tacitly declared war on Hindustan', and to counteract their threat 'our state must raise a mighty force exclusively constituted by Hindus alone, must open arms and munitions factories exclusively manned by Hindus alone and mobilize everything on a war scale'.[35] This call for the recovery of Hindu strength was enunciated by Golwalkar with uncompromising forthrightness: 'We want a "Man" with a capital "M" … Now

[31] Roland Miller, 'Indian Muslim Critiques of Gandhi' in Harold Coward (ed.), *Indian Critiques of Gandhi* (Albany: SUNY Press, 2003), pp.193–216.

[32] Nathuram Godse, *May It Please Your Honour: Statement of Nathuram Godse* (Pune: Vitasta Prakashan, 1977), p. 42.

[33] Christophe Jaffrelot, 'Opposing Gandhi: Hindu Nationalism and Political Violence' in Denis Vidal, Gilles Tarabot, and Eric Meyer (ed.), *Violence/Non-Violence: Some Hindu Perspectives* (Delhi: Manohar, 2003), pp. 299–34, 312.

[34] Savarkar, *Hindu Rashtra Darshan*, p. 29.

[35] Lise McKean, *Divine Enterprise: Gurus and the Hindu Nationalist Movement* (Chicago: Chicago University Press, 1996), p. 89.

our [Hindu] people are feminine men'.[36] However, these configurations of a unified Hindu nation were threatened by various movements among the 'untouchables' who claimed that they did not belong to the Hindu body politic. Therefore, organisations such as the Arya Samaj and the Mahasabha, fearing that these subaltern groups would move towards Islam or Christianity, started massive campaigns aimed at bringing them to declare their formal allegiance to the Hindu 'community'.

Thus, around the time of the census of 1931, the 'untouchables' in various parts of western and northern India began to claim that their socio-historical origins were different from those of the upper-caste Hindus. For instance, members of the Ad Dharm movement in Punjab in the 1920s declared that they were a distinct religious 'community' (*qaum*) and did not wish to be listed as 'Hindus'. In response, the Arya Samaj launched movements of socio-ritual purification (*shuddhi*) through which the 'untouchables' would be given access to Vedic rites and village wells, taught the *Gāyatrī* mantra, and allowed to wear the sacred thread.[37] During 1907–1910, the Samaj launched *shuddhi* programmes directed at Rajputs who had converted to Islam, and the Rajput Shuddhi Sabha claimed to have reconverted 1052 individuals.[38] However, the influx of 'untouchables' led to severe conflicts over their sociocultural positions within the Samaj. Most members of the Samaj remained attached to their caste-structured brotherhood (*birādarī*). Therefore, the initiation of commensal and connubial relations with those who had been recently 'purified' could lead to a dissolution of their social associations. For instance, the Meghs of Sialkot began to address the Rajputs with the Samaj greeting '*namaste*', rejected deferential forms of address such as '*garīb-navāz*' ('saviour of the poor'), claimed access to village wells, and refused unpaid labour (*begār*) to their landlords. The upper-caste Hindus often responded to these challenges to rural power structures with violent retaliation.[39]

These VAU-shaped anxieties – relating to *adharmic* destabilisation by Muslim 'outsiders' and subaltern 'insiders' – recur through ongoing mobilisations of Hindu socio-political identity. The socioeconomic shifts

[36] S.P. Udayakumar, *'Presenting' The Past: Anxious History and Ancient Future in Hindutva India* (London: Praeger, 2005), p. 37.

[37] Cassie Adcock, *The Limits of Toleration: Indian Secularism and the Politics of Religious Freedom* (Oxford: Oxford University Press, 2014), pp. 48–49.

[38] Kenneth W. Jones, *Arya Dharm: Hindu Consciousness in 19th-century Punjab* (Berkeley: University of California Press, 1976), p. 304.

[39] Adcock, *The Limits of Toleration*, pp. 127–28.

associated with the upwardly mobile lower castes ('Dalits' in present-day terminology), who were the beneficiaries of affirmative action instituted by the Constitution (1950), were concurrent with the rise of Hindu nationalist parties such as the BJP (1980), which often reflect the concerns of the assertive middle classes. Towards national unity, the VHP (founded in 1964) organised in 1983 an *Ekātmatā Yātrā* ('March Towards One-Souledness'). This event evoked various traditional Hindu idioms – carrying statues of Mother India (*Bhārat Mātā*) and ritual pots with the water of the Ganges, chariots traveled along three pilgrimage routes.

The premodern *Purāṇic* paradigm continues to suffuse constructions of the past in the embattled town of Ayodhya, where a mosque was demolished in December 1992. In these narratives, usually written in Hindi, 'Hindus' and 'Muslims' are pitted against each other in a mortal conflict, thus recapitulating the archetypal battle between gods and demons. In their chronologies, God Rāmā was born in Ayodhya around 9,00,000 years ago, the 'Hindu' king Vikramāditya constructed a temple there, which was destroyed by the 'Muslim' emperor Babar in 1528, and this demolition was followed by 76 'wars of liberation'.[40] These accounts combine *Purāṇic* cosmology with a strong emphasis on human agency. A righteous reign centred around Rāma, who is the embodiment of *dharma*, is to be realised in the immediate present. In these calamitous conjunctures – inherited from colonial stereotypes and reworked through postcolonial idioms – the *pacification* of Indian Muslims is envisioned as an essential moment in the establishment of the Hindu *peace*.

Conclusion

Against ahistorical generalisations such as 'Hindus are essentially peaceful folk' (or its conceptual cousin, 'All Hindus are vegetarians'), this essay has pointed to the intertwining of spiritual visions of peace and violent consolidations of identity in the 'deep history' of Hindu sociocultural formations. To craft an extended metaphor, our essay has sketched a spectrum of the afterlives of VAB-imaginations when they hit the rough ground of VAU-deprivations – some raised the drawbridge in enterprises of

[40] Gyanendra Pandey, 'The Appeal of Hindu History' in Vasudha Dalmia and Heinrich von Stietencron (ed.), *Representing Hinduism: The Construction of Religious Traditions and National Identity* (New Delhi: Sage Publications, 1995), pp. 369–88, 373–80.

self-fortification during the nightmare of history, while others continued to dream that another world of peace is somehow possible.

Thus, after pointing out that western observers are often surprised to see Hindus engaged in violent conflict, W. Doniger argues that 'it is what Hindus have said, and what they have seemed to believe, rather than what they have done, that had led to the European and American expectation of Hindu tolerance'.[41] For instance, groups of Daśanāmī ascetics appeared in the premodern centuries to protect the lands of temples and monasteries at a time of the dissolution of imperial authority, and during the latter half of the eighteenth century, they often entered as mercenaries into armies with Hindu, Muslim or English employers.[42] The point of these reflections is, of course, not to generate a neo-Orientalist stereotype such as 'Hindus are essentially violent'. It is to reinforce recent scholarship which has highlighted the interweaving between sacred cosmology and socio-political organisation in religiously motivated violence. For instance, C. Tyerman notes that sudden enthusiasm on the part of individuals would not supply the momentum for a full-scale Crusade, which would involve various forms of political, social, and financial networks. He indicates the nexus in these terms: '[A]ll the passion in the universe could not, cannot, create war, crusading or not, without the organization and manipulation of recruitment, finance, logistics, military structure – and ideas'.[43] While 'religion' itself is not *the* causal variable in religious violence, aspects of religious universes can significantly transform the nature of historical conflicts, by relocating these conflicts on transcendental horizons, supporting institutional mobilisations, and shaping collective identities.[44] Thus, enacting biblical variations on VAU, Oliver Cromwell drew parallels between the Catholics in Ireland and the Canaanites, while the Puritans in New England represented the native Indians as the Canaanites and the Amalekites.

[41] Wendy Doniger, 'Moral Paradoxes in Hinduism' in Anna Lannstrom (ed.), *Promise and Peril: The Paradox of Religion as Resource and Threat* (Notre Dame, Ind.: University of Notre Dame Press, 2003), pp. 106–124, 111.

[42] David Lorenzen, 'Warrior Ascetics in Indian History', *Journal of the American Oriental Society*, 1978, vol. 98, pp. 61–75.

[43] Christopher Tyerman, *The Crusades: A Very Short Introduction* (Oxford: Oxford University Press, 2005), p.87.

[44] Linell E. Cady and Sheldon W. Simon, 'Introduction: Reflections on the Nexus of Religion and Violence' in Linell E. Cady and Sheldon W. Simon (ed.), *Religion and Conflict in South and Southeast Asia* (London: Routledge, 2007), pp. 3–20, 16.

Thus, as we have argued, the dense interconnections between *ideational* reconstructions of primordial purity and *institutional* mobilisations of Hindu unity are vital to the representations of an intrinsically 'nonviolent' Hindu*ism*. For instance, when after the carnage of the First Afghan War (1839–1842), Governor-General Ellenborough ordered a general to retrieve a set of gates from Ghazni by claiming that they had been seized by Mahmud of Ghazni, and declared that with their return an 'insult of 800 years is at last avenged',[45] he was laying the ground for an edifice that would, in a tragic twist of history, outlast the British Empire itself – namely, the imagination of one unified Hindu self that is subjugated by one alien Muslim force. The vehement denunciations of Muslims as fifth-columnists and the frenetic movements to generate Hindu solidarity were dialectically interrelated in colonial spaces where political power was mediated through 'communal' representation. For the proponents of *Hindutva* in postcolonial India, the self-assertive movements among Dalits are a source of dismay, given their commitment to the civilisational unification of Hindustan through a solidarity where the castes would be 'organically' interconnected. Hence the rallying cry of the Motherland in distress which would unite all Hindus who consider the land to be imbued with divinity. Therefore, the markers of ethno-political unity are motifs drawn from Hindu religious archetypes such as Lord Rāma, Lord Kṛṣṇa, the Goddess, and so on.

However, as various social scientists have noted, socio-religious interactions between Hindus and Muslims in South Asia have been marked by various layers of complexity. These dimensions are obscured by the projections of an inevitable antagonism between the Hindu 'kingdom' and the Islamic 'brotherhood'. For instance, the common description of Benares as a 'Hindu' city ignores the presence of a sizeable Muslim population – while some Hindus participate in Sufi shrine veneration, Muslims contribute to the Hindu pilgrimage economy by supplying saris, sacrificial animals, and so on. In nearby Aligarh, which has witnessed endemic Hindu-Muslim riots, institutionalised systems of riot production have been generated. Through these systems, disputes are often fabricated by individuals who draw upon the discourse of threat to Hindus and interpret violence as a 'natural' Hindu response of self-defence. Therefore, such conflicts have to be viewed through the dynamic lenses of caste, class, occupation,

[45] Barbara Metcalfe, 'Preface' in Barbara Metcalfe (ed.), *Islam in South Asia in Practice* (Princeton: Princeton University Press, 2010), pp. xvii–xxv, xx.

language, and so on. In the wake of invasions by Muslim armies from around the eleventh century, Hindu kings were not united by a sense of 'holy war' and often fought amongst themselves. Hindu and Muslim rulers sometimes struck alliances for strategic reasons while, conversely, 'the brutal invasions of Persians (1739) and Afghans (1748–1767) from the northwest made no distinction on the grounds of religion; they attacked Muslims and non-Muslims alike'.[46] Such socio-historical densities are systematically effaced in the narrations, through *Purāṇic* prisms, of two monolithic blocs as perennially locked in a mortal combat. On these militarised landscapes, the trope of the 'violent Muslim' becomes a dialectical foil for the consolidation of a Hindu identity which must rise – in ethnonationalist imaginations if not quite in concrete reality – above caste-shaped divisions in the *dharmic* body.

Thus, across Hindu milieus, there are visions of superabundance which are rooted in a spiritual continuity across God, humanity, and world. There are also visions of scarcity which are structured by socio-political upheavals, demographic shifts, and socioeconomic deprivation. Both visions can – and often do – claim scriptural legitimation. It is from within this volatile crucible that we should seek to understand how multiple patterns of Hindu living have alternately become enmeshed in violent antagonism with religious outsiders and envisioned peaceful horizons of interreligious harmony.

Further Reading

Paul M. Brass, *The Production of Hindu-Muslim Violence in Contemporary India* (Seattle: University of Washington Press, 2003).

Adam Roberts and Timothy Garton Ash (ed.), *Civil Resistance and Power Politics: The Experience of Non-violent Action from Gandhi to the Present* (Oxford: Oxford University Press, 2011).

Peter Gottschalk, *Beyond Hindu and Muslim: Multiple Identity in Narratives from Village India* (New York: Oxford University Press, 2000).

Bhikhu Parekh, *Gandhi's Political Philosophy: A Critical Examination* (London: Macmillan, 1989).

Mrinalini Sinha, *Colonial Masculinity: The 'Manly Englishman' and the 'Effeminate Bengali' in the Late Nineteenth Century* (Manchester: Manchester University Press, 1995).

Gene Thursby, *Hindu-Muslim Relations in British India* (Leiden: E.J. Brill, 1975).

[46] Barbara Metcalfe, 'Introduction' in Barbara Metcalfe (ed.), *Islam in South Asia in Practice* (Princeton: Princeton University Press, 2010), pp, 1–39, 17.

CHAPTER 4

Jewish Interpretations of Biblical Violence

Alan Mittleman

The Problem of Biblical Violence

The Bible is full of violence. The violence comprises the normal operations of law, which include several dozen cases of capital punishment, corporal punishment, slavery, commanded war rising to the level of genocide against the indigenous peoples of Canaan, as well as against a marauding desert people, Amalek, divine threats (and sometimes realizations) of annihilation against wayward Israelite groups, and divine experiments on the character of discrete individuals, such as Abraham and Job. There are also violent incidents with violent consequences of a more 'secular' character, such as Shechem's rape of Dinah,[1] or the grisly rape of the Levite's

Positionality: I write as a scholar of Jewish Thought and Ethics, and as a Jewish philosophical theologian committed to purging violence from the concept of the sacred.

[1] Gen 34:1–31.

A. Mittleman (✉)
Jewish Thought, The Jewish Theological Seminary, New York, NY, USA
e-mail: almittleman@jtsa.edu

M. Power, H. Paynter (eds.), *Violence and Peace in Sacred Texts*,
https://doi.org/10.1007/978-3-031-17804-7_4

concubine at Gibeah,[2] which precipitates a massive war by all of the other tribes against the tribe of Benjamin.[3]

Genesis starts with the story of a serene and sovereign God who brings order out of indeterminacy, but the backstory, as we learn from academic scholarship, is a long history of divine conflict with the forces of chaos, comparable to the theomachy of ancient near eastern myths.[4] In fragments of creation stories made marginal by Genesis 1, such as Ps 74:12–17, God drove back the sea with all his might and crushed the heads of monsters. That's what it took to make a world. The unopposed God of the first, majestic creation story is the literary coda to earlier essays in cosmic conflict. Before God was sublime and serene, he was a victorious *warrior*.[5]

In the Bible, violent conflict seems fundamental to the warp and woof of human experience. With the first humans, violence manifests in human affairs. After creation, there follows betrayal. Temptation, disobedience, dissembling, blame, and guilt lead to expulsion into a harsh world where survival is not assured. Before there is law, there is punishment. And soon enough, there is fratricide—the first fully articulated relationship among brothers. Cain's humiliation by God—God rejects his offering for reasons known only to God—leads to murderous rage against his brother, Abel, whose offering is accepted. The Bible does not minimize or sugarcoat violence. It mirrors—it may even amplify—the violence that infects the human world. Assuming, as we should, that the Bible gives us a 'religion for adults' rather than comforting fictions, how could it be otherwise?[6] In confronting biblical violence, we confront ourselves. Nonetheless, biblical violence is disturbing. For the Bible does more than mirror our violence. In crucial instances, it legitimates it; God sometimes calls for it. That, to say the least, is troubling.

[2] Judges 19:22–30.

[3] Judges 20:1–48.

[4] Jon D. Levenson, *Creation and the Persistence of Evil: The Drama of Divine Omnipotence* (Princeton: Princeton University Press, 1988), 14–25.

[5] Levenson, *Creation and the Persistence of Evil*, XXV.

[6] Emmanuel Levinas, *Difficult Freedom: Essays on Judaism*, trans. Sean Hand (Baltimore: Johns Hopkins University Press, 1990), 11–23.

Rabbinic Readings of Violent Texts

It is not only modern 'enlightened' readers who are troubled by the violence of biblical stories and laws. Ancient and medieval Jewish interpreters were troubled by them, too. In what follows, let us look at some attempts by ancient, medieval, and modern Jewish interpreters to cope with violent biblical episodes or legal norms. Since antiquity, Jewish interpreters have deployed several strategies for diminishing, sidelining, or justifying violent norms. One strategy is to interpret a law out of existence, even though the original, ethically problematic law remains 'on the books.' I shall call this denial. Other strategies include what I shall call legalization, moralization, politicization, and historicization. In each instance, a biblical datum is put into a context—law, ethics, politics, or history—which brings, or attempts to bring, both intelligibility and greater acceptability. All of these depend on the relative freedom of rabbinic interpretation to depart from the obvious meaning of a scriptural text.

From the rabbinic point of view, God gave both a written Torah and an Oral interpretation of that Torah at Mt. Sinai.[7] Without the Oral Torah, the written scripture would be routinely misconstrued. The inherited Oral tradition looks to us, from our modern, historicist point of view, as an 'invented tradition.' But for the rabbis, it is not only co-eval with scripture, it is the divinely intended key to its meaning. A famous example of this dynamic is the law of talion, which itself entails a certain violence. The law of talion stipulates that one who assaults another and injures him shall be commensurably injured himself. Its famous phrase is 'an eye for an eye and a tooth for a tooth'.[8] This is rough justice, although it is justice of a kind. The Talmud, however, understands 'eye' as the monetary value of an eye, which is much less harsh.[9] From the (majority) rabbinic point of view 'eye' never meant 'eye.' (There were, of course, dissenters among the rabbis. Interpretive pluralism is also part of the hermeneutic picture.) What God always had in mind, so to speak, was monetary compensation for damages. Keeping the rabbinic tradition of interpretation in mind, let us look at how Jewish commentators and legists coped with violent texts.

[7] In the twelfth century, Maimonides formulated the belief in the divine origin of both the written and the oral law into a dogma. See his Perek Helek, on Mishnah, Sanhedrin, chapter 10; principle #8 in Isadore Twersky, *A Maimonides Reader* (Springfield, NJ: Behrman House, 1972), 420.

[8] Lev 19:20.

[9] b. Bava Kamma 83b.

Interpretive Strategy I: Denial

Consider first an example of **denial**. A law in Deut 13:13–19 requires the obliteration of an idolatrous Israelite city (*ir hanidaḥat*). Its inhabitants were to be killed with the sword, and the city itself burned to the ground, never to be rebuilt. The Talmud has it that *there never was such a city, nor will there ever be one*. The law exists only to be studied and to gain benefit therefrom.[10] What benefit could accrue from the study of such a morally problematic law? Rashi writes that the seven terms used in Deut. 13:15 (and two other Deuteronomy texts) form the basis for the rabbinic understanding of how investigations in capital cases should proceed. The idolatrous city case is a textbook example meant to generate norms of procedural justice. The rabbis then use these strenuous evidentiary and procedural norms to virtually eliminate the possibility of judicial execution in ordinary cases. This was one of the benefits of studying this problematic law.

Interpretive Strategy II: Legalization

Far more common is the strategy of **legalization**. To see how this works, consider the pericope mentioned above, the rape of Jacob's daughter, Dinah, by Canaanites (Hivites) in Shechem (Genesis, chap. 34). The son of the local Hivite chieftain, Shechem, saw her as she was visiting the women of the town and 'lay with her by force'.[11] He soon warmed to her and asked his father to acquire her legally for him as a wife. The father approaches Jacob and asks for his daughter's hand for his son: 'Please give

[10] b. Sanhedrin 71a .Rabbi Nathan Lopes Cardozo writes: 'It is most ingenious how the Sages justified this ruling [that the law was never meant to be operable]. They argued that it was impossible to destroy the entire city, since no doubt there must have been *mezuzot* on the doorposts of some of its inhabitants. (You can be a Jewish idol worshipper, but what Jew doesn't have a *mezuzah* on their doorpost?) Since it is forbidden to destroy the name of God, which is found in the *mezuzah*, and *everything* in the city had to be utterly destroyed, the law of *ir hanidachat* could not be enforced and was meant to be purely theoretical. That the mezuzah could be removed before the city would be destroyed was something the Sages did not want to contemplate! They must surely have been aware of this possibility. But since they believed that God could never have meant this law to be applied, they found an extremely far-fetched loophole and based their whole argument on a minor detail, which they could easily have solved and which they knew made little sense. It was deliberate trickery rooted in an unequalled moral awareness.' See Nathan Lopes Cardozo, 'The Deliberately Flawed Divine Torah,' 5, in TheTorah.com, https://www.thetorah.com/article/the-deliberately-flawed-divine-torah, accessed 8 June 2022.

[11] Gen 34:2.

her to him in marriage. Intermarry with us; give your daughters to us, and take our daughters for yourselves: You will dwell among us and the land will be open before you…(Gen 34:8–10).' The bride price can be as high as Jacob chooses to ask for. Shechem 'longed for' Dinah. Jacob's sons, who are seething with outrage at this indecency, speak to the Hivites deceitfully. They claim that Dinah cannot marry Shechem because he is uncircumcised. Until all of the male Hivites are circumcised, the deal is off. This was, to say the least, disingenuous. The sons had other plans. Shechem, his father, and eventually all of their townsmen agree. On the third day after the circumcision, with the Hivites still consumed by pain, Simeon and Levi, two of Dinah's brothers, came into the town and killed every male with their swords and brought Dinah home. Then the rest of the brothers came and took all of the women, children, animals, and other possessions as booty—a disproportionately violent consequence to a violent act.

Jacob is chagrined not so much by the violence per se but by its possible repercussions. 'You have brought trouble on me, making me odious among the inhabitants of the land…my men are few in number so that if they unite against me and attack me, I and my house will be destroyed.' The brothers were not mollified: 'But, they answered: "Should our sister be treated like a whore!"'[12] Later, on his deathbed, Jacob curses Simeon and Levi: 'Simeon and Levi are a pair; Their weapons are tools of lawlessness. Let not my person be included in their council, Let not by being be counted in their assembly. For when they are angry, they slay men… Cursed be their anger so fierce, and their wrath so relentless. I will divide them in Jacob, scatter them in Israel'.[13]

Two major medieval thinkers, Maimonides and Nachmanides disagree about how to understand this incident. Maimonides justifies Simeon and Levi's actions not so much for what Shechem did, but for what his townsmen failed to do. Explicating the Noachide Laws—the seven commandments incumbent upon all human beings—Maimonides claims that they failed to set up 'courts of justice.' The town's failure to prosecute Shechem could not go unmarked:

[12] Gen 34:30–31. All biblical translations, unless otherwise noted, are from *Tanakh: The Holy Scriptures* (Philadelphia: The Jewish Publication Society, 1985). (This is known as The New JPS translation or NJPS.)

[13] Gen 49:5–7.

> What must they [i.e. non-Jews] do to fulfill their requirement regarding the Law of Justice? They have to set up magistrates and judges in each district to judge the people with regard to these Six Commandments; and they must issue warnings (about them) to the people. A non-Jew who violates one of the Seven Commandments is executed by means of the sword. How is this so? Anyone who worships idols or blasphemed or murdered or had sexual relations with one of those forbidden to him or stole even less than the value of a Prutah or ate any amount from a limb or the flesh of a live animal or saw someone else violate one of these and failed to judge and execute him, is himself executed by means of the sword. It was for this reason all residents of the City of Shechem deserved to be executed. For Shechem kidnapped Dinah and they saw and knew and failed to judge him.[14]

Maimonides sees the brothers' act not as wanton revenge but as *just punishment*, absent an institutional legal system. This employs the rabbis' legalization strategy. Whenever a violent event in the Bible seems spontaneous, the rabbis tend to see it as the result of a legal process that they interpolate into the text.[15]

Nachmanides finds this unconvincing. He disagrees with Maimonides's interpretation of the Noachide laws and the consequences of violating the one positive law—setting up courts of justice. There can be no death penalty for an omission (i.e., failing to set up a legal system) only for committing criminal acts. Furthermore, if the brothers were acting out of an obligation to impose justice, shouldn't Jacob have done so first? Even if he were afraid to act, why would Jacob have been angry with them for doing what was right? But how could it have been right? At most, in Nachmanides's opinion, the rapist alone deserved death, not everyone else. Nachmanides thinks that the Hivites' agreement to become 'one kindred' with Jacob's

[14] *Mishneh Torah*, Laws of Kings and Their Wars IX:14.

[15] An especially striking example of this tendency is found in the rabbinic interpretation of the Phinehas incident in Numbers, chap 25. Phinehas executes Zimri and his Midianite consort, Cozbi, spontaneously in the Bible, spearing them through their bellies while they are having intercourse. But the Talmud places so many conditions on such punitive action that Phinehas himself could have become a murderer and liable to execution by a court had he not complied with those conditions. For an analysis, see Alan Mittleman, *Does Judaism Condone Violence?: Holiness and Ethics in the Jewish Tradition* (Princeton: Princeton University Press, 2018), 168. For a thorough review of all the rabbinic sources, see David Bernat, 'Pinchas' Extrajudicial Execution of Zimri and Cozbi,' at: https://www.thetorah.com/article/pinchas-extrajudicial-execution-of-zimri-and-cozbi, accessed 8 June 2022.

family through circumcision[16] was not disingenuous. Their agreement implied that they were open to choosing a godly way of life. They might have become proper worshippers of God. Thus, Simeon and Levi killed the townspeople for nothing; they 'had not done Jacob's sons any harm.' Thus, Nachmanides explains Jacob's lingering anger toward his sons. It goes beyond his initial dismay at his precarious position into a principled critique of their wanton violence. Nachmanides here rejects the legalization strategy. He does not give us an easy resolution to this morally fraught story.

Neither Maimonides' nor Nachmanides' readings remove the horror of the events, whether that of the rape or that of the slaughter, but they show how the interpretive tradition engages with a morally difficult text. Maimonides tries to justify the brothers' actions through an appeal to legal procedure; violence is normed by law. Nachmanides tries to criticize the brothers' actions as themselves violative of legal and ethical norms. Both take the actions out of the realm of mere vengeance and subject them to reasoned analysis. Their disagreement displays the open-ended, dialectical quality of the tradition. It invites us into a conversation about what can be justified and what cannot. Nor is the dispute resolved. We are left to make the best sense of it, that we can by reflecting on what constitutes violence, what attempts can be made to justify it, and what the differences between justification and mere post-facto rationalization are.

Another instance of legalization is the pericope of the wood gatherer of Numbers 15:32–36.

> Once, when the Israelites were in the wilderness, they came upon a man gathering wood on the sabbath day. Those who found him as he was gathering wood brought him before Moses, Aaron, and the whole community. He was placed in custody, for it had not been specified what should be done to him. Then the LORD said to Moses, 'The man shall be put to death: the whole community shall pelt him with stones outside the camp.' So the whole community took him outside the camp and stoned him to death—as the LORD had commanded Moses.

This is a violent text, but it is not a savage one. The wood gatherer is not the victim of a lynch mob but of a judicial procedure. The man is apprehended by some anonymous Israelites. Perhaps they knew the law,

[16] Gen 34:22.

propounded in Exodus 31:15, which mandated capital punishment for Sabbath violation. Or perhaps they sensed something taboo. But what precisely should be done to the wood gatherer was unclear. The legal tradition was not yet definite. They brought the wood gatherer before Moses, Aaron, and the whole community. Moses had to consult the Divine author of the law. God decreed death by stoning, effectuated by the entire community. The sin/crime affects the whole people; the whole people participate in the punishment.

In the hands of the rabbis, layers of legal procedure are added to the spare narrative. The overall thrust of rabbinic law is to diminish, to the vanishing point, the possibility of imposing a death sentence. One way that the law does this is through the device of *hatra'ah*: the requirement to give a warning to the would-be offender that what he is about to do bears a penalty of death (b. Sanhedrin 8b). The witnesses, no fewer than two, must also tell him the manner of death. If he persists and acts in a culpable way, which would indicate that he understands the consequences of his actions and accepts them, then he is liable to the death penalty.[17] (It is unrealistic that all of these conditions could obtain, particularly in the paradigm case of murder.)

One of the main sources for this procedure is the current story. As the rabbis read it, those who found him did more than find him; they *warned* him. The Talmud (b. Sanhedrin 41a) takes the verb ('as he was gathering'—a single word in Hebrew) to imply that while they were warning him, he persisted in gathering twigs; he heard what they were saying but was not swayed. With full awareness, he thus accepted the consequences of his action. What the finders did not know was what manner of execution the wood gatherer should face. They couldn't fully warn him in the proper way. The great medieval commentator, Rashi, speculates that they therefore had to tell him all of the possible ways that he might be killed. Moses himself wasn't sure what the punishment should be because he wasn't sure of his exact sin; there are a number of possible violations in play. The man had to be imprisoned until a determination of the legality and outcome of the whole process could be made. That is why Moses had to consult God, who ratified the criminal procedure and determined the punishment. The stress on proper procedure—legalization—counts toward the justification of the norm and its application. The criterion of

[17] b. Sanhedrin 40b.

procedural justice, the rabbis imply, has been satisfied. (Whether the norm is substantively just is not addressed.)

Interpretive Strategy III: Moralization

As is often the case, ancient midrash and medieval biblical commentary explore the human dimensions of the case or the characters, lending greater ethical depth to the norm or story. Here, we see the strategy of **moralization**. The gatherer, according to Kimhi, was collecting twigs that were similar to straw so that he could kindle a fire—a major Sabbath violation—and cook his manna on the Sabbath (another violation). The people who came upon him didn't just do so coincidentally—Moses knew that he was a troublemaker and told people to track his whereabouts and check on what he was doing (Hizkuni).[18] The man was someone, whose behavior had previously aroused suspicion; he was a bad influence on society. Indeed, some commentators see Moses as having established a whole system of oversight, a public police function to patrol for Sabbath violations. (If Moses had to set up a public morality squad, doesn't that imply that violations were widespread? If the wood gatherer were not an outlier in his flouting of Sabbath norms, does that diminish or enhance his guilt?) By adding ethical complexity, the midrash discredits the wood gatherer's motives, character, and conduct. It thus makes his punishment even more appropriate. In addition to the legal proceduralism, the rabbis craft an ethical context for the story—indeed, for almost every story.[19]

But why such a horrendous punishment for gathering sticks on the Sabbath? Why does violating the Sabbath—denigrating its holy status and rendering it profane and unholy—warrant the death penalty? Where is the substantive justice in that? Maimonides, following ancient midrash, likens the desecration of the Sabbath to the most extreme instance of biblical sin: idolatry. Just as idolatry implies utter rejection of God, so too does Sabbath violation. Maimonides writes:

[18] Michael Carasik, ed. and trans., *The Commentators' Bible: Numbers* (Philadelphia: The Jewish Publication Society, 2011), 112.

[19] A striking instance of this is the bizarre story in II Kings 2:23–24 about the prophet Elisha being insulted by a group of boys due to his baldness. Elisha summons bears to come out of the forest and maul the boys. The Talmud tries to justify the violence by painting the boys as wicked, irredeemable people. Fabulous backstories about the 'boys' (one of the rabbis ages them into adults who should have known better) darken their moral character and destiny. See B. Sotah 46b.

> Observance of the Sabbath and abstention from idolatry are each equivalent to the sum total of all other commandments of the Law. Furthermore, the Sabbath is an eternal sign between the Holy One, blessed be He, and ourselves. Accordingly, if one transgresses any of the other commandments, he is merely a wicked Israelite (*b'khlal rishei yisrael*), but if he publicly desecrates the Sabbath, he is the same as an idol worshipper (*k'oved avodat khokhavim u'mazalot*).[20]

Idolatry negates the biblical/Jewish project at its most fundamental level. Maimonides understands the Torah, indeed, the entirety of Judaism, as an ongoing rebellion against the human tendency toward idolatry. Abraham, the first Jew, as it were, launches a spiritual/moral rebellion against idolatry. He achieved a blazing intellectual insight into the truth of monotheism and sought to convince his contemporaries, through argument and moral example, of the pernicious error of idolatry. Moses, subsequently, through prophetic communion with the divine mind, received a law that gave definitive form to the rejection of idolatry.[21] It mobilized an entire nation to fight idolatry. That fight is its very *raison d'être*. Many of the laws of the Torah should be understood, according to Maimonides, as educational devices to train Israel to repudiate idolatry. Thus, the Sabbath, a sign of God's transcendence of the created world, severs any link between God and the things that human beings idolatrously worship. The Sabbath reminds Jews that idolatry is an intellectual and ethical arrest; it stops at the pseudo-ultimacy of some existent thing, say, the sun, moon, or stars, rather than going on to the Ultimate, their Creator. Desecrating the Sabbath is tantamount to affirming the validity of idolatry, hence the justification of its harsh punishment.

Interpretive Strategy IV: Politicization

Maimonides presents a highly intellectualized Judaism. But it is also a highly **politicized** one. Abraham founds a movement, but Moses founds a nation. The laws of all nations seek to secure the material and moral conditions of life for their inhabitants, but a divine law also brings them to true beliefs. The Torah encompasses and surpasses natural and civil laws by aiming both at the 'welfare of the body' and the 'welfare of the soul'.[22]

[20] *Mishneh Torah*, Laws of the Sabbath, 30:15.

[21] *Guide of the Perplexed*, III:29.

[22] *Guide* III:27.

Thus, the punishments that the Torah enacts for religiously perverse, viz., idolatrous beliefs and practices, are of a piece with its fundamental political orientation. Politics, unlike for moderns but very much like for Plato of the *Laws*, is meant to perfect human beings insofar as that is possible. (It is possible only for a very few, in Maimonides's opinion.[23]) Maimonides's overall framing of the Torah as a kind of constitution for the Jewish people establishes a broad political context. It makes individual laws the laws of a state (or, in medieval parlance, of a city—*medinah*). Since living in a polis or *medinah*, as Aristotle understood, is essential to the well-being of human beings, God's law, the supreme expression of law, is justified by its contribution to human perfection.

The establishment of a political context for Jewish legal norms continues into modernity.[24] Spinoza adopted this political framing of the Torah-constitution—and much else—from Maimonides. Spinoza notes that in the ancient Israelite/Jewish commonwealth,

> the enemies of this state were the enemies of God; citizens who aimed to seize the sovereignty were guilty of treason against God, and the laws of the state were the laws and commands of God. So in this state civil law and religion...were one and the same thing; the tenets of religion were not just teachings but laws and commands; piety was looked upon as justice, impiety as crime and injustice... There was considered to be no difference whatsoever between civil law and religion.[25]

In Spinoza, politicization of the law is complete. The entire legal order is meant to support a project of this worldly political life—a flawed and self-defeating project, by Spinoza's lights. The violence of any given biblical law is understood as part of the necessary violence of political life. Spinoza, excommunicated by the Amsterdam Jewish community, took the stance of an outsider. He didn't so much justify problematic laws as explain their purported ancient function and subsequent obsolescence. He both

[23] For a comprehensive view of Maimonides's political philosophy and the functions of law and punishment within it, see Haim Kreisel, 'Maimonides' Political Philosophy,' in Kenneth Seeskin, ed., *The Cambridge Companion to Maimonides* (New York: Cambridge University Press, 2005), 198.

[24] For an overview, see Alan L. Mittleman, *The Scepter Shall Not Depart from Judah: Perspectives on the Persistence of the Political in Judaism* (Lanham, MD: Lexington Books, 2000), 19–45.

[25] Baruch Spinoza, *Theological-Political Treatise*, trans. Samuel Shirley (Indianapolis: Hackett Publishing Company, 1998), 117.

politicizes and historicizes. The latter move, also anticipated by Maimonides, opens the way for modern Jews, who will try to nullify problematic norms by relegating them to an abandoned past.[26] Although ancient and medieval Jewish scholars did this too, modern historicism does not invoke their pious claim that history reveals divine providence. Modern historians assume Spinoza's outsider stance. They seek explanation more than normative justification.

Unlike Spinoza, Moses Mendelssohn continued to live within the normative universe of rabbinic Judaism. He maintained an internal point of view. But he also relegated the problematic norms to a past that, while not triumphantly overcome, was no longer pertinent; it must remain past. Like Spinoza, he accepts that the ancient Jewish state had a unique constitution. Judaism, he claims, is a revealed law, not a 'religion' in the Enlightenment sense. Its doctrines are the basic philosophical and moral beliefs of natural religion. What is particular to Judaism are its laws, which have a broadly moral, educational function. The laws and ceremonies are a script, the enactment of which shapes the moral conscience of the Jew and brings the individual to felicity. The civil and criminal laws of the ancient Jewish society were pertinent only to that bygone era when God was the actual sovereign of Israel. Mendelssohn writes that 'in this original constitution, state and religion weren't conjoined—they were one. They weren't connected, but identical. Man's relation to society and his relation to God coincided and could never come into conflict. God, the creator and preserver of the world, was also the king and administrator of this nation…'[27] Mendelssohn tries to undermine the standard categories of religion, state, and even theocracy. The ancient Mosaic constitution was

[26] Maimonides sometimes appealed to 'historical' explanations for certain Jewish norms and practices, such as the sacrificial system. Because the Israelites lived in a world where sacrifice was the normal means of approaching and communing with God, God's law could not have instituted a religion without sacrifice. It would have been too jarring a transition for the Israelites. Were God to have given his law at a later date, installing a sacrificial cult would not have been necessary. The law enshrines but constrains sacrifice, anticipating its eventual obsolescence. See *Guide* III:32. Maimonides thus provides a basis for contemporary traditionalists to see the Torah as both true and dependent on the cultural level of its human recipients. Torah might be thought of as 'a stage in God's plan at a particular moment in Jewish history.' See Nathan Lopes Cardozo, Ibid., 2.

[27] Moses Mendelssohn, *Jerusalem: Religious Power and Judaism*, trans. Jonathan Bennett accessible at: https://www.earlymoderntexts.com/assets/pdfs/mendelssohn1782.pdf, accessed 8 June 2022, 56.

incomparable, a singularity. Applying his framework to our case of Sabbath desecration, he writes:

> The same can be said of crimes. Every sacrilege against the authority of God, as the lawgiver of the nation, was high treason and therefore a state crime. Whoever blasphemed against God was insulting the monarch; whoever desecrated the Sabbath was setting himself against a fundamental law of civil society, for the establishment of this day was the basis for an essential part of the constitution… Under this constitution these crimes could be—indeed, *had to be*—punished by the state; not as wrong opinion, not as *unbelief*, but as *misdeeds*, outrageous crimes against the state, aimed at abolishing or weakening the lawgiver's authority and thereby undermining the state itself. And yet how leniently even these high crimes were punished![28]

Mendelssohn goes on to extol the rabbinic diminution of capital sentences through reliance on *hatra'ah* and other legal devices. When someone, like the wood gatherer, is punished for Sabbath desecration, what he was really punished for was a political rebellion against the authority of the state and its divine lawgiver.

When the civil bonds of the ancient Jewish nation were dissolved through foreign conquest, 'all corporal and capital punishments ceased to be legal…'[29] Judaism was able to become what it has been ever after: a religion based on a revealed law, the overriding purpose of which is moral improvement and spiritual felicity in this world and the world to come. There is no longer state power, sanctions, or punishment. The only 'sanction' is an individual sinner's conscience, which leads him voluntarily to change his ways. He then fully re-enters the non-coercive moral community which is Judaism. Mendelssohn leaves little doubt that this is a more fitting, ennobling expression of Judaism than the bygone Mosaic constitution, while at the same time rejecting the idea of moral progress. Mendelssohn has one foot in Maimonides's insider world of using history and politics to justify violent norms and the other in Spinoza's outsider world of using history to debunk them.

[28] Mendelssohn, *Jerusalem*, 57.
[29] Ibid., 57.

Interpretive Strategy V: Historicization

For Mendelssohn's nineteenth and twentieth-century descendants, the Jews of modernity, the insider-outsider use of history led eventually to the assumption that Judaism is nothing but a contingent historical product. One effect of this shift to modern historical consciousness is that, unlike for Mendelssohn, the authority of the Torah is fundamentally reconfigured. Rather than a definitive divine revelation that imparts an eternal law to the Jews, the law becomes a human product that develops, like all cultural artifacts, within the push and pull of lived human historical experience. Authority becomes a kind of cooperation between generations; the wisdom and custom of the past are kept alive through voluntary appropriation in the present. **Historicization**, at least in the academic realm, has become the dominant modern Jewish way of dealing with sacred texts, including the morally problematic ones. Let us consider some modern scholarship on the biblical phenomenon of 'holy war' to see how this mode of justification works.[30]

The commandment to obliterate the Canaanite people that dwell in the land God promised to the Israelites is given in Deut. 7:1–4.

> When the LORD your God brings you to the land that you are about to enter and possess, and He dislodges many nations before you—the Hittites, Girgashites, Amorites, Canaanites, Perizzites, Hivites, and Jebusites, seven nations much larger than you— and the LORD your God delivers them to you and you defeat them, *you must doom them to destruction: grant them no terms and give them no quarter*. You shall not intermarry with them: do not give your daughters to their sons or take their daughters for your sons. For they will turn your children away from Me to worship other gods, and the LORD's anger will blaze forth against you and He will promptly wipe you out.

[30] The term 'holy war' as a leading historian of religious warfare in Judaism admits is a misnomer. Reuven Firestone writes that '…there exists no *traditional* term for holy war in the vocabulary of either religion [Islam or Judaism]. 'Holy war' is a slippery term, and some have cautioned against using it in scholarship because of its current politicization and because the traditional context for its discussion is within Christian thought and practice. Moreover, holy war in the Western imagination is war for conversion, while neither Judaism nor Islam condones engagement in war for that purpose.' Nonetheless, Firestone takes the Jewish notion of 'divinely sanctioned war…war that is justified by divine authority' as a kind of holy war. Reuven Firestone, *Holy War in Judaism: The Fall and Rise of a Controversial Idea* (New York: Oxford University Press, 2012), vii–viii.

God will deliver the Canaanites into the Israelites' hands but the Israelites, for their part, must utterly destroy them (*ha-ḥareim taḥarim*)—man, woman, and child—as well as all of their possessions. The text tries to justify the enormity of this course of action, by portraying the Canaanites as incorrigibly idolatrous and the Israelites as prone to defect if they fall under Canaanite influence. If the Canaanites remain in the land, the Israelites will abandon God, who has made them His treasured people.[31]

This text, as well as Deut 20:16–18, which repeats the commandment of proscription (*ḥerem*) of the Canaanite nations and Deut 25:19, which commands the genocide of a related people, the Amalekites, presents these groups as *morally deserving* of destruction.[32] God's desire for their destruction is a matter of justice. The sin of these peoples is so great that, given how they have lived to date, they will not change and will only corrupt the Israelites moving into their midst. They are presented as moral monsters deserving of destruction through divine justice, executed by Israel. As Susan Niditch points out, however, within the Bible itself, this attempted justification was preceded (and accompanied) by another approach, rooted in priestly thought. The idea of *ḥerem* is drawn from the vocabulary of sacrifice. Animals or other possessions dedicated to God become holy (*kodesh*). Holiness cannot be reversed. Sacrificial animals that have been 'proscribed for the LORD' cannot be withdrawn for profane use.[33] They must be given to God through immolation on the altar. This scenario of vowing to sacrifice something to God, designating it as *ḥerem*, and then wholly destroying it, comes into play at Numbers 21:2–3.

> Then Israel made a vow to the LORD and said, 'If You deliver this people into our hand, we will proscribe (*haḥaramti*) their towns.' The LORD heeded Israel's plea and delivered up the Canaanites; and they and their cities were proscribed. So that place was named Ḥormah.

In this war text, Israel vows that if God lets them conquer the Canaanites in the Negev, they will proscribe the inhabitants and their towns, offering them as a sacrifice. This implies that the Canaanite other is 'human and

[31] Deut. 7:6.

[32] It is noteworthy that the general import of Deut, chapter 20 in which the commandment to proscribe the Canaanites occurs is one of limiting warfare. The chapter begins with a list of Israelites who can claim exemptions from having to fight and ends with an injunction not to the destroy the fruit trees of cities under siege.

[33] Lev 27:28–29.

valuable and does not turn him into a monster worthy of destruction, a cancer that must be rooted out. The enemy is not the unclean 'other' but a mirror of the self, which God desires for himself.'[34] The irony is, as Niditch points out, that Deuteronomy's ethicizing approach, which might seem more advanced than the Priestly author's holiness-based, sacramental approach, *does* see the Canaanites as a cancer, a morally evil people. The more ethically salient text diminishes the enemy's humanity. Nonetheless, ascribing agency to the Canaanites, seeing them as moral beings who are so degraded that they deserve ultimate punishment also attests to their humanity. Punishing them as an act of justice is not convincing but it is an attempt at justifying a law. It shows the biblical authors trying to work out different ethical models and justificatory strategies.

In the hands of the rabbis, holy war, like murder, becomes almost impossible to prosecute. The rabbis distinguish a 'war of commandment' from a 'discretionary war'.[35] The latter, like the wars of King David to expand the borders of his kingdom, are irrelevant, absent a Jewish state. The rabbis develop so many deferments from service that it is questionable whether an army could even be raised. The commanded wars, principally those against the Canaanites in order to conquer the land, have already been accomplished. The rabbis historicize the command into irrelevance. History has made it a dead letter.[36] Commenting on this nullification by historicization, Moshe Greenberg writes:

> [T]he sages left the ancient *ḥerem* law as they found it: applying to seven extinct nations, while radically meliorating other terms of the obsolete law. The rabbis adjusted its meaning to their moral sentiments. Since Deuteronomy expressly grounds the *ḥerem* in the warning 'lest you learn their evil ways and they cause you to sin to the LORD,' the rabbis concluded reasonably enough, that if the Canaanites reformed they should be allow to remain. The moral sensibility of postbiblical Judaism cancelled the indiscriminate inevitable application of the *ḥerem* (which is the plain sense of

[34] Susan Niditch, *War in the Hebrew Bible: A Study in the Ethics of Violence* (New York: Oxford University Press, 1993).

[35] Mishnah Sotah 8:7; b. Sotah 44b.

[36] Firestone, *Holy War in Judaism*, 77–90.

Scripture): it did not justify it by political or military reasons of public security or living space.[37]

To the extent that the texts bear any ongoing normative weight, it is because they were once God's will and—given an eventual messianic age and Jewish ingathering to the Land of Israel, they may well become God's will again. Some level of human participation in a messianic conquest may be required.[38] The war against Amalek, however, at least on some interpretations, remains obligatory. Furthermore, an opinion in the Jerusalem Talmud holds that wars of self-defense, unrelated to the conquest, are commanded and remain obligatory. These keep the possibility of *milḥemet mitzvah* (commanded war) notionally alive. If contemporary wars between the modern State of Israel and its neighbors can be characterized as wars of self-defense or wars against the ideological, but not biological, descendants of Amalek, then aspects of the ancient paradigm could be applied.[39] The possibility of 'sacralizing' contemporary warfare is, to state the obvious, deeply troubling and morally problematic.

The text of Deuteronomy chapter 20 distinguishes between towns that are 'very far off from you' and towns that are 'hereabout'.[40] The former should be offered peace terms; the latter must simply be proscribed. If the inhabitants of the former towns agree to surrender, then they shall be allowed to live, albeit as slaves to the Israelites. The latter, Canaanite

[37] Moshe Greenberg, 'On the Political Use of the Bible in Modern Israel,' in *Pomegranates and Golden Bells: Studies in Biblical, Jewish, and Near Eastern Ritual, Law, and Literature in Honor of Jacob Milgrom*, ed. David P. Wright, David Noel Freedman, and Avi Hurwitz (Winona Lake, IN: Eisenbrauns, 1995), 469. The aim of Greenberg's study is to repudiate the legitimacy of nationalistic and militaristic readings of the ḥerem commandment by modern Israeli extremists.

[38] An important dissenter is the medieval scholar Nachmanides, who claims that there is a commandment to conquer the land of Israel incumbent upon all Jews in every generation. That will involve war, although a genocidal war against contemporary inhabitants would not be commanded. Nachmanides, unlike Maimonides ties the ḥerem commandment to the conquest of the land rather than to the elimination of idolatry, as Maimonides does. Thus, since conquest of the land is an ongoing, valid commandment, war against it present occupiers is an ongoing desideratum. For texts and analysis, see Firestone, *Holy War in Judaism*, 128–131.

[39] On the tradition's construction of Amalek as a category of eternal, evil enemy rather than an historical people, see Firestone, *Holy War*, 101–104. See also Zev Garber, 'Amalek and Amalekut: A Homiletic Lesson,' in Isaac Kalimi, ed., *Jewish Bible Theology: Perspectives and Case Studies* (Winona Lake: Eisenbrauns, 2012), 147–160.

[40] Deut 20:15.

towns, however, are to be destroyed with all of their inhabitants. Based on some rabbinic precedents, Maimonides applies the leniency to be shown to the far-off towns to the Canaanites as well. 'A war is never waged against *anyone* before peace is offered,' he writes.

> This applies both to an obligatory war and to a permitted war, as it is written 'when you get near a city to wage war against it, you must offer peace. If they agree and accept upon themselves the seven mitzvot given to the children of Noah, not a single soul is to be harmed, and they are to pay taxes, as it is written 'they will pay taxes and serve you'.[41] If they accepted taxes but not servitude, or servitude and not taxes, we don't listen to them until they accepted both.[42]

Maimonides even includes Amalek under the category of 'anyone,' an innovation that drew some criticism within his own lifetime. Maimonides, through legal interpretation, effectively nullified the *ḥerem* against the seven Canaanite nations and Amalek. In principle, their treatment would depend upon their choice; they are portrayed as rational agents who can decide upon their future. Of course, in history, as the Bible presents it, other than the Gibeonites mentioned in Joshua 11:19–20, who were spared, the other Canaanite groups did not decide to surrender. They, therefore, deserved extirpation. The logic tracks that of Deut, chapter 20.

But were they actually extirpated? Are the texts that call for genocide, as well as the depictions of total war in Joshua, based on credible traditions? Are they idealizations, retrojections, or rhetorical warnings that, as scholars have suggested, are directed to idolatrous Israelites in the author's present more than to imagined Canaanites in an already remote past? Contrary biblical texts and traditions, as well as archeological evidence, strongly imply that the conquest of Canaan and the total destruction of the Canaanites, as depicted in Joshua, chapters 1–11, never occurred.[43] The ḥerem never took place. The biblical scholar Steven Geller, whose view is typical of contemporary academic scholarship, sees holy war as a fantasy retrojected onto the 'supposed 'conquest' of Canaan.' Its true purpose is to serve as a metaphor for God's 'fight against his own sinful

[41] Deut. 20:11.

[42] Maimonides, *Mishneh Torah*, Laws of Kings and Their Wars, 6:1.

[43] For a summary, with attention to the ethical implications, see Michael Walzer, 'The Idea of Holy War in Ancient Israel,' *The Journal of Religious Ethics*, 1992, Vol. 20, No. 2, 215–228.

people.'[44] Similarly, John Collins sees Deuteronomy as a text promulgated to support the work of King Josiah, who centralized the sacrificial cult in Jerusalem and destroyed idolatrous shrines around the country. Josiah's campaign against idolatry was directed not against actual Canaanites but against 'Israelites whose cultic practice did not conform to Deuteronomic orthopraxy.' Thus, 'there is much to be said then for the view that neither Deuteronomy nor Joshua, in the historical context of their composition, was intended to 'incite literal violence against ethnic outsiders,' but rather they were directed at 'insiders who pose a threat to the hierarchy that is being asserted'.'[45] Given the polemical, historically contextualized purposes of the text, they may tell us more, to quote Collins again, 'about the purposes of their human authors than about the purposes of God.'[46]

In these modern historical framings, the ḥerem is purely notional. It served highly ideological purposes in the seventh-century BCE world of the Deuteronomist. This dissolves some of the ethical problems by taking the norm out of the register of divine command and putting it into the register of political-religious rhetoric and polemic. But it also takes the divine commandments out of the register of divine command. What is left of revelation, authority, normativity as modern historicism does its work? The ascription of genocidal intent to God is no theological scandal on this view; God is just a character in a human drama of religious reform. But is there anything left of divine intent at all? The typical move of modern Jewish interpreters is to take the texts that teach generosity, compassion, welcoming the stranger, social solidarity, and so forth and to give them ethical primacy, to let them set the tone against which the violent texts are wanting. The rabbis did this, too, and it is all for the best. But I am not sure how this approach avoids the Euthyphro problem—by making God synonymous with the good, don't we also make God redundant? This question must remain open.

[44] See Geller's 'Prophetic Roots of Religious Violence,' David A. Bernat and Jonathan Klawans, eds., *Religion and Violence: The Biblical Heritage* (Sheffield, UK: Sheffield Phoenix Press, 2007), 51.

[45] John J. Collins, 'The Zeal of Phinehas: The Bible and the Legitimation of Violence,' *The Journal of Biblical Literature*, 2003, vol 122, no. 1, 11.

[46] Collins, The Zeal of Phinehas, 10.

In Lieu of a Conclusion: Open Questions

Do the various strategies for coping with violence in the Bible and the Rabbis go far enough? To my mind, they move in the right direction, but they do not fully achieve their goal. The texts remain a provocation. The overall approach of the classical and medieval traditions toward the most troubling texts of the Torah is to minimize their violence through reading the texts in context, in the contexts of law, ethics, politics, and history. The Torah points toward what a modern philosopher, Avishai Margalit, calls the decent society.[47] That is the pole star. A decent society is one in which violence, both routine and extraordinary, is rare. It is a society in which people have dignity and standing, and where the institutional humiliation and the denigration of others are condemned. It is a more modest ideal than a good society. It recognizes that violence is to some extent ineliminable, but that it should be delimited to the greatest extent possible. The Bible initiates that recognition and that effort at containment. Of course, it also points beyond, to a good, even to a perfected society where violence has been eliminated because 'the earth shall be filled with awe for the glory of the LORD as waters cover the sea.'[48]

But in the here and now, violence remains, both in our lives and in our inherited scriptural texts. For religious Jews, to enter the world of the text is to enter a fertile intergenerational conversation. The Torah is unfinished; it too remains open. The violent texts serve to sharpen our moral attunement and capacity for ethical critique. Better a scripture with glimpses of the uncanny and inassimilable than a Jefferson Bible, trimmed to the preferences of an 'enlightened' age. Modern readers should not approach these glimpses with a smug sense of their own moral superiority, but rather with humble perplexity as to how a good God could command or tolerate such seemingly bad things. That question too must remain open.

Further Reading

Robert Eisen, *The Peace and Violence of Judaism: From the Bible to Modern Zionism* (New York: Oxford University Press, 2011)

Reuven Firestone, *Holy War in Judaism: The Fall and Rise of a Controversial Idea* (New York: Oxford University Press, 2012)

Alan Mittleman, *Does Judaism Condone Violence? Holiness and Ethics in the Jewish Tradition* (Princeton: Princeton University Press, 2018)

[47] Avishai Margalit, *The Decent Society*, (Cambridge: Harvard University Press, 1996).

[48] Habakkuk 2:14.

CHAPTER 5

A Hermeneutic of Violence in Jewish Legal Sources: The Case of the Kippah

Laliv Clenman

מי איכא מידי דרחמנא פטריה ואנן ניקום וניקטול ליה?
Is there any case where the Merciful One exempts him and we rise up and kill him?
Babylonian Talmud Sanhedrin 82b

'We don't know what you've done,
but we wouldn't have you starved to death for it,

Positionality: As a scholar of rabbinic law and literature, I engage in the struggle to understand the most difficult and troubling of texts in a way that embraces the fullest and most forthright vision of the sacred and its connections to the divine and to human experience, acknowledging the integral significance of even the most violent legal and narrative traditions.

L. Clenman (✉)
Rabbinic Literature, Leo Baeck College, London, UK

King's College London, London, UK
e-mail: Laliv.Clenman@lbc.ac.uk

M. Power, H. Paynter (eds.), *Violence and Peace in Sacred Texts*,
https://doi.org/10.1007/978-3-031-17804-7_5

poor miserable fellow-creatur.'
Great Expectations, Charles Dickens[1]

Introduction

The early works of rabbinic Judaism, such as the Mishna, Tosefta, early exegetical works known as the midrashim, and the Palestinian and Babylonian Talmuds, comprise the rich and complex literary and legal traditions of late antique Judaism that continue to form the basis for much of Judaism.[2] The proper understanding of violent law in early rabbinic Judaism has been a matter of much debate, even within these classical sources, as well as amongst their later religious interpreters and in the analysis of contemporary scholarship. The study of such violent laws can also be viewed in the context of an increasing contemporary interest in the role of violent sacred traditions in religion. Is religious textual violence connected to the real-world violence that is associated with religious movements and, if so, how? In this chapter, I seek to enrich our understanding of the function and importance of violent legal texts in Jewish law beyond a discourse of apologetics or erasure. By exploring a case study of exceptionally violent sources in early rabbinic literature, I aim to contribute to the conversation on violence in rabbinic Judaism and religious law more broadly by arguing for the significance of violence as an inherent, necessary and even desirable characteristic of religious legal traditions.

[1] Charles Dickens, *Great Expectations* (London: Penguin Classics, 1860–61, 1996), 40.

[2] The Mishna and Tosefta are closely related works of early rabbinic Judaism hailing from the earliest layer of rabbinic literature, known as the tannaitic layer, which spans the end of the Second Temple period in 70 CE through their redaction circa 200–250 CE. On the Mishna see Martin Goodman 'The Presentation of the Past in the Mishna' and others in *What is the Mishnah?: The State of the Question,* Shaye J.D. Cohen, ed., forthcoming from the Julis-Rabinowitz Program on Jewish and Israeli Law at Harvard Law School and the Center for Jewish Studies, Harvard University Press. On the Tosefta see, Tirzah Meacham and Harry Fox, eds., *Introducing Tosefta* (New Jersey: Ktav, 1999) and Robert Brody, *Mishnah and Tosefta Studies* (Jerusalem: Magness Press, 2014). On rabbinic sources more generally, see Gunter Stemberger and Herman L. Strack, *Introduction to the Talmud and Midrash*, ed. and trans. Markus Boekmuehl (Edinburgh: T & T Clark, 1996), and N.S. Hecht, B.S. Jackson, et al eds., *An Introduction to the History and Sources of Jewish Law* (Oxford: Clarendon Press, 1996).

I have argued previously that normative rabbinic hermeneutic traditions can and do seek to mitigate the scriptural violence they encounter.[3] Alan Mittleman, in his chapter, in this volume on Jewish interpretive methodologies for dealing with the wide range of biblical violence that readers inevitably encounter, has skillfully analysed the diversity of approaches to this problem amongst interpreters. This chapter complements his work by considering the problem of violence in rabbinic texts when there is in fact no biblical violent precedent and no scriptural violence with which to engage. To this end, I will relate to a very different sort of case, namely, where rabbinic tradition appears to innovate violence when it is not biblically mandated.

The focus of this study will be on an explicitly violent case, the punishment of the *kippah* in early rabbinic law. In particular, I will examine the punishment of the *kippah* as found in the Mishna and Tosefta, with a brief consideration of the reception of these laws in the Palestinian and Babylonian Talmuds (or Yerushalmi and Bavli). The Mishna and Tosefta are early rabbinic legal sources, which came to form the basis of the later talmudic discussions. The Palestinian and Babylonian Talmuds both engage with these earlier rabbinic teachings.

The punishment of the *kippah* involves placing the individual in a small cell and subjecting him either to a subsistence/starvation diet or causing him to suffer death via ruptured intestines; this despite the fact that the legal violations in question would not otherwise be subject to capital punishment according to biblical or indeed rabbinic law. Meesh Hammer-Kossoi has argued that the *kippah* in the tannaitic period was a form of imprisonment that served a diverse range of functions, from 'a short term holding cell, a long-term punitive prison, or an indirect death penalty,' with placement in the *kippah* combined with a variety of other punishments.[4] Hammer-Kossoi argues that this early diversity was also character-

[3] See Laliv Clenman, 'Texts and Violence in Modern Israel: Interpreting Pinchas,' in *Scripture and Violence*, Julia Snyder and Daniel Weiss, eds., (New York: Routledge, 2021), 60–75. Through a study of a range of texts produced in relation to the murder of sixteen-year-old Shira Banki by Yishai Schlissel at the Jerusalem Pride parade in 2015, I proposed that even real-world violence that is connected to violent scripture by contemporary interpreters does not necessarily exist in a causative relationship with said scripture. The multiplicity that characterises much of rabbinic traditions' responses to such violent scripture serves to limit and supplant this violence, perhaps with the aim of discouraging and isolating actual violence.

[4] Hammer-Kossoi, *Divine Justice*, 230.

istic of imprisonment in the Greco-Roman period and that only in the later talmudic (amoraic) period did the *kippah* come to be understood exclusively as a form of indirect killing.

This apparently unjustified and extremely violent response by the religious court has troubled both traditional and modern scholarly readers. By addressing this explicitly and seemingly unnecessarily violent Jewish religious law (*halakhah*), I aim to broaden our understanding of the role of violence in religious legal sources as well as the manner in which the wider tradition engages with them. What can we learn from a case where a religious legal text calls for extreme violence even though it does not appear to have any mandate? If rabbinic sources tend to mitigate violence in encounters with scripture, why might *halakhah* generate such violent legal texts? [5] I shall ultimately propose that what appears to be creative jurisgenesis actually reflects a jurispathic instinct, whereby the law destroys itself in its attempt to protect its institutions and due process from harm.[6] In other words, the violence of these laws is a protective response to the threat of serious violent harm posed by the very individual placed in the *kippah*.

A Field of Pain and Death: Theories of Legal Violence

Robert Cover in his seminal essay, 'Violence and the Word', wrote elegantly that 'Legal interpretation takes place in a field of pain and death.'[7] Beth Berkowitz has subsequently applied Cover's theories to the study of rabbinic law, and this chapter heeds her call to examine violence in rabbinic sources anew.[8] Berkowitz writes,

[5] I am grateful to Tali Artman, Jacob Adler, Mark Solomon, Lucetta Johnson, Sari Kisilevsky, Martina Loreggian, Cassy Sachar, Binyanim Katzoff, Neil Janes, Sacha Stern, Nathan Alfred, Wendy Filer and Anthony Lazarus-Magrill for their inspiration and insight at various stages of this project. Any errors are the author's own. All translations are the author's own unless otherwise noted.

[6] On the jurispathic instinct in law, see Austin Sarat and Thomas R. Kearns, 'Making Peace with Violence: Robert Cover on Law and Legal Theory,' in *Law's Violence*, ed. Sarat Austin and Thomas Kearns (Ann Arbor: Michigan, 1993), 211–250.

[7] Robert Cover, 'Violence and the Word,' *The Yale Law Journal*, 1986, vol. 95, no. 8, 1601–1629.

[8] Beth Berkowitz, 'Negotiatimg Violence and the Word in Rabbinic Law,' *Yale Journal of Law and the Humanities* 2005, 17, no. 125, 125–150. See also, Thomas R. Kearns, 'Making Peace with Violence: Robert Cover on Law and Legal Theory,' 211–50.

> I suggest that the Mishnah establishes a close relationship between the rabbinic judge and violence, but at the same time creates some distance between the two. According to Cover, such strategies are typical of law, which in order to maintain legitimacy must appear to be capable of violence yet not unduly eager to resort to it. I suggest that Cover's work, when applied to rabbinic law, helps to dispel the romanticism of rabbinics scholarship.[9]

On the question of capital punishment more specifically, Berkowitz notes a similar process. 'Cover's work helps us to move beyond the romantic view of the Rabbis as impossibly enlightened proto-abolitionists and allows us to take them more seriously as lawmakers vigorously seeking legitimacy within the competing nomoi of their day.'[10] Scholars of rabbinic history have long wrestled with the question of whether or not capital punishment was actually practiced in the early rabbinic period. It is difficult to determine whether rabbinical courts had the capacity to act violently in the tannaitic era. These debates necessarily depend in part on historical theories about the influence and authority of the rabbis in late antiquity, as well as how scholars answer the question of whether such rabbinic legal material reflects or intends legal practice, as opposed to being largely rhetorical and academic in nature. I propose that we remain open to the possibility that laws related to capital punishment in the tannaitic period were indeed what Bernard Jackson has called a live institution.[11]

In favour of taking such a straightforward view of the early rabbinic presentation of capital punishment, Beth Berkowitz argues similarly that, 'The Mishnah does not ask its audience to see its death penalty in a

[9] Berkowitz, 'Negotiating,' 126.

[10] Berkowitz, 'Negotiating,' 147. My approach could also be described, in Tal Ilan's terms, as a so-called provocative view that accepts the content of a text at 'face value' rather than taking an apologetic approach to reading rabbinic texts. See, Tal Ilan, 'Premarital Cohabitation in Ancient Judea: The Evidence of the Babatha Archive and the Mishnah (Ketubbot 1.4)' in *The Harvard Theological Review* 86 no. 3 (1993), 247.

[11] Jackson, 'Testes Singulares,' 192. See below for the specific case to which Jackson refers. For an excellent review of capital punishment in Judaism and of the difficulty of determining whether early rabbinic discussions reflect historical practice or academic fiction, see the entry by Haim Cohn, Louis Rabinowitz, and Menachem Elon, 'Capital Punishment,' in *Encyclopaedia Judaica*, 2nd ed., edited by Michael Berenbaum and Fred Skolnik, 445–451. Vol. 4. Detroit, MI: Macmillan Reference USA, 2007. *Gale eBooks* (accessed January 14, 2022). https://link.gale.com/apps/doc/CX2587503929/GVRL?u=leobaeck&sid=bookmark-GVRL&xid=00b69d5c. For an argument against rabbinic authority in this period, see Seth Schwartz, *Imperialism and Jewish Society:200 B.C.E.-640 C.E.* (New Jersey: Princeton University Press, 2001).

context of disempowerment; it represents itself, quite shockingly given our knowledge of the period, as a perfectly legitimate and practiceable law code.'[12] With regard to the particular case of the murderer in mSanhedrin 9:5, Jackson writes, 'The rabbinic evidence provides support for the view that mSanhedrin 9:5b represents a live tannaitic institution. Its inclusion in the Mishna is (despite some contemporary views) prima facie evidence of that.'[13]

Is this religious legal violence, as Cover might have argued, a necessary and integral part of any legal tradition, and by extension, perhaps, any religious legal tradition? Dare we ask whether we should be seeking a religious tradition that is all peace while condemning all violence? I propose that our notions of peace and justice are intimately bound up with religious law's ability to enforce its rules and judgements through violent means.

[12] Berkowitz, 'Negotiating,' 145.

[13] Jackson, 'Testes Singulares,' 192. Meesh Hammer-Kossoi has argued that the lack of scriptural, midrashic and aggadic (narrative) engagment with the the *kippah* means that it was not a live or institution or a practical concern, *Divine Justice in Rabbinic Hands*, 226. Lack of midrash and lack of scripture certainly concerns the Bavli, but might rather suggest the *kippah* is part of an early tradition for which authoritativeness is not contingent upon scripture. Non-scriptural tannaitic traditions may have been independently authoritative in the early halakhah, as per the proposal of Azzan Yadin Israel, *Scripture and Tradition: Rabbi Akiva and the Triumph of Midrash*, (Philadelphia: University of Pennsylvania Press, 2015). For later midrashic and talmudic interpreters this presents a serious problem that must be solved, but in its own context it need not have been problematic.

A Case Study: The Kippah *and Its Punishments*

The case study of the kippah is found in two early rabbinic legal works, Mishna Sanhedrin Chapter 9:5 and Tosefta Sanhedrin 12:7–8.[14] The punishment described includes two stages, first placing a person in the *kippah*, apparently, a small cell, followed by a second element, either a starvation/ bare subsistence diet or feeding the person barley until their belly bursts.[15] Mishna Sanhedrin 9:5, which relates to the rabbinical court's violent punishment of these unusual cases, appears in the context of a series of mishnaic rules dealing with problems and irregularities related to the rabbinical court's (*beit din*) judgement of capital cases.[16] The Mishna continues in Sanhedrin 9:6 with other cases that are punishable by extreme violence, though by authorities other than the *beit din*, including by zealots and the priesthood.[17] It is instructive to read these rules within their immediate literary-legal context, therefore we will begin by briefly addressing Mishna Sanhedrin 9:6. This Mishna acknowledges that religious entities or bodies,

[14] Perhaps all that may be safely said of the *kippah* is that it was a non-standard form of imprisonment. In the Babylonian Talmud Sanhedrin 81b, Rav Yehuda explains that the *kippah* is the fullness of a man's height. It is entirely possible that medieval commentators and perhaps even the talmudic sages, did not know what the *kippah* was. Maimonides described it as a cell within the prison in which a person could just barely stand, but could neither lie down nor sleep. The verbal root for the term *kippah* may refer to something doubled or something rounded. On the *kippah* see, '*Kippah*' in The Talmudic *Encyclopedia*, (Jerusalem: Yad Harav Hertsog c. 2014, 5774), 933–968 [Hebrew], Aryeh Reich, 'Onesh Ha*kippah*' in *Maaliot* 7: 31–41, (c. 1985) and the response by Menachem Elon, 42–43 [Hebrew]. See also Haninah Ben-Menahem 'Anishah shelo minhadin,' in *Misphpetei Eretz*, (2001): 152–163. On Mishna Sanhedrin 9:5 amongst others, see Shaul Lieberman, 'Peirushim bamishnayot in *Tarbiz* 40 no. 1 (1970): 9–17 [Hebrew].

[15] I am most grateful to Jacob Adler for sharing a forthcoming essay on the belly-bursting punishment, and his discovery of numerous accounts of realia involving death caused by ingestion of barley through to the modern period, 'The mystery of the Bursting Belly' (unpublished). Barley may have also been considered a food more suitable for animals than humans, signifying lowly status. For example, the ancient Aramaic insuffiency curses in the Tel Fekherye inscription include the people gleaning and eating barley from rubbish heaps.

[16] On capital punishment and criminal law, see Beth Berkowitz, *Execution and Invention: Death Penalty Discourse in Early Christian Cultures.* (Oxford: Oxford University Press, 2006), Devorah Steinmetz, *Punishment and Freedom: The Rabbinic Construction of Criminal Law* (Philadelphia: University of Pennsylvania Press, 2008).

[17] This mishna refers to zealots or *qanaim*. For more on the zealots as a political faction as well as rabbinic usage of the term, see Martin Hengel, *The Zealots: Investigation into the Jewish Freedom Movement in the Period from Herod I until 70 AD.* (Edinburgh: T&T Clark, new edition 1997).

other than the rabbinical court, have particular, perhaps unique, legal concerns and deal with offenders violently.

Mishna Sanhedrin 9:6[18]

> The one who steals the *qisvah*, the one who curses with divination, and the one who has sexual relations with an Aramean woman, zealots attack them. A priest who served [while] in [a state of] ritual impurity, his brothers the priests do not bring him to the rabbinical court [*beit din*], rather the youth of the priesthood take him out of the [Temple] courtyard and take out his brain with clubs. A stranger [i.e. a non-priest] who served in the Temple, Rabbi Akiva says [he is liable to capital punishment] by strangulation, and the sages say, [he is liable to death] at the hands of heaven.[19]

If the extent of the violence of the zealot attack might be unclear, the removal of the brain of the priest is not. The manner in which these rules are edited in the Mishna suggests that each punishment – by the rabbinical court, the zealots and the priestly youth – is not only brutally violent, but fatal.[20] Following this view, they may all be viewed as non-standard capital punishments. While Bernard Jackson has argued persuasively that in the Mishna, the starvation/dehydration diet was a less-than-fatal alternative to capital punishment, and proposed a general principle 'that a lesser sanction may be imposed where the evidence is less than sufficient,' he also made a strong case for reading this punishment as a slow death offering

[18] This text of mSanhedrin 9:6 follows the version in MS Kaufmann A 50, which follows a Palestinian tradition of the Mishna. Shaul Lieberman argued that the former is a preferable reading in the Palestinian tradition, 'Peirushim bamishnayot, 9–17. Note that mSanhedrin 9:6 does not have a parallel in Tosefta. This avoids the numerous legal and interpretive problems generated by the integration of a zealot rule into a rabbinic legal work.

[19] On this violent and fatal punishment for the priest who served in the Temple while in a state of ritual impurity see, Yehonatan Reiner, '*Oneshin she-lo'min had din?! Iyun besugyat kohen sheshimesh bitumah bemasekhet Sanhedrin*,' *Maagalim* 5, 5767: 89–115 [Hebrew].

[20] Berkowitz argued that the rabbis 'create a death penalty tailored specially for priests' in Mishna Sanhedrin 9:6, though I would argue the Mishna rather describes a priestly practice and clarifies that it is no business of the rabbinical court, '*Negotiating*,' 129. I hesitate to say that these priestly and zealot rules are innovative cases of rabbinic violence *per se*, as they do not appear to stem from within rabbinic tradition, rather from competing or complementary religious spheres. See also Berkowitz's recent translation of Mishna Sanhedrin with notes in *The Oxford Annotated Mishnah: A New Translation of the Mishna With Introduction and Notes*. Volume II, Shaye J.D. Cohen, Robert Goldenberg and Hayim Lapin, eds. Oxford: Oxford University Press, 2022.

much opportunity for the offender to repent.[21] In this sense, the *kippah* might be viewed as a method for encouraging contrition and adherence to normative due process in the most intransigent of legal subjects. Of the use of torture as a means of forcing confession, Elaine Scarry has written, 'in compelling confession, the torturers compel the prisoner to record and objectify the fact that intense pain is world-destroying.'[22]

The rules presented in Mishna Sanhedrin 9:5 (and its parallel in Tosefta 12:7–8) involve two cases that *are* brought before the *beit din*:

Mishna Sanhedrin 9:5

> One who was flogged [for a transgression] and repeated [said transgression] in the *beit din* one puts him into the *kippah* and feeds[23] him barley until his belly explodes. The one who kills *nefashot* [i.e. people] without witnesses, one puts him into the *kippah* and gives him 'meager bread and scant water' (Isaiah 30:20 New JPS).[24]

Tosefta Sanhedrin 12:7–8[25]

12:7

> They warn him and he is silent, they warn him and he nods his head: they warn him a first time and a second and on the third, they put him into the *kippah*. Abba Shaul says, also on the third they warn him, and on the fourth they put him into the *kippah* and they feed[26] him 'meager bread and scant water' (Isaiah 30:20).

12:8

[21] See Bernard Jackson, 'Testes Singulares in Early Jewish Law and the New Testament,' in *Essays in Jewish Comparative Legal History* (Leiden: Brill, 1975) 190. The use of the *kippah* for murderers and oxen who have killed a person, but cannot be properly identified and punished, also suggests that it is a means to an end, in that case waiting for the murderer to be distinguished so that normative due process can unfold.

[22] Elaine Scarry, *The Body in Pain: The Making and Unmaking of the World* (Oxford: Oxford University Press, 1998) as cited in Robert Cover, 'Violence and World,' 1603.

[23] Other versions read 'gives.'

[24] The broader context of the verse in Isaiah suggests divine provision of a clear path, 'This is the road; follow it!' (Isaiah 30:21). This could support the notion that the *kippah* was intended as a means towards repentance on the part of the transgressor. Trans., New JPS.

[25] Ed. Zuckermandel p. 433.

[26] Other versions read 'give.'

> Like this case, ones who are liable to lashes [for their transgression] who were lashed and they repeated [the transgression], one lashes them a first time and a second and on the third one puts them into the *kippah*. Abba Shaul says even on the third one lashes them and on the fourth one puts them into the *kippah* and feeds him barley until his belly explodes.

Mishna Sanhedrin 9:5 relates to the punishment by *kippah* of two offenders. The first is a recidivist, who repeatedly transgresses and is punished by the *beit din* in an apparently endless cycle of crime and punishment, which the rabbinical court is otherwise powerless to bring to an end. This case is identical to the second case in the Tosefta. The second mishnaic case is the murderer without witnesses, who I propose, following Palestinian rescensions of the Mishna, is actually a serial murderer, though with insufficient witnessing to each particular murder to allow for capital punishment to proceed.[27] Tosefta's first case is an offender who refuses to properly accept the warning that must precede any punishment according to due process in rabbinic law.[28]

A central problem in each of these cases is the criminal's stubborn refusal to allow the court to mete out its violence, as s/he flagrantly and shamelessly makes a mockery of the process of the *beit din*. These individuals impede the process of the *beit din* by preventing it from meting out the violence that is due, in particular by taking advantage of highly particularistic elements of the due process, leaving the *beit din* with no recourse. We can see these laws as having a deterrent intent, putting pressure on the individual to submit to the punishment at hand or to relent.

[27] MS Kaufmann A 50 of the Mishna reads 'who kills people' while the mishna as presented in the Babylonian Talmud reads 'who kills a person.'

[28] Some understand that the refuser in the Tosefta is in fact a murderer, akin to the murderer without witnesses in the Mishna.

In this sense, these punishments may very well be an ordeal more terrible and torturous than standard capital punishments – not lesser but worse.[29]

Bernard Jackson argued that 'the offender has (presumably on sufficient evidence) received the legally appropriate punishment for each of his several offences. He "deserves" the death penalty only on the basis of public safety. Jewish law provides the judges with no general discretion to increase a punishment because of the offender's previous record. Hence, the present extraordinary measure.'[30] The law of the *kippah* is called for in the case of the recidivist precisely because there is no normative legal framework which would enable punitive action. With regards to the serial murderer without witnesses, Jackson argues that the death penalty is 'deserved' in 'an entirely different sense.' In this case, the law *does* provide a capital sanction, but the sanction cannot be imposed due to a lack of evidence. Palestinian traditions, including the Talmud Yerushalmi, read 'the persons' (*hanefashot*) in the plural 'which may include the case where there is only one witness to each of a series of homicides.'[31] So, contra talmudic discourse, we need not be speaking of merely formal inadequacies of testimony. We could be speaking of single witnesses to multiple murders. As Jackson concludes, 'In Mishnaic law, two [witnesses] are required for the death penalty, but one suffices for imprisonment [in the *kippah*] and *lehem zar umayim lahaz*.'[32]

Each of these offenders not only threatens communal peace, proper due process, judgement and justice, but directly challenges the authority

[29] Judiciously placed quotation marks in Binyanim Katzoff and Adiel Schremer's commentary to Tosefta Sanhedrin 12:7 express this sense of contradiction, 'And since in the case judged here he did not say 'I know etc.' it is not possible to judge him on his deeds and to punish him according to the official law, rather 'merely' to place him in the *kippah* based on a *taqanah* of the sages' (Original in Hebrew, my translation). The halakhic basis – *taqanah* (a type of corrective legal ordinance) or otherwise - for these rules is debated. I am most grateful to Binyamin Katzoff for generously sharing a prepublication version of the eagerly awaited critical edition and commentary to Tosefta Sanhedrin by Adiel Schremer and Binyanim Katzoff. See Adiel Schremer and Binyanim Katzoff, *JSIJ* 20 (2021) (*Jewish Studies – An Internet Journal*) https://jewish-faculty.biu.ac.il/files/jewish-faculty/shared/JSIJ20/schremer_katzoff.pdf.

[30] Jackson, '*Testes Singulares*,' 189. On the scope for deviation in the ruling of the rabbinic judge, see Haninah Ben-Menahem. *Judicial Deviation in Jewish Law: Governed by Men not by Rules*. New York: Harwood Academic Publishers, 1991.

[31] Bernard Jackson, 'Testes Singulares,' 189.

[32] This is the starvation or subsistence diet of scant bread and water. Jackson, 'Testes Singulares,' 190.

and impedes the functioning of the rabbinical judge and his court. Each of these cases is met with irregular innovative violence that appears to be out of context within biblical and ensuing rabbinic tradition.[33] This suggests rabbinic jurisgenesis independent of biblical tradition, following Berkowitz's claim that tannaitic law on capital and corporal punishment more generally was 'strikingly innovative.'[34]

Of the tannaitic law of *kippah*, Meesh Hammer-Kossoi writes that it is,

> ...in the rabbinic context, a radical institution with shocking power. Not only is *kipah* essentially legislated by the tannaim as a form of indirect execution and torture, it is prescribed in cases that from a biblical perspective do not justify death at all. Even uses of *kipah* that do not lead to indirect death can be considered calculated torture. In this sense, it is not surprising that the amoraim [rabbis of the Talmuds] felt it necessary to remove much of the force from these sources.[35]

The Tosefta records a disagreement about the technicality of how many chances the individual is granted by the *beit din* prior to being placed in the *kippah*. This suggests a reluctance to enact this punishment and an interest in providing third (and fourth) chances. Berkowitz notes that such reluctance need not be understood as a rejection of capital or other violent punishment *per se*, but rather, as Cover argued, as characteristic of the law's relationship with its violence.[36] Aside from this variance regarding the number of chances, there is no recorded disagreement regarding the punishment itself (unlike, for example, in the case of the stranger who served in the Temple, or other uses of the *kippah*, where alternative punishments are proposed).

While I have framed these laws as innovative jurisgensis, we should consider that they may have been understood and accepted as non-standard punishments within their own contexts or *nomos*. Bernard Jackson has argued, for example, that the case of the murderer in mSanhedrin 9:5 has parallels in legal works of the earlier Second Temple period, which he suggests provided for less-than-capital punishments if there was

[33] See Beth Berkowitz, 'Reclaiming Halakhah: On the Recent Works of Aharon Shemesh,' *AJS Review* 35 no. 1 (April 2011): 125–135.

[34] Berkowitz, 'Negotiating,' 129.

[35] Michelle (Meesh) Hammer-Kossoi, *Divine Justice in Rabbinic Hands: Talmudic Reconstitution of the Penal System,* (PhD diss., New York University, 2005), 230–231.

[36] Cover, 'Violence and the Word,' 1613–1615 and Berkowitz, 'Negotiating,' 126.

a single witness to a murder, but more witnesses were required for capital punishment to be implemented. If true, at least part of these rules may find their origins prior to the tannaitic period. It is therefore possible that these rules were, strictly speaking, no more innovative than other second-temple legal rules. The violence of these laws only becomes problematic for those interpreters who lack this shared *nomos*.[37] It is this lack of shared meaning that causes interpretive (both antique and modern) dissonance that tends to erase or mitigate the obvious and straightforward violent meaning of these texts.

The manner in which the Mishna and the Tosefta present these cases suggest a symbolic pattern to the punishments suffered in the *kippah*.

Mishna:

Recidivist = barley until his stomach explodes
Murderer sans-witnesses = *kippah* + scant food and water

Tosefta:

Refuser of warnings = *kippah* + scant food and water
Recidivist = barley until his stomach explodes

In both versions, the recidivist is either force-fed or eats barley, so as to cause death. The symbolism of the measure-for-measure punishment is evident, as the one who sinned too much dies of eating too much. The murderer in the Mishna and the refuser in the Tosefta, in contrast, each deliberately and presumably knowingly, prevent the *beit din* from meting out the violence that it should. This withholding of a confession or of the acceptance of the warning is met with the insufficiency of the diet in the

[37] Robert Cover, 'Foreward: Nomos and Narrative,' *Harvard Law Review*, 97 no. 1, (November 1983): 4–68.

kippah. Therefore, each of these cases might be seen as an example of measure-for-measure punishment.[38]

The understanding of these texts depends partly on one's understanding of the relationship between the Mishna and the Tosefta. Bernard Jackson argues that the Tosefta is interpreting the Mishna and its refuser of warnings is indeed the murderer. While this is a possible reading, I prefer to read each text on its own terms. For example, when Tosefta Sanhedrin 8:3 (ed. Zuckermandel, 427) deals with the case of a murder witnessed by a single person, the single witness states, 'What shall I do to you, your judgement (law) is not transmitted to my hand' [due to the Torah's requirement for two or three witnesses] and continues, 'rather The One Who Knows Thoughts, He shall exact revenge from that very man.' He did not move from there until a snake bit him and he died.'[39] This source suggests that the Tosefta (if indeed we can read these different laws in the Tosfeta coherently in this manner) sees the murderer sans-sufficient-witnesses as punishable by the divine rather than by the human court. This could be a point of disagreement with the Mishna, which sees this murderer as punishable by the *kippah* and scant food and water. Such a reading would support an interpretation of the cases in tSanhedrin 12:7–8 such that the first case is the refuser of warnings and the second is the recidivist, but neither the murderer without witnesses, because the murderer is dealt with elsewhere and punishable by the divine rather than the court. This position in the Tosefta is similar to the Bavli's statement

[38] The symbolism and of these unique individual punitive elements is lost in the Bavli, where they are combined. I am grateful to Mark Solomon for two insights related to this punishment. First, that this talmudic combination of punishments is ultimately more severe than the earlier sources because it is necessarily fatal. Second, for his observation of some similarities to the test of the bitter waters for the Sotah in Numbers 5, which also involves barley, in the form of an offering of barley flour, and swelling of the belly. The case of the Sotah is similarly imbuded with uncertainty and dispenses with normal due process.

[39] See also *Mekhilta d'Rabbi Ishmael Masekhta d'Kaspa* 20 (ed. Lauterbach, 170, ed. Horowitz-Rabin, 327).

that in place of human punishment, one might 'leave him that he might be killed at the hands of heaven.' [40]

The *kippah* also serves as a location for placing unknowable or insoluble cases that defy human resolution or action. Such problems cannot be dealt with through normative procedures and have no structured place in the established order of the *nomos*. Their very existence metes a kind of violence upon the religious sphere. Take, for example, the case where a murderer has been mixed up with other individuals and presumably cannot be recovered or identified (mSanhedrin 9:3). The legal response to this situation is that all are exempted and released (from capital punishment), but the dissenting opinion (R. Yehudah) holds that they should all be placed in the *kippah*.[41] In Tosefta Bava Qamma 5:5, we find a similar case of mixing in the case of a cow who has killed a person; all the cows are placed in the *kippah* 'until the time that they die.'[42] The dissenting option is that all of them are stoned to death, a standard capital punishment. The problem is that it proves impossible to designate the appropriate object of the violence, not unlike the manner in which it is impossible to effectively act violently in the case of the recidivist, the murderer without witnesses, and the refuser of warnings. This suggests that the *kippah* served as an alternative form of capital punishment where the normally correct procedure proved impossible, and that the subject was left there indefinitely until its demise, repentance or confession, unless the barrier to appropriate punishment was removed and the punishment could be implemented.

The use of the *kippah*, in these instances, offers a solution to these hard legal cases. This violence eliminates an irresolvable legal problem. By placing the body of the person or the ox in the *kippah*, the individual in whom this problem is embodied is eliminated. At the same time, the due process that led to the problem is maintained, and the court asserts its ability to

[40] bSanhedrin 82b. As Jacob Neusner wrote of the Pharisaic response to problems of witnessing, 'The solution was to rely on the heavenly court to accomplish what was beyond the power of the earthly one.' Jacob Neusner, ' 'By the Testimony of Two Witnesses' in the Damascus Document IX, 17–22 and in Pharisaic-Rabbinic Law,' *Revue de Qumrân* 8 no. 2 (March 1973): 216. Bernard Jackson further notes that evidentiary insufficiency is not included amongst the cases subject to heavenly punishment, 'Testest Singulares,' 193. I am grateful for Nathan Alfred's research on the concept of the 'rabbinic snake'.

[41] The mishna does not state the next steps, but commentators propose that they would be held there until such time as they could be distinguished.

[42] *Tosefta*, ed. Lieberman, 19. See also *Mekhilta d'Rabbi Shimon bar Yochai Mishpatim* to Exodus 21:28 (ed. Epstein-Melamed, 178, ed. Nelson, 296) where all the oxen are placed in the *kippah* 'until the time that they die' as an alternative to being stoned.

act violently rather than being forced into inaction. In the face of the unknowable and the insoluble, this violence keeps the peace.

These cases expose weaknesses in the due process of the religious law and leave the *beit din* and its judges helpless as the transgressors perhaps take advantage of the law itself to defy the court and its judges and, by extension, those they may have harmed in the community. The court is prevented from acting and punishing violently as it should or as it means to. As Robert Cover wrote, 'Very often the balance of terror in this regard is just as I would want it. But I do not wish us to pretend that we talk our prisoners into jail. The "interpretations" or "conversations" that are the preconditions for violent incarceration are themselves implements of violence.'[43] The recidivist renders his punishment meaningless as it clearly serves neither as deterrent nor as atonement, rendering what should be a moment of repentance and absolution into a loophole to enable endless transgression. The (serial) murderer may be lacking sufficient witnessing, but it is nevertheless obvious he is (repeatedly) guilty.[44] Were this murderer to go free without any action taken by the *beit din*, perhaps multiple times, it would clearly demonstrate the powerlessness of the *beit din* and its inability to punish and prevent murders in the community. Jackson has noted that such an eventuality could encourage family members to seek a remedy in the Roman courts, which the rabbinical courts opposed.[45] I would add that it might also result in extra-judicial remedies such as vigilante killing of the murderer by the family or community.

Why would a tradition that tends to mitigate biblical violence, in turn, innovate violence of its own? These tannaitic rules, I would argue, allow for irregular and exceptional iterations of violence, even in the absence of any biblical basis or scriptural compulsion to act violently, in order to stem violent damage, as a kind of harm-reduction policy protecting the court and the community it claims to serve.

[43] Cover, 'Violence and the Word,' 1608.

[44] This follows well from Jackson's reading, where a witness has indeed witnessed the murder, but the single witness is deemed insufficient for enacting capital punishment. He notes, for example, that Roman law in the tannaitic period still accepted a single witness in capital cases, 'Testes Singulares,' 191.

[45] Bernard Jackson, 'Testes Singulares,' 191.

Talmudic Interpreters: Dead Man Walking

Turning now to Talmudic discourse, we will explore the engagement of the Palestinian and Babylonian Talmuds with these punishments. The Palestinian Talmud was redacted approximately 200 years after the Mishna and Tosefta, while the Babylonian Talmud subsequently underwent an extended period of development and redaction. Both works are intimately concerned with interpreting and framing earlier rabbinic material, such as we find in the Mishna and Tosefta.[46] Unfortunately, the Palestinian Talmud (Yerushalmi or Jerusalem Talmud) has virtually nothing to say regarding Mishna Sanhedrin 9:5, though it tends to frame these cases as formalities.[47] This technique is also taken in the Bavli, and I would argue that it dispenses with any sense of any wilful threat to the *beit din* on the part of the offender. The Yerushalmi does cite a baraita (a tannaitic or early rabbinic source that is not included in the Mishna) that appears in Tosefta 12:8 when it discusses the case of a murderer who refuses to properly accept the warning given to him.

Palestinian Talmud Sanhedrin 5:1[48]

> They would warn him and he [remained] silent, they warned him and he nodded his head (tSanhedrin 12:8), Even though he says, 'I know' he is exempt. Until he should say, 'on that condition I am doing [it].' They saw him spilling blood [i.e. murdering someone]. They said to him, 'Woe! Do [you] know that he is a son of covenant and the Torah said, 'if the human [*adam*] spills blood, his blood shall be spilled'?' (Genesis 9:6). Even though he says, 'I know' he is exempt until he should say, 'on that condition I am doing [this].'

The Yerushalmi frames the Mishna's question for witnesses – have you warned him? – within a very stringent and formal due process. The murderer must acknowledge the punishment and act with full acceptance of his imminent capital punishment, almost as if he were killing in expectation of that violence and deliberately seeking it out. His act of murderous violence against another becomes a means to the end of his own inevitable

[46] For a review of the scholarly study of the Palestinian and Babylonian Talmuds, see Tal Ilan and Ronit Nikolsky, 'An Introduction,' in *From There to Here: Rabbinic Traditions Between Palestine and Babylonia*, Tal Ilan and Ronit Nikolsky eds. (Leiden: Brill, 2014), 1–31.

[47] For a similar disagreement regarding the case of a murderer who became mixed up with others, see ySanhedrin 9:3 (ed. Sussman, 1313, ed. Venetsia 27b 16:7 and 16:9).

[48] Text follows MS Leiden as per ed. Sussman, 1289, see also ed. Venetsia 5:1 22d.

death. The warner even quotes scripture, articulating a clear biblical basis for the capital punishment that awaits the murderer, but all is for nothing if the murderer fails to comply. [49] This would appear to make it rather possible for a murderer to evade punishment, even when caught and warned in the act. The Yerushalmi's insistence on accepting the burden of punishment in this manner, perhaps distances the *beit din* from its violence, for the murderer then claims to be committing murder as a means to his own execution. In this sense, we might understand this discourse as a means of conceptually justifying and enabling the court's ability to enact capital punishment rather than circumscribing it, even if it necessarily poses pragmatic limitations on the court's power to act.

Of course, the Mishna's law in turn appears to resist such an eventuality by rendering it straightforward for the court to put such a person in the *kippah.* The Yerushalmi, however, does not mention the *kippah* here. Any argument from silence is necessarily speculative, but I would suggest that the failure to mention the *kippah* reflects two contrary possibilities. First, an unspoken assumption on the part of the Yerushalmi that putting this man in the *kippah* is a plan B, which permits the Yerushalmi's stringency in the area of accepting warnings. Second, that the Yerushalmi opposed the notion of *kippah* and so neglected to mention it. Following the first, the violence of the *kippah* permits stringency and rigidity elsewhere, acting as a safety valve; following the second, the violence of the *kippah* is erased. Haninah Ben-Menahem has argued that the Yerushalmi tended (more so than the Bavli) to reject tannaitic teachings that appear to contradict biblical law. If so, this could very well be an instance of the Yerushalmi quietly rejecting the tannaitic institution of the *kippah.*

In contrast to the Yerushalmi's relative silence, the Babylonian Talmud (Bavli) acknowledges the potentiality of innovative rabbinic violence in these tannaitic sources but tends towards closing off this avenue in favour of constructing the religious court's human violence as a mere

[49] See Targum Onqelos and Targum Pseudo-Jonathan to Gen 9:5–6, which both apply heavenly punishment to murder without witnesses in their translations of this verse that the Yerushalmi calls for the witness to recite to the murderer. Jackson, 'Testes Singulares,' 192–193.

redundancy.[50] I would argue that the Bavli is troubled by these earlier rabbinic sources and the powerful human violence that they represent. This is perhaps best expressed by the query in bSanhedrin 82b, 'Is there a case where the Merciful One exempts him, and we rise up and kill him?' The Divine, cast as the Merciful One, is lenient and exempts, while the human realm is stringent and acts violently, rendering the person culpable when God would not. While the Babylonian Talmud recognizes this feature of its tannaitic (early rabbinic) inheritance, it is ultimately unwilling to accept this notion of a violent human action in the excess of and in the absence of a divine punishment.[51] For the Babylonian Talmud, the *beit din*'s punishment of the *kippah* or indeed of the priestly youth or the zealot is hardly required. Human violence is rendered superfluous and divine violence is enough.

The Bavli argues, for example, that the recidivist who would be subject to the *kippah* and belly bursting via barley, is essentially a dead man walking (*gavra bar qatla hu*).[52] His flogging is deemed to be a punishment for a severe transgression punishable by excision (*karet*) and his death at the hands of heaven is considered predetermined, so that any torture, killing or exploding of his body by the *beit din* becomes a sort of appetiser to the

[50] It is possible to understand this talmudic approach in various ways. In his study of the murderer without witnesses in mSanhedrin 9:5, Bernard Jackson argued that this early law may have been driven by practical rabbinic concerns that no longer applied in the talmudic era. Jackson further argued that the Bavli was reluctant to contravene biblical laws regarding witnessing, even though tannaitic sources seem comfortable doing so, 'Witnessing,' 188. Haninah Ben-Menahem, however, suggests rather that the Bavli was driven by a very pragmatic question, namely 'if there were no witnesses how do we know who committed the crime?' Viewing the Bavli as largely driven by this practical problem, he proposes that it is the Yerushalmi that is more hesitant to deviate from biblical law, Haninah Ben-Menahem, *Judicial Deviation in Talmudic Law: Governed by Men not by Rules*, (New York: Harwood, 1990), 83 n. 96.

[51] Rav Sheshet, who is represented in the Bavli as a great expert on tannaitic teachings, cites mSanhedrin 9:6 as proof that the priest who served while ritually impure is not subject to death at the hands of heaven, but rather death at the hands of the priestly youth (bSanhedrin 82b). While this idea that the human punishment exceeds the divine is eventually refuted (bSanhedrin 83a), according to Rav Sheshet's view, this would appear to the be the sense of the mishna itself.

[52] bSanhedrin 82b.

main course, hastening or prefiguring the inevitable.[53] While the recidivist is constructed as one awaiting death, normally a person who accepts the court's flogging for his severe transgression thereby avoids the punishment of *karet*, and so spares his own life. An intransigent recidivist, however, takes advantage of this legal loophole as a means to an end of further transgression. The human court may then preserve its due process by using the *kippah* to put an end to this leniency that seemingly allows for the endless circumvention of the divine punishment of *karet*. In this respect, the Bavli may also understand the *kippah* as a method of resolving legal uncertainty. The notion that evildoers will wreck their own self-destruction serves a similar purpose in the Bavli, which cites Psalm 34:22, 'Evil shall kill the wicked' (JPS).[54] The *beit din* is therefore merely taking a life that the person has already renounced. Each of these claims seeks to justify his killing in the *kippah* at the hands of the court in apparent violation of standard due process. [55] The Bavli thus transforms troubling human violence into a mere epilogue to that which has already been established by the Divine or the transgressor himself. It might appear as if humans rise up and kill when the Divine remains merciful, but indeed, for this Talmudic

[53] This narrow interpretation limits the application of the punishment to severe cases punishable by excision and is therefore far more lenient than the general scope suggested by the Mishna. Excision was generally held by the sages to be a punishment of premature death. See, Ta-Shma, Israel Moses. "Karet." In *Encyclopaedia Judaica*, 2nd ed., edited by Michael Berenbaum and Fred Skolnik, 806–807. Vol. 11. Detroit, MI: Macmillan Reference USA, 2007. *Gale eBooks* (accessed June 22, 2022). https://link.gale.com/apps/doc/CX2587510755/GVRL?u=leobaeck&sid=bookmark-GVRL&xid=faab4787. I am grateful to Mark Solomon for his insights on the *kippah*, excision and uncertainty in the Bavli.

[54] The new JPS translation reads, 'One misfortune is the deathblow of the wicked.' Rashi argues along similar lines, that the subject abandons himself to transgression or is legally presumed to be irredeemably evil, and has thereby surrendered his own life (*s.v.* Rashi bSanhedrin 81a *d'mevater nafsheih* and *aveirot machziqot*). This perhaps serves to allay any concerns regarding normative expectations of atonement and redemption. Indeed, flogging for transgressions liable to excision is meant to have an atoning effect, in place of the severe punishment of excision. A recidivist, however, makes a mockery of this understanding of the process. There is also a rabbinic notion that death itself atones (see for example, Tosefta Yoma 4:5). Though this notion is not explicitly mentioned in reference to our cases, it is possible that it might play a role in framing these deaths as having an atoning function.

[55] I am indebted to Tali Artman for suggesting a tantalising similarity to the Roman legal concept of *homo sacer* and its treatment in the work of Giorgio Agamben. See Giorgio Agamben, *Homo Sacer: Sovereign Power and Bare Life*, trans. Daniel Heller-Roazen (California: Stanford, 1998).

discourse, they do not. Both Talmuds, using different methodologies, ultimately dismiss or constrain the violence of the *kippah* punishment.

Conclusion

Inspired by the legal theoretical work of Robert Cover, Beth Berkowitz has challenged scholars to move beyond an apologetic and romanticised view of violence in rabbinic sources. These religious legal texts do not appear to apologise for themselves, to state that they are not doing what they propose to do, or that it should not be done. I propose that as readers, we also meet this violence directly and without any attempt at erasure. This analysis of these tannaitic cases demonstrates that the sages were well aware of the strictures that rabbinic penal procedure placed on their ability to act violently. This violence is called for, but stymied by the offenders who would ultimately be subjected to the *kippah*. Such rules reflect the religious law's ability to counter that hindrance and act violently regardless. Through its violence, the law keeps its peace.

I would argue that the Mishna and Tosefta's apparent jurisgenesis in these rules of the *kippah* actually reflects a jurispathic instinct; it is willing and ready, threatening, to destroy its own law in these cases, in order to protect its capacity to judge and act violently in general. One might argue that the person who finds themselves in the *kippah* has failed to respect the common meanings and commitments that combine to make the 'cooperative enterprise of law possible' as Austin Sarat and Thomas Kearns write on Robert Cover's approach to the violence of the law. Sarat and Kearns explain that 'these commitments and meanings, while never wholly cogent nor wholly shared and common, must be respected if law's fragile capacity to do (controlled and temperate) violence is to be sustained.' They argue that this 'homicidal' tendency in the law renders it jurispathic. [56] It is not only the recidivist, the one who killed persons without witnesses, and the one who refuses to acknowledge the warning of punishment as he knows he should, who are destroyed in one way or another. It is also the religious law and its due process – this law in which the Talmuds and so many other interpreters are so invested. For a moment, the rabbinical court acts with particular shocking violence, not unlike a zealot or a young priestly mob.

[56] Austin Sarat and Thomas R. Kearns, 'Making Peace with Violence: Robert Cover on Law and Legal Theory,' in *Law's Violence*, ed. Sarat Austin and Thomas Kearns (Ann Arbor: Michigan, 1993), 249.

Acting to protect its own interests, it momentarily destroys its own law in order to eliminate the person in whom the threat is embodied.

This death in the *kippah* serves as a hermeneutic tool for engaging with these insoluble problems. As Cover wrote, the legal interpretation is death, but I would propose that this death is a legal interpretation. The death serves as a hermeneutic device for the resolution of what would otherwise remain an insoluble legal and social problem. We need not resurrect the dead in order to redeem the religious law; he is dead for a reason. By attempting to apologise for, erase, romanticise or otherwise revive the dead, we eviscerate the power of the court to preserve itself in the face of its most recalcitrant threat. Let us rather acknowledge this violence, however troubling, and its attempt to keep this uneasy peace.

Further Reading

Berkowitz, Beth. *Execution and Invention: Death Penalty Discourse in Early Rabbinic and Christian* Cultures. Oxford: Oxford University Press, 2006.

Cover, Robert. *Narrative, Violence and the Law: The Essays of Robert Cover*, edited by Austin Serat, Martha Minow, Michael Ryan, eds. Ann Arbor: University of Michigan Press, 1992.

Cohn, Haim. *Human Rights in Jewish Law*. London: Ktav Publishing, 1984.

Horowitz, Elliott. *Reckless Rites: Purim and the Legacy of Jewish Violence*. New Jersey: Princeton University Press, 2006.

Snyder, J and D. Weiss, eds. *Scripture and Violence*. London: Routledge, 2020.

Austin Sarat and Thomas R. Kearns. *Law's Violence*. Ann Arbor: University of Michigan Press, 1993.

CHAPTER 6

Buddhism and the Dilemma of Whether to Use Violence in Defence of a Way of Peace

Peter Harvey

The Historical Buddha on Violence

Our earliest complete set of sources on Buddhism is the Pali Canon, preserved by the Theravāda school, consisting of texts on *Vinaya*, or monastic discipline, *Sutta*s, or discourses of the Buddha, and *Abhidhamma*, or systematic analyses of mental and physical states and their causal interactions. The Theravāda school is also known as Southern Buddhism and is found mainly in Sri Lanka, Thailand, Myanmar/Burma, Cambodia and Laos. Also in Chinese are the *Āgama*s, translations of texts very similar to the *Sutta*s preserved in Pali. The monastic codes used in China, Vietnam, Korea and Tibet are also similar to the Pali Vinaya. *Abhidhamma*

Positionality: I write as a scholar of Buddhism, especially Buddhist ethics, a Theravāda Buddhist, and a teacher of mindfulness of breathing. I am currently involved with the International Committee of the Red Cross in a project on Buddhist ethics and International Humanitarian Law (the law of war).

P. Harvey (✉)
Department of Culture, University of Sunderland, Tyne and Wear, UK

M. Power, H. Paynter (eds.), *Violence and Peace in Sacred Texts*,
https://doi.org/10.1007/978-3-031-17804-7_6

traditions are more diverse, and the Mahāyāna movement, which began to develop from the first century BCE, developed many more discourses (*Sūtras*) ascribed to the Buddha, as well as systematic philosophical schools. This became the dominant form of Buddhism in the 'Eastern Buddhism' of East Asia (China, Vietnam, Korea, and Japan). It is also very influential in 'Northern Buddhism' (of ancient north India, then Tibet, Bhutan, and Mongolia), where the Vajrayāna is also very influential. The Vajrayāna also draws on later texts, known as *Tantras*, to use such things as visualisations, symbols and mantras as powerful means to accelerate progress on the spiritual path.

The Pali *Suttas* are perhaps the best accessible sources for ascertaining the Buddha's attitude toward the use of violence. The Buddha taught lay followers to live by five ethical precepts, the first of which is to avoid the intentional killing of any sentient being, human or otherwise. For a monk or nun to deliberately kill a human also entails their expulsion from the monastic order, as well as any secular punishments. Key values include patience, non-anger, and friendly kindness and compassion for all beings. As is said in the *Dhammapada*[1] of the *Sutta* collection:

> 'He abused me, he beat me, he defeated me, he robbed me', the enmity of those
> who harbour such thoughts is not appeased.
> 'He abused me, he beat me, he defeated me, he robbed me', the enmity of those
> who do not harbour such thoughts is appeased.
> Enmities never cease by enmity in this world; only by non-enmity (loving kindness)
> do they cease. This is an ancient law.

There is a realistic assessment, though, of the negative mental states and tendencies that exist in the human mind, so that fully living up to such ideals is recognised as being a long-term project. While one should nurture generosity, kindness, and mindful clarity of mind and understanding, often humans act from the opposite of these: greed and clinging; hate, ill-will and anger; and fuzzy-minded confusion, ignorance, delusion and stupidity. The Buddhist project, though, is to recognise this, restrain the negative 'unwholesome/unskilful' (*akusala*) states and actions, cultivate

[1] vv.3–5.

the positive (*kusala*) ones, and in time end the deep psychological roots of the negative states, so as to end how we inflict suffering on ourselves and others. Practices that help towards this are:

- *dāna*: generosity, giving, and sharing of food, resources, support and wise advice.
- *sīla*: moral virtue, ethical discipline, especially in living by the ethical precepts.
- *bhāvanā:* cultivation of wholesome mental qualities, through chanting and meditation, to bring the mind to *samādhi*, or focused stillness imbued with such qualities as mindfulness, non-attached joy, and equanimity; and also the cultivation of wisdom that directly sees the nature of reality and cuts the roots of unwholesome states.

A set of qualities which are seen to obstruct the development of wholesome states and actions is the 'five hindrances':

- desire for sense-pleasures, an expression of greed and grasping,
- ill-will, an expression of hatred and aversion, whether directed at others, oneself, or in aversion to beneficial practices.
- dullness and lethargy, as in laziness, passivity, and disengaged mental dullness.
- restlessness and unease, forms of emotional agitation.
- vacillation, as in wavering doubt about what is truly wholesome and worth engaging in.

These hindrances have both obvious and subtle forms, and can be seen as akin to confidence tricksters that can even come to influence religious and spiritual practice, such as getting angry at someone one sees as having disturbed one's meditative calm, or at people who one sees as threatening 'us and our religion'.

Related to the latter is the harmful quality of attachment to views: beliefs, theories, opinions or world-views, especially when they become fixed or dogmatic, so that one identifies fully with a way-of-looking at something, a way of explaining it.[2] One's attachment is then such that one is wounded if that theory is criticized, and one is willing to be underhand

[2] Paul Fuller, *The Notion of Diṭṭhi in Theravāda Buddhism* (London and New York: Routledge Curzon, 2005).

or not fully honest in the theory's defence. One is also limited in one's vision by the theory or belief: it is like a pair of blinkers which only enables one to see certain things, narrowing one's whole outlook on life, like a blind man who mistakes the part of an elephant that he has felt for the whole of what an 'elephant' is.[3] It may contain some truth, but one always needs to be open to a deepening of that truth, or balancing by a complementary one. The Buddha was clearly very wary of mere theories or 'views', holding that they led to quarrels[4] and conceit. Such views are seen as hidden forms of self-assertion, which lead to conflict with those of other opinions, be this in the form of verbal wrangling or ideological wars and bloody revolutions. In this context, it is worth noting that the atrocities carried out by Hitler, Stalin and the Khmer Rouge were initiated by people who were convinced of a theory which demanded and 'justified' their actions. Indeed, Buddhism holds that the wrong view feeds bad behaviour[5] and that the worst way of doing a bad act is if accompanied by a view that perversely sees it as 'right'.[6]

To be sure, there are what might be called 'Buddhist views', such as belief in the goodness of giving and in karma and rebirth. Such beliefs are termed 'ordinary' (*lokiya*) 'right view', and, though they lead in the right direction, they are still associated with clinging,[7] as they can be clung to, if not tested by wisdom.[8] Views, like all else in the conditioned world, are seen to be arisen according to conditions, to be impermanent, and bringing suffering if clung to.[9]

Clearly, clinging attachment to the views of a particular religion, including Buddhism, and the view that 'this alone is true, all else is falsehood' has fed many conflicts that have a religious aspect to them, as they have conflicts rooted in different political worldviews. Sometimes, it is just a matter of belonging to a nation, ethnic or social group that broadly shares certain views and related customs, so those who are perceived not to share these views, or to oppose them, are seen as a threat to '*us*'.

[3] *Ud*.67–9.

[4] *A*.I.66.

[5] *A*.I.30–2.

[6] Peter Harvey, *An Introduction to Buddhist Ethics: Foundations, Values and Issues* (Cambridge: Cambridge University Press, 2000), 5–6.

[7] *M*.III.72.

[8] *M*.I.133.

[9] *A*.V.187–8.

And of course when it comes to matters of religion, where 'getting it right' is seen as vital, co-religionists who have different interpretations and applications of key beliefs, can be seen as particular threats, especially when such differences are allied to rival focusses of political and social power – for example in the conflict between Protestants and Catholics in Europe from the sixteenth to early eighteenth centuries, or between different Buddhist sects in Japan from the twelfth to the sixteenth centuries.

On war, the Buddha said, after his follower, king Pasenadi, was defeated in battle by king Ajātasatu: 'Victory breeds hatred; the defeated live in pain. Happily the peaceful live, giving up victory and defeat'.[10] This clearly implies that conquest results in tragedy for the defeated, which may lead to hatred and the likelihood of a desire to overcome the conqueror. In the second battle, Pasenadi wins. Capturing Ajātasattu, he spares his life but confiscates all his weapons and army. Here are the Buddha's comments:

> A person may plunder so long as it serves his ends,
> but when they plunder others, the plundered (then) plunder.
> So long as evil's fruit is not matured, the fool thinks he has an opportunity,
> but when the evil matures, the fool suffers.
> The slayer gets a slayer (in his turn), the conqueror gets a conqueror,
> the abuser gets abuse, the wrathful gets one who annoys.
> Thus by the evolution of karma, he who plunders is plundered.[11]

Without justifying defensive violence, this points out that aggression often leads to defensive counter-violence, which can be seen as a karmic result for the aggressor. Such a response happens, whether or not it is justified. Thus, aggression is discouraged. Yet Pasenadi, the generally peace-loving defender, is not free of censure. To spare the life of a defeated enemy is surely good, but leaving him defenceless, without an army, is seen as storing up trouble.

Buddhism and Politics

In the *Suttas*, the ideal political ruler is known as a *Cakravartin*, a 'Wheel-turning' Universal emperor, who has an army but avoids going to war, by inspiring lesser rulers to come under his sway by his ruling ethically and

[10] *S.*I.83; *Dhp.* 201.
[11] *S.*I.85.

justly, and protecting all sections of society, in accordance with Dharma, Buddhist teachings, especially on ethics.[12] It is said that the Buddha had been such a ruler in the past,[13] and at birth had the potential to be one again, or, as he did, to go on to become a Buddha.[14]

Such, then, is the ideal of non-violent rule as expressed in the early Buddhist texts. Yet, it seems to be acknowledged that this is an ideal that can be fully lived up to only by an exceptional person. Thus Elizabeth Harris, after an investigation of such texts, holds:

> That lay people should never initiate violence where there is harmony or use it against the innocent is very clear. That they should not attempt to protect those under their care if the only way of doing so is to use defensive violence is not so clear . . . The person who feels violence is justified to protect the lives of others has indeed to take the consequences into account. He has to remember that he is risking grave [karmic] consequences for himself in that his action will inevitably bear fruit . . . Such a person needs to evaluate motives .... Yet that person might still judge that the risks are worth facing to prevent a greater evil.[15]

The Indian emperor Ashoka (268–239 BCE) is widely revered by Buddhists as a great exemplar of Buddhist social ethics,[16] partly because of his emphasis on non-violence. While encouraging his people in this and other Buddhist moral norms, he himself abandoned his forebears' custom of violent expansion of the realm. Indeed, the Hinduism, the *Manu-smṛti*[17] holds that a king should make war when he thinks that all his subjects are contented and that he is most exalted in power, with the *Mahā-bhārata* holding that there is no evil in a king killing enemies. In the early part of his reign, prior to becoming a committed Buddhist, Ashoka had conquered the Kaliṅga region, but his Kaliṅga Rock Edict[18] expressed horror at the carnage that this had caused. He therefore resolved to abandon such conquests – even though he was the head of a very powerful empire. He retained his

[12] *D*.III.61–2.

[13] *A*.IV.89–90; cf. *D*.I.88–9; *D*.III.59.

[14] *Lakkhaṇa Sutta*, *D*.III.142–79.

[15] Elizabeth J. Harris, *Violence and Disruption in Society: A Study of the Early Buddhist Texts* (Wheel booklet no. 392/393, Kandy: Buddhist Publication Society, 1994), 47–8.

[16] Harvey, *Introduction to Buddhist Ethics*, 115–17.

[17] 7.169–70.

[18] N.A.Nikam and Richard McKeon, *The Edicts of Asoka* (Chicago: The University of Chicago Press, 1959. Midway Reprint 1978), 27–30.

army, though, and in one edict warned troublesome border people that, while he preferred not to use force against them, if they harassed his realm, he would, if necessary, do so. He retained the goal of spreading the influence of his empire, but sought to do so by sending out emissaries to bring about 'conquests by Dharma' – what is in accord with ethical values – to spread the influence of his way of ruling and thus form alliances. The most famous instance of this was his link with Sri Lanka, where his son, the monk Mahinda, transmitted Buddhism in its Theravāda form.

The Bodhisattva When Involved in Conflicts

The early Buddhist schools have many stories, known as *Jātakas*, of the Buddha in some of his previous lives, when he was a Bodhisattva, building up the qualities that would enable his future Buddhahood. These do include some in which he was involved in armed conflict. In the *Asadisa Jātaka*[19] for instance, the Bodhisattva as prince Asadisa has a strong reputation as an effective warrior and prevents several kings from attacking the weaker king of Benares by warning them that he would come to his assistance and defeat them if they did so. This averted a war which would have resulted in heavy loss of life. So, the *Jātaka* concludes saying: 'Thus did our Prince put to flight seven kings, without even shedding so much blood as a little fly might drink.'[20] In the *Kusa Jātaka*[21] king Kusa, the Bodhisattva, defeats seven kings who attacked his father-in-law, king Madda. Although Madda then says that Kusa may kill all seven rival kings, Kusa chose instead to form alliances with them through the traditional method of intermarriage, by arranging for them to be married to his wife's sisters.[22]

The *(Mahā)-Ummagga Jātaka*[23] relates the story of the Bodhisattva as Mahosadha, a wise counsellor of king Vedeha. Cūḷani Brahmadatta, a powerful neighbouring king planned to capture king Vedeha's kingdom by armed force, under the advice of his counsellor, Kevaṭṭa. Kevaṭṭa's plan is first, through deception, to unite 100 weaker kings against Vedeha, and

[19] no.181, *Jat.*II.87–90.

[20] *Jat.*II.90.

[21] no. 531, *Jat.*V.247–311.

[22] *Jat.*V.311.

[23] no. 546, *Jat.*VI.329–478. Also known as the *Mahosadha Jātaka*; see Naomi Appleton and Sarah Shaw, *The Ten Great Birth Stories of the Buddha; The Mahānipāta of the Jātakavaṇṇanā* (Chiang Mai: Silkworm, 2 volumes, 2015), 187–333.

then poison them, to remove possible rivals. Mahosadha, through his network of informants, becomes aware of Kevaṭṭa's plans, and although the 100 kings were known adversaries, he very skillfully spoils the plot of Kevaṭṭa to kill them by poisoning. A later plan of Kevaṭṭa is to offer Brahmadatta's daughter's hand in marriage to king Vedeha, but have him killed when he comes to marry her. Again, Mahosadha's informants warn him. He carefully plans an ingenious strategy to save the life of king Vedeha and in the end frustrates the military ambitions of king Brahmadatta, doing the least harm to life and property. Finally, king Vedeha succeeds in obtaining Brahmadatta's daughter in marriage, and the skillful and wise strategies adopted by Mahosadha result in the cessation of all hostilities, the prevention of colossal loss of life, and then new bonds of friendship between all the kings.

So, in such literature, there is acceptance of violence in limited circumstances, if it is kept to a minimum. Steven Collins, in his weighty study, *Nirvana and Other Buddhist Felicities*, talks of two modes of Dhamma[24] (Pali equivalent of Sanskrit Dharma) in Buddhist texts:

> *Mode 1* Dhamma is an ethics of reciprocity [the principle that good is to be returned for good and bad for bad], in which the assessment of violence is context-dependent and negotiable. Buddhist advice to kings in Mode 1 tells them not to pass judgement in haste or anger, but appropriately, such that the punishment fits the crime. [By implication, warfare can sometimes be acceptably engaged in.] To follow such advice is to be a Good King...
>
> *Mode 2* Dhamma is an ethic of absolute values, in which the assessment of violence is context-independent and non-negotiable ... The only advice possible for kings in Mode 2 might seem to be 'Don't be one!,' 'Renounce the world!' . . . . Many stories recommend just this. Others, however, envision the utopia of a non-violent king[25].

Here, Rupert Gethin comments, 'This is a useful distinction but I would suggest that it is *dhamma* in the second mode that is normative for early

[24] On which, see also: Gananath Obeyesekere and Frank Reynolds, *The Two Wheels of Dhamma: Essays on the Theravada Tradition in India and Ceylon* (Chambersburg, Penn.: American Academy of Religion, 1972).

[25] Steven Collins, *Nirvana and Other Buddhist Felicities* (Cambridge: Cambridge University Press, 1998), 420.

Buddhist thought. The first mode is more characteristic of later, post-canonical texts; in the Pāli canon, it is restricted to certain *Jātaka* stories'[26],[27] which, in the form we have them, consist mainly of commentarial prose embedding a lesser amount of canonical verses.

The Dilemma of Defensive Violence

Just as modern democratic societies have to face the dilemma of the degree to which their valued tolerance should tolerate intolerance, so any religion or society that greatly values peace has to deal with the dilemma of how to deal with violent threats to it. States which have been or are majority Buddhist have had to deal with this dilemma, and have sometimes chosen to use violence in defence of themselves.

Violence in the *Mahāvaṃsa*, the Theravāda Buddhist Chronicle of Sri Lanka

Daniel Kent reports[28] that during the 1983–2009 civil war in Sri Lanka, in which the Sinhalese majority state was fighting Tamil separatists, soldiers were urged to fight to defend *raṭa, jātiya* and *āgama*, which he translates both as 'country, nation and religion' and 'country, race and religion'. These three entities derive from the *Mahāvaṃsa* (Great Chronicle) which has been interpreted by many as describing the lineage of the Sinhala ethnic group and its enduring relationship with Buddhism. The earlier *Dīpavaṃsa* (Chronicle of the Island) discusses explicitly how the ancestors of the Sinhalese came to the island called Laṅkā. Yet, of course, such a melding of state and Buddhist interests has, in different countries and times, been variable in extent and effects, and in any instance is subject to debate. In Sri Lanka, where the population is 74% Sinhalese and 72% Buddhist, the government has never been exclusively Sinhalese or Buddhist but has always included others, including Christians, Hindus, Tamils and Muslims.

[26] As discussed in Ibid., 451–466.

[27] Rupert Gethin, 'Buddhist Monks, Buddhist Kings, Buddhist Violence', in *Religion and Violence in South Asia: Theory and Practice*, edited by John R. Hinnells and Richard King. (London: Routledge, 2007: 62–82), 71.

[28] Daniel Kent, 'Onward Buddhist Soldiers: Preaching to the Sri Lankan Army', in Michael K. Jerryson and Mark Juergensmeyer, editors, *Buddhist* Warfare (Oxford: Oxford University Press, 2010, 157–177), 158, 160.

The *Mahāvaṃsa* focuses on the actions of Buddhist kings and the fate of Buddhism from its arrival on the island in 250 BCE. The *Mahāvaṃsa* was composed by the Buddhist monk Mahānāma in the fifth century CE. More than a quarter of it (chapters 22–32) concerns the reign of king Duṭṭhagāmaṇī (Sinhala Duṭugämuṇu; 101–77 BCE.), glorifying him as the greatest of Sinhala heroes. Chapter 25 tells how he defeated Eḷāra, a non-Buddhist Damiḷa (Tamil) of South Indian origin who had invaded the island from south India, and established an enclave in the north which had lasted 44 years. While Eḷāra is presented as not an unbenevolent ruler, who is occasionally portrayed as even offering some patronage to Buddhism, the *Mahāvaṃsa* sees him nevertheless as having been a threat to the health of Buddhist institutions on the island. That said, Duṭṭhagāmaṇī refrained from resorting to any insulting behaviour or cruelty towards the defeated enemy camp.

Duṭṭhagāmaṇī is said to have fought not for the 'joy of sovereignty', but to 'bring glory to the teachings'[29], to save and protect the teachings of the Buddha and associated institutions.

In a controversial passage, the *Mahāvaṃsa* says that, after defeating the Tamils, the king was distressed at the deaths of a 'very large number/ complete army' (*akkhohiṇī*)[30] he had caused – as Ashoka had been after his defeat of Kāliṅga – but it is claimed[31] that eight enlightened monks (*Arahats*) re-assured him that:

> That deed presents no obstacle on your path to heaven. You caused the death of just one and a half people [*manujā*], O king. One had taken the refuges [i.e. were Buddhist], the other the Five Precepts [of Buddhist ethics] as well. The rest were wicked men of wrong view [*micchādiṭṭhī ca dussīlā*] who died like (or: as considered as) beasts [*pasu*[32]*-samā*]. You will in many ways illuminate the Buddha's teaching, so stop worrying.[33]

[29] *jotetuṃ sāsanam*, *Mvm*.25.2–3.

[30] *Mvm*.25.103, 108.

[31] 25.108–11.

[32] *Pasu* generally means cattle.

[33] Transl. (with Pāli added) Richard F. Gombrich, *Theravāda Buddhism*, 2nd edn (London and New York: Routledge, 2006): 141. See also: Mahinda Deegalle, 'Is Violence Justified in Theravada?' *Current Dialogue* 39 (2002), 8–17; and Rupert Gethin, 'Buddhist Monks, Buddhist Kings, Buddhist Violence', in *Religion and Violence in South Asia: Theory and Practice*, edited by John R. Hinnells and Richard King. (London: Routledge, 2007: 62–82), 63, 75–8.

This was written many centuries after the events it purports to describe, at a time of renewed threat from South India; indeed H.L. Seneviratne says, 'the entire story is probably fictional',[34] while Gethin describes it as 'largely legendary'.[35] The surprising nature of the claim, put in the mouth of supposed *Arahats* – saints who are incapable of lying – strongly indicates that if this was said, it was *not* by any *Arahat*. Gethin comments on these '*Arahats*', or rather Mahānāma, the text's author, 'How did these ... come to get their Buddhism so wrong?'.[36] Now it would have been appropriate for King Duṭṭhagāmaṇī to regret the deaths he and his army had caused; but the actual issue here is this surprising claim: that most of the people killed were not *really*, or not *fully*, human, so that there was little problem in killing them.

The account provides a very questionable and highly charged reflection of the Buddhist doctrine that it is less bad to kill a person deemed less virtuous person than a virtuous one,[37] for in Early Buddhist and Theravāda teachings, it is always worse to intentionally kill a human than an animal. To gain a human or divine rebirth, or have two in a row, is said to be rare.[38] However, some early schools other than the Theravāda seem to have accepted that, sometimes, killing an animal could be worse than killing a human.[39]

In any case, the king was said to have sought to make amends for his actions by a life of good works of benefit to the community, before being reborn in heaven – though this would not preclude any bad karma of his catching up with him later, as the *Sutta*s say that one who does bad action *may* still be reborn in heaven in their next life before their bad karma later catches up with them.[40]

Duṭṭhagāmaṇī may in fact have been the first to unify the island: even the *Mahāvaṃsa* says that not all who fought against him were Tamil and that he had to fight 32 kings before reaching Eḷāra's kingdom from the far

[34] H.L. Seneviratne, *The Work of Kings: The New Buddhism in Sri Lanka* (Chicago: The University of Chicago Press, 1999), 21.

[35] Gethin, 'Buddhist Monks, Buddhist Kings, Buddhist Violence', 75.

[36] Ibid., 63 and 76–7

[37] Ibid., 78.

[38] *S*.V.75–6; cf. *Dhp*.182.

[39] Ann Heirman, 'Protecting Insects in Medieval Chinese Buddhism: Daoxuan's *Vinaya* Commentaries'. *Buddhist Studies Review*, 2020, vol. 37, no. 1, 27–52.

[40] *M*.III.209–15; Harvey, *An Introduction to Buddhist Ethics*, 24–5.

south.[41] Thus, the chronicle's attempt to portray his actions as simply a defence of the Sinhalese nation and its Buddhism is over-played. The alignment of the Sinhalese to Buddhism and the Tamils to a threatening alien force was probably the product of a later period. There was racial and cultural mixing from an early time, and this only began to be undermined in the fifth century, when rulers of three powerful South Indian kingdoms succeeded in undermining the influence of Buddhism on Hindu society in South India, and threatened the political stability of the island's Sinhalese kingdom, generating real fear for the plight of Buddhism. There were notable destructive invasions of the island by militantly Hindu South Indian states in the fifth, ninth, tenth, eleventh and thirteenth centuries.

Many of the ideas popularly associated with the *Mahāvaṃsa* are in fact not found in the text itself; with multiple new interpretations found frequently in popular literature for mass consumption, all of which warrants scholarly scrutiny and serious challenge. Even those elements that are found in the *Mahāvaṃsa* often have different meanings in the context of its compilation. Recent work by Sven Bretfeld,[42] comparing the *Mahāvaṃsa* with archaeological records, highlights constructions from disparate sources underlying stories now taken as historical and identity-forming facts. This suggests that much can therefore be done to deconstruct this text.

In twentieth-century Sri Lanka, an influential book arguing for the involvement of Buddhist monks in social and political matters was Walpola Rāhula's *Bhiksuvage Urumaya* (1946).[43] In a colonial context, this talked of Sinhalese-Buddhist 'religio-nationalism' and 'religio-patriotism'[44] and referred to Duṭṭhagāmaṇī's campaign against General Eḷāra as a 'crusade' to 'liberate the nation and the religion from the foreign yoke' which was arresting the 'progress of Buddhism'.[45]

[41] S.J. Tambiah, *Buddhism Betrayed? Religion, Politics and Violence in Sri Lanka* (Chicago and London: University of Chicago Press, 1992), 134.

[42] Sven Bretfeld, 'The Story of Mahinda in the Politics of Transnational Representation'. Paper delivered at the inaugural meeting of the Transnational Network of Theravada Studies, Trondheim, Norway, November 2018. To be published in *The Making of Theravada*, in preparation.

[43] Walpola Rahula, *The Heritage of the Bhikkhu: A Short History of the Bhikkhu in the Educational, Cultural, Social, and Political Life* (New York, Grove Press, 1974 – revised version of the original 1946 translation from Sinhalese *Bhiṣuvagē Urumaya*).

[44] Tambiah, *Buddhism Betrayed?*, 27–8.

[45] Rahula, *The Heritage of the Bhikkhu*, 20.

> From this time the patriotism and the religion of the Sinhalese became inseparably linked. The religio-patriotism at that time assumed such overpowering proportions that both *bhikkhus* and laymen considered that even killing people in order to liberate the religion and the country was not a heinous crime.[46]

On the *Mahāvaṃsa*'s claim that supposed *Arahats* had said that most of the Tamils killed were not fully human, Rāhula says:

> Nevertheless, it is diametrically opposed to the teaching of the Buddha. It is difficult for us today either to affirm or to deny whether *arahants* who lived in the second century BCE did ever make such a statement. But there is no doubt that Mahānāma Thera, the author of the *Mahā-vaṃsa*, who lived in the fifth century A.C., recorded this in the *Mahā-vaṃsa*.[47]

He held that this shows that responsible monks of this time had accepted such an idea and that they 'considered it their sacred duty to engage themselves in the service of their country as much as in the service of their religion'.[48]

When Richard Gombrich interviewed Sinhalese monks in the 1960s, he found that

'most (but not all) of them were reluctant entirely to accept the view propounded to Duṭṭhagāmaṇī, for they realized its incongruence with Buddhist ethics. The stereotypes are, however, too strong to be easily demolished, and least of all by historical fact.'[49] When monks were asked about the ethics of Duṭṭhagāmaṇī's war, the answers varied slightly, but typical was the reply that his 'killing of Tamils was sin [*pava*], but not great, because his main purpose (*paramārtha*) was not to kill men but to save Buddhism; he did not have full intention to kill. But to say that he will not pay for his sin ... is wrong.'[50] Only one monk said that the king was

[46] Ibid., 21.

[47] Ibid., 22.

[48] Ibid., 22.

[49] Gombrich, *Theravāda Buddhism*, 141–42.

[50] Richard F. Gombrich, *Precept and Practice: Traditional Buddhism in the Rural Highlands of Ceylon* (Oxford: Clarendon Press, 1971): 157. I would prefer the translation 'evil' to that of 'sin', as 'sin' implies an action which offends a creator God. For further information on the use of the Duṭṭhagāmaṇī legend in the context of the current ethnic conflict in Sri Lanka, see Tessa J. Bartholomeusz's, 'In Defense of Dharma: Just-War Ideology in Buddhist Sri Lanka', *Journal of Buddhist Ethics*, 1999, vol. 6, 1–16; and *In Defense of Dharma: Just-War Ideology in Buddhist Sri Lanka* (London: Routledge Curzon, 2002).

wrong in thinking that his ultimate purpose made his action right. It was wrong. Only two monks said that he did not 'sin'. One, a kindly but very unsophisticated monk, said that it had not been a 'sin' for the king to kill Tamils as they were of the wrong view, since it was not wrong to kill in order to save religion. Another held that killing is not a 'sin' if it is done to defend Buddhism, as with Duṭṭhagāmaṇī.[51]

As a background to the Tamil-Sinhala tensions that fuelled the 1983–2009 civil war, it can be noted that after independence from the British in 1948, Sinhalese Buddhists rightly sought to revive and strengthen their culture after the colonial period, and they also sought to overcome the colonial legacy of the Tamils being a relatively privileged minority. Yet a side-effect of building their nationalism around a Buddhist identity rooted in perceptions of past Sinhalese Buddhist civilisations has been to exclude the mainly non-Buddhist Tamils from this ideal. Buddhist values have become distorted as 'Buddhism' has become increasingly identified, by sections of the population, with the Sinhalese people and the territory of the entire island.[52] While the *Mahāvaṃsa* has the Buddha predict that Buddhism would flourish in Sri Lanka, this has wrongly been taken by some to support a drive to restore all, and only, Buddhists to prominence.[53] This perspective has led to Buddhists exploiting their majority position and alienating Tamils, who are still perceived as a privileged minority. Sinhalese party politicians have 'played to the gallery' and made capital out of religion, producing a communalisation of politics.[54] Often, the party in opposition has objected when the party in power has made moves to address Tamil grievances. There are Buddhists who object to this, though: both the All Ceylon Buddhist Congress and the Young Men's Buddhist Association have passed resolutions for the government to revoke the party system.[55] The division of the *Saṅgha* along political lines has not helped either, though there is a swell of opinion against this.

But for extremists on both sides – including some Buddhist monks who have demonstrated against 'concessions to the Tamils' – moderates could have resolved the ethnic problem by taking into account the concerns of both sides and encouraging mutual forgiveness of past wrongs.

[51] Gombrich, *Precept and Practice*, 258.

[52] Cf. the rise of 'Hindutva', a kind of Hindu fundamentalism, in India.

[53] George D. Bond, *The Buddhist Revival in Sri Lanka – Religious Tradition, Reinterpretation and Response* (Columbia: University of South Carolina Press, 1988). 9.

[54] Ibid., 121–22.

[55] Ibid., 118.

In their drive to protect Buddhism, Sinhalese Buddhists need to pay more attention to the contents of what they are 'protecting', and less to the need for a strong political 'container' for it. A re-emphasis on the Buddhist values of non-violence and tolerance is needed, as is a more pluralistic model of Buddhist nationalism.[56]

Defence of Violence in Some Mahāyāna Texts

From perhaps the first century BCE to around the sixth century CE, the Mahāyāna movement developed in India and generated a range of new *Sūtra* texts, mainly based on meditative experiences in which people felt that they were inspired and taught by heavenly Buddhas. Due to the Mahāyāna's central emphasis on the virtue of compassion, it was more willing to over-ride Buddhist ethical precepts in the name of this virtue. This means that it contains various textual passages which validate killing in certain circumstances, if this may help prevent further suffering.

That said, the *Ārya-satyaka-parivarta Sūtra*, an early Mahāyāna text perhaps influenced by Ashokan edicts, and in turn influential in Tibet, teaches that the righteous ruler should seek to avoid war by using negotiation or placation, or having strong alliances. If he has to fight to defend his country, he should seek to attain victory over the enemy only with the aim of protecting his people, also bearing in mind the need to protect all life, and having no concern for himself and his property. In this way, he may avoid the usual bad karmic results of killing.[57] In war, he should not vent his anger by burning cities or villages, or destroying reservoirs, fruit trees or harvests as these are 'sources of life commonly used by many sentient beings who have not produced any faults', including local deities and animals.[58]

Upāya-kauśalya Sūtra

The archetypal practitioner of compassion is a Bodhisattva: one on the long path to perfect Buddhahood. An influential text is the *Upāya-kauśalya Sūtra*, the Discourse on Skill in Means,[59] in which the Buddha, in a past life, as a Bodhisattva, is a captain who reluctantly kills a thief who

[56] Tambiah, *Buddhism Betrayed?*, 125.
[57] *ASP.*206–8.
[58] *ASP.*197; cf.70.
[59] Mark Tatz, *The Skill in Means (Upāyakauśalya) Sūtra* (Delhi: Motilal Banarsidass, 1994).

is about to kill 500 good men on his ship, both to save them and to save the thief from generating much bad karma by killing them.[60] The captain was willing to be reborn in hell from his act of killing, but his compassionate motivation in risking this fate is seen to have meant that he avoided hell, or only spent a very short time there.[61]

While this story of acceptable killing is about a very special person, driven by difficult circumstances to reluctantly kill someone, it sets an example that has often been cited by Mahāyānists, and is open to misuse, in that it might be used in circumstances that are less pressing, and in which the motive for killing is not really, or sufficiently, compassionate.

Mahā-parinirvāṇa Sūtra

Moreover, the Mahāyāna contains less guarded justifications for killing, several of which are contained in the *Mahā-parinirvāṇa Sūtra,* which is not the same as non-Mahāyāna texts of the same name, including the *Mahā-parinibbāna Sutta* in Pali. Its early form may have developed in India in or by the second century CE. There is a 418 CE translation into Chinese by Faxian[62] and a 430 CE one translated by Dharmakṣema.[63] The latter, more popular, translation is four times longer than the former, and unlike it, argues that *all* sentient beings have the potential to become Buddhas in some lifetime of theirs.[64] The former sees deeply evil beings known as the '*icchantikas*' as incapable of this, whereas the latter sees them as, in time, capable of it.

In one passage of the Dharmakṣema version, the Buddha says that in a previous life, he was a king who found that several Brahmins were slandering Mahāyāna teachings. To save them from the bad karma entailed in this (!), and to protect Buddhism, 'I had them put to death on the spot. Men

[60] Ibid., 73–6.

[61] Harvey, *An Introduction to Buddhist Ethics,* 135–38; Stephen Jenkins, 'On the auspiciousness of compassionate violence', *Journal of the International Association of Buddhist Studies,* 2011, vol. 33, nos. 1–2, 299–331.

[62] Taishō 376.12.853–899.

[63] Taishō 374.12.365c–603c.

[64] Taishō 374.12.573c. See: Paul Williams, *Mahāyāna Buddhism: The Doctrinal Foundations,* 2nd edn (London and New York: Routledge and Kegan Paul, 2009), 107; and P. B. Yampolsky, *Selected Writings of Nichiren,* edited with an introduction by Yampolsky; translated by Burton Watson and others (New York: Columbia University Press, 1990), 120–21.

of devout faith, as a result of that action, I never thereafter fell into hell.'[65] Further:

> O good man! You asked if one could gain this 'bhumi' [stage on the Bodhisattva path] or not when one has killed a Brahmin … the Bodhisattva-mahasattva acts likewise for reasons of protecting Wonderful Dharma. Should beings slander Mahayana, he applies kindly lashings, in order to cure them. Or he may take life in order that what obtained in the past could be mended, thus seeing to it that the law [Dharma] could be accorded with. The Bodhisattva always thinks: 'How might I best make beings aspire to faith? I shall always act as is best fitted to the occasion.' The Brahmin fell into Avichi Hell after his death. … He then came to realise that things had taken this turn because of his slandering of the vaipulya Mahayana sutras and by his not believing, and by his being killed by the king – thus had he been born there. Thinking in this way, respect arose towards the Mahayana vaipulya sutras. Then, after his death, he was born in the world of Tathagata [Buddha] Amrta-Drum. There he lived for 10 kalpas [eons]. O good man! I thus, in days gone by, gave this person a life of 10 kalpas. How could it be said that I killed him?'.[66]

In any case, says the *Sūtra*, the Brahmins (non-Buddhist priests) were each an *icchantika*, so there was no evil in killing them to protect the Dharma. While killing even an animal can lead to rebirth in hell or as an animal or hungry ghost:

> All those Brahmins are of the class of the icchantika. For example, such actions as digging the ground, mowing the grass, felling trees, cutting up corpses, ill-speaking, and lashing do not call forth karmic returns. Killing an icchantika comes within the same category.[67]

[65] Taishō 374.12, 434c; quoted in Yampolsky *Selected Writings of Nichiren*, 32; and see Williams *Mahāyāna Buddhism*, 167.

[66] Kosho Yamamoto, and Tony Page, *The Mahayana Mahaparinirvana Sutra* (translated into English by Kosho Yamamoto, 1973 from Dharmakshema's Chinese version. (Taisho Tripitaka Vol. 12, No. 374). Edited, revised and copyright by Dr. Tony Page, 2007: http://lirs.ru/do/Mahaparinirvana_Sutra,Yamamoto,Page,2007.pdf, accessed 8 June 2022, 219, cf.37.

[67] Yamamoto and Page, *The Mahayana Mahaparinirvana Sutra,* 220 (Taishō 374, 12. 459a–460b), and as cited in: Yampolsky, *Selected Writings of Nichiren*, 32, Paul Demiéville, 'Le Bouddhisme et la guerre: postscriptum a 'L'Histoire des moines guerriers du Japon' de G. Renondeau', *Melanges*, Vol. I (Paris, L'Institut des Hautes Etudes Chinoises, Presses Universitaires de France, 1957, 347–85. Reprinted in Jerryson and Juergensmeyer, *Buddhist Warfare*, 17–57), 378, and Holmes Welch, *Buddhism Under Mao* (Cambridge, Mass.: Harvard University Press), 281.

An *icchantika* is otherwise described as 'perfect in his obstacles to present and future good',[68] being a monastic or lay person who: 'slanders the true Dharma' repeatedly and without any signs of remorse; or enacts a monastic offence entailing defeat [expulsion]; or does one of the five deadly actions, such as killing one of one's parents, without contrition. He is a companion to Māra, the embodiment of evil.[69] Thus, 'Sentient beings possess the five good roots such as faith, but the *icchantika* has eternally severed those roots. Thus, while it is a fault to kill an ant, it is not a fault to kill an *icchantika*.'[70]

Paul Williams sees the permission to kill those who slander the Dharma as the kind of passage which might be used to justify killing those who opposed one's own sect of Buddhism,[71] as happened in medieval Japan. McFarlane comments, 'the arguments are hardly convincing in terms of Mahāyāna or more general Buddhist principles',[72] and such attempts to justify Buddhist involvement in violence have been rare.[73]

In another passage of the *Mahā-parinirvāṇa Sūtra*, it is said that the true follower of the Mahāyāna should ignore the moral precepts, if the need to protect monks (who uphold them) from attack makes this necessary.[74] Nevertheless, the passage goes on to say that they should never use the weapons that they carry to take life.[75]

The *Sūtra* contains over 100 references to bad people slandering the 'Wonderful Dharma', by which it mainly means Mahāyāna teachings. This may well reflect criticisms of Buddhism from the resurgent Hinduism at the time of later phases of the *Sūtra*'s development. That said, earlier Mahāyāna *Sūtra*s refer to criticisms from non-Mahāyānists, saying that the newly appeared *Sūtra*s were not really teachings of the Buddha. In any case, it is notable that criticisms of Buddhism in pre-Mahāyāna texts receive a much calmer response than in some Mahāyāna texts. In the Pali

[68] Taishō 374.12.562b.

[69] Taishō 12, 425a–b, 419a and 421c–422a, as cited in Yampolsky *Selected Writings of Nichiren*, 31–2, 124.

[70] Taishō 12, 562b.

[71] Williams, *Mahāyāna Buddhism*, 164.

[72] Stewart McFarlane, 'Buddhism', in E. Laszlo and J. Y. Yoo (eds.), *World Encyclopaedia of Peace* (Oxford, Pergamon Press, vol. I, 1986), 97–103, 101.

[73] Ibid., 102.

[74] Taishō 374.12.383b–384a, as cited in Demiéville, 'Le Bouddhisme et la guerre', 378–9, in turn cited by Welch, *Buddhism Under Mao*, 281, and Williams, *Mahāyāna Buddhism*, 167.

[75] Taishō 374.12.383b–384b, as cited in Yampolsky, *Selected Writings of Nichiren*, 33–5.

Canon, the Buddha advised his disciples not to react emotionally when they heard people speaking in blame or praise of him, the Dharma or Saṅgha, but to assess calmly the degree to which what was said was true or false.[76]

It might be thought that the relatively easy acceptance of killing in the above text may be facilitated by Buddhism's non-acceptance of a permanent Self in humans and other beings. However, the Mahāyāna *Mahāparinirvāṇa Sūtra* is one of the few *Sūtras* to talk of there being a true Self within beings, as it sometimes refers in this way to the Buddha-nature:[77] the potential for Buddhahood in all beings, which is sometimes seen as a full-fledged Buddhahood already hidden by obscuring defilements within beings. It sees the non-Self teaching as only applying to the impermanent things of saṃsāra, but not to the Tathāgata/Buddha, which is the eternal Self,[78] so non-Self is not a definitive teaching.[79] The Self is the Buddha-nature.[80] '"Self" means "Tathagatagarbha" [Buddha-Womb, Buddha-Embryo, Buddha-Nature]. Every being has Buddha-Nature. This is the Self'.[81] Unlike the five kinds of impermanent process of body and mind, 'The True Self of the Buddha-Nature is like the diamond, which cannot be crushed'.[82] This is rather reminiscent of the idea in the Hindu *Bhagavad Gītā* that the killing of people in battle does not really kill them as their Self is inviolable.

Buddhism and Violence in East Asia

In China, kings occasionally gave a 'Buddhist' justification for violence. In 581, after Wen-ti had established the Sui dynasty, he pronounced himself a *Cakravartin* emperor, saying 'We regard the weapons of war as having become like incense and flowers' as offerings. He took the Bodhisattva vows, claimed that his battles had promoted Buddhism, and was a lavish patron of Buddhism.[83]

[76] *D.*I.3.
[77] Williams, *Mahāyāna Buddhism*, 108.
[78] Yamamoto and Page, *The Mahayana Mahaparinirvana Sutra*, 29–32, in ch. 3.
[79] Ibid., 107, ch. 12.
[80] Ibid., 99, ch.11
[81] Ibid., 101, ch 12.
[82] Ibid., 103, ch 12.
[83] Welch, *Buddhism Under Mao*, 297.

Amongst the schools of Buddhism that developed in China, an influential one was the Tiantai (T'ien-t'ai), founded by Zhiyi,[84] which emphasized the notion of the Buddha-nature as present in all things, and that the world is non-different from the ultimate 'One Mind', *Nirvāṇa*.[85] It saw the Buddha as having taught different teachings at a variety of levels of truth, culminating with the *Lotus* (*Saddharma-puṇḍarīka*) and *Mahāparinirvāṇa Sūtra*s as the highest teaching: on the Buddha-nature in all beings, and the Buddha as the saviour of all. In Japan, where it was known as the Tendai School, it was even more influential.

In Japan, Buddhists intervened in the life of the nation more openly than in China; indeed, there was a connection between Buddhism and the state from the time of the coming of Buddhism to the country, in 538 CE. In the tenth century, during the Heian era (794–1185), social order began to break down, and a strong central government was not re-established until the Tokugawa era (1603–1867). In the intervening period, a feudal society developed in which clan and regional loyalties were dominant, yet the project of attaining national unity urged the parties on to attain such dominance.[86] This was also a time when *sōhei*, or warrior-monks, were a recognized part of national life.[87] One factor in this was the fact that monasteries were centres of power and donated land at a time of social unrest, when political power was up for grabs. Another was the fact that Japanese Buddhists came to identify strongly with one or other school or sub-school, these becoming more like sects, so that sectarian differences were far more strongly drawn than in other Buddhist countries.[88]

In the Heian era, a demanding and oppressive aristocracy put high demands for taxes and labour on the population, which sought refuge in Buddhist monasteries, which were exempt from these. Many inhabitants of the monasteries were 'monks' in name only, and were used by the monasteries to develop land donated to them. They also came to be used in armed defence of these lands against the state or the nobility, and then

[84] Chih-i; 539–97.

[85] Williams, *Mahāyāna Buddhism,* 161–5.

[86] Winston L. King, *Zen and the Way of the Sword: Arming the Samurai Psyche* (Oxford and New York: Oxford University Press, 1993): 39.

[87] G. Renondeau, 'Histoire des moins guerriers du Japon', in *Melanges*, vol. I (Paris, L'Institut des Hautes Etudes Chinoises, Presses Universitaires de France, 1957, 159–346), Demiéville, 'Le Bouddhisme et la guerre', 369.

[88] Demiéville, 'Le Bouddhisme et la guerre', 369–70.

armed monks rebelled against their abbots, who were often of noble origin or connected to the court. By 1100, all the great monasteries of the well-established, broad-based Tendai school had armies to protect their interests.[89]

For the Tendai school, the emphasised *Mahā-parinirvāṇa Sūtra* contains, as we have seen, several passages allowing violence 'in defence of the Dharma'. At the same time as these developments, military barons of the provinces were launching revolts against the court.[90] Thus, feudal conflicts and clan rivalries arose in which there was fighting between sects and the imperial court, between sects and feudal lords, and between sect and sect.[91]

During the troubled Kamakura period (1192–1333), central state power almost completely disappeared. Rule was by military Shōguns and the *bushi*, or warrior-knight, class. The latter helped Buddhism spread to the people, however, and thus put down deep roots. Zen's meditational and ethical self-discipline, and indifference to death, helped the *bushi* to resist two attempted Mongolian invasions in 1274 and 1281.[92] Eisai (1141–1215), founder of Rinzai Zen, gained the protection of a Shōgun at the capital Kamakura and helped establish the long-lasting alliance between Rinzai and the *bushi*. Rinzai Zen monks began to teach some of the *bushi* knights how to be calm, self-disciplined fighters, with no fear of death. This can be seen as an example of 'skilful means', in the form of an adaptation of Buddhism to the way of life of a particular group of people. The *bushi* also appreciated Zen discipline, simplicity and directness. This continued in a later period, when the *bushi* had evolved into *samurai* knights. Takuan Sōhō Zenji (1573–1645) was not averse to applying Zen principles to their swordsmanship:

> The uplifted sword has no will of its own, it is all of emptiness. It is like a flash of lightning. The man who is about to be struck down is also of emptiness, as is the one who wields the sword . . . Do not get your mind stopped with the sword you raise, forget about what you are doing, and strike the enemy. Do not keep your mind on the person before you. They are all of emptiness, but beware of your mind being caught in emptiness.[93]

[89] King, *Zen and the Way of the Sword*, 451.

[90] Demiéville, 'Le Bouddhisme et la guerre', 370.

[91] Ibid., 371.

[92] Daisetzu T. Suzuki, *Zen and Japanese Culture* (New York: Bollingen Foundation, 1959), 64–79.

[93] Robert Aitken, *The Mind of Clover: Essays in Zen Buddhist Ethics* (San Francisco: North Point Press, 1984), 5.

Such ideas sound morally dangerous, but Takuan was adapting the Mahāyāna idea of all as 'empty' of independent reality for those who were already committed by birth to fighting – neglecting to point out that one's 'own' side is likewise empty and not to be attached to! Nevertheless, he also emphasized the virtues of sympathy and human-heartedness.

The militant and nationalistic reformer Nichiren (1222–82), ex-Tendai founder of a school named after him, unsuccessfully called for the government to suppress other Buddhist sects, which he regarded as undermining the Japanese nation, citing various passages from the *Mahā-parinirvāṇa Sūtra* in support of this. The school fell into conflict with the Pure Land Jōdo school, and especially its offshoot, the Jōdo-shin school, both of which focussed on faith in the heavenly Buddha Amitābha (Amida in Japanese), whereas Nichiren focussed on the saving power of the *Lotus Sūtra*, and the heavenly Buddha Śākyamuni who is seen to have delivered this.

The Ashikaga period (1333–1573) was one of almost constant turmoil, with simultaneous rule by two emperors followed by rule by rival warring Shōguns. The Jōdo-shin school became centred on fortified temples, with its armed followers, both priests and laity, acting to defend its single-minded 'true faith' in the saving power of Amida Buddha. They could be fanatical in battle, believing that they would be reborn in Amida's Pure Land if they were killed. In the sixteenth century, the school organized and led peasant uprisings and became the ruling power in one region of Japan.[94] This century also saw Nichiren Buddhists attack the headquarters of the Jōdo-shin and the Tendai School.

The Tendai School continued to maintain troops, as did the Tantric Shingon school. In 1409, Tendai monks published the following, which they attributed to Ryōgen (912–85): 'Without literate culture, there are no rites which show love for superiors; without arms, there is no virtue which impresses inferiors. The world is therefore only well-ordered if literate culture and arms mutually complement each other.'[95] They went on to say that, in their day, the true Dharma had declined, and people did not respect religion. It was thus necessary for *shuto*, troops drawn from the less able monks, to prevent disorder in monastic domains, and protect against 'heretical' sects, so as to maintain the facilities for study and meditation.[96]

[94] Demiéville, 'Le Bouddhisme et la guerre', 373.
[95] Ibid., 377.
[96] Ibid., 377.

A biography of Ryōgen from around the same time has him urging Tendai monks to take up arms to protect their true version of the Mahāyāna against 'heresies'.[97]

Conclusion

A common theme in violence-supporting perspectives is a blending of religion and nationalism, or a tendency to equate the 'Buddhism' that must be defended with a particular form of Buddhism; the equivalent, of course, also occurs in other religious communities. In both cases, something that is seen as precious and sacred is linked to a container or embodiment that is seen as somehow under threat and in need of forceful protection. Of course, such defence can have a noble aspect if genuine, but there is always the danger that a perceived 'enemy' is seen as not just *different* from one's own community, but as somehow less human and worthy of little respect.

Abbreviations

A *Aṅguttara Nikāya*; tr. F. L. Woodward and E. M. Hare, *The Book of Gradual Sayings*, 5 vols., London, PTS, 1932–6; tr. Bhikkhu Bodhi, *The Numerical Discourses of the Buddha*, Boston: Wisdom, 2012.

ASP *Ārya-satyaka-parivarta*; tr. L. Jamspal, *The Range of the Bodhisattva: A Mahāyāna Sūtra*, 2010, New York: American Institute of Buddhist Studies.

D *Dīgha Nikāya*; tr. by T. W. and C. A. F. Rhys Davids, *Dialogues of the Buddha*, 3 vols., London, PTS, 1899–1921; tr. M.Walshe, *Long Discourses of the Buddha*, 2nd revised edition, Boston: Wisdom, 1996, one vol..

Dhp *Dhammapada*; tr. K.R.Norman, *The Word of the Doctrine*, London, PTS, 1997; tr. V. Roebuck, *The Dhammapada*, London: Penguin, 2010. Buddharakkhita and Ṭhānissaro translations on Access to Insight website.

Jat *Jātaka with Commentary*; tr. by various hands under E. B. Cowell, *The Jātaka or Stories of the Buddha's Former Births*, 6 vols.,

[97] Ibid., 377–78.

	London, PTS, 1895–1907. Sarah Shaw, *The Jātakas: Birth Stories of the Bodhisatta*, New Delhi: Penguin, 2006, translates 26 of the *Jātakas.*
M	*Majjhima Nikāya*; tr. by I. B. Horner, *Middle Length Sayings*, 3 vols., London, PTS, 1954–9; tr. Bhikkhu Ñāṇamoli and Bhikkhu Bodhi, *The Middle Length Discourses of the Buddha*, Boston: Wisdom, 1995.
Mvm	*Mahāvaṃsa*; tr. W. Geiger and M. H. Bode, *The Mahāvaṃsa or Great Chronicle of Ceylon*, London: PTS, 1912.
PTS	Pali Text Society
S	*Saṃyutta Nikāya*; tr. C.A.F. Rhys Davids and F.L. Woodward, *The Book of Kindred Sayings*, 5 vols., London, PTS, 1917–30; tr. Bhikkhu Bodhi, *The Connected Discourses of the Buddha*, Boston: Wisdom, 2005, in one vol.
Ud	*Udāna*; tr. P.Masefield, *The Udāna*, London: PTS, 1994.

References to above, except ASP, Dhp and Mvm, are to page number of PTS edition of Pali text, preceded by volume number, where relevant.

Further Reading

Harvey, Peter. *An Introduction to Buddhist Ethics: Foundations, Values and Issues.* Cambridge: Cambridge University Press, 2000): pp. 239–85

Harvey, Peter, et al (eds). 'Exploratory Position Paper on Buddhism and IHL', for 2019 conference on 'Reducing Suffering During Conflict: The Interface Between Buddhism and International Humanitarian Law (IHL)': https://www.icrc.org/en/document/reducing-suffering-during-conflict-interface-between-buddhism-and-international, accessed 8 June 2022.

Harris, Elizabeth J. *Violence and Disruption in Society: A Study of the Early Buddhist Texts* Wheel booklet no. 392/393, Kandy: Buddhist Publication Society, 1994: https://www.accesstoinsight.org/lib/authors/harris/wheel392.html, accessed 8 June 2022.

Jerryson, Michael K., and Mark Juergensmeyer (eds). *Buddhist Warfare.* Oxford: Oxford University Press, 2010.

CHAPTER 7

Apologists and Appropriators: Protestant Christian Reckoning with Biblical Violence

Helen Paynter

Since its earliest days, Christianity has had to reckon with the violence which its sacred text contains. In very broad terms, Christians have been exercised by two main questions with regard to this issue. First, to what extent is violence in the world of the reader condemned, justified, or indeed commanded by the biblical text? Second, how is the violence of the text to be reconciled with the conventional Christian view of God as all-loving? This chapter will attempt to sketch out the contours of the modern debate within Protestant Christian scholarship, with more attention being given to the second of these questions. First, however, it is important to briefly delineate the parameters of the issue. What is the biblical witness to violence and peace in both testaments? The chapter will begin

Positionality: I write as a biblical scholar and a Non-conformist Christian minister (accredited by the Baptist Union of Great Britain).

H. Paynter (✉)
Centre for the Study of Bible and Violence, Bristol Baptist College, Bristol, UK
e-mail: paynterh@bristol-baptist.ac.uk

M. Power, H. Paynter (eds.), *Violence and Peace in Sacred Texts*,
https://doi.org/10.1007/978-3-031-17804-7_7

with a broad overview of both of these issues, and then briefly consider some of the traditional ways in which these texts have been viewed before moving on to a consideration of the contemporary debate.

Violence and Peace in the Bible

Contrary to popular opinion, which we will consider further below, it is not possible to distinguish the Old Testament from the New in regard to its representations of God's character. The popular imagination of an Old Testament angry God and a New Testament loving God revealed by Jesus is a gross parody. Likewise, the notion that the Old Testament is full of violence, and the New Testament is full of peace, is also an entirely unfair oversimplification. The injunction to love one's neighbour, for example, although quoted by Jesus, originates in Leviticus 19:18. Rather, both testaments reveal an overall trajectory of peace, with frequent instances of violence intruding.

Peace in the Bible: The Trajectory of Shalom

The closing chapters of Revelation, the final book of the New Testament, self-consciously reflect the opening two chapters of Genesis, which portray the creation of the Garden of Eden. Eden, of course, has become paradigmatic in the popular imagination as a place of peace and harmony among humans and between humans and nature. In contrast to the extant Ancient Near-Eastern creation myths, the one offered by Genesis is remarkably irenic.[1] Rather than the earth being created through cosmic conflict, the God of the Bible creates by the simple divine fiat.[2] Rather than humans being created to be as slaves of the gods, as in the Babylonian *Atraharsis Epic,* for example, in Genesis, humans are recipients of divine hospitality, to whom the treasures of the earth and the fruit of the paradisical orchards are given.[3] The divine command is explicitly about human flourishing.[4] Within this garden, humans are represented as living in non-hierarchical gender relationships,[5] and in an intrinsically non-violent world, where

[1] For a helpful discussion of these themes, see J. Richard Middleton, *The liberating image: The imago Dei in Genesis 1.* (Grand Rapids: Brazos Press, 2005).

[2] Gen 1.

[3] Gen 2: 10–16.

[4] Gen 1:28.

[5] Gen 1:27.

even the eating of animals has not yet been sanctioned.[6] Although the Hebrew word *shalom* (weakly rendered 'peace' in many English translations of the Bible) is not used, this is a powerful depiction of the holistic well-being which the noun represents.

Genesis 3, of course, introduces the complications in the plot. The man and the woman take the fruit which has been forbidden to them, and as a direct result, violence enters the world. Gender relationships become disordered,[7] the relationship with nature is disrupted,[8] and very shortly afterwards, the first murder takes place.[9] The flood that is unleashed upon the world shortly afterward is a direct consequence of its violence;[10] note that the world is already 'ruined' by violence and so God chooses to 'ruin' it.[11]

From here on, the biblical trajectory is aiming towards the restoration of that lost *shalom*. The Old Testament law can be understood, in part, as an attempt to model the nation along the lines of *shalom*; legislating for neighbourly co-operation,[12] the limitation of vengeance,[13] and the maintenance of law and order, though this is sometimes effected by violent means.[14] In a similar vein, though a different genre, the book of Proverbs offers advice from personified 'Wisdom' towards those who will listen, teaching them how to live well in God's world with advice on matters such as gossiping, the impartiality of judges, and marital fidelity.[15]

The prophets have an even bigger vision for *shalom*, strongly condemning societal injustice[16] and setting out a vision for an eschatological [17] reign of peace. In this society, which they envision, *shalom* will once again be the norm. Their imagery is Edenic: animals will no longer prey on one another,

[6] Gen 1:29, cf. 9:3.

[7] Gen 3:16.

[8] Gen 3:17–19

[9] Gen 4:8.

[10] Gen 6:11–14.

[11] See L. Daniel Hawk, *The Violence of the Biblical God*. (Grand Rapids: Eerdmans, 2019): 30–37.

[12] E.g. Exodus 22:14–15.

[13] E.g. Leviticus 24:19–21.

[14] E.g. Numbers 35:30–31.

[15] See, for example, Prov 16:28; 18:5 and chapter 5.

[16] E.g. Amos 2:6–8.

[17] The eschaton refers to the Christian belief of the end of the world, heralded by the return of Jesus Christ and the final judgement.

or be a threat to humanity;[18] and humanity will no longer be a threat to itself.[19] This paradisical world will be inaugurated by a true king who will reign victoriously, presiding over a kingdom of peace. The prophet Isaiah, for example, envisions a king emerging from the broken family tree of King David, who will govern with wisdom, mercy, and pity for the downtrodden.[20] One of the great prophecies of Isaiah, which is understood by Christians to refer to Jesus and is especially quoted at Christmas, is in this vein:

> To us a child is born, to us a son is given; and the government shall be upon his shoulder, and his name shall be called Wonderful Counselor, Mighty God, Everlasting Father, Prince of Peace.[21]

This vision of peace is evident throughout the New Testament. Jesus's words in the Sermon on the Mount extend the Old Testament's limitation of vengeance to an appeal for enemy love and forgiveness, 'turn the other cheek'.[22] He describes peacemakers as children of God.[23] When his followers try to defend him with violence, he sternly warns that those who live by the sword will die by the sword.[24]

In addition to this ethic of human non-violence, the New Testament speaks clearly and often of the possibility of peace (reconciliation) with God. At the birth narrative of Jesus, the angels announce to the shepherd's good news of peace (from God) to those on earth.[25] This divine-human peace is achieved by Jesus' death on the Cross and is the means of reconciliation between former enemies. Paul, an apostle to the Gentiles, is credited with these words concerning the unity between Jews and Gentiles in the early church.

> But now in Christ Jesus you who once were far off have been brought near by the blood of Christ. For he himself is our peace, who has made us both one and has broken down in his flesh the dividing wall of hostility… that he

[18] E.g. Isaiah 11:6–8.
[19] E.g. Micah 4:3–4.
[20] Isa 11:1–10.
[21] Isa 9:6, ESV.
[22] Matt 5:39–48.
[23] Matt 5:9.
[24] Matt 26:52.
[25] Luke 2:10–14.

> might reconcile us both to God in one body through the cross, thereby killing the hostility. And he came and preached peace to you who were far off and peace to those who were near.[26]

The Book of Revelation, written within and to the early church as a persecuted minority, positions the Kingdom of God as diametrically opposed to the bloody empire of Rome. Victory, in this context, is achieved through self-sacrifice.[27] Finally, in the closing chapters, which foretell the New Jerusalem, the imagery returns to the Edenic paradise. The curse of Genesis 3 is undone;[28] the tree of life, put out of human reach in Genesis 2:33, is given for the healing of the nations;[29] and murderers are excluded,[30] showing that this is a vision of a wholly non-violent society.

Biblical Violence

But throughout this idyllic-sounding trajectory, violence continually intrudes. Indeed, arguably, it is only in Genesis 1 and 2 (pre-Fall), and Revelation 21 and 22 (post-eschaton) where it is not in view. However, not all violence serves the same purpose, and it is important to delineate the types of violence that the text is representing. I have argued elsewhere that the failure to do this results in un-nuanced reading and the application of blunt hermeneutical instruments.[31]

So, violence is frequently *portrayed* by the text, reflecting its setting in, and composition within, a violent world. Thus, we encounter stories of individual violence[32] and of battles.[33] There are also a number of instances

[26] Ephesians 2:13–18, ESV.

[27] Rev. 12:11.

[28] Rev. 22:3.

[29] Rev. 22:2.

[30] Rev. 22:15.

[31] Helen Paynter, *Crucifixion of the Warrior God by Gregory Boyd: Review*, 2019 Crucifixion of the Warrior God by Gregory Boyd: Review - CSBV (csbvbristol.org.uk) Accessed on 15 February 2021. See also Helen Paynter, *God of Violence Yesterday, God of Love Today? Wrestling Honestly with the Old Testament* (Abingdon: BRF, 2019).

[32] E.g. 2 Samuel 20:8–13.

[33] E.g. Genesis 14:1–12.

of sexual violence.[34] Sometimes the narration of such violence contains explicit or implicit criticism of it.[35]

Violence is also *implored* by the text, particularly in the so-called psalms of imprecation. In such psalms, the song-writer appeals to God for violent action against his enemies; for example, 'Oh that you would slay the wicked, O God!'[36] It can be argued that making such an appeal to God requires the one praying to lay down their own ambition to violence.[37]

Violence is also *attributed* to God in both testaments, usually in the context of judgment. For instance, in Numbers 16:35, fire comes out from the Lord and burns up 250 men who had attempted to usurp the authority of Moses. In the New Testament, some of the parables of Jesus have the God-figure acting violently.[38] And Revelation, notwithstanding the theme of non-violence outlined above, also uses torrid metaphors of violence.[39]

For many Christians, the most problematic type of violence encountered in the Bible is the *directive* of violence; places where God's people are commanded to act violently. The largest cluster of such texts, and arguably the most problematic, relates to the Conquest of Canaan by Joshua and his armies.[40] This is often an aggressive war and appears, on plain reading at least, to command the slaughter of non-combatants.[41]

Historic Christian Attitudes Towards Biblical Violence

For many Christians, these texts, particularly the ones where God appears to command violence, evoke significant ethical discomfort – we will shortly consider some of the apologetics which are offered. However, this is not

[34] E.g. Judges 19.

[35] The egregious story of Judges 19 amounts to a sharp critique of the nation of Israel in the time of the Judges. See Helen Paynter, *Telling Terror in Judges 19: Rape and Reparation for the Levite's Wife*. (Abingdon: Routledge, 2020).

[36] Ps 139:19.

[37] For example, David Firth says that the individual laments 'reject all forms of human violence. Within the 'I' psalms only the violence that may be enacted by Yahweh is acceptable.' David Firth, *Surrendering Retribution in the Psalms*, (Milton Keynes: Paternoster, 2007), 3.

[38] E.g. Luke 12:46

[39] E.g. Revelation 17–18.

[40] This is mainly found in Joshua 1–12, and also prefigured in Deuteronomy.

[41] E.g. Deut 20:16.

always the case. Historically (and still sometimes today), interpretations have sometimes been offered which instrumentalize the texts in ways which maintain an oppressive *stati quo* or justify violence in the world of the interpreter. We will here consider two examples.

Some Interpretations of a Text of Sexual Violence

Judges 19 contains an appalling story of the gang rape and murder of a low-status wife who has run away from her husband. She is thrown out to a baying mob by her husband, who is himself facing the threat of rape. There is no narratorial comment to suggest that God is approving of the woman's suffering. However, this has not prevented commentators from victim-blaming her. For example, it has been used as a cautionary tale to warn prospective brides about obeying their husbands. This is from the fourteenth-century writer, Geoffroy de la Tour-Landry:

> And therfor euery woman aught to restraine wrathe, and to plese and suffre her husbonde, and he be wroth, with faire langage, and not to go away from hym, as ded that woman, of the whiche come moche sorugh, as the dethe of her selff and of so gret nombre of pepill.[42]

Regrettably, such attitudes are still to be found today. In a Bible commentary written in 2009, Keith Brooks leaps to the brutal conclusion, 'In the miserable end of this woman, we see the hand of God punishing her for her uncleanness.'[43]

Because of the averted threat of male-on-male rape, the text has sometimes been used as part of an anti-homosexual polemic:

> Here one could ask whether the old man should be excused from guilt for exposing or offering his own daughter and the Levite's wife to the lust of

[42] In more modern English: "And therefore every woman ought to restrain wrath and to please and suffer her husband, if he be wroth, with fair language, and not to go away from him, as that woman did, of which came much sorrow, as the death of herself and of so great number of people." Geoffroy de la Tour Landry, *The Book of the Knight of La Tour-Landry, Compiled for the Instruction of his Daughters*, transl. Thomas Wright (London: Kegan Paul, Trench, Trubner & Co, 1906), Chapter LXII, 94.

[43] Keith L. Brooks, *Summarized Bible: Complete Summary of the Old Testament* (Los Angeles: Bible Institute of Los Angeles, 2009), 55.

these impious men to avoid a more serious crime, namely the crime against nature.[44]

Many further examples of historical interpretations like this could be given. In more contemporary Protestant scholarship, texts like this are read with much more sensitivity to the experience of the woman, and with an eye to the way that the text in fact criticises the violence against her.

Some Historic Readings of the Conquest of Canaan

With regard to the battles of Joshua, these texts have at various points in history been used to attempt to justify acts of violence against others. In 1095, Pope Urban II stirred up crusaders by telling them, 'It is our duty to pray, yours to fight against the Amalekites'.[45] The Amalekites were one of the chief foes of ancient Israel, intended to be subject to total extermination.[46] Here, the term is being used of Muslims.

More recently, such texts were quoted to promote the ideology of degeneracy, the fore-runner of the eugenics movement, which sought to eliminate people with 'defective' genetic traits. Massachusetts clergyman John Hayley wrote this in 1876:

> Had the women and children been spared, there would soon have been a fresh crop of adult Amalekites, precisely like their predecessors. Or suppose merely the children had been saved... they might, from their hereditary disposition and proclivities to evil have proved a most undesirable and pernicious element in the nation. It was, doubtless, on the whole, the best thing for the world that the Amalekite race should be exterminated.[47]

The name of another of Israel's ancient enemies, the Ammonites, was used to incite violence against the Natve Americans during the White colonialization of North America. The New England Puritan minister, Cotton

[44] Denis the Carthusian, *Enarrationes in Judicum*. Quoted in Joy A. Schroeder, *Dinah's Lament: The Biblical Legacy of Sexual Violence in Christian Interpretation* (Minneapolis: Fortress Press, 2007), 127 (emphasis added).

[45] Quoted in P. Jenkins, *Laying Down the Sword: Why we can't ignore the Bible's violent verses*. (New York: Harper Collins, 2011), 125.

[46] E.g. Deut 25:17–19.

[47] Quoted in Jenkins, *Laying Down*, 114.

Mather, referred to them as 'these Ammonites who perceived that they had made themselves to stink before the New-English Israel'.[48]

Many other such examples could be provided. However, such appetite for violence was by no means universal in church history. In fact, during the first three centuries of the Christian church, it appears that official teaching was unanimously non-violent.[49] These remarks from the Church Father Origen of Alexandria (c.184–c.254 CE) are indicative:

> We came in accordance with the commands of Jesus to beat the spiritual swords that fight and insult us into ploughshares, and to transform the spears that formerly fought against us into pruning-hooks. No longer do we take the sword against any nation, nor do we learn [the art of] war any more, since we have become sons of peace [cf. Luke 10:6] through Jesus who is our leader.[50]

One of the ways in which Origen achieves this stance is by reading the Conquest narratives allegorically, to refer to the personal battle of the Christian against evil. To quote from Origen once again:

> I myself think it is better that the Israelite wars be understood in this way, and it is better that Jesus [Joshua][51] is thought to fight in this way and to destroy cities and overthrow kingdoms... Would that the Lord might thus cast out and extinguish all former evils from the souls who believe in him—even those he claims for his kingdom—and from my own soul, its own evils; so that nothing of a malicious inclination may continue to breathe in me... For thus, purged from all former evils and under the leadership of Jesus, I can be included among the cities of the sons of Israel.[52]

[48] Quoted in Jenkins, *Laying Down*, 133–4.

[49] Kalantzis, George. *Caesar and the lamb: early Christian attitudes on war and military service*. (Eugene: Wipf and Stock, 2012).

[50] Origen, *Contra Celsus 5.33*. Quoted in Kalantzis, *Caesar and the Lamb*, 136.

[51] The names 'Jesus' and 'Joshua' are the same in Hebrew.

[52] Origen, 'Homily on Joshua 13:3'. In Franke, J. R. (ed) *Ancient Commentary on Christian Scripture, Volume IV. Joshua, Judges, Ruth, 1-2 Samuel* (Downers Grove, IL: InterVarsity Press, 2005), 63.

Contemporary Interpretations of the Conquest of Canaan

This very brief consideration of some of the ways that biblical texts of violence have been interpreted historically brings us to the question of the contemporary interpretation of biblical violence in Christian (Protestant) scholars. In order to limit the field of enquiry, we will focus on perspectives taken towards the Conquest of Canaan, generally regarded as the most ethically challenging texts to interpret. Four different approaches will be described, in an attempt to reflect something of the diversity of thought and the state of the contemporary debate. We begin with one approach which is sometimes expressed (usually in far less sophisticated terms than the scholarly approach described below) by Christians in the church: God commanded it, so it must be good.

Sui Generis

The term *sui generis*, which means 'of its own kind', can be used as a summary of a number of approaches towards the Conquest. Their argument—which has been proposed in various forms for 100 of years—is that God's commands, and the actions of Joshua, were righteous because the Canaanites were wicked. This would be supported by certain elements of the Old Testament text, such as Deuteronomy 9:5.

> Not because of your righteousness or the uprightness of your heart are you going in to possess their land, but because of the wickedness of these nations the LORD your God is driving them out from before you.

By this argument, the Canaanites deserved death (and, indeed, it had been mercifully held back for generations), and so the actions of Joshua in slaying them were the righteous enactment of God's judgment. Moreover, the Canaanites represented a serious moral threat to the incoming Israelites, and so they had to be eliminated for safety's sake. As one proponent, Eugene Merrill says, 'they were irretrievably lost to anti-God idolatry and was certain to proselytise Israel to do the same.'[53]

[53] Eugene H. Merrill, 'The case for moderate discontinuity.' In C.S. Cowles, Eugene H. Merrill, Daniel L. Gard and Tremper Longman III *Show them no mercy. 4 views on God and Canaanite genocide* (Grand Rapids: Zondervan, 2003): 61–96 (83).

But modern scholars who present this perspective take care to point out that this represents a singular moment in the history of the world, never to be repeated. This is because of the particularity of Israel, as shown in the covenant promises which God had made to Abraham and his descendants, Israel.[54] Again, we quote Merrill,

> Israel's role in the implementation of Yahweh war needs careful attention because *only Israel was authorised to carry it out in Old Testament times.* The reason for this dubious privilege is clear: Israel was the elect people of God, chosen not just to mediate the message of Salvation to the world but also to serve as his agent in bringing to pass his will on the earth... And even Israel could do so only when God gave special mandate and instruction in each case.[55]

In the end, Merrill concedes that he has to fall back on an unresolvable tension.

> The moral and ethical dilemma of Yahweh war must [...] remain without satisfying rational explanation. At the risk of cliché, all that can be said is that God if God is all the Bible says he is, all that he does must be good – and that includes his authorization of genocide [56]

The contemporary Christian scholars who have explored this approach in most detail are undoubtedly Paul Copan and Matthew Flannagan, in their careful, almost forensic, examination of the question: did God really command genocide?[57] As is true for all of the scholars, we are examining in this chapter, Copan and Flannagan's work is far broader and more nuanced than I am able to give justice to here. They argue that the Canaanites could have responded favourably to God, or at least fled without fighting Israel, and they lay stress on the rhetorical and hyperbolic nature of the text. They also argue, partly on legal grounds, that no true genocide occurred. Nonetheless, they concede that some innocent people were killed. The heart of their argument then lies in a pair of questions, both of

[54] E.g. Genesis 15:7–15.

[55] Eugene H. Merrill, 'The case for moderate discontinuity.' In Cowles, *Show them no mercy*, 84–85.

[56] Eugene H. Merrill, 'The case for moderate discontinuity.' In Cowles, *Show them no mercy*, 94.

[57] Paul Copan, and Matthew Flannagan. *Did God really command genocide?: Coming to terms with the justice of God*. (Grand Rapids: Baker Books, 2014).

which are examined carefully from a philosophical and theological, sometimes almost a judicial perspective. I set them out, in extreme summary, here.

- Question: can one *coherently* claim that [a morally perfect] God commanded the killing of innocents?
  Answer: yes. Based on the argument that the killing of innocent people can, in rare cases of supreme emergency, be overridden, there is nothing inherently incoherent about this position.[58]
- Question: is it *rational* to believe God commanded the killing of innocents?
  Answer: yes. Even if the reasons given in the 'annihilation' texts are considered inadequate, they do not reveal God's reasons, only the incentive or explanation that he offers to Israel. 'If we can't justifiably attribute a command to God unless we know why he commands it, then we won't be able to attribute any commands to God, even a command to not kill.'[59] And it is perfectly reasonable to expect God to act through human mediators even though he could take direct action himself.

Copan and Flannagan then pose the rhetorical question: what if someone claimed that God commanded killing the innocent today? Like Merrill, they conclude that although God commanded it back in the time of the conquest, he never will again. Their reasons are slightly different from Merrill's, and centre on the epistemological issue of how God can be heard to speak today. Because the biblical canon is closed, it is not possible anymore to proclaim infallibly 'thus says the Lord'. Therefore, nobody today can satisfy the four biblical criteria of prophetic authenticity, which would be required to validate such a claim.

This approach proves satisfying to some Christians and unhelpful to others. Indeed, some would express significant antipathy to such arguments. Moving to the other extreme of the debate, then, we will now consider the approaches that seek to weaken the voice of the Old Testament in contemporary interpretation.

[58] Copan, *Did God really command genocide?*, 186–193.
[59] Copan, *Did God really command genocide?*, 210–232, quotation from p.244.

Marginalising or Relativising the Old Testament

A controversial figure in the early church was Marcion, who was active in the early part of the second century.[60] He was so offended by the representation of God that he found in the Old Testament that he rejected it entirely from the canon. He then selected a group of texts which he considered to amount to true scripture; these were Luke's gospel and ten of the Pauline epistles. Even these were subject to his editorial scissors, such that his contemporary Irenaeus described him as mutilating the text. Marcion had a dualistic cosmology, with the good god of the New Testament set against the evil god of the Old Testament. His views were vigorously opposed by many of the church fathers, including Irenaeus and Tertullian, whose arguments prevailed, and Marcion was relegated to the status of heretic.

While I am not aware of any Christian scholar explicitly resurrecting the arguments of Marcion today, driving a wedge between the Old and New Testaments is one of the solutions proposed by modern apologists. One prominent scholar who seeks to do this is Eric Seibert. Like the majority of Christian interpreters, Seibert proposes that the representation of God found in Jesus Christ is the controlling hermeneutic (interpretive tool) for all of the rest of Scripture. Siebert's approach becomes more distinctive in his solution, where he proposes that where the textual God differs from this, the reader should infer that human error has influenced the writing of the text. For instance, Seibert writes,

> Old Testament portrayals that correspond to the God Jesus reveals should be regarded as trustworthy and reliable reflections of God's character, while those that do not measure up should be regarded as distortions.[61]

Seibert calls this approach a 'Christocentric' hermeneutic. Similar, but crucially different, is an approach offered by Greg Boyd, which he calls a 'cruciform hermeneutic'. Boyd also sees the Old Testament texts of violence as misrepresentations of the true character of God, but he goes further than Seibert in attempting to address them. He argues that these texts

[60] A good summary of what is known about Marcion's life and theology can be found in Paul Foster, 'Marcion: His life, works, beliefs, and impact.' *The Expository Times* 121, no. 6 (2010): 269–280.

[61] Eric A. Seibert, *Disturbing Divine Behavior: Troubling Old Testament Images of God*. (Philadelphia: Fortress Press, 2009), 185.

reveal the character of God in a different way, likening it to the way that Jesus silently suffered the false accusations at his trial and then the punishment for them. A similar humility towards the maligning of his character has led God to allow himself to be utterly misrepresented in parts of the Old Testament text, and in these false representations, we see the gentle meekness of God revealed.[62] This leads, then, to the paradoxical suggestion that '[t]he more a scriptural accommodation conceals God's true nature on its surface, the more profoundly it reveals God's true nature in its depths'.[63]

Both Seibert and Boyd wish to be clear that they are not advancing a Marcionite hermeneutic. Indeed, Eric Seibert is a professor of the Old Testament. On this matter he says,

> Rather than rejecting the Old Testament, I have proposed an interpretive approach that can help us evaluate the appropriateness of various portrayals of God in the Old Testament… Just because we find some portrayals of God problematic, we should not repeat the mistake of Marcion. Marcion treated the Old Testament as though it came from one cloth, so to speak, equally bad and problematic from start to finish. In doing so, he robbed himself of many valuable and unobjectionable insights that can be derived from the pages of the Old Testament.[64]

Perhaps unsurprisingly, these methodological approaches have been welcomed and condemned in equal measure among Christian scholars. It is fair to say that centralising the life and death of Jesus Christ as a hermeneutical principle for the whole of Scripture is a standard approach for Christian scholarship.[65] However, what this actually means is far more diversely understood. Both Seibert and Boyd have been criticised for

[62] Gregory A. Boyd, *The Crucifixion of the Warrior God: Volumes 1 & 2*. Vol. 1. (Philadelphia: Fortress Press, 2017), 502.

[63] Boyd, *The Crucifixion of the Warrior God*, 651.

[64] Seibert, *Disturbing Divine Behavior*, 211.

[65] See, for example, Goldsworthy, Graeme. *Gospel-centered hermeneutics: foundations and principles of evangelical biblical interpretation.* (Downers Grove: InterVarsity Press, 2014), 296–317.

centralising certain aspects of Jesus—the 'meek and mild' elements of his character—to the neglect of others.[66]

The relationship between the Old Testament and the New, and the force which Old Testament commands have for Christians, is a source of ongoing debate among Protestant scholars. A good example of this with regard to the Conquest of Canaan is found in a book published in 2003, where four Christian scholars each offered a different perspective on the question.[67] At one end of the spectrum of thought is CS Cowles. Writing much earlier than Seibert and Boyd, he offers what might be considered an early version of their argument, in what he describes as 'The Case for Radical Discontinuity' between the Old and New Testaments.[68]

At the other end of the spectrum, Tremper Longman III argues for 'spiritual continuity' between the testaments, outlining five phases of holy war in the Bible. The Conquest of Canaan falls into the first phase, where God fights the flesh-and-blood enemies of Israel. Later in the story, however, God is prepared to fight *against* Israel, by means of human agents, when they are disobedient to him. Longman's third phase is the Old Testament prophets' vision of God as an eschatological warrior, who will one day arise majestically to free his oppressed people. Moving into the New Testament, Longman points out the spiritualization of the language of 'enemies', with passages such as these words of Paul's; 'We do not wrestle against flesh and blood, but against the rulers, against the authorities, against the cosmic powers over this present darkness, against the spiritual forces of evil in the heavenly places'.[69] Here, Jesus Christ is the warrior who defeats those powers and authorities, not with the weapons of war, but by his death and resurrection. The fifth phase is the eschatological battle of, for example, Revelation 19:11–21, which represents the final judgment and the beginning of the age of peace. Longman locates the narratives of the Conquest of Canaan in the first of these phases.

[66] For a critique of Seibert along these lines, see John Anderson, 'Eric A. Seibert, Disturbing Divine Behavior: Troubling Old Testament Images of God', *Review of Biblical Literature* [http://www.bookreviews.org] (2011) Accessed on 16.02.21. For a similar critique of Boyd, see Paul Copan, 'Not Cruciform Enough: Getting Our Hermeneutical Bearings in the Wake of a Boydian Reinterpretation' in Helen Paynter and Trevor Laurence (eds) *Hermeneutics of Violence* (Sheffield: Sheffield Phoenix, 2022).

[67] We have already considered Eugene Merrill's contribution to this book.

[68] C.S. Cowles, 'The case for radical discontinuity.' In Cowles, *Show them no mercy*, 13–44.

[69] Eph 6:12.

> While in the Old Testament the Israelites were often used by God as an instrument of his judgment, it is now a betrayal of the gospel to take up arms to defend or promote the interests of Christ. However, this discontinuity is not absolute. There is also continuity, especially as we look to the New Testament's picture of the final judgement... All *ḥerem*[70] warfare, spiritual and physical, derives from the conflict anticipated in the curse against the serpent at the time of the Fall [Genesis 3:15].[71]

For Longman, then, the Conquest is the physical precursor of the spiritual triumph of good over evil at the eschaton.

Historically Minimising Approaches

The rise of the historical-critical method in the nineteenth century opened up a more sceptical approach to scripture. Narratives were no longer understood to be, per se, accurate representations of underlying events. Indeed, the discipline of history studies was itself undergoing a revolution, and all of this fed into scholarly approaches to scripture, which started asking questions about the events which lay behind the text. Some of these questions related to the literary sources which had been spliced together to form the final text. More pertinently to our question, some of those questions lay around the historical accuracy of the traditions.[72]

With regard to the events of the book of Joshua, there is little extra-biblical material to support the stories. An Egyptian victory memorial called the Merneptah Stela, dated to around 1230 BCE, lists 'Israel' as one of several city-states in Palestine at that time. However, the archaeological evidence for the sort of *Blitzkrieg* Conquest event which the book

[70] *Ḥerem* is the one of the Hebrew words used in the conquest accounts. It is sometimes translated 'utterly destroy' but more accurately could be rendered 'devote to the deity'. It neither mandates nor precludes death as an outcome. See Paynter, *God of Violence Yesterday, God of Love Today?*, 128–9.

[71] Tremper Longman III, 'The case for spiritual continuity.' In Cowles, *Show them no mercy*, 161–187 (187).

[72] For a balanced, representative analysis of some of the issues by a confessional scholar, see David M. Howard, 'History as history: the search for meaning.' In David A. Howard and Michael A. Grisanti (eds) *Giving the Sense: Understanding and Using Old Testament Historical Texts* (Grand Rapids: Apollos, 2003), 25–53.

of Joshua appears to describe is largely lacking.[73] Some theories suggest, then, that Israel was part of the indigenous population, which gradually displaced the other people groups, rather than scorching through the land as the text appears to claim.

While more conservative Christian scholars normally tend to resist the de-historicising move,[74] there is something in this argument which appeals to many of those charged with providing an apologetic for the Canaanite Conquest. Further evidence for a lack of 'photographic' accuracy can be adduced in the obvious rhetorical structure of the text, which conforms to Ancient Near-Eastern forms of battle rhetoric. K. Lawson Younger gives an example of such hyperbole, from Egyptian archive material.

> All the ground was ablaze with his fire; he burned all the countries with his blast... He took no note of the millions of foreigners; he regarded them as chaff... His majesty slew the entire force of the wretched foe... as well as all the chiefs of all the countries that had come with him... I was after them like a griffin; I defeated all the foreign countries, I alone. For my infantry and my chariotry had deserted me; not one of them stood looking back.[75]

However, such arguments have their limitations. The apologetic, which argues that the actual death count of the Conquest was lower than the biblical narrative implies, fails to address some important issues, not least because for many Christians, one such death is one too many. Further, in historical terms, any 'behind the text' reconstruction of events that we attempt will necessarily be conjectural, and therefore form an unreliable foundation for building hypotheses upon.

Perhaps most importantly, however, the *Christian* (as opposed to the secular) scholar will typically be attempting to draw theological conclusions from the text; that is, she will be attempting to listen to the theological message that the text is seeking to communicate. And this, axiomatically, cannot be deduced from a reconstruction—accurate or otherwise—of the events underlying the narrative. As L. Daniel Hawk suggests,

[73] A notable exception is the city of Hazor, where there is a clear burn layer in the 13th stratum, consistent with the biblical account in Joshua 11:10–11. Ben-Tor, Amnon. "Who Destroyed Canaanite Hazor?" *Biblical archaeology review* 39, no. 4 (2013), 27–36, 58.

[74] See, for example, Kenneth Kitchen, *On the reliability of the Old Testament.* (Grand Rapids: Eerdmans Publishing, 2006).

[75] K. Lawson Younger, Jr., *Ancient Conquest Accounts: A study in Ancient Near Eastern and biblical history writing* (JSOT Press, 1990), 245.

> Although I practice historical-critical interpretation and agree that we can detect biblical authors' intentions to a certain extent, I do not believe that historical criticism can bear the theological weight placed on it by these and similar studies… It is one thing to draw upon the fruit of historical research to elaborate aspects of the world presented by the biblical text. It is quite another to construct a hypothetical historical scenario in support of a theological reading, to set that scenario over against the biblical narrative, and then to use it to judge the theological witness of the biblical text as plainly rendered.[76]

The situation is more complex than the mere enquiry about 'what actually happened', however. In addition to its undoubted rhetorical flourishes, the book of Joshua itself appears to represent more than one view of the Conquest. The *Blitzkrieg*-type account mentioned above is only one part of the story. At times, the text feels as if it is constructed in the dialogue between a polemical, 'totalising' narrator and a more cautious, moderate one. Take, for example, the two accounts of the fate of the inhabitants of Debir, which occur in two halves of the same verse:

> When Joshua and the sons of Israel had finished striking them with a great blow until they were wiped out, and when the remnant that remained of them had entered into the fortified cities…[77]

When the claims of the text are being evaluated for their ethical significance, the *polyphony* of these voices should be allowed to play. Polyphony is a term coined by literary critic Mikhail Bakhtin to describe divergent voices which debate within a text, with neither having the privilege of the final word. It is a tool which some biblical scholars are beginning to use, and which may continue to enlighten our reading of texts such as Joshua.[78]

[76] Hawk. *The Violence of the Biblical God*, 14.

[77] Josh 10:20, ESV.

[78] Anthony Thiselton, 'Polyphonic Voices in Theological Fiction: Job, Eliot and Dostoyevsky on Evil' in Roger Lundin, Anthony C. Thiselton, and Clarence Walhout (eds). *The promise of hermeneutics.* (Grand Rapids: Eerdmans, 1999), 172–182. Much of the pioneering work in this field has been performed by the Dominican scholar Barbara Green.

Comparative Approaches

A fourth apologetic approach to the question of the Conquest can be termed the comparative approach. Some of the best work in this area has been done by John Walton. Walton is interested in the history, archaeology, literature and language of the Ancient Near East, because it provides a window into the shared cultural worldview in the region. Israel's sacred literature is at certain times a product of this worldview, and at other times a reaction against it.[79] We have already seen that Ancient Near Eastern Conquest accounts generally followed a stylised, hyperbolic pattern, and that this provides insight into the ways in which the biblical writers are framing their own discourse.

In a book co-written with his son, J. Harvey Walton, John Walton offers some careful work around the meaning of a particular Hebrew word, *ḥerem*, which is one of the chief ways that the actions of Joshua and his soldiers at the Conquest are described. *Ḥerem* is often translated as 'utterly destroy',[80] and therefore taken to be the equivalent of mass slaughter. English Bibles vary in the way that they handle this word. Compare these three translations of Joshua 8:26, where the translation of the word *ḥerem* is rendered in bold.

> But Joshua did not draw back his hand with which he stretched out the javelin until he had **devoted** all the inhabitants of Ai **to destruction**. (ESV)
>
> For Joshua did not draw back his hand, with which he stretched out the sword, until he had **utterly destroyed** all the inhabitants of Ai. (NRSV)
>
> Joshua kept his spear pointed at Ai and did not put it down until every person there had been **killed**. (GNB)

By means of the technique of comparative studies and building on the work of philologists, the Waltons show that the root meaning of *ḥerem* relates to the removal of an object from normal use.[81] This is why it can also be translated as 'devote to the deity'. Designating an object *ḥerem* means that it is either taken into the sanctuary or destroyed; it is not

[79] John H. Walton, *Ancient Near Eastern thought and the Old Testament: Introducing the conceptual world of the Hebrew Bible.* (Nottingham: Apollos, 2007), 15–28.

[80] E.g. Deut 20:17

[81] John H., Walton, and J. Harvey Walton. *The Lost World of the Israelite Conquest: Covenant, Retribution, and the Fate of the Canaanites.* (Downers Grove: InterVarsity Press, 2017), 169–194.

available for everyday purposes. With regard to the exercise of this verb upon people groups, the Waltons argue that it is the *identity* of the people which is to be expunged, not necessarily the people themselves. This is why the Canaanites are not eligible as marriage partners, because this would be a 'normal' means of interaction.[82] So Walton and Walton write,

> The combination of the hyperbolic rhetoric with the successful *ḥerem* of the city does not mean "they didn't really kill all of them, but they left some of them in the city". Rather it means "they decisively cleared them all out of the city, one way or another".[83]

They offer a helpful example of how they believe *ḥerem* was viewed in the character of Rahab. Rahab is a Jerichoite, which means that she is subject to the *ḥerem* order against her city.[84] However, she does not die, but is brought into the heart of the nation of Israel, and ultimately into the ancestry of Jesus Christ.[85] The Waltons argue that Rahab is not *exempted* from *ḥerem* by these means, but that by being absorbed into the nation of Israel, she experiences *ḥerem* just as truly as those who die experience it. [86]

The reason that the Canaanites are subject to the *ḥerem* order, according to Walton and Walton, is that they are viewed in the same way that most ancient societies regarded people groups who existed on the margins of their experience: as demiurges, abominable others, who represented the chaos that was continually pushing back against the created order.[87] There is therefore a mythic element to the events of the book of Joshua, whereby, in the ancient mind, the people of Israel are participating with their deity in clearing aside chaotic otherness in order to participate with God and establish a new world. The events of the Conquest, the Waltons' argue, are charged with new creation imagery.[88]

As with the other readings, the extent to which the Waltons' theories have proved satisfying to Christians troubled by these texts is various. It is probably fair to say that they may have reframed the questions that the Conquest poses, but for most readers, they have not removed them.

[82] See Deuteronomy 7:1–6, which legislates for herem and against intermarriage.
[83] Walton, *The Lost World of the Israelite Conquest,* 177.
[84] Josh 6:17.
[85] Josh 6:22–25; Matt 1:5.
[86] Walton, *The Lost World of the Israelite Conquest,* 212–4.
[87] Walton, *The Lost World of the Israelite Conquest,* 137–156.
[88] Walton, *The Lost World of the Israelite Conquest,* 157–168.

A different type of comparative approach is offered by William Webb and Gorde Oeste, in their book *Bloody, Brutal, and Barbaric: Wrestling with Troubling War Texts*. This is building upon a methodology previously published by Webb alone, where he demonstrates the existence of what he calls 'redemptive trajectories'.[89] He argues that the ethical standards of the Old Testament laws are advancing the practice of the nation of Israel in comparison with the nations around them. However, this ethical advance does not represent a final destination, but a step on the way toward a perfect ethical standard. The Old Testament ethics should not, therefore, be evaluated against modern ethical standards (since we are—generally—further advanced along the trajectory), but against what they would have been without the restraint of the law.

In their book on war texts, Webb and Oeste examine the practices of the other Ancient Near-Eastern nations, with particular attention to their treatment of male and female prisoners of war. They conclude:

> Israel's war measures would have been considered mild or comparatively moderate within its larger ancient context. Repugnant as the biblical war texts are for modern readers (we cannot escape our ingrained Hague/ Geneva horizon), they were markedly restrained in their day. To put it another way, the clear movement away from well-known war atrocities of the ancient world betrays significant incremental movement in a good, redemptive direction.[90]

Rather than the Old Testament being a text that glories in bloody warfare, Webb and Oeste represent the God of the Old Testament as an 'uneasy war God', providing a detailed analysis of the ways in which militaristic patterns are subverted by the Old Testament text.[91] One such example is found in 2 Kings 6:8–23, where the plans of an attacking group of Arameans are thwarted by the prophet of God. Through a burlesque series of events, the prophet leads the Aramean army into the court of the King of Israel. But rather than ending in battle or slaughter, there is an

[89] William J. Webb, *Slaves, women & homosexuals: Exploring the hermeneutics of cultural analysis*. (Downers Grove: InterVarsity Press, 2001).

[90] William J Webb, and Gordon K. Oeste. *Bloody, Brutal, and Barbaric?: Wrestling with Troubling War Texts*. (Downers Grove: InterVarsity Press, 2019), 285.

[91] Webb, *Bloody, Brutal, and Barbaric?*, 288–316.

unexpected feast, and the Arameans are sent on their way in peace. This is one of a number of examples offered by Webb and Oeste in defence of their argument that the God of the Old Testament is highly reluctant to go to war.

Conclusion

This chapter has attempted to sketch out a broad view of some of the key contemporary Protestant Christian responses to the ethical problem raised by the conquest of Canaan in the biblical book of Joshua. It is fair to say that the range of opinions in the churches will be at least as broad. Speaking personally for a moment, when I went on a lecture tour around the country a few years ago speaking on this subject, I encountered the range of opinions at close hand. I met people who shrugged and told me that the conquest did not challenge their view of the goodness of God, with about the same frequency that I encountered people who were ready to tear the Old Testament out of their Bibles. And in between were a whole range of Christians who had come to their own accommodation with the issue.

The matter is of relevance to the church today for two important reasons. First, Christian leaders are increasingly concerned about a lack of confidence in the Bible in some circles. This is not necessarily referring to the question of biblical inerrancy (though there will be a range of opinions about that, too), but rather to a general reduction in biblical literacy, and in some places, a reduced confidence in Scripture's value to address the present. It is this concern which drives much of the scholarship that we have considered above.

The second reason lies in Scripture's capacity to inspire contemporary violence when it is interpreted carelessly or cynically. We began with some historical examples where biblical violence had been used to endorse violence in a more modern setting. Such abuses continue today; the Capitol riots of 6th January 2021, with their highly visible use of Christian symbolism and practice, prove the point. For these reasons, it is imperative to Christian scholars that we continue to wrestle with these texts. It does not appear that the conundrum will be resolved any time soon.

Further Reading

Boyd, Gregory A., *The Crucifixion of the Warrior God: Volumes 1 & 2*. Vol. 1. (Philadelphia: Fortress Press, 2017)

Cowles, C.S., Eugene H. Merrill, Daniel L. Gard and Tremper Longman III *Show them no mercy. 4 views on God and Canaanite genocide* (Grand Rapids: Zondervan, 2003)

Copan, Paul, and Matthew Flannagan. *Did God really command genocide?: Coming to terms with the justice of God.* (Grand Rapids: Baker Books, 2014)

Paynter, Helen, *God of Violence Yesterday, God of Love Today? Wrestling Honestly with the Old Testament* (Abingdon: BRF, 2019).

Walton, John H., and J. Harvey Walton. *The Lost World of the Israelite Conquest: Covenant, Retribution, and the Fate of the Canaanites.* (Downers Grove: InterVarsity Press, 2017)

Webb, William J., and Gordon K. Oeste. *Bloody, Brutal, and Barbaric?: Wrestling with Troubling War Texts.* (Downers Grove: InterVarsity Press, 2019)

CHAPTER 8

Roman Catholic Teachings on Violence and Peace: The Credible Re-enactment of the Kingdom

Maria Power

When Pope Francis announced at his now traditional press conference on the flight home from his Apostolic Visit to Japan in November 2019 that he was declaring the use of nuclear weapons immoral and adding a

Positionality: I write as a scholar of Catholic social ethics and a practising Roman Catholic.

M. Power (✉)
Las Casas Institute for Social Justice, University of Oxford, Oxford, UK
e-mail: Maria.power@bfriars.ox.ac.uk

M. Power, H. Paynter (eds.), *Violence and Peace in Sacred Texts*,
https://doi.org/10.1007/978-3-031-17804-7_8

prohibition of their use to the Catechism of the Catholic Church,[1] he was continuing the evolution of teachings on violence and peace that has been occurring within Catholicism since the times of the earliest Christian communities. The teaching of the Catholic Church on all matters is subject to considered and regular reinterpretation as the institution seeks to 'explain to all how it understands the presence and function of the Church in the world today.'[2] From the Second Vatican Council (1962–1965) onwards, the Church transformed its self-understanding, no longer viewing itself as a state actor but rather as 'a witness to the truth', with its role being 'to save, not to judge, to serve not to be served.'[3] This was and is achieved by a continual examination 'of the signs of the times' which are interpreted 'in the light of the Gospel.'[4] Whilst this has resulted in developments in teaching and practice in a number of areas of Catholic social teaching, such as the creation of the preferential option for the poor, nowhere can this be seen more clearly than in Catholic social teachings on violence and peace. Here, the Church has tethered itself increasingly firmly to the concept of Just Peace—a definition of which it finds in particular in the Gospels. Thus, whilst still acknowledging that direct violence, at times, can be inevitable but not condoning its practice, the Catholic Church now uses the teachings of both the Old and New Testaments to offer the

[1] 'The Pope: not using or possessing nuclear arms will be added to the Catechism', https://www.vaticannews.va/en/pope/news/2019-11/pope-francis-press-conference-japan-airplane.html, accessed 18 March 2021. The updated passage has yet to be included in the Catechism which is currently being updated. However, in his most recent encyclical, he once more emphasised the immorality of nuclear weapons. *Fratelli Tutti: On Fraternity and Social Friendship,* 3 October 2020, http://www.vatican.va/content/francesco/en/encyclicals/documents/papa-francesco_20201003_enciclica-fratelli-tutti.html, accessed 18 March 2021, §262.

[2] Second Vatican Council, *Gaudium et Spes: Pastoral Constitution on the Church in the Modern World,* 7 December 1965, http://www.vatican.va/archive/hist_councils/ii_vatican_council/documents/vat-ii_cons_19651207_gaudium-et-spes_en.html, accessed 18 March 2021, §2.

[3] *Gaudium et Spes,* §3. To understand this change in attitude and its consequences see: Kenneth R Himes, *Christianity and the Political Order: Conflict, Cooptation, and Cooperation,* (Maryknoll NY, Orbis, 2013), Emile Perreau-Saussine, *Catholicism and Democracy: An Essay in the History of Political Thought,* trans. Richard Rex, (Princeton, NJ: Princeton University Press, 2011) and Maria Power, *Catholic Social Teaching and Theologies of Peace in Northern Ireland: Cardinal Cahal Daly and the Pursuit of the Peaceable Kingdom,* (Abingdon: Routledge, 2021).

[4] *Gaudium et Spes,* §4.

concepts and practices needed to overcome the structural violence[5] that so frequently acts as a precursor to conflict and war. This chapter, which I write as a Roman Catholic and a scholar of Catholic social teaching, will argue that Roman Catholic teaching on violence and peace now focuses on dealing with the causes of violence, and that the 'responsibility to protect' can, and should, be achieved by creating a social order based upon the teachings of Christ. First, however, we will turn to the relationship of scripture to tradition in Catholicism, seeking to explain how the interplay between these two elements led to the creation of Catholic social teaching of which teaching on violence and peace forms a vital part.

Scripture and Tradition in the Roman Catholic Church

> In discerning the canon of scripture, the church was also discerning and defining [its] own identity. Henceforth scripture was to function as a mirror in which the church could continually rediscover [its] identity and assess, century after century, the way in which [it] constantly responds to the Gospel and equips itself to be an apt vehicle of its transmission.[6]

For Roman Catholics, scripture is the single source of divine revelation that is passed down through generations through tradition.[7] As a community of believers, Roman Catholics are 'servants of the word of God'.[8] The Gospels have pre-eminence as they are the 'principal witness to the life and teaching of the word incarnate.'[9] But, the Roman Catholic Church stresses that the bible must be approached as a whole. Since 1943 and the

[5] Structural violence refers to a form of violence wherein some social structure or social institution may harm people by preventing them from meeting their basic needs and denying their human dignity. The term was first used in 1969. See Johan Galtung, 'Violence, Peace, and Peace Research', *Journal of Peace Research,* 1969, vol. 6, no. 3, 167–191.

[6] Pontifical Biblical Commission, *The Interpretation of the Bible in the Church*, 23 April 1993, https://www.bc.edu/content/dam/files/research_sites/cjl/texts/cjrelations/resources/documents/catholic/pbcinterpretation.htm, accessed 19 March 2021, 32.

[7] Second Vatican Council, *Dei Verbum: Dogmatic Constitution on Divine Revelation,* 18 November 1965, https://www.vatican.va/archive/hist_councils/ii_vatican_council/documents/vat-ii_const_19651118_dei-verbum_en.html, accessed 19 March 2021, §7.

[8] *Dei Verbum,* §10.

[9] Ibid., §18.

promulgation of the encyclical,[10] *Divino Afflante Spiritu,*[11] Catholic biblical scholars have been allowed to make full use of the methods and tools of modern biblical scholarship. This has resulted in a deepening of 'the Bible's influence on theology' with 'interest in the Bible [growing] among Catholics with the resultant progress in Christian life.'[12] The influence of this upon our understanding of violence and peace has been clear, with the move towards a just peace approach being the result. Tradition, which is the 'process by which revelation and grace are mediated',[13] resulting in the teachings of the Roman Catholic Church, enables scripture to be read with the fresh eyes demanded by the new challenges facing each generation.[14] Scripture and tradition are accepted as equals.[15] A teaching which Yves Congar explains thus: 'Tradition is not a secondary source, alongside scripture from which comes a part not contained in scripture, of the truths of faith but another and complimentary way of handing on these truths.'[16] Together, they form the 'deposit of faith.'[17]

Roman Catholics believe that 'scripture does not interpret itself.'[18] All members of the Church have a role to play in the interpretation of scripture. This is approached with a 'hermeneutic of trust' as 'it is interpreted in a way that presumes its status as an authentic means of divine self-communication.'[19] Scripture must be read in faith and with deep prayer as a service to the community and the mission of the Church. Roman Catholic interpretation of scripture involves three steps:

[10] An encyclical is the highest form of papal communication, and the contents are official Roman Catholic teaching.

[11] Pius XII, *Divino Afflante Spiritu: On Promoting Biblical Studies,* 30 September 1943, http://www.vatican.va/content/pius-xii/en/encyclicals/documents/hf_p-xii_enc_30091943_divino-afflante-spiritu.html, accessed 19 March 2021.

[12] *The Interpretation of the Bible in the Church,* p. 4.

[13] Stephen F Miletic, 'Sacred Tradition' in Russell Shaw (ed.), *The Encyclopaedia of Catholic Doctrine,* (Huntington, IN: Our Sunday Visitor Publishing, 1997), 603–606, 603.

[14] Thus, 'the development of tradition does not produce new scriptural texts, but rather leads us to read these texts with new eyes.' Frederick C Bauerschmidt and James J Buckley, *Catholic Theology: An Introduction,* (Oxford: Wiley-Blackwell, 2017), 20.

[15] *Dei Verbum,* §9.

[16] Yves Congar, *Tradition and Traditions: A Historical and Theological Essay,* trans. Michael Naseby and Thomas Rainborough, (London: Macmillan, 1967), 64.

[17] 1 Tim 6:20.

[18] Archbishop Charles Chaput, 'Introduction', *Dei Verbum: Dogmatic Constitution on Divine Revelation,* (London: Catholic Truth Society, no date), 3–7, 5.

[19] Bauerschmidt and Buckley, *Catholic Theology,* 19.

1. To hear the word from within one's own concrete situation;
2. To identify the aspects of the present situation highlighted or put in question by the biblical text;
3. To draw from the fullness of meaning contained in the biblical text, those elements are capable of advancing the present situation in a way that is productive and consonant with the saving will of God.[20]

Through this process, Roman Catholics must try to discern 'what riches God, in his generosity, has bestowed on the nations; at the same time, they should try to shed the light of the Gospel on these treasures, to set them free and bring them under the common dominion of the Saviour.'[21] The teaching manifest in scripture is viewed as evolving over time and therefore has to be reinterpreted for each new age. This is because 'God is constantly speaking to his Christian people a message that is ever relevant for their time.'[22] And as the Second Vatican Council's Constitution, *Dei Verbum* teaches, biblical interpretation provides the data with which the Church's judgement may be matured.[23]

Jus ad Bellum: Christian Realism and the Just War Tradition

Roman Catholic teachings on violence and peace reflect the lived reality of faith, and in particular, the pressures that Christians face in trying to reconcile scripture and tradition with the demands of living in, and encountering the modern world. Consequently, teachings on violence and peace are full of tensions regarding understandings of the nature and meaning of the Christian vocation. In terms of war and conflict, such tensions amount to a fundamental question: should Catholic responses to violence and peace be driven by an ideal of gospel perfection or by socio-political realities? At present, the Roman Catholic Church addresses this question by operating as a dual-tradition institution, with just war and pacifist[24] stances both being taught by the magisterium. Matthew A Shadle describes the

[20] *The Interpretation of the Bible in the Church,* 33.

[21] Second Vatican Council, *Ad Gentes: Decree on the Mission Activity of the Church,* 7 December 1965, http://www.vatican.va/archive/hist_councils/ii_vatican_council/documents/vat-ii_decree_19651207_ad-gentes_en.html, accessed 19 March 2021, §22.

[22] *The Interpretation of the Bible in the Church,* 33.

[23] *Dei Verbum,* §12.

[24] The teachings on pacifism will be discussed in a later section of this chapter.

influence of scripture on these stances thus: 'The words of Jesus in the Gospels have inspired pacifists throughout the centuries, whereas those committed to the just war theory have had to situate those sayings in the context of other New Testament passages and natural law thinking.'[25] Both sets of teachings share a belief that peace is paramount, but the means of achieving it are different.

The Roman Catholic Church is known for its defence of just war teaching, which begins with a presumption against violence. This is a teaching that emphasises the futurity of the kingdom of God as the 'Christian just war tradition has been built on the premise that the present world so entangles the disciple in conflict and "brokenness" that gospel fidelity requires compromise action.'[26] Thus, war and violent conflict are seen as sometimes necessary to secure peace. As John Courtney Murray, a leading advocate for realism in Roman Catholic approaches to war puts it, the just war position expresses 'a will to peace, which in the extremity, bears within itself a will to enforce the precept of peace by arms.'[27] However, 'the fact that war is justified does not mean that all actions in it are morally permitted'[28] resulting in a 'rules-based' approach for political leaders contemplating a resort to war. As Augustine teaches, the concepts of mercy, forgiveness, and love must lie at the heart of any decision to enter into war.[29] At present, both the *Catechism of the Catholic Church* and the *Compendium of the Social Doctrine of the Church*,[30] list the preconditions for a just war as the following:

> The strict conditions for *legitimate defence by military force* require rigorous consideration. The gravity of such a decision makes it subject to rigorous conditions of moral legitimacy. At one and the same time:

[25] Matthew A Shadle, *The Origins of War: A Catholic Perspective*, (Washington DC: Georgetown University Press, 2011), 7.

[26] Lisa Sowle Cahill, *Love your Enemies: Discipleship, Pacifism, and Just War Theory*, (Minneapolis, MN: Fortress Press, 1994), 19

[27] John Courtney Murray, *Morality and Modern War*, (New York, NY: Council on Religion and International Affairs, 1959), 16.

[28] David Carroll Cochran, *Catholic Realism and the Abolition of War*, (Maryknoll, NY: Orbis Books, 2014), 10.

[29] Ibid., p. 8.

[30] Pontifical Council for Justice and Peace, *Compendium of the Social Doctrine of the Church*, 2004, https://www.vatican.va/roman_curia/pontifical_councils/justpeace/documents/rc_pc_justpeace_doc_20060526_compendio-dott-soc_en.html, accessed 24 March 2022.

- The damage inflicted by the aggressor on the community of nations must be lasting, grave, and certain;
- All other means of putting an end to it, must have been shown to be impractical or ineffective;
- There must be serious prospects of success;
- The use of arms must not produce evils and disorders graver than the evil to be eliminated. The power of modern means of destruction weighs very heavily in evaluating this condition.

The evaluation of these conditions for moral legitimacy belongs to the prudential judgement of those who have responsibility for the common good.[31]

These conditions have recently been scrutinised by Pope Francis in *Fratelli Tutti: On Fraternity and Social Friendship,* in which he argues for an even tighter interpretation of these rules, arguing that they have been abused by those in power. In an oblique reference to the 2003 invasion of Iraq by collation forces as well as recent instances of cyber warfare, he states that 'War can easily be chosen by invoking all sorts of allegedly humanitarian, defensive or precautionary excuses, and even resorting to the manipulation of information.'[32] This has prompted a renewed debate around the efficacy of just war theory within Catholicism, especially as in footnote 242 of the document, Francis states that 'we no longer uphold' Augustine's concept of just war. In doing so, Francis stops just short of rejecting the just war conditions, but places a major question mark above its role in, and usefulness to, Catholic social teaching. In this, Francis joins his predecessors and the Magisterium who have argued that 'moral reflection on the use of force calls for a spirit of moderation rare in contemporary political culture.' Consequently, the responsibility to protect remains the only

[31] *Catechism of the Catholic Church,* 1994, https://www.vatican.va/archive/ccc_css/archive/catechism/ccc_toc.htm, accessed 24 March 2022, §2309. Note that this section is entitled *avoiding war.*

[32] *Fratelli Tutti,* §258. In a speech to the Vatican Diplomatic Corps on 13 January 2003, John Paul II counselled against the invasion of Iraq, stating that the detrimental consequences for civilians would outweigh any benefits the conflict could bring. www.vatican.va/content/john-paul-ii/en/speeches/2003/january/documents/hf_jp-ii_spe_20030113_diplomatic-corps.html, accessed 25 March 2022.

legitimate reason for the use of violence but even this is being questioned.[33] This evolution, for the most part, is the challenge presented by the nature of modern warfare and, in particular, the threat that it poses to non-combatants.[34]

Jus in Bello: The Challenges Presented by Modern Warfare

One of the main criteria set out in Just War theory is *Jus in Bello,* which governs conduct in war. The twentieth century has seen changes in the nature, mechanisms, scale and impact of warfare, which have concerned pontiffs since the outbreak of the Great War in 1914. Technological and social advances bring new challenges, which must be reflected on using the wisdom of scripture and tradition as outlined earlier in this essay. As the United States bishops argued in 1983, 'Modern warfare threatens the obliteration of human life on a previously unimaginable scale.'[35] In addition, the twenty-first century has seen the advent of new forms of weaponry, such as drones and cyber warfare, the nature and scale of which are only just being confronted by Christian ethicists.[36]

The influence of changes in the conduct of war can be seen in evolutions in a number of areas governing Roman Catholic teachings on violence and peace. As early as 1922, Pius XI felt the need to teach that the world was in a state of negative peace: 'The nations today live in a state of armed peace which is scarcely better than war itself, a condition that tends to exhaust national finances, to waste the flower of youth, to muddy and

[33] Drew Christiansen, 'Fratelli Tutti and the Responsibility to Protect', 14 October 2020, https://berkleycenter.georgetown.edu/responses/fratelli-tutti-and-the-responsibility-to-protect, accessed 24 March 2022. Francis discusses the responsibility to protect in §262 of *Fratelli Tutti.*

[34] For a history of the development of modern warfare see Margaret MacMillan, *War: How Conflict Shaped Us,* (London: Profile Books, 2020).

[35] United States National Conference of Catholic Bishops, *The Challenge of Peace: God's Promise and Our Response,* 3 May 1983, https://www.usccb.org/upload/challenge-peace-gods-promise-our-response-1983.pdf, accessed 23 March 2022, §15.

[36] See for example, Kenneth R Himes, *Drones and the Ethics of Targeted Killing,* (Lanham, MD: Rowman and Littlefield, 2016) and Matthew A Shadle, 'Towards a Just-War Ethic for Cyber War: Defining Cyber Warfare', 15 June 2018, https://politicaltheology.com/towards-a-just-war-ethic-for-cyber-war-defining-cyber-warfare/, accessed 25 March 2022. These threats were alluded to in paragraph 262 of *Fratelli Tutti* but the Magisterium has yet to produce a full response to the implications of these new technologies of warfare.

poison the very fountainheads of life, physical, intellectual, religious and moral.'[37] Violence is now endemic within society, not something contained on the battlefield as it was previously believed. The most influential of these scientific and technological advances was the creation of nuclear weapons, deployed by the United States of America in Japan to such devastating effect as a means of bringing the Second World War to an end in August 1945 and still used as a 'deterrent' against armed combat today. The existence of nuclear weapons and the capability for annihilation that they pose caused the Fathers of the Second Vatican Council to teach that: 'The increase in scientific weapons has increased the wickedness of war immensely. Action carried out with those weapons can cause vast and indiscriminate destruction which goes far beyond the limits of legitimate defence.'[38] In doing so, they were echoing John XXIII who, in the wake of the 1962 Cuban Missile crisis wrote, 'in this age which boasts of its atomic power, it no longer makes sense to maintain that war is a fit instrument with which to repair the violation of justice.'[39] The *use* of nuclear weapons could never, in Roman Catholic teaching, justify the damage that they would do to humanity, and many Roman Catholics now see campaigning for nuclear disarmament as a necessary outworking of their faith and use non-violent methods to do so.[40]

Developments in the field of psychiatric medicine have also advanced understandings of the impact of war upon the combatant, with PTSD[41] now acknowledged as a common consequence of military service. The

[37] Pius XI, *Ubi Arcano Dei Consilio,* 23 December 1922, §11, http://w2.vatican.va/content/pius-xi/en/encyclicals/documents/hf_p-xi_enc_23121922_ubi-arcano-dei-consilio.html, accessed 12 August 2019.

[38] *Gaudium et Spes,* §80.

[39] John XXIII, *Pacem in Terris: On Establishing Universal Peace in Truth, Justice, Charity and Liberty,* 11 April 1963, http://www.vatican.va/content/john-xxiii/en/encyclicals/documents/hf_j-xxiii_enc_11041963_pacem.html, accessed 25 March 2022.

[40] One example of such activism is the work of Fr Martin Newell CP who has carried out several ploughshare actions and who highlights the influence of the Gospels on his work when he says: 'I believe Jesus was a pacifist, and I believe that means I should be one as well. And the implications of that are using non-violent means to work for justice; I'm convinced that non-violent action is a legitimate and positive way of standing up for what I believe in.' 'Fr Martin Newell, Priest-Protester', no date, https://www.alivepublishing.co.uk/2018/05/fr-martin-newell-priest-protester/, accessed 25 March 2022.

[41] Edgar Jones and Simon Wessely, *Shell Shock to PTSD: Military Psychiatry from 1900 to the Gulf War,* (Hove: Psychology Press, 2005).

concept of moral injury[42] sustained in war has moved the Roman Catholic Church even further away from viewing any combat as just. Cardinal Cahal Daly summed this up when he described the impact of the Northern Ireland conflict on combatants and non-combatants alike: 'The worst consequences of violence, however, have been moral and spiritual, rather than material. The foundation of all moral principle and the source of all human rights is absolute respect from the sacredness of human life. Human life is now cheaper and more expendable than an armalite rifle.'[43] Such attitudes prevent people from experiencing the true purpose of living which is 'to know and love God.'[44] They result from a failure to recognise God in themselves as well as in those that they maim and kill.[45]

Throughout the twentieth century, war and other forms of violent conflict have also increasingly impacted upon non-combatants, with their deaths being euphemistically referred to as 'collateral damage' by the military. It is now estimated by the United Nations that 90 per cent of the victims of war are civilians.[46] Rape is a standard weapon of war,[47] and the use of child soldiers is now commonplace. In addition to killing and psychologically and physically injuring people, war also destroys the structure of societies and prevents human flourishing. John Paul II described the process thus:

[42] According to Purcell et al, 'moral injury refers to a lasting sense of guilt, shame, and disillusionment that arises from participating in acts that violate or undermine one's deeply held moral beliefs of sense of justice.' Natalie Purcell, Kristine Burkman, Jessica Keysen, Philip Fucella and Shira Maguen, 'Healing from Moral Injury: A Qualitative Evaluation of the *Impact of Killing* Treatment for Combat Veterans,' *Journal of Aggression, Maltreatment and Trauma,* published online 18 April 2018, 2. https://www.tandfonline.com/doi/abs/10.1080/10926771.2018.1463582, accessed 22 August 2019.

[43] Cardinal Cahal Daly 'Peace is Mightier than the Bomb.', Address for 1979 World Day of Peace', 1 January 1979, Northern Ireland Political Collection, Linen Hall Library, *Addresses on Peace in Northern Ireland, 1976–1983, Volume 2,* P13579.

[44] *Catechism,* §31.

[45] *Gaudium et Spes,* §19, translation taken from *Catechism,* §27.

[46] Alexandre Marc, 'Conflict and Violence in the 21st Century: Current Trends as Observed in Empirical Research and Statistics', https://www.un.org/pga/70/wp-content/uploads/sites/10/2016/01/Conflict-and-violence-in-the-21st-century-Current-trends-as-observed-in-empirical-research-and-statistics-Mr.-Alexandre-Marc-Chief-Specialist-Fragility-Conflict-and-Violence-World-Bank-Group.pdf, accessed 29 March 2021.

[47] Christina Lamb, *Our Bodies, Their Battlefield: What War Does to Women,* (London: William Collins, 2020).

> Recourse to violence, in fact, aggravates existing tensions and creates new ones. Nothing is resolved by war; on the contrary, everything is placed in jeopardy by war. The results of this scourge are the suffering and death of innumerable individuals the disintegration of human relations and the irreparable loss of an immense artistic and environmental patrimony. War worsens the suffering of the poor; indeed, it creates new poor by destroying the means of subsistence, homes and property, and by eating away at the very fabric of the social environment.[48]

The 2003 invasion of Iraq, which subsequently destabilised the entire region, creating further conflict and the rise of ISIS, is a clear example of John Paul II's teachings. Here, papal teachings on violence and peace can be seen to be moving much closer to the teachings of the Gospels. In emphasis on the rights and needs of the poor and oppressed members of society, and the creation of a stable social order that promotes human flourishing, the teachings of the Catholic Church on peace are echoing the message of Christ.

Pacifism and Nonviolence: A Legitimate Alternative to Just War

Such changes in the nature of warfare and the reaction of the Roman Catholic Church to them have led to a recognition of pacifism and contentious objection as legitimate stances to be taken by the faithful. As recently as 1956, Roman Catholics were denied the right to refuse to participate in war. But in 1965, the Council Fathers acknowledged the right to contentious objection, stating: 'We cannot but praise those who renounce violence in defending their rights and use means of defence which are available to the weakest, so long as this can be done without harm to the rights and duties of others or of the community.'[49] This recognition of pacifism is crucial to the role of scripture in teachings on violence and peace. Himes demonstrates that Catholic teaching on pacifism makes three claims:

[48] John Paul II, 'If you want peace, reach out to the poor', XXVI World Day of Peace Message 1993, 8 December 1992, http://www.vatican.va/content/john-paul-ii/en/messages/peace/documents/hf_jp-ii_mes_08121992_xxvi-world-day-for-peace.html, accessed 23 March 2022, §4.

[49] *Gaudium et Spes*, §78.

1. Pacifism is an option that individuals may choose based on sincere belief that war is incompatible with Christian discipleship;
2. Pacifism requires a clear commitment to resist injustice and a desire to promote human rights and the common good; and
3. Pacifism is based on the freedom of the person and the right of individual conscience.

It is not a duty for all but a legitimate option for those who discern a moral calling to oppose the war.[50] However, I would suggest that in 'reading the signs of the times', papal teaching has now moved. The establishment of the positive conception of peace inherent in Catholic definitions of pacifism with their emphasis upon justice and the common good is now the primary focus of Roman Catholic teachings on violence and peace rather than a 'legitimate option'. This means that violence and peace are viewed through a different lens, one which focuses on the prevention of violence rather than its containment inherent in just war theory. As the Council Fathers taught, 'Peace is never achieved once and for all, but has to be constantly fashioned'[51] and it is this, which forms the basis of Roman Catholic conceptions of Just Peace.

Just Peace: 'Fostering a Positive Conception of Peace'[52]

> Peace is not merely the absence of war; nor can it be reduced solely to the maintenance and balance of power between enemies; nor is it brought by dictatorship. *Instead, is it rightly and appropriately called an enterprise of justice.* Peace results from that order structured into human society by its divine Founder, and actualised by men as they thirst after ever greater justice.[53]

[50] Himes, *Christianity and the Political Order,* p.331.

[51] *Gaudium et Spes,* §78.

[52] *The Challenge of Peace,* §234.

[53] *Gaudium et Spes,* §78, emphasis added. Cf 'For peace is not simply the absence of warfare, based on a precarious balance of power; it is fashioned by efforts directed day after day toward the establishment of the ordered universe willed by God, with a more perfect form of justice among men.' Paul VI, *Populorum Progressio: Encyclical Letter on the Development of Peoples,* 26 March 1967, http://www.vatican.va/content/paul-vi/en/encyclicals/documents/hf_p-vi_enc_26031967_populorum.html, accessed 31 March 2022, §76.

The teachings of the Second Vatican Council thus demand that Christians seek to free society from war and violence by working for justice. In doing so, it moved the focus of the institution's teachings from just war and its containment of violent conflict to a focus on eradicating structural violence, which was defined by Pope Paul VI in 1967 as:

> The material poverty of those who lack the bare necessities of life, and the moral poverty of those who are crushed under the weight of their own self-love; oppressive political structures resulting from the abuse of ownership or the improper exercise of power, from the exploitation of the worker or unjust transactions.[54]

Structural violence, then, is that which prevents human flourishing and stops the achievement of the common good[55] from being the goal in political, economic and social decision-making. Through such words, the Magisterium was firmly placing teachings on violence and peace on a scriptural footing. The form of positive peace described here can only be achieved by a credible re-enactment of the kingdom of God. Through His incarnation, Christ modelled the form of societal perfection that is required for justice and peace to flourish. An example that, through our baptism, we are compelled to follow. In his 2013 Apostolic Exhortation, *Evangelii Gaudium,* Francis added another layer to the command, thus:

> The Christian ideal will always be a summons to overcome suspicion, habitual mistrust, fear of losing our privacy, all the defensive attitudes which today's world imposes on us. Many try to escape from others and take refuge in the comfort of their privacy or in a small circle of close friends, renouncing the social aspect of the Gospel. For just as some people want a purely spiritual Christ, without flesh and without the cross, they also want their interpersonal relationships provided by sophisticated equipment, by screens and systems which can be turned on and off at command. Meanwhile,

[54] *Populorum Progressio,* §21.

[55] Although the concept of the common good has been present in the vocabulary of the Catholic Church from the Pontificate of Leo XIII, it was not until the Pontificate of John XXIII that a definition was provided. In both *Mater et Magistra* and *Pacem in Terris* he described the common good as 'the sum total of conditions of social life, by which people may reach their perfection more fully and easily.' John XXIII, *Mater et Magistra: On Christianity and Social Progress,* 15 May 1961, http://www.vatican.va/content/john-xxiii/en/encyclicals/documents/hf_j-xxiii_enc_15051961_mater.html, accessed 31 March 2022, §65, and *Pacem in Terris,* §58.

> the Gospel tells us constantly to run the risk of face-to-face encounter with others, with their physical presence which challenges us, with their pain and their pleas, with their joy which infects us in close and continuous interaction. True faith in the incarnate Son of God is inseparable from self-giving, from membership in the community, from service, from reconciliation with others. The Son of God, by becoming flesh, summoned us to the revolution of tenderness.[56]

Hence, as well as improving the material conditions of the poor and the oppressed, we must enter into a Christ-centred relationship with them. In doing so, we can ensure that both the principles of solidarity[57] and subsidiarity[58] so crucial to the creation of justice and peace are enacted.

Through such a process, we are expected to create a common vision for the future of humanity that is grounded in scripture; a vision of a society in which the causes of war, conflict and violence no longer exist, and the common good and human flourishing are the norm. This

> involves building a human community where men can live truly human lives, free from discrimination on account of race, religion or nationality, free from servitude to other men or to natural forces which they cannot yet control satisfactorily. It involves building a human community where liberty is not an idle world, where the needy Lazurus can sit down with the rich man at the same banquet table.[59]

In doing so, we are committing ourselves to 'the ceaseless pursuit of the just ordering of human affairs.'[60] This in-breaking of the kingdom into history requires ongoing work, the realisation of which we are unlikely to

[56] Francis, *Evangelii Gaudium: The Joy of the Gospel,* 24 November 2013, http://www.vatican.va/content/francesco/en/apost_exhortations/documents/papa-francesco_esortazione-ap_20131124_evangelii-gaudium.html, accessed 31 March 2022, §88.

[57] The concept of solidarity compels people to take into account the effect of their actions on others, asking them to strive to promote the common good, whilst standing and working *with* the poor and marginalised rather than myopically focusing on their own desires and needs.

[58] Subsidiarity affirms the idea that each person has the right to shape their own destiny rather than it being solely subject to external forces. When at all possible, therefore, power and decision-making processes should be exercised at the lowest possible level.

[59] *Populorum Progressio*, §47.

[60] Benedict XVI, *Caritas in Veritate,* 29 June 2009, http://www.vatican.va/content/benedict-xvi/en/encyclicals/documents/hf_ben-xvi_enc_20090629_caritas-in-veritate.html, accessed 23 March 2022, §78.

experience. It is the complete example of the 'already but not yet,'[61] the meaning of which is perfectly summed up by Gustavo Gutiérrez OP: 'the Kingdom is the final meaning in history; its total fulfilment takes place beyond history, and at the same time is present from this moment on.'[62] But, whilst 'some would regard these hopes as vain flights of fancy. ...[such] adversity, when endured for the sake of one's brothers and out of love for them, can contribute greatly to human progress.'[63]

The concept of just peace is taught through Catholic social teaching, which indicates the different steps that Christians can take to create a new social order. These teachings are produced through prayerful reading and interpretation of scripture, and they are disseminated in the case of teachings on peace through encyclicals and the Pope's annual world day of peace messages.[64] Each of these messages concentrates on a different theme, for example nonviolence (2017) and politics (2019), and in doing so, provides material that can be contextualised by the laity and put into action in a manner appropriate to their own situations. As I argue elsewhere, within Catholicism, this moral vision is born from the combination of three elements: the gospel and magisterium, empirical analysis, and most crucially dialogue.[65] Such a combination is crucial because, as Johan Verstvaeten points out:

> Judgements on the world cannot be made merely on the basis of faith propositions. Without social and economic analysis, the faith perspective loses touch with reality or leads to the construction of a world of pious ideas,

[61] George E Ladd, *The Gospel of the Kingdom,* (Grand Rapids, MI: Eerdmans Publishing Co, 1959), pp. 13–23. This concept has become popularized within Catholic 'popular' spirituality see for example James Martin, *Jesus A Pilgrimage,* (New York: Harper, 2014), 170–171.

[62] Gustavo Gutiérrez OP, 'The Option for the Poor Arises from Faith in Christ', *Theological Studies,* 2009, vol. 70, 317–326, 323.

[63] *Populorum Progressio,* §79.

[64] Francis's messages can be found here: https://www.vatican.va/content/francesco/en/messages/peace.index.html, accessed 31 March 2022. See also Maria Power and Christopher Hrynkow, 'Qualified Advocacy for Just Peace: The Pope's World Day of Peace Messages (1968–2020) in Historical and Ethical Perspective', *Peace and Change: A Journal of Peace History,* vol. 45, no. 3, 339–368.

[65] Maria Power, 'Alternative Possible Futures: Unearthing a Catholic Public Theology for Northern Ireland', in Christopher R Baker and Elaine Graham (eds.), *Theology for Changing Times: John Atherton and the Future of Public Theology,* (London: SCM, 2018), 158–174.

> which risks being an expression of social alienation rather than a solution to it.[66]

Through the use of such a method, the 'already but not yet' emerges for each particular milieu, enabling the binary goals of the church for individuals of personal and communal salvation, or the individual attainment of a place in the heavenly kingdom combined with a contribution to the creation of the earthly peaceable kingdom, to be achieved. At this point in this chapter, it might be useful to outline Roman Catholic teachings on a particular topic and relate them to the definition of peace offered by the Magisterium. Doing so will allow us to understand the form of material and its relationship to Scripture that Catholics are expected to work with as they seek the kingdom of God.

In 1967, Pope Paul VI told us that 'development is the new name for peace'.[67] In doing so, he showed that employment of the techniques of development was key to the eradication of structural violence and was the route to justice and peace. Indeed, development was so key to Roman Catholic understandings of peace, that Paul VI created the Pontifical Commission on Justice and Peace[68] in 1967 to ensure that human dignity and flourishing in the Global South remained a key focus of the church's attention. However, the form of development espoused by the Roman Catholic Church focuses on empowerment and equality rather than dependency. Since the papacy of John XXIII, Catholic social teaching has underscored the fundamental need to build a more just global economic system and has been critical of policies that hurt the poor and marginalised. The overarching argument behind this teaching is that every person should be allowed to live in a manner that recognises their dignity and which allows them to flourish.[69] The massive inequalities between countries, in the Global North and South, must therefore be addressed in a manner that allows less economically robust countries to retain their autonomy. In 1963, John XXIII stated:

[66] Johan Verstvaeten, 'Towards Interpreting the Signs of the Times, Conversation with the World, and Inclusion of the Poor: Three Challenges for Catholic Social Teaching', *International Journal of Public Theology*, 2011, 5, 314–330, 317.

[67] *Populorum Progressio*, §76.

[68] Information about this commission can be found here: http://www.vatican.va/roman_curia/pontifical_councils/justpeace/index.htm, accessed 19 April 2022.

[69] *Pacem in Terris*, §122.

> Again and again We must insist on the need for helping these peoples in a way which guarantees to them the preservation of their own freedom. They must be conscious that they are themselves playing the major role in their economic and social development; that they themselves are to shoulder the main burden of it.[70]

The teachings on the causes of global inequality have been consistent: the economic system, with its focus on profit margins and the creation of a 'civilisation of consumerism and waste'[71] has led to the subordination of the human person to a world where 'a profit-based economic model [dominates] that does not hesitate to exploit, discard and even kill human beings. While one part of humanity lives in opulence, another part sees its own dignity denied, scorned or trampled upon, and its fundamental rights discarded or violated.'[72] Through this, human beings are no longer allowed to be active subjects in their own lives, and their dignity is violated—a situation which is *the* embodiment of structural violence. This criticism of economic structures (be they capitalist, socialist, or communist) has been a consistent feature of Catholic social teaching throughout the last six papacies.

The Roman Catholic Church has stated that 'The present state of affairs must be confronted boldly, and its concomitant injustices must be challenged and overcome. Continuing development calls for bold innovations that will work profound changes. The critical state of affairs must be corrected without delay.'[73] These profound changes are to be expressed through a global solidarity based upon the teachings of the gospel,[74] which manifests itself as the preferential option for the poor—that is, to take the

[70] Ibid., §123.

[71] John Paul II, *Sollicitudo Rei Socialis: On Social Concerns*, 30 December 1987, http://www.vatican.va/content/john-paul-ii/en/encyclicals/documents/hf_jp-ii_enc_30121987_sollicitudo-rei-socialis.html, accessed 19 April 2022, §28.

[72] *Fratelli Tutti*, §22.

[73] *Populorum Progressio*, §32.

[74] In 1971, the World Synod of Catholic Bishops stated the following: 'Listening to the cry of those who suffer violence and are oppressed by unjust systems and structures, and hearing the appeal of a world that by its perversity contradicts the plan of its Creator, we have shared our awareness of the Church's vocation to be present in the heart of the world by proclaiming the Good News to the poor, freedom to the oppressed, and joy to the afflicted. The hopes and forces which are moving the world in its very foundations are not foreign to the dynamism of the Gospel, which through the power of the Holy Spirit frees people from personal sin and from its consequences in social life.' *Justice in the World*, §5.

side of the powerless and the oppressed and to work for their liberation—teaching solidly rooted in the Bible.[75]

But how can this vision or teaching be translated into reality? For a just peace to emerge, human society needs to bear the closest possible resemblance to the kingdom of God, as outlined in the Sermon on the Mount and demonstrated by Jesus' actions throughout His ministry. But how is this to be brought into reality? The entire people of God proclaim the message of the Gospel. Therefore, in the Roman Catholic tradition, the laity is expected to work to bring about the constructive change needed to eradicate the structural violence that is preventing human flourishing and the common good from emerging. This is because just peace is a historical reality, something that Christians can work to bring about as well as an eschatological offer of hope to believers. In *Gaudium et Spes* the laity's vocation in this regard is described thus:

> Christians who take an active part in present-day socio-economic development and fight for justice and charity should be convinced that they can make a great contribution to the prosperity of mankind and to the peace of the world. In these activities let them, either as individuals or as members of groups, give a shining example. Having acquired the absolutely necessary skill and experience, they should observe the right order in their earthly activities in faithfulness to Christ and His Gospel. Thus their whole life, both individual and social, will be permeated with the spirit of the beatitudes, notably with a spirit of poverty.[76]

For the laity then, life and faith are to be integrated, and they are expected to work towards a society that realized the Gospel's teachings.

But although the Gospel and Catholic social teaching demand that Catholics work to build a new social order, they do not offer a programme or blueprint for action. This is achieved by a further reading of the 'signs of the times' which allows the teachings of the Gospel and the Magisterium to be translated into any given context. The starting point should be a belief that the world should not be as it is. This was one of the main reasons for Christ's life and His death on the Cross. Catholics are therefore

[75] See for example Ex 3:9; Ex 8:1; Isa 3: 14–15; Isa 10: 1–2; Lk 4: 18–21; Lk 6: 20–21; Mt. 15: 1–5; and Mk 2: 23–3:6. For a fuller discussion of this, see Donal Dorr, 'Preferential Option for the Poor' in Judith A Dwyer (ed.), *The New Dictionary of Catholic Social Thought*, (Collegeville, MN: The Litugical Press, 1994), 755–759.

[76] *Gaudium et Spes*, §72.

taught that they must use the ideals raised by the Gospel and Magisterium to engage in a critical and ethical reflection on the social order. But because of the position taken by Jesus in the gospels towards the poor and marginalised, there is little room for impartiality.[77] Consequently, this means that the lived realities of the poorest members of our society must be understood if we are going to work to challenge the structural violence that leads to war and conflict. Once this consciousness-raising is complete, a new moral vision which shows what a just social order would look like must be developed and a method for achieving this decided upon. Then the work of building a just peace begins.

However, the creation of a just peace is something which must emerge in partnership. This stance is best summed up by the phrase 'active solidarity'[78] used by John XXIII in *Pacem in Terris.* Solidarity with the poor must be combined with subsidiarity so that Catholics are working with the poor rather than enacting a form of noblesse oblige which serves merely to disempower all of those involved. This is because 'the promotion of peace flows steadily from our self-understanding as a community centred on the person of Christ.'[79] The fundamental question that lies at the heart of all Catholic activity orientated towards the establishment of a just peace is *who is my neighbour*? 'The Gospel makes no distinction between the love neighbour and justice',[80] therefore neither should we. The answer to this question is found in the Gospel of Luke and, in particular, the Parable of the Good Samaritan.[81] This parable models for us the creation of a new community that knows no boundaries or outcasts; in which compassion, care, and practical action for those in need are the marks of a life lived in communion with Christ. This parable shows us how we should be in relationship with one another in order to create a just peace. As Pope Benedict XVI teaches:

[77] This is a foundational element of Catholic social teaching. For example Francis states that 'while it is quite true that the essential vocation and mission of the lay faithful is to strive that earthly realities and all human activity may be transformed by the Gospel, none of us can think that we are exempt from concern for the poor and for social justice: "Spiritual conversion, the intensity of love of God and neighbour, zeal for justice and peace, the Gospel meaning of the poor and of poverty, are required for everyone.", *Evangelii Gaudium,* §201.

[78] *Pacem in Terris,* §98.

[79] Pádraig Corkery, *Companion to the Compendium of the Social Doctrine of the Church,* (Dublin: Veritas, 2007), 101.

[80] Simone Weil, *Wating for God,* (New York: Harper Modern Classics, 1951, 2009), 85.

[81] Lk 10:25–37. Pope Francis recently used this parable in his encyclical *Fratelli Tutti* to explain why we should 'resolve our conflicts and care for one another.' §57.

> The Samaritan, the foreigner, makes himself the neighbour and shows me that I have to learn to be a neighbour deep within and that I already have the answer in myself. I have to become like someone in love, someone whose heart is open to being shaken up by another's need. Then I find my neighbour, or – better – then I am found by him.[82]

The process of changing understandings of the concept of neighbourliness is itself as important as the action of working for a just peace. Here, the intersection of the cross (God (the vertical) and neighbour or community (the horizontal)) becomes real: 'the love of God and the love of one's neighbour converge in the encounter with the other',[83] and the mandate given at baptism is enacted and a new community is created.

Conclusion

It cannot be denied that there are significant tensions within Roman Catholicism regarding teachings on violence and peace, with a fault line developing between those who espouse just war and those who focus on the structural change that just peace brings. The Roman Catholic Church has, however, been moving towards a just peace approach since the Second Vatican Council (1962–1965) and the Pontificate of Paul VI (1963–1978)—a stance which is firmly rooted within scripture. As a result, Roman Catholics must now try and find a balance in their attitudes towards violence and peace; a balance which takes into account the temporal obligations that Christ's incarnation brings as well as its eschatological hope. This can be achieved by approaching matters of violence and peace through the lens of scripture and tradition to create contextualised solutions that seek to deal with the causes of violence before they become uncontainable.

Further Reading

Gregory Boyle SJ, *Barking to the Choir: The Power of Radical Kinship,* (New York, NY: Simon & Schuster, 2017)

[82] Benedict XVI, Jesus of Nazareth, trans. Adrian J Walker, (London: Bloomsbury, 2007), 197.

[83] R Zimmerman, 'The etho-poietic of the parable of the good Samaritan (LK 10:25–37). The ethics of seeing in a culture looking the other way', *Verbum et Ecclesia*, 2008, vol. 29, no. 1, 269–292, 280.

David Carroll Cochran, *Catholic Realism and the Abolition of War,* (Maryknoll, NY: Orbis Books, 2014)
Donal Dorr, *Option for the Poor and for the Earth: From Leo XIII to Pope Francis,* (Maryknoll, NY: Orbis Books, 2016)
Eli S McCarthy (ed.), *A Just Peace Ethic Primer: Building Sustainable Peace and Breaking Cycles of Violence,* (Washington DC: Georgetown University Press, 2020)
Marcus Mescher, *The Ethics of Encounter: Christian Neighbour Love as a Practice of Solidarity,* (Maryknoll, NY: Orbis Books, 2020)
Maria Power, *Catholic Social Teaching and Theologies of Peace: Cardinal Cahal Daly and the Pursuit of the Peaceable Kingdom,* (Abingdon: Routledge, 2021).
Lisa Sowle Cahill, *Love your Enemies: Discipleship, Pacifism, and Just War Theory,* (Minneapolis, MN: Fortress Press, 1994)

CHAPTER 9

Interpretations of Qur'ānic Violence in Shī'ī Islam

Ali Hammoud

A sacred text is a source of guidance, beauty and spiritual nourishment – a text that directly addresses the heart and soul of the reader. So far as this is true, anyone – believer or otherwise – can browse through the pages of a sacred text, and perhaps scent an otherworldly musk, glimpse moments of self-transcendence, or encounter verses that resonate deeply within their very core that demand immediate introspection. For the believer, the sacred text is all of this. But it is also much more. It is not limited to the prescription of doctrinal beliefs, ritual observances, and general moral precepts. It goes beyond merely influencing the believer's actions; rather, it formulates their entire worldview and directs their practical affairs to attain true felicity. This breadth and depth of sacred texts is simultaneously

Positionality: I write as a scholar of Islamic intellectual history and as a Shī'ī Muslim committed to spreading peace and justice.

A. Hammoud (✉)
School of Humanities and Communication Arts, Western Sydney University, Sydney, NSW, Australia
e-mail: a.hammoud3@westernsydney.edu.au

M. Power, H. Paynter (eds.), *Violence and Peace in Sacred Texts*, https://doi.org/10.1007/978-3-031-17804-7_9

comforting and challenging for the believer. The comfort lies in the belief that the answers to life's mysteries, to the questions that have perpetually probed and prodded humanity, are contained within the text. The challenge arises, however, when one engages with the tension inherent in all sacred texts: the revelation of eternal truths within a particular spatio-temporal context. Sacred texts chronicle specific events that relate to the context in which they were revealed, and present injunctions related to those events. Some injunctions confront believers with challenging moral dilemmas and, on the surface, appear to blatantly contradict our modern understanding of human rights. Do these injunctions persist throughout time? How is one to differentiate between the eternal and the contextual?

The questions posed relate directly to the problem of violence and peace in sacred texts. All religious traditions must confront these questions, and Islam is no different. As a faith tradition with more than one billion adherents globally, Islam is incredibly influential in the modern world. Yet despite its global impact, much has been said about Islam in the public sphere that demonstrates a lack of critical engagement with its intellectual traditions. Be it, ardent critics of Islam who portray the faith as inherently possessing a violent streak, or well-meaning Muslims who wish to placate an increasingly anxious public with platitudes that misconstrue Islam as endorsing pacifism, both do a disservice to the intellectual heritage of Islam and its engagement with critical questions concerning violence and peace. It is the lack of attention paid to Islam's nuanced positions concerning violence and peace that this chapter seeks to address. In particular, the chapter will focus on Shīʿī Islam and the interpretations of Qurʾānic violence offered by Shīʿī scholars.

Although the Qurʾān contains numerous references to violence, the framing of the topic is often centred on jihād, often erroneously translated as 'Holy War'. According to ElSayed, jihād is 'striving or exerting one's utmost effort to do something'.[1] This struggle, however, is not limited to physical exertion; there is also a spiritual dimension associated with jihād. The physical and spiritual dimensions of jihād are clarified in a narration from the Shīʿī Ḥadīth corpus, in which it is recorded:

> Al-Sukuni relates on the authority of al-Ṣādiq: On seeing the returning armies from the battlefront, the Prophet of God said, 'Blessed are those who

[1] Amin ElSayed, *Reclaiming Jihad: A Qurʾānic Critique of Terrorism* (United Kingdom: The Islamic Foundation, 2015), 80.

have performed the minor jihād, and have yet to perform the major one.' When asked, 'What is the major jihād?' the Prophet replied, 'the jihād of the self' (struggle against the self).[2]

Jihād then, is a multidimensional concept, one that incorporates both a spiritual and intellectual striving, as well as a physical striving that may take the shape of violence. In its physical manifestation, jihād is also related to terms such as *qitāl* (fighting) and *ḥarb* (war), as the terms often appear together in verses. For the purposes of this chapter, these terms, as well as warfare, will be used interchangeably.[3] The analysis of jihād in the Qur'ān by both exegetes and jurists has mostly focused on the distinction between defensive jihād and offensive jihād. Defensive jihād refers to the jihād that is waged in defence of one's homeland, faith and freedom, whereas offensive jihād is the pre-emptive attack launched without provocation. Whilst defensive jihād is acknowledged by all scholars to be a valid form of jihād, scholars have debated the validity, or lack thereof, of offensive jihād. It is this particular discussion, namely, that of defensive/offensive jihād within Shīʿī Islam, that this chapter aims to illuminate.

Shīʿīsm: Historical Evolution of Theology and Qur'ānic Exegesis

This chapter will focus exclusively on Shīʿī Islam and the interpretations of Qur'ānic violence put forward by Shīʿī scholars. Shīʿī Islam differs from Sunnī Islam in a variety of ways, although the primary difference between them is the concept of Imāmāh.[4] Shīʿīsm holds that the successorship to the Prophet is limited to 12 individuals from the Prophet's family, known as Imams. Each Imam – with the exception of the second and third Imams, who were brothers – is the son of the former, and succeeds the former after their death. The first Imam is Alī, the cousin and son-in-law of the Prophet Muhammad, and the final Imam is the messianic twelfth Imam, al-Mahdī.[5] Shīʿī Muslims believe that the twelfth Imam went into

[2] Ruhollah Khomeini, *Forty Ḥadīths: An Exposition of Ethical and Mystical Traditions* (Tehran: Institute for Compilation and Publication of Imam Khomeini's Works, 2003), 35.

[3] Asma Afsaruddin, *Striving in the Path of God: Jihad and Martyrdom in Islamic Thought* (Oxford: Oxford University Press, 2013), 2.

[4] Mohammad Ali Amir-Moezzi et al., *What Is Shi'i Islam? An Introduction* (London: Routledge, Taylor & Francis Group, 2018), 13.

[5] Amir-Moezzi et al., *What Is Shi'i Islam?*, 37.

occultation in the year 874 CE, and will re-appear at the end of time with Jesus to establish justice upon the earth.

The function of Imāmāh in Shīʿīsm vastly differs from the ideals of successorship in Sunnī Islam. In Shīʿīsm, the Imam is chosen exclusively by God and not the populace. Popular acceptability, however, is a condition for the Imam to assume political power. The Imam is also held to be infallible, and as such, represents the supreme model of emulation for Shīʿī Muslims. In this capacity, the Imam is not only the political successor to the Prophet, but also the spiritual leader of the Muslim community.[6] This entails that religion is to be understood and received exclusively through the teachings of the Imams and not Muhammad's companions, as is the case within the Sunnī Islamic tradition. This caused a divide between the structure and development of Islamic sciences within these two intellectual traditions. Although there is much overlap, this crucial theological tenet ensured that the Shīʿī tradition would evolve in a unique manner.

Another key historical event that significantly altered the Shīʿī consciousness was the martyrdom of Ḥusayn, the third Imam, in Karbalā in the year 680 CE. Ḥusayn, along with his band of 72 warriors, was brutally massacred by the military force of the Calīph Yazīd, numbering some 30,000 men.[7] The consequences of the massacre of Karbalā were not only evident in the immediate aftermath of the event, but have reverberated throughout Islamic history. Its effects have served to both support and delegitimise violence. With regard to the former, the martyrdom of Imam Ḥusayn brought the doctrine of martyrdom to the fore of Shīʿīsm, where it has continued significance and influence in times of revolt and warfare for Shīʿī Muslims throughout history.[8] With regard to the effect of delegitimising violence, this can be seen in the general attitude of distrust that the Imams following al-Ḥusayn held towards politics and the ruling elite. After al-Ḥusayn's martyrdom, the Shīʿī Imams exercised more caution in publicising their political activities, and did not directly engage in any political revolts and uprisings.

One of the fields in which Shīʿī theology and history have had a significant impact is Tafsīr (Qurʾānic exegesis). The structure of Shīʿī Tafsīr

[6] Najam Iftikhar Haider, *Shīʿī Islam: An Introduction* (New York: Cambridge University Press, 2014), 63.

[7] Haider, *Shīʿī Islam*, 66.

[8] Mohammad Hassan Faghfoory, *Ethics of War and Peace in Islam: A Shi'a view* (Chicago: Kazi Publications Inc., 2019), 9.

mirrors the broader evolution of Shīʿīsm through the centuries, oscillating between ḫadīṯh-based commentary, and works evincing the philosophical-mystical flavour inherent within Shīʿīsm. The formative centuries of Islamic history bore witness to a Shīʿīsm that eschewed personal interpretation in favour of traditions and opinions ascribed to either Muhammad or an Imam.[9] The subsequent occultation of the Imam in 874 CE would drastically alter the course of Shīʿī intellectual history. Shīʿī scholars, in lieu of the Imam, began to exert more authorial influence and employed a variety of methodologies and approaches to interpreting the Qurʾān.

The process of interpreting a verse of the Qurʾān is complex and multifaceted. The exegete must study a verse in its linguistic, hermeneutical, historical, theological and jurisprudential dimensions to arrive at a sound reading. This will – at a minimum – involve: consulting lexicons to determine the precise meaning of a word as understood in seventh century Arabia; consulting the Ḥadīṯh corpus and *sīrah* (biography) literature to identify the *asbāb al-nuzūl* (occasions of revelation), as well as whether *naskh* (abrogation) is applicable; and, referring to earlier tafsīrs to compare explanations.[10] An exegete will usually employ their own approach in interpreting the Qurʾānic text, depending on both their expertise and areas of interest. These differing approaches have led to the production of countless Qurʾānic exegetical works, the collective sum of which have fleshed out the linguistic, historical, philosophical and mystical elements of the text.

Violence and Peace in the Qurʾān

Any attempt to critically engage with the Qurʾān, and with the question of violence and peace, is confronted by two challenges. The first challenge is that one must decipher the historical context of the verses in question. The Qurʾān is not structured in a sequential manner, making it difficult to weave together a coherent narrative. Although there are myriad references to both violence and peace, they are scattered throughout the text, often with little background or context provided. To address this, secondary

[9] Husayn Alawi Mehr and Hamid Hussein Waqar, *An introduction to the history of Tafsīr and commentators of the Quran* (Qum: Al-Mustafa International Translation and Publication Center, 2012), 22.

[10] Ġulām ʿAlī Ḥaddād ʿĀdil, Muḥammad Jaʿfar ʿIlmī, and Ḥasan Ṭārimī Rād, eds., *Tafsīr: An Entry from Encyclopaedia of the World of Islam* (London: EWI Press, 2012), 15.

sources, such as the Ḥadīth corpus and *sīrah* literature must be consulted to distill a clearer picture and provide the broader context.[11] The second challenge revolves around the issue of *naskh*.[12] A surface reading of the Qur'ānic text may reveal apparent contradictions between certain rulings and injunctions.[13] To explain this, Muslim scholars argue that some later verses abrogate earlier verses, with the distinction based primarily upon the Meccan and Medinan sections of the Qur'ān.[14] For example, some medieval jurists opined that the two 'sword verses' (9:5, 9:29) abrogated the earlier verses calling for peace or limited warfare, and established a new policy of dealing with non-believers.[15] Other jurists however, would contend that the 'sword verses' were limited to their specific context, and were associated with certain conditions.[16] Perspectives on both the contextual understanding of the respective verses and the application of abrogation are crucial to the formation of different positions concerning violence and peace.

Traditional readings of the Qur'ānic perspective on violence and peace present a four-stage schema, with each stage successively granting more permission for Muslims to engage in warfare. These four stages are: peaceful co-existence and dealings; discussion and debate; defensive warfare with conditions; and finally, what appears to be permission to engage in offensive warfare.[17] It would be pertinent to mention, however, that not all Muslim scholars concur with this schema. Based on different views concerning the occasion of revelation, the potential application of abrogation and context of the verse, scholars have offered competing schemas for assorting verses that deal with violence and peace.[18] Shīʿī scholars however—and in particular Murtaḍa Muṭahharī, whose views will be analysed

[11] Michael David Bonner, *Jihad in Islamic History: Doctrines and Practice* (Princeton: Princeton University Press, 2006), 37.

[12] Abbas Jaffer and Masuma Jaffer, *An Introduction to Qur'anic Sciences* (London: ICAS Press, 2009), 147–65.

[13] Reuven Firestone, *Jihad: The Origin of Holy War in Islam* (New York: Oxford University Press, 1999), 49.

[14] Richard Bonney, *Jihad: From Qur'ān to Bin Laden* (New York: Palgrave Macmillan, 2004), 24.

[15] Bonner, *Jihad in Islamic History*, 26.

[16] Mohammad Hassan Khalil, *Jihad, Radicalism, and the New Atheism* (Cambridge: Cambridge University Press, 2018), 15–16.

[17] Bonney, *Jihad*, 25–26.

[18] Firestone, *Jihad*, 69.

in greater detail further—mostly adhere to the traditional schema. In this regard, he writes:

> One set of verses appear in absolute terms to tell us to wage war, such that if we were only acquainted with these verses and not others, we may have assumed that Islam is a religion of war. The second set of verses allow for war with others under certain conditions, such as being in a state of war with an opposing group, or if another group has trampled upon the rights of the commonfolk – both Muslim and non-Muslim alike – that live under their rule. The third set of verses explicitly state that invitation towards Islam cannot be based on compulsion or force. The fourth set of verses are those in which Islam explicitly announces itself as a supporter of peace.[19]

The first set of verses, namely, those that deal with peaceful co-existence, were revealed during Muhammad's life in Mecca. Mecca was the birthplace of Muhammad, who belonged to a powerful Meccan tribe, the Quraysh.[20] The Meccan period coincided with the first 53 years of Muhammad's life. Muslim scholars hold that the first revelation of the Qur'ān—and the subsequent commencement of Prophethood—occurred when Muhammad was 40 years old. Following this, Muhammad spent 13 years in Mecca, preaching the faith secretly for the first 3 years, before eventually proclaiming the new faith within the public arena. The fledgling religion struggled to attract newcomers, as the Meccans were hostile to any perceived threat to their established customs and traditions.[21] Muhammad's familial prestige protected him from excessive harm or murder; his followers however, were not afforded the same luxuries, and were constantly assaulted during his time in Mecca.[22] Muhammad, however, stuck firmly to the Qur'ānic injunctions at that time, which forbade violence. Some of these verses include:

> The servants of the All-beneficent are those who walk humbly on the earth, and when the ignorant address them, say, 'Peace!'[23]

[19] Murtaḍa Muṭahharī, *Jihād* (Tehran: Sadra Publications, 2016), 60–61.

[20] Marshall G. S. Hodgson, *The Venture of Islam, Volume 1: The Classical Age of Islam* (Chicago: University of Chicago Press, 1977), 158.

[21] Ibid., 170–71.

[22] 'Abd al-Malik Ibn Hishām, Muḥammad Ibn Isḥāq, and Alfred Guillaume, *The Life of Muhammad: A Translation of Isḥāq's Sīrat Rasūl Allāh* (New York: Oxford University Press, 2001), 205.

[23] Qur'ān 25:63.

> And be patient over what they say, and keep away from them in a graceful manner.[24]

> Good and evil [conduct] are not equal. Repel [evil] with what is best. [If you do so,] behold, he between whom and you was enmity, will be as though he were a sympathetic friend. But none is granted it except those who are patient, and none is granted it except the greatly endowed.[25]

The second set of verses were also revealed in the Meccan phase, although their contents indicate that they were revealed towards the latter stages of Muhammad's period in Mecca. By this time, the number of adherents to the new faith had increased, necessitating a new mode of engagement with non-believers. To this end, these verses called for dialogue with the non-believers of Mecca, with Muslims still ordered to abstain from violence. These verses include:

> Invite to the way of your Lord with wisdom and good advice and dispute with them in a manner that is best. Indeed your Lord knows best those who stray from His way, and He knows best those who are guided.[26]

> Do not dispute with the People of the Book except in a manner which is best, barring such of them as are wrongdoers, and say, 'We believe in that which has been sent down to us and has been sent down to you; our God and your God is one [and the same], and to Him do we submit.'[27]

The third set of verses were revealed in the second year of Muhammad's life in Medina, just prior to the Battle of Badr. These verses constitute a sharp break from the previous two stages. For the first time, a Qur'ānic injunction permits violence, albeit violence that is defensive and retaliatory in nature.[28] The verses read as follows:

> Those who are fought against are permitted [to fight] because they have been wronged, and Allah is indeed able to help them. Those who were expelled from their homes unjustly, only because they said, 'Allah is our Lord.' Had not Allah repulsed the people from one another, ruin would

[24] Qur'ān 73:10.
[25] Qur'ān 41:34–35.
[26] Qur'ān 16:125.
[27] Qur'ān 29:46.
[28] Khalil, *Jihad, Radicalism, and the New Atheism*, 10.

> have befallen the monasteries, churches, synagogues and mosques in which Allah's Name is mentioned greatly. Allah will surely help those who help Him. Indeed Allah is all-strong, all-mighty.[29]

The fourth set of verses were revealed in the final years of Muhammad's life, and go a step beyond in stipulating permission for warfare. Up until this juncture, little criticism is leveled at Islam's stance *vis-à-vis* warfare, as the Qur'ān had hitherto promoted peace or defensive warfare.[30] These verses indicate a radical departure from previous protocol, as they – on the apparent – permit offensive warfare. Scholars have robustly debated whether these verses abrogate the earlier verses that call for peace or defensive warfare, spawning multiple interpretations and positions vis-à-vis jihād.[31] The verses are as follows:

> Fight in the way of Allah those who fight you, but do not transgress. Indeed Allah does not like transgressors.[32]

> And kill them wherever you confront them, and expel them from where they expelled you, for faithlessness is graver than killing. But do not fight them near the Holy Mosque unless they fight you therein; but if they fight you, kill them; such is the requital of the faithless. But if they relinquish, then Allah is indeed all-forgiving, all-merciful. Fight them until faithlessness is no more, and religion becomes [exclusively] for Allah. Then if they relinquish, there shall be no reprisal except against the wrongdoers. A sacred month for a sacred month, and all sanctities require retribution. So should anyone aggress against you, assail him in the manner he assailed you, and be wary of Allah, and know that Allah is with the Godwary. Spend in the way of Allah, and do not cast yourselves with your own hands into destruction; and be virtuous. Indeed Allah loves the virtuous.[33]

Debate surrounds not only the meaning of the verses, but whether they were revealed together or on separate occasions. Although most scholars believe that 2:190 was revealed separately from 2:191–195, ʿĀllamah Ṭabāṭabāʾī, the most prominent Shīʿī exegete of the twentieth century—whose views will be analysed below—argues that they were all revealed at

[29] Qur'ān 22:39–40.
[30] ElSayed, *Reclaiming Jihad*, 89–90.
[31] Khalil, *Jihad, Radicalism, and the New Atheism*, 13.
[32] Qur'ān 2:190.
[33] Qur'ān 2:191–195.

once. Other verses such as 4:89–91 and 9:5–6 that are pertinent to the discussion of peace and violence in Islam are believed to have been revealed after 2:190–195. These verses are:

> They are eager that you should disbelieve like they have disbelieved, so that you all become alike. So do not make friends [with anyone] from among them, until they migrate in the way of Allah. But if they turn their backs, seize them and kill them wherever you find them, and do not take from among them friends or helpers, excepting those who join a people between whom and you there is a treaty, or such as come to you with hearts reluctant to fight you or to fight their own people. Had Allah wished, He would have imposed them upon you, and then they would have surely fought you. So if they keep out of your way and do not fight you, and offer you peace, then Allah does not allow you any course [of action] against them. You will find others desiring to be secure from you, and secure from their own people; yet whenever they are called back to polytheism, they relapse into it. So if they do not keep out of your way, nor offer you peace, nor keep their hands off [from fighting], then seize them and kill them wherever you confront them, and it is such against whom We have given you a clear sanction.[34]

> Then, when the sacred months have passed, kill the polytheists wherever you find them, capture them and besiege them, and lie in wait for them at every ambush. But if they repent, and maintain the prayer and give the zakat, then let them alone. Indeed Allah is all-forgiving, all-merciful. If any of the polytheists seeks asylum from you, grant him asylum until he hears the Word of Allah. Then convey him to his place of safety. That is because they are a people who do not know.[35]

Shīʿī Interpretations of Violence

Preliminary Remarks

Prior to analysing the opinions of Shīʿī scholars on the aforementioned verses, it would be pertinent to identify the traditional classifications of Shīʿī scholars *vis-à-vis* their positions concerning warfare. Shīʿī scholars are traditionally grouped into four main categories pertaining to jihād: offensive jihād has and always will be a valid form of jihād; only defensive jihād is valid, offensive jihād has never existed; both defensive and offensive

[34] Qurʾān 4:89–91.
[35] Qurʾān 9:5–6.

jihād exist and are valid; both defensive and offensive jihād exist, but only an Imam can declare offensive jihād.[36] As is evident from the above classifications, defensive jihād is viewed as valid by all scholars; the debate concerns the permissibility and scope of offensive jihād.[37] Faghfoory argues that for most of Shīʿī history, a balance persisted between the proponents of defensive and offensive jihād; the former, however, is more favoured in contemporary discourse, whereas the latter was more popular in pre-modern Islamic societies.[38]

The current popularity of the former position, as well as the renewed discourse surrounding war and peace owes its emergence to three phenomena. First, the study of Tafsīr continued to progress and evolve, with significant strides made in the twentieth century. Scholars and exegetes applied new methodologies and engaged more critically with the Qurʾānic text, resulting in more refined interpretations. Second, the experience of modern warfare, and in particular, the Iranian Revolution and the Iran-Iraq war shaped emerging perspectives in the contemporary period in novel ways. Finally, the elevation of the jurists into positions of political authority following the Iranian Revolution necessitated that traditional concepts be appropriated to suit modern conventions.[39] Collectively, this has led to an increased rigour in the articulation of modern perspectives on jihād; perspectives that are not only more nuanced than classical perspectives, but are more relevant for contemporary readers. As such, we will focus exclusively on the opinions of modern scholars.

This section will focus on the engagements of ʿĀllamah Ṭabāṭabāʾī (d.1981), Murtaḍa Muṭahharī (d.1979) and Neʿmatollāh Sālehī-Najafābādī (d.2006). Ṭabāṭabāʾī was a remarkable exegete, philosopher and jurist, with his 20-volume masterpiece *Tafsīr al-Mīzān* acclaimed by many scholars as the finest Shīʿī exegesis ever authored. Murtaḍa Muṭahharī, a student of Ṭabāṭabāʾī, was also a noted theologian and philosopher who authored several influential works, amongst them a collection of his lectures pertaining to jihād. Sālehī-Najafābādī was an influential, high-ranking jurist noted for holding unorthodox views that have sparked robust debate in Iranian intellectual circles.

[36] Faghfoory, *Ethics of War and Peace in Islam*, 40–41.

[37] Ibid., 46.

[38] Ibid., 65.

[39] Mohammad Jafar Amir Mahallati, *Ethics of War and Peace in Iran and Shi'i Islam* (Toronto: University of Toronto Press, 2016), 8–9.

Before we begin our analysis, there are two points to make: first, there have been noteworthy interventions in the field from non-seminary trained scholars and intellectuals that merit analysis. Despite this, we have chosen to focus exclusively on these three thinkers as they represent the primary Shīʿī perspectives on jihād in contemporary discourse. Notwithstanding the criticisms leveled at their positions, their works have remained critical reading for any thinker intending on contributing to the discourse. Second, the discussions contained herein operate on a theoretical level; practical application does not necessarily follow, particularly if the jurist takes into consideration external factors that can alter their ruling/ position on a particular issue.

Ṭabāṭabāʾī

Ṭabāṭabāʾī covers the issue of jihād most comprehensively within *Tafsīr al-Mīzān* when analysing 2:190–195. Ṭabāṭabāʾī critiques the concept of offensive warfare, decrying its misapplication by Muslim rulers after Muhammad to justify their expansionist policies.[40] Furthermore, he asserts that no wars or battles launched by Muhammad were purely offensive or unprovoked.[41] His understanding of defensive warfare however, and the potential shape it might take warrants further analysis. Ṭabāṭabāʾī's interpretation of defensive warfare allows for the possibility of pre-emptive attacks, provided that it acts to protect moral obligations.

Ṭabāṭabāʾī begins his commentary on violence in the Qurʾān by analysing verses 2:190–195. He argues that they were revealed on one occasion, and not separately, as other scholars adduced. This is because the subject matter of the verses is consistent throughout—namely, permission to fight with the polytheists of Mecca.[42] The verses provide several clues as to the context in which this fighting is to occur. First, the claim 'fight those who fight you' does not carry the condition of 'if they fight you', implying that the fighting is already occurring, and that the Muslims are obliged to counter the violence. The second implication of the verses is that fighting is restricted to those that are engaged in warfare; non-combatants are not to be harmed.

[40] Ibid., 149.

[41] Ibid., 150.

[42] Muhammad Husayn Ṭabāṭabāʾī, *Al-Mīzān, An Exegesis of the Qurʾān*, trans. Sayyid Sa'eed Akhtar Rizvi, vol. 3 (Tehran: World Organisation for Islamic Services, 1982), 76.

When analysing verses 9:5–6 however, Ṭabāṭabā'ī negates the application of abrogation. Contrary to many exegetes, who posit that 9:5–6 abrogated 2:190–195, and expanded the rights of Muslims to engage in warfare against all non-believers, Ṭabāṭabā'ī instead argues that abrogation does not apply in this instance; verses 9:5–6 did not abrogate 2:190–195, but instead de-contextualised them, and made them applicable at all times.[43] If however, offensive jihād is deemed impermissible by Ṭabāṭabā'ī, how are the injunctions of 9:5–6 to be understood?

Ṭabāṭabā'ī grounds his position vis-à-vis defensive jihād on the truthfulness of Islam. If Islam is considered to be the ultimate truth, then jihād in defence of this truth is deemed defensive warfare. In this regard Ṭabāṭabā'ī writes:

> In short, the Qur'ān says that Islam—the religion of monotheism—is based on the foundation of true nature, and is responsible for the well-being of humanity in this life. Allah says: Then set your face uprightly for the (right) religion—the nature made by Allah in which He has made men; there is no alteration (by anyone else) in the creation of Allah; that is the established religion, but most people do not know (30:30). Therefore, establishing and maintaining this religion is the most important right for humanity which has been laid down.[44]

It follows then, that the ability to defend this right must also be enshrined, and that the warfare engaged in by Muslims is for the sake of humanity. Ṭabāṭabā'ī elaborates on this when he states:

> Here the war and fighting, to which the believers are called, has been termed as something giving them life. It means that fighting—whether waged for the defence of the Muslims, or that of the Islamic territory or even that which is initiated—is in reality in defence of the right of humanity in this life. Polytheism is the death of humanity and a corruption of nature, and it is the defence of its right that resurrects it and gives it a new lease of life.[45]

Following this, Ṭabāṭabā'ī anticipates that criticisms will be leveled at his argument, claiming that it validates the notion that Islam is an inherently violent religion spread by the sword. He rebuts these claims in two ways.

[43] Ṭabāṭabā'ī, *Al-Mīzān*, 3:79.
[44] Ibid., 84.
[45] Ibid.

First, he argues that criticism directed by adherents to other faiths – and in particular the Abrahamic faiths – are futile, as their scriptures detail the battles and wars waged by prophets.[46] In the case, however, that they did not wage war, it was due to the lack of opportunity or power. Granted, Ṭabāṭabāʾī concurs that prophets sought to guide their communities through dialogue and peaceful engagement; they were not, however, limited to this method of propagating the faith. The second line of argument employed by Ṭabāṭabāʾī rests on his appeal to Islam's concordance with human nature. This concordance, however, can only come about through adherence to God's laws. To bring about this concordance then, is the right of humanity, as its abandonment will lead to chaos and discord. Muslims, however, must follow the protocol of Muhammad and begin by exhibiting patience and engaging in peaceful dialogue, escalating towards violence only so far as the enemy elects to escalate the situation.

Ṭabāṭabāʾī's perspective on Islam's concordance with human nature has significant implications for his discussion on compulsion. For Ṭabāṭabāʾī, compulsion should not be deemed immoral so long as its purpose correlates to the truth. He argues that all nation-states engage in a degree of compulsion in order to maintain public order and that, likewise, compulsion designed to acclimatise the human to the ultimate truth should not be morally questionable.[47] In this regard, he writes:

> There is no need to feel alarmed if jihād has in it an element of compulsion. When explanations, discussions and exhortations fail to bring a group of people onto the right path, and humanity is in disorder and turmoil because of that group's disregard for the basic right mentioned above, then there is no way but to compel them to come onto the right path of truth. This is the strategy adopted by all societies and states throughout the world. The outlaws who flout the laws of the state are first called to accept the authority of the state and obey its laws. Then, if they do not listen, they are compelled by all possible means to do so, even if it leads to killing and fighting. A point to ponder: The compulsion will remain for one generation only. Coming generations will be so taught and trained that they will gladly accept the religion of nature and the creed of the Oneness of God. It is not objectionable if one generation is compelled to see reason, if by that action all coming generations will gladly follow the right path till the end of the world.[48]

[46] Ibid., 87–88.

[47] Ibid.

[48] Ibid.

Muṭahharī

We begin our analysis of Muṭahharī's position on offensive/defensive jihād by outlining his general perspective on war. Muṭahharī sharply rebukes the opponents of war, arguing that their inactivity and cowardice allow injustice to thrive unopposed. He notes that these arguments are illogical in light of the modern world, where all nation-states dedicate a significant portion of their economy to train and maintain an army, so as to defend their state and deter potential aggression. This is not, of course, intended to vindicate or justify offensive warfare. Muṭahharī condemns those who wage war for reasons emanating from ambition or an inflated sense of superiority; nor can one justify a war intended to subjugate others' lands and peoples and exploit their resources. Warfare is only justified if it retaliates against aggression – a defensive measure that seeks to protect, rather than to conquer. In so far as it relates to the offensive/defensive jihād debate, Muṭahharī firmly situates himself within the latter camp.

Muṭahharī goes on to tackle the issue of whether the 'sword verses' are restricted or absolute. Muṭahharī presents the two positions below:

> We can suggest two views here. One view is that we can say that the command is absolute. Because the People of the Book (Jews and Christians) are not Muslims, we are permitted to wage war with them. Further, we are permitted to wage war against any non-Muslim until we subdue them. If they are neither Muslim nor People of the Book, we must wage war with them until they become Muslim or are killed, and if they are People of the Book we must wage war with them until they become Muslim or submit to Muslim rule and pay the jizya (tax for non-Muslim living in Muslim territory). If somebody states that the command is absolute, then they will hold this view. However, somebody could also say that the absolute must be interpreted in light of the restricted. They could argue that, through the use of other Qur'anic verses that mention jihād and its conditions, we are able to understand that the command is not absolute.[49]

Muṭahharī argues that the 'sword verses' should be read as restrictive. As evidence for his position, he posits a jurisprudential maxim concerning the relationship between the restricted and absolute. The maxim posits that if there is an absolute instruction in one part of the Qurʾān, and a restrictive instruction related to it in another part, the former must be interpreted

[49] Muṭahharī, *Jihād*, 13.

through the latter.[50] One example of a restrictive verse that would subsume the absolute verses is:

> Fight in the cause of Allah those who fight you, but do not transgress limits; for Allah loveth not transgressors.[51]

This verse places restrictions on fighting, forbidding the combatants from transgressing limits. As such, absolute verses must be understood through the lens of this verse and the limits that it prescribes. In explaining what these limits are, Muṭahharī writes:

> Its explanation is that you are only to engage in war with those who wage war with you, and this warfare is to take place solely on the battlefield. For example, you and a group of soldiers are to wage war with the enemy soldiers who are prepared and ready for war with you . . . in this situation you are to strike and fight, to wage war, but as for those who are not soldiers, who are not in a state of battle, for example the elderly, women, children, do not oppose them. Do not perpetrate any transgressions against their property, for example do not cut down their trees . . .'[52]

Muṭahharī links this discussion to that of abrogation. Contrary to many exegetes, Muṭahharī argues that the notion that the 'sword verses' in Chap. 9 of the Qur'ān abrogated all previous verses concerning violence and peace is incorrect. He bases his reasoning upon the argument that abrogation is only valid if there is a contradiction between the abrogating and abrogated verse. He explains:

> We can say that a verse functions as an abrogation for a previous verse only if it opposes the abrogated verse. For example, suppose that a verse is revealed and says that you must not engage in war with non-Muslims, and after this another verse is revealed that henceforth grants permission to engage in war. The meaning of this verse would be that God has nullified the former verse and has issued a new order in its place. The meaning of abrogation and abrogated is that the first order has been nullified and a second order has been revealed to replace it. So, the second order must be completely contrary to the first order so that it may be perceived to be the abro-

[50] Ibid., 5.
[51] Qur'ān 2:190.
[52] Ibid., 44–45.

> gation of the earlier order. However, if the verses can be reconciled, so that one explains the other in more detail, then abrogation does not apply.[53]

Based on this reasoning, Muṭahharī argues that the 'sword verses' of Chap. 9 do not abrogate the earlier verses concerning violence and peace, as they attach certain conditions to jihād, rather than completely nullifying earlier verses.

Muṭahharī also outlines the definition and scope of defensive warfare. A nation-state certainly has the right to defend itself against aggression and injustice. Can a nation-state, however, intervene in a foreign conflict to aid an oppressed group or party? Muṭahharī answers in the affirmative. He writes:

> Requesting help is another issue to consider. If an oppressed person or nation requests help from us, is our help permissible or obligatory? If they do not ask for our assistance, is it still permissible, or perhaps obligatory for us to come to their aid? It is not necessary for them to request our assistance. The mere fact that they are oppressed, that oppression [imposed by a government] has formed a barrier to their felicity, a barrier which does not allow the call [to Islam]—that is the source of felicity for the people—to be heard; the call that, if they were made aware of it and were to hear it, would be surely accepted. In this situation, Islam says that you are allowed to break this barrier.[54]

This position is substantiated by Muṭahharī's elevation of sacred values of humanity, and within that framework, the value of freedom. Being universal, freedom is not limited to a particular individual or nation; rather, it transcends artificial boundaries and binds humans together in a sacred pact.[55] As such, it possesses greater significance, and its defence is greater than the defence of one's individual liberties. This position entails an extension of the meaning of the term 'defence': jihād is not solely lawful *in* defence, but also *for* defence. In explaining these points, he writes:

> ...however from the perspective of human ideals a right has been transgressed. Within the society that he lives in, neither his material rights nor his personal rights have been transgressed, yet a right that relates to the better-

[53] Ibid., 91–92.
[54] Ibid., 49.
[55] Ibid., 24.

> ment of humanity has been transgressed. For example, in a society in which both good and evil exist, the good must surely be established, whereas the bad must be driven out of society. Now, under these conditions, if a person were to see that the good was viewed as evil, and that evil were seen to be good, and for the sake of enjoining good and forbidding evil, decided to stand up and take a stance. What exactly are they protecting or defending? Is he defending his personal rights? No. Is he defending the civil rights of the people? No. He defends the spiritual right that transcends nations or tribes, a right that is connected to humanity at large. Do we condemn this man's jihād, or do we view it as sacred? Surely, we must view it as sacred, for it concerns the defence of human rights.[56]

This section concludes with Muṭahharī's foray into compulsion and freedom of religion. Muṭahharī begins by outlining the different opinions that scholars hold concerning this issue. He acknowledges that some believe that monotheism belongs in the category of general human rights, as Ṭabāṭabā'ī previously argued; others however, deem it a personal right in which no other individual possesses the right to infringe upon or coerce another individual to alter their beliefs. Muṭahharī adopts a unique stance, one that perhaps places him between the two positions. Muṭahharī believes that monotheism, much like freedom, is a universal human right that transcends individual rights. However, as it is a matter of faith and personal belief, it is not something that can be imposed. He explains further:

> Faith—regardless of whether it is a human right or not—by its very nature cannot be instilled through compulsion. Even if we desired to instil faith through force, we should know that faith cannot be established this way. Faith is belief and disposition. Faith is attraction to, and acceptance of an idea or belief. Attraction to a belief rests upon two pillars. The first relates to the intellectual aspect of the belief, in that the idea or belief must correlate with one's intellect. The second relates to the emotional aspect of the belief, in that the human heart must be inclined towards that belief. Neither the intellectual nor emotional aspects of belief can be instilled through compulsion…When the Qur'an states that there is no compulsion in religion, it does not mean that religion can be imposed through force, but that you must not use force and allow the people freedom of choice in religion. Rather, what the Qur'an is saying is that religion cannot be imposed by force, as whatever is imposed by force is no longer religion.[57]

[56] Ibid., 71.
[57] Ibid., 77–78.

Muṭahharī also brings forth some Qur'ānic verses to support his position. They include:

> There is no compulsion in religion: rectitude has become distinct from error. So one who disavows the Rebels and has faith in Allah has held fast to the firmest handle for which there is no breaking; and Allah is all-hearing, all-knowing.[58]

> And say, '[This is] the truth from your Lord: let anyone who wishes believe it, and let anyone who wishes disbelieve it.'[59]

> And had your Lord wished, all those who are on earth would have believed. Would you then force people until they become faithful?[60]

For Muṭahharī, these verses illustrate that compulsion is futile; one must be truly convinced of the truth of Islam to accept it. Compulsion contradicts the Qur'ānic ethos, which endows the human with the choice to accept or reject faith.

Sālehī-Najafābādī

Of the three scholars analysed in this chapter, Sālehī-Najafābādī represents the reformist strand, and is harshly critical of the jurisprudential discourse concerning jihād. In his works, Sālehī-Najafābādī not only examines and analyses the verses pertaining to jihād, but also offers insights as to how the traditionally dominant view of offensive jihād and its permissibility crystallised within the Shi'i tradition.

Sālehī-Najafābādī is a staunch critic of offensive jihād in all its forms, and inveighs against the interpretations of offensive jihād that justify compulsion of religion. He grounds his interpretation of Qur'anic verses pertaining to violence within two arguments. First, he argues that peace is the default state of affairs between nations – in contrast to earlier jurists who argued that war was the default state.[61] Second, Qur'anic verses and injunctions pertaining to war and killing, particularly those advanced as

[58] Qur'ān 2:256.
[59] Qur'ān 18:29.
[60] Qur'ān 10:99.
[61] Ne'matollāh Sālehī-Najafābādī, *Jihād dar Islam* [Jihād in Islam] (Tehran: Nashre Ney, 2014): 17–18.

evidence for the legitimacy of offensive jihād, are restricted by both context and conditions. Rather than adhering to a schema of abrogation, he argues instead that the restrictive verses function as elucidations of the absolute verses.[62] This is particularly evident in the interpretations he puts forward of the most contentious verses that deal with jihād.

In his interpretation of 2:190–193, Sālehī-Najafābādī mentions several points that reinforce the general thrust of his argument. First, the verses make it abundantly clear that the non-Muslims in this scenario were the aggressors, and that responding to their advances is permitted.[63] Second, the verses forbid Muslims from initiating war, regardless of intent, with only the response to a military offense a valid justification for violence.[64] His analysis of 22:39 mirrors the interpretation offered for 2:190–193. He again emphasises the context of the verse, arguing that it is not only one's right, but one's obligation to defend themselves if militarily attacked by an enemy. However, just as 2:191 explains, there is no justification for initiating war, and it is absolutely forbidden to shatter the peace, even if it is for the purpose of spreading religion.[65] These verses, according to Sālehī-Najafābādī, were not abrogated by later verses that appear to unconditionally support offensive jihād, but act as expositions of those verses, highlighting the necessary conditions to be met for jihād to be justified.

In his critique of the justification of offensive jihād to impose religion, Sālehī-Najafābādī directly addresses the arguments put forward by Ṭabāṭabā'ī. Although he concurs with Ṭabāṭabā'ī that Islam and monotheism accord with human nature and are therefore, human rights, the right to accept or reject them is concurrently a human right. He argues that Islam has never sought to remove the freedom to choose faith, as evidenced by 2:256, and that it contradicts logic to dictate that one human right must be violated so that another can be fulfilled.[66] As well as contradicting the Qur'ānic text and logic, Sālehī-Najafābādī asserts that the imposition of faith contradicts the conduct of Muhammad. In this regard, he writes:

[62] Ibid., 32.
[63] Ibid., 20.
[64] Ibid., 20.
[65] Ibid., 27.
[66] Ibid., 58.

> If launching offensive jihād for the sake of imposing religion were obligatory…then the Prophet of God would have done this, and the best opportunity to do this would have been during the conquest of Mecca, which he conquered and had complete power over it and its inhabitants. However, he did not demand that one choose between accepting Islam or death; rather, he announced that all who remained indoors would be safe…he said to them that they could go, and that they were the freed ones… it is known from this that the Prophet left the non-Muslims to their disbelief, and did not impose Islam in the name of jihād.[67]

How then, did such erroneous interpretations enter and dominate mainstream juristic discourse? The adoption of these false positions, he argues, can be attributed to al-Shāfiʿī, the eponymous founder of the (Sunnī) Shāfiʿī school of law. According to Sālehī-Najafābādī, Shāfiʿī argued – on weak grounds – for not only the permissibility of offensive jihād to impose religion, but also for the obligation to engage in offensive jihād annually.[68] These views were upheld, according to Mahallati, to justify the expansionist policies of the Abbasid Empire.[69] Following his lead, some classical Shi'i scholars uncritically adopted Shāfiʿī's views on offensive jihād.[70] He argues, however, that they contradict the ethos of the Qur'an and the teachings and conduct of the Prophet Muhammad and the 12 Imams. He writes:

> The jurists have said that offensive jihād with peace-seeking non-Muslims is obligatory annually…if this were truly the ruling of God, then surely Imam Alī in his years as ruler would have initiated offensive jihād with peace-seeking non-Muslims, and would have viewed it as a priority. Why then, did the Imam not pursue this line of action? Is this not evidence that this ruling is not sanctioned by God, as if it were, then surely the Imam would not have abstained from performing his duty?[71]

Conclusion

Shīʿī scholars throughout history have engaged with the Qurʾān, each attempting to make sense of their world in relation to the eternal. Their engagements have built a tremendous intellectual heritage, one that

[67] Ibid., 60.
[68] Ibid., 83.
[69] Mahallati, *Ethics of War and Peace in Iran and Shi'i Islam*, 168.
[70] Faghfoory, *Ethics of War and Peace in Islam*, 67.
[71] Sālehī-Najafābādī, *Jihād*, 92.

extends far beyond the material covered in this chapter. This chapter sought to demonstrate their understanding of violence and peace, and its relation to their worldviews. The understanding of violence and peace, as articulated through the Qurʾān, developed and evolved significantly over time, as reflected by the approaches and methodologies of the exegetes. One can perhaps predict that current and future understandings will continue to evolve, reflecting their attempts to grapple with harmonising the eternal and contextual. For the believer, however, the sense of the sacred will continue to permeate the text, as will the challenges of interpreting difficult verses. In this sense, the engagement with the sacred will continue to both comfort and challenge the believer in equal measure.

Further Reading

Meir Hatina, *Martyrdom in Modern Islam: Piety, Power and Politics* (New York: Cambridge University Press, 2014)

Mohammad Jafar Amir Mahallati, *Ethics of War and Peace in Iran and Shīʿī Islam* (Toronto: University of Toronto Press, 2016)

Mohammad Hassan Khalil, *Jihād, Radicalism and the New Atheism* (Cambridge: Cambridge University Press, 2018)

CHAPTER 10

Sacralized Violence in Sufism

Minlib Dallh O. P.

The mystical dimension of Islam (Sufism) has had an ambivalent relationship with the use of force and violence to achieve religious and political objectives. Sufism vacillated between quietism/pacifism and active political involvement. Even though many a Sufi master warned against the dangers of political implications, rulers and sultans used them to secure their worldly power. For many other Sufis, their tasks and duty included the 're-arranging' and 'improvement' of earthly affairs of their communities.[1] This chapter is concerned with this latter strain of Sufism, whose political

Positionality: I write as a Dominican friar, whose field of research focuses on the mystical dimensions of Christianity and Islam, with a keen interest in the complexity of the mystical and esoteric expressions of the Abrahamic faith traditions.

[1] Omid Safi, 'Bargaining with Baraka: Persian Sufism, "Mysticism," and Pre-Modern Politics', *The Muslim World*, 90 (2007), 264.

M. Dallh O. P. (✉)
Candler School of Theology, Emory University, Atlanta, GA, USA

M. Power, H. Paynter (eds.), *Violence and Peace in Sacred Texts*,
https://doi.org/10.1007/978-3-031-17804-7_10

involvement justified armed jihad (God-sanctioned warfare).[2] These Sufis see a complementarity between spiritual (greater jihad) and martial (lesser jihad). Most of them agree that spiritual jihad not only supersedes armed jihad but must be realized before one engages in martial jihad. The Bektashi, Naqshbandi, Qadiri, Tijani, Sanusi and many other Sufi orders in South and Central Asia, the Caucasus and Africa spearheaded martial jihad.

The Qadiri Abdel Qader al-Jaza'iri (d. 1883) led an armed jihad against French colonial invaders in his native Algeria. The Naqshbandi-Khalidiyya Imam Shamil (d. 1871) spearheaded the Caucasian armed resistance against Russian imperial forces. In West Africa, the Tijani al Hajj Umar Tall (d. 1864) headed an army which fought to impose Islamic reforms and later waged a war against French colonial invasion. This contribution focuses on the call for spiritual and armed jihad in the name of Islamic revival, renewal and reform in nineteenth-century West Africa. From 1804 to 1808, the Qadiri Sufi master, Usman dan Fodio (d. 1817), launched a martial jihad which resulted in the establishment of the Sokoto Caliphate. First, the concept of jihad must be clarified.

Jihad: A Polyvalent Concept

Debates over the evolution of the concept of jihad and Sufis' involvement in God-sanctioned warfare or sacred violence (armed jihad) are pervasive. In pre-modern and modern periods, a peace-loving and quietist image of Sufis, who eschewed the use of force and violence, is challenged by the tradition of Sufi warriors. In his book, *Jihad in Pre-modern Sufi Writings*, Harry S. Neal argues that despite the diversity of practices, Sufi writings have advocated both spiritual and armed jihad.[3] Many Sufis were peaceful mystics, while others were exemplary warriors who combined spiritual discipline and martial commitment. Neal seems to conclude that armed jihad had become even more prevalent in the classical period.

In his multiple contributions, David Cook makes a similar argument. He cites the case of 'Abdallah b. al-Mubarak (d. 797) who authored

[2] Christian Décobert, 'Ascéticisme et jihad', *La Guerre juste dans le Proche-Orient ancient et médievale. Approaches historique, philosphique, et juridique*, in Mélanges de l'Université St. Joseph vol. 62 (2009), 253–282.

[3] Harry S. Neal, Jihad *in Premodern Sufi Writings* (New York: Palgrave Macmillan, 2017). See his introduction. The entire book argues for a complementary understanding of Jihad as both spiritual and military endeavour in the classical writings of Sufism.

treatises on asceticism as well as martial jihad. Ibrahim b. Adham (d. 777), one of the earliest ascetics, engaged in jihad of the soul, the tongue and the sword.[4] Cook acknowledges these three forms of jihad.[5] The first form of jihad is a struggle against the lower soul, or purification, to overcome earthly temptations (via *purgativa* in Christian terms). The second is to speak truth and justice in the face of oppression and repression that is 'enjoining the right and forbidding the wrong' (Q 3:104, 110). The third type is the jihad of the sword or armed jihad.

Likewise, al-Raghib al-Isfahani (d. c. 1108) wrote a lexicon of Qur'anic vocabulary, *mufradat al-Quran*, in which he identifies three forms of jihad as well: the jihad of the soul, of the tongue/pen and of the sword. He defines '*Jihad* and *mujahad* [as] to exert the utmost of one's ability to oppose the enemy'. He continues:

> Jihad is of three kinds: fighting the outward enemy, fighting Satan, and fighting the lower self. The three aspects [of jihad] are included in what God has said: strive for God with the striving that is His due [Qur'an 22: 78]; Strive with your property and your lives in God's path [Qur'an 9: 41]; Verily those who have believed and emigrated and striven with their property and lives in God's path [Qur'an 8: 72]; and [the prophet] said 'Fight your passions as you have fought your enemies.' Striving is [accomplished] by means of the hands and the tongue, [the prophet] said 'Fight the unbelievers with your hands and tongues.[6]

Throughout Islamic history, Sufis have advocated jihad of the tongue and pen, jihad against the lower self and jihad of the sword. Regrettably in current literature, the jihad of the sword seems to have supplanted the first two.[7]

Asma Afsaruddin, in her book, *Striving in the Path of God. Jihad and Martyrdom in Islamic Thought*, and her article 'Jihad and Martyrdom in Islamic Thought and History', insists on the evolution of the concept and its polyvalent meanings. She rejects the reduction of jihad (effort) only to

[4] David Cook, *Sufism, the Army and Holy War*, ed. Alexander Papas (Leiden: Brill, 2020), 316.

[5] Cook, *Sufism*, 315.

[6] Al- Raghib al-Isfahani, *Mufradat alfaz al-Qur'an* (Damascus: dar al-Qalam, 1992), 208.

[7] Many classical Muslim scholars wrote extensively about the different types of jihad.

See Ibn Rush al-Jadd, (the grandfather of Ibn Rushd), Ibn Khaldun, Ibn Qayyim al-Jawziya, to name but three.

qital (fighting) and *harb* (war). She directs attention to the Qur'anic ethics of refraining from armed combat, peace-making and patient endurance of hardship and persecution. She explains the historical relationship between a *mujahid* (the person who engages in jihad) and a *shahid* (a martyr).[8] The interplay between martyrdom and jihad sheds light on Sufi's understanding of armed jihad as an act of piety.

A quick look at the etymology of the word is helpful. Jihad means to exert an effort, to strive hard against, to engage in a meritorious struggle (*une conduite vertueuse*). It is the *masdar* [verbal noun] of the fourth form of the root j-h-d, and the form *fi'al* (active participle) is reciprocal, 'exerting effort in the face of an exertion by something or someone else'.[9] The one who exerts effort or engages in a meritorious struggle, effort, or strives hard against something or someone is the *mujahid*. In the Qur'an, jihad (struggle, striving, exertion) is frequently conjoined to the phrase '*fi sabil Allah*' ('in the path of God'), *al-jihad fi sabil Allah*, which means 'struggling/striving on the path or for the sake of God'.[10] Also, the Qur'an often refers to those who 'strive with their wealth and their selves' (*jahadu bi-amwalihim wa-anfusihim*; or 'using one's wealth to support a cause' (Q. 8:72, and 9:20). In Q. 25:52, the Prophet is instructed to not give in to the disbelievers but to strive hard against them with this [Qur'an] (*jadhidhum bihi jihadan kabiran*).

Indeed, jihad as struggle, or strain, or exhaustion, or effort, includes jihad by the tongue/pen, the heart/soul and the sword. Hence, jihad should not be reduced to *qital* (fighting or armed combat) or *harb* (war). Afsaruddin reminds us that 'The term (*harb*) is never used with the phrase "in the path of God" and has no bearing on the concept of jihad.'[11] She continues:

> According to the Qur'anic worldview, human beings should be constantly engaged in the basic moral endeavour of enjoining what is right and forbidding what is wrong (Qur'an 3:104, 110, 114; 7:157; 9:71, 112, etc.). The 'struggle' implicit in the application of this precept is jihad, properly and

[8] Asma Afsaruddin, *Striving in the Path of God. Jihad and Martyrdom in Islamic Thought*, (Oxford: Oxford University Press, 2013), and her article 'Jihad and Martyrdom in Islamic Thought and History', published online by *Oxford University Press*: 3 March 2021, 448–469.

[9] M. A. S. Abdel Haleem, Qur'anic '*jihad*': a Linguistic and Contextual Analysis, *Journal of Qur'anic Studies*, vol. 12 (2010), 147.

[10] Abdel Haleem, 'Qur'anic '*jihad*",148. See Q. 61: 11.

[11] Afsaruddin, 'Jihad and Martyrdom', 450.

> plainly speaking, and the endeavour is both individual and collective. The means for carrying out this struggle vary according to circumstances, and the Qur'an often refers to those who 'strive with their wealth and their selves' (*jahadu bi-amwalihim wa-anfusihim*; e.g. Qur'an 8:72).[12]

Muslim scholars developed the theory of jihad from the Qur'an and Sunnah. By the period of Abdallah b. al-Mubarak (d. 797), who authored the earliest extant book on jihad, the lore associated with the term was consolidated and included references to specific rewards for martyrs who die in battle, spiritual rewards for fighters and prescriptions concerning the protected status of fighters and their families.[13]

Over a millennium, the concept of jihad took different expressions, at times, contradictory meanings were provided. I would agree with Afsaruddin that jihad is not a monovalent concept in the Qur'an or Sunna nor in Islamic mystical thought nor in its legal tradition nor among the commentators of the sacred texts. In her book, *Striving in the Path of God*, Afsaruddin shows convincingly that during the Meccan period, jihad meant a non-violent and patient endurance of hardship. In the Medinan period, Muslims were given permission to engage in armed combat to defend themselves against all attacks or oppression. Since the death of Muhammad, many interpretations of the concept were held. Under the Umayyad (661–750) and then the Abbasid period (750–1258), the concept had a layered meaning, and its political manipulation was even more apparent. Muslim scholars, however, continued to disagree on the exact meaning of the concept.

In addition, it was the jurist Muhammad b. Idris al-Shafiʿ i (d. 820), the eponym of the Shafa'i school of jurisprudence, who was responsible for the key concepts of the abode of Islam (*dar al-Islam*) and the abode of war (*dar al-harb*), referring to the land of non-Muslims where offensive martial jihad was permitted. Imam Shafa'i added a third possibility *dar al-ʿahd* ('the abode of treaty') or *dar al-sulh* ('the abode of reconciliation'). These are territories which signed treaties with Muslim empires. This tripartite division of the world is not found in the Qur'an or Sunna of the prophet.

Afsaruddin notes:

[12] Afsaruddin, 'Jihad and Martyrdom', 449.

[13] Abdel Haleem, 'Qur'anic *'jihad'*', 146. Cook, 'Sufism', 316.

These terms were coined by al-Shafiʿi himself and have no precedent either in the Qur'an or in the hadith literature. Rather they reflect the Realpolitik of his time; international law (*siyar*) was predicated on an existing state of 'cold war' between realms inhabited by Muslims versus those inhabited by non-Muslims, which required constant vigilance on the part of the former against the latter.[14]

Almost five centuries after al-Shafa'i divided the world into three abodes, Ibn Kathir, the fourteenth-century Mamluk hanbali historian and Qur'an commentator, qualified verse 5 of Qur'an suara 9, 'the verses of the sword' (*ayat al sayf*). In the context of persistent attacks by Crusaders and Mongols during the Seljuk and Mamluk periods, jihad as a defensive military activity against external aggressors was promoted and particularly encouraged by certain jurists and scholars. It is in this period that the application of Qur'an 9:5 was extended to non-Muslims and aggressors of Muslim communities, in contradistinction to earlier Muslim exegetes, who applied the verse exclusively to Arab pagans during the Prophet's lifetime.[15] In addition, many jurists and exegetes declared that Qur'an 9: verse 5 abrogated other peace-making verses, such as Qur'an 60:7–8 and 8:61, which required Muslims to coexist peacefully with all those who showed no hostility towards them, regardless of their religious affiliation.[16] The debate is further complicated by the distinction between greater and lesser jihad.

Greater and Lesser Jihad

The best-known hadith (report attributed to Muhammad) associated with the concept of greater and lesser jihad is the following: 'a number of fighters came to the Messenger of God, and he said: "You have done well in coming from the 'lesser jihad' to the 'greater jihad'". They said: What is the "greater jihad"? He said: For the servant [of God] to fight his passions.'[17] The weighty debates concerning the greater and lesser jihad stem from this questionable (or weak) hadith. According to Neal, the

[14] Al- Shafa'i, *al- Risala* ed. Ahmad Shakir (n.p., 1891) 430–432. See also Afsaruddin, 'Jihad and Martyrdom', 462.

[15] Afsaruddin, 'Jihad and Martyrdom', 455.

[16] Ibid., 454.

Neal, *Jihad in Premodern*, 4. John Renard, 'Al-Jihad al-Akbar: Notes on a Theme in Islamic Spirituality', 78 *The Muslim World*, 2007, vol. 78, 228–9.

[17] Neal, *Jihad in Premodern*, 4.

earlier extant source of this hadith is attributed to Abu Bakr Ibn Husayn al-Bayhaqi (d. 1066) in his *al-zuhd al- Kabir*, but none of the six Sunni canonical hadith collections mention it.[18]

In his book, Neal makes a sustained argument concerning the distinction between jihad and *mujahad*, two verbal nouns from the Arabic verb *jahada*. He writes 'while *mujahada* refers to the austerities and ascetic practices employed by Sufis to subdue the lower self, jihad generally refers to the Islamic doctrine of jihad and its primary martial aspect as developed and elaborated in Islamic scripture and juristic treatises'.[19] Many Sufi masters used jihad to mean both martial and spiritual. Abu'l Qasim al-Qushayri in his *Risala* (the Epistles) refers to *mujahada* (spiritual struggle) and Hujwuri in *Kashf al-mahjub* (The Unveiling of the Veiled) mentions the questionable hadith concerning the greater and lesser jihad, 'We have returned from the lesser jihad—meaning from warfare—to the greater jihad… the prophet regarded the struggle (*mujahada*) against the lower self as superior to jihad because the tribulation of *mujahada* was greater than the tribulations of jihad and military campaigns …'.[20]

In his article, 'al-Jihad al- Akbar: Notes on a Theme in Islamic Spirituality', John Renard explains that 'the greatest jihad has meant interior struggle against the baser tendencies and proclivities of the self'.[21] For most Sufis, the demand of spiritual struggle or constant moral and virtuous striving is unquestionably the greater jihad. In his article, Renard discusses (1) 'the mystical interpretations of the prophets and saints, … as exemplary [spiritual] combatants', (2) 'the ongoing definition of "spiritual struggle" … how Muslims have coined a language in which to speak of the subtleties and nuances of that unique challenge that life in the way of God poses to seeker' and (3) 'the three principal methods the spiritual tradition has developed: the phenomenon of spiritual guidance, methods of spiritual discernment, and the use of retreat or seclusion'.[22]

Remarkably, the distinction between greater and lesser jihad crystalized the heart of the debate in Islamic mystical tradition. In the following section, I will focus on a specific modern case which represents Sufi orthopraxis of greater and lesser jihad.

[18] Ibid.; John Renard, 'al-Jihad al-Akbar', 228–9.

[19] Neal, *Jihad in Premodern*, 48.

[20] Hujwuri, Kashf trans. Nickleson

[21] John Renard, 'Al-Jihad al-Akbar: Notes on a Theme in Islamic Spirituality', The Muslim World, vol. 78, no. 3–4 (2007), 225.

[22] Renard, 'Al-Jihad al-Akbar', 225.

Armed Jihad of Uthman Dan Fodio and the Advent of the Sokoto Caliphate

Even though Islam arrived in Sub-Saharan Africa as early as the eleventh century, a major shift occurred in the eighteenth and nineteenth centuries. About a century before the Western colonial conquest of West Africa, a number of notable Islamic Caliphates were established by Muslim scholars and mystics under the banner of Islamic revival, reform and renewal. West Africa was swept by a wave of Islamic revolutionary movements resulting often in the establishment of major Caliphates.

The Qadiri Usman dan Fodio (d. 1817) founded the Sokoto Caliphate in Hausaland (1804–1904). The Tijani al-Hajj Umar Tall (d. 1864) established a Tukulor Emirate and Masina or Hamdallahi Caliphate was founded by the jurist and mystic Ahmad Lobbo (d. 1845) in the Middle Niger region (1818–62).[23] The advent of these politico-religious entities was the result of armed jihad spearheaded by powerful spiritual and political leaders. In this chapter, only the most remarkable one will be considered: the Sokoto Caliphate, which influenced both Masina and Tukulor Emirates.

In 1804, Shehu Usman dan Fodio led an armed Islamic revival movement (jihad), which changed radically the religious landscape of Hausaland and brought into existence the Sokoto Caliphate, which led to profound socio-economic and political transformations in the region and undeniable development in learning and scholarship. The advent of the Caliphate was a defining event and a reference point in the history of Sub-Saharan Africa. Sokoto was the largest imperial power since the collapse of the Songhay dynasty in 1591. The Caliphate was pivotal for Shehu Usman and his successors for the success of Islamic revival and renewal. The jihad was directed primarily against Hausa Muslim rulers resisting reform and intended to root out unorthodox practices in the population.

It is important to remember that Sokoto's armed jihad lasted only 4 years (1804–08), while Usman dan Fodio's itinerant preaching, or jihad of the tongue, across Hausaland took almost 30 years. In the history of West Africa, four years of armed jihad seemed to have eclipsed three decades of painstaking calls for the practice of orthodox Islam based on the Qur'an and Sunna of the prophet.

[23] Hamdallahi is situated in present-day Mali. Although Hamdallahi was the centre of considerable political and economic importance in its day, it has attracted limited scholarly attention. See Mauro Nobili, *Sultan, Caliph, and the Renewal of Faith: Ahmad Lobbo, the tarikh al-fattash and the Making of an Islamic State in West Africa* (Cambridge: C.U.P., 2020).

Sufism and Islamic Revival in West Africa

During the sixteenth century, West Africa underwent a series of changes mainly due to the rise of the Atlantic slave trade. There was a shift of commercial routes from the Sahara Desert towards the Atlantic coasts. In the Sub-Saharan region, the locus of political power changed, and the stabilizing effects of the medieval empires disappeared with the fall of the Songhay Dynasty in 1591. As a result, many smaller political entities emerged to compete over access to the growing Atlantic trade. The increase in the slave trade led to a militarization of West African societies and to political and social volatility, and at times, chaos in certain parts of the region. Thus, Islam in West Africa entered a new phase which was marked by the popularization of Islam via Sufism and Sufi orders, and with it, a strong impetus for reform and revival.[24]

The promotion of armed jihad as a means of reforming society was the most obvious expression of this transformation within Islam in West Africa. The leaders of these armed movements had an obvious religious motive but also a zeal to correct the doctrine and conduct of West African Muslims, particularly those who held political power. The jihad was a legitimate critique of the social, political, and economic conditions within West African societies, which were devastated by the Atlantic slave trade.[25]

John Glover believes that '*Jihad* in this context takes on the aspect of a revolution complete with grievances, a guiding ideology, an organizational structure, and a vision of a post-revolution future'.[26] Sufism played a crucial role in the ideological and organizational realms in most of the reform movements of this epoch. The long-term result of the expansion of Sufism and Sufi orders (Qadriyya, Tijaniyya, Mouridiyya, etc. ...) and the various efforts for Islamic reform and revival were the formation of a new sense of Islamic identity which was discernible prior to western colonial conquest.

The first instance of Islamic reform and revolt in West Africa after the fall of the great medieval empires (Ghana, Mali, Songhay) was initiated by Nasir al-Din, a Berber marabout (religious leader), in 1673. The revolt

[24] See Paul E. Lovejoy's works on Jihad and slavery during the age of Islamic revolutions of the nineteenth century. For example, *Jihad in West Africa During the Age of Revolutions* (Ohio: Ohio University Press, 2016).

[25] H. F. C. Smith, 'A Neglected Theme of West Africa History: the Islamic Revolution of the 19th Century', *Journal of the Historical Society of Nigeria*, vol.2, no. 2 (1961), 169–185.

[26] John Glover, *Sufism and Jihad in Modern Senegal*, (Rochester: University of Rochester Press, 2007), 24.

became nothing less than a revolution against the contemporary political, social and economic situation on the northern bank of the Senegal River valley. His revolution soon spilled over to the southern bank of the river and the 'War of the Marabouts' briefly toppled the Wolof kingdoms of northern Senegambia. This reform was illustrative of the historical context in which later religious conflicts took place.[27]

These religious revolts, in many cases termed as jihad, are not to be viewed as wars of Muslims versus non-Muslims or as holy wars per se. Rather, the Islamic reform movements of West Africa, regardless of whether or not they were violent or peaceful, successful or unsuccessful, are expressions of vigorous critiques of the existing political, social and economic conditions. The goals of the movement were to change the *status quo* by enforcing orthodox Islamic rules and practices.

Like many reformers, the significant character of Usman dan Fodio's movement was the integration of Sufism into his conception of revival. In his case, Sufism was limited to beliefs and practices, vision and miracles but did not include the organizational and hierarchical structure of the Qadiriyya Order. The brotherhood did not serve as the primary vehicle of jihad. Unlike the Murid experience in Senegal, where Amadu Bamba utilized the organization of the Sufi order in addition to Sufi beliefs and practices and made initiation into the order a priority. Usman dan Fodio did not pursue induction into the Qadiriyya order for his followers or utilize the brotherhood to help guide the revolution.[28]

However, for Usman dan Fodio, 'Umar ibn Said Tal, and Ahmad Bamba the mystical experiences of Sufism were an important legitimizing factor for the movement and secured a symbolic capital for the reform leaders. This symbolic capital galvanized disciples for the difficult task ahead and supported the calls for reform made to the ruling class. Throughout West Africa and Senegambia, the nineteenth century witnessed the apex of Islamic reforms and the remarkable growth of Sufism within reformist ideology and Islamic society at large. The historical context behind these trends is quite complex. In spite of the decline of the Atlantic slave trade in the early decades of the 1800s, the disruptive effects of the slave trade continued to plague many parts of the region. Unfortunately, with the rise of cash crop agriculture in the form of peanuts, gum Arabic and palm oil destined for the European market, new life

[27] Glover, *Sufism and Jihad,* 34.
[28] Glover, *Sufism and Jihad,* 52.

was given to an intracontinental slave trade.[29] This intracontinental slave trade was no less devastating for the Sub-Saharan Africans than the Atlantic one.

Boubacar Barry, in his important book, *Senegambia and the Atlantic Slave Trade*, offers a comprehensive background to understanding the emergence and development of Islamic reform movements in the region. Barry argues that from the fifteenth to the nineteenth centuries, a commercial reorientation occurred, which shifted trade routes away from the Sahara Desert towards the Atlantic coast. The reason for the change in trade routes was the ever-increasing volume of commerce with various European powers with their bases on the coast. The shift disrupted the economy of Senegambia, which in turn caused political and social mayhem.[30]

Of course, this new commerce was mainly about the Atlantic slave trade, and its commercial traffic included not only slaves but also grain, hides and other products of the interior meant to support the slave trade or supplement it. The growth of the Atlantic slave trade was accompanied by an increase in war and conflict in the region. In some cases, the upsurge of violence was connected directly to supplying captives for sale on the coast, and in others, the conflicts reflected the changing political fortunes of states and societies that were trying to cope with the rise of the coastal trade and the subsequent shifts in political and economic power.[31]

The advent of the Sokoto Caliphate was a product of these changing political fortunes and above all, Usman dan Fodio's zeal for Islamic revival. His military endeavour as an armed jihad contrasts with Lamin Sanneh's description of a peaceful assimilation of Islam in West Africa in the initial period.[32] Jihad as rebellion against an existing state had Islamic legal precedent, but many rulers in Hausaland didn't foresee the gravity of Usman's rebellion.

[29] Ibid., 53, see also Marilyn Robinson Waldman, 'The Fulani Jihad: a Reassessment', *The Journal of African History*, vol. 6, no. 3 (1965), 333–355.

[30] Boubacar Barry, *Senegambia and the Atlantic Slave Trade*, (Cambridge: C. U. P., 2009); Glover analyzes Barry's seminal contribution to the debate, see Glover, *Sufism and Jihad*, 34.

[31] Glover, *Sufism and Jihad*, 35.

[32] Lamin Sanneh, *Beyond Jihad: The Pacifist Tradition in West African Islam* (Oxford: Oxford University Press, 2016). See also John Philips, 'Causes of the Jihad of Usman dan Fodio: a Historiographical Review', *Journal of Islamic Studies*, 2017, vol. 36, 24. 'Muslim scholars in West Africa had traditionally been peacemakers. Many groups such as the Jakhanke and the Kunta of the Sahara were pacifists and considered themselves above jihad.'

The Establishment of the Sokoto Caliphate

The socio-economic, ethnic and religious reasons of the reform and the *jama'a's* military triumph are considered in this section.[33] By the late eighteenth century, the once powerful Kanem-Borno Emirate was faced with numerous problems. The decline of its military effectiveness was attributed to the neglect of its professional corps, both in terms of training and preparedness. The coup de grace was the nineteenth-century Sokoto Jihad, which led to the demise of one of Africa's oldest ruling dynasties, the Saifawa Dynasty, which ruled from the end of the eleventh century to the nineteenth century.[34]

The thrust of Usman's jihad lies in the people's dissatisfaction with the local Muslim rulers and their allies. The Shaykh felt that Muslim communities departed from the original message of the Qu'ran and Sunna of the Prophet both in their ideology and conduct. Nana Asma'u grew up in a transitional age during which Islamic practices were excessively relaxed and her father's reform and revival movement (jihad) sought to return Muslims to the fundamentals of orthodox Sunni Islam. The shaykh denounced local practices as 'innovation' which endangered the vital tenets of Islam.

According to Jean Boyd, 'The fascination of the Shehu's personality is that it combined the fundamental characteristics of two different kinds of men, one the Sufi seeing life as a pilgrimage to a spiritual Mecca, the other the lawyer-theologian who derives his knowledge from his understanding of the Shari'a and wrestles with the realities of building an Islamic state.'[35] Shehu Usman dan Fodio was born in Maratta in 1754 before his family moved to Degel in the state of Gobir. His father, Muhammad Fodiyo, looked after his early Islamic education. Then, as customary, Usman began to move from one master to another to gain advanced knowledge in the Islamic sciences. His influential masters were 'Uthman Bidduri after whom the Shehu moulded himself; Muhammad Sambo, Muhammad Raji,

[33] Usman dan Fodio refers to his community as the *jama'a* meaning community or congregation of believers.

[34] H. M. Maishanu and I. M Maishanu, 'The Jihad and the formation of the Sokoto Caliphate', *Islamic Studies*, vol. 38, no. 1, (1999), 119. Murray Last, 'Contradiction in Creating a Jihad Capital: Sokoto in the 19th Century and Its Legacy', *African Studies Review*, 2013, vol. 56, no. 2, 1–20.

[35] Jean Boyd and Beverly B. Mack, *Collected Works of Nana Asma'u, Daughter of Usman 'dan Fodiyo (1793–1864)*, (East Lansing: Michigan State University, 1984), 1.

Hashimu al-Zamfari. Above all, Shaykh Jibril ibn 'Umar had a central influence on the Shehu's conception of an ideal Muslim community. Shaykh Jibril's uncompromising attitude and his attack on local practices prepared the way for Usman. Let me consider the socio-economic, ethnic and religious reasons of the jihad.

Socio-economic, Ethnic and Religious Reasons of Sokoto Jihad

In his book, *The Sword of Truth: The Life and Times of the Shehu Usman dan*, M. Hiskett notes 'the causation behind the *jihad* and the nature of the Shehu's support may be thought of as a mosaic: some of its pieces are by now clearly delineated, others only dimly discernible, and many more have yet to be discovered'.[36] If the jihad's causes can be compared to a mosaic, the motives of those who joined the fight are equally complex. Muhammad Bello, who led the war on his father's behalf, listed no less than ten different reasons which motivated those who took part in the battles. His account ranges from those who joined to escape the grip of their previous rulers to the most trustworthy ones, that is those who fought to bring about genuine reform and revival of Islam in the region.

In addition to these two groups, the fighters included Fulani bigots who despised non-Fulani and religious scholars who supported the jihad because it was intellectually fashionable. Still other Muslim scholars joined because their students left and became members of Shehu's community. Likewise, many parents supported the jihad because their children responded favourably to Usman's call. Also, worldly benefits and war booty attracted many others. Even fighters who had honest motives at the beginning succumbed to worldly riches later. Finally, young people who grew up in Usman's community had no alternative but to become foot soldiers. Bello believes the true fighters were those who gave up all for the love of God and joined the community in the hope of spreading Islam.[37] In Bello's own assessment, a complex mix of religious, ethnic and socio-economic causes brought people into the community. Undoubtedly, many joined for various causes, but Usman's jihad was motivated by three main reasons: socio-economic, ethnic and religious.

[36] Mervyn Hiskett, *The Sword of Truth: The Life and Times of the Shehu Usman dan Fodio* (New York: Oxford University Press, 1973), 80.

[37] John Philips, 'Causes of the Jihad of Usman dan Fodio', 19.

Socio-economic Causes

On the eve of the jihad, the society of Hausaland was divided by contradictions and conflicts, a mixture of prosperity, social violence and dislocation. Many significant tribal groups were alienated and unrepresented among the ruling elites. In the face of socio-economic injustice, some Muslim scholars were successful in voicing people's grievances and in so doing gained their loyalty. Society was in such a state that even a minor event could ignite a sweeping revolution.[38] In his article 'The Jihad and the Formation of the Sokoto Caliphate', Maishanu describes the socio-political situation of Northern Nigeria at the time. In Hausaland, he observes, the eighteenth century saw the decline of Borno and the rise of Zamfara and Gobir states to political prominence. Though situated in the western part, the rise of these states had repercussions throughout the region.[39]

Indeed, the Borno emirate at the turn of the eighteenth century was militarily weak, its central unity undermined, and vassal states like Bagirmi challenged the central authority. In 1759, the Taureg raids of the northern fringes of Borno intensified and the Emirate lost the control of Bilma Salt mines and the Trans-Sahara trade routes to Ahir.[40] These internal wars led to major population displacement. Shuwa Arabs, Kanembu, Fulani, Manga people and many others were forced to move. The social pressure brought about by these demographic movements culminated in a number of revolts in the region. Towards the end of the eighteenth century, Borno was exhausted by almost half a century of warfare, raids and revolts.[41]

Usman's call to jihad was supported by a large number of Fulanis who settled around Borno and who had, for a long period, felt estranged from the ruling elites. The socio-economic concerns of the local people became obvious to Usman as he travelled around the countryside. He became a critic of corruption, unjust taxation and oppression. Indeed, the propensity of the local rulers for extortion made life unbearable for the commoners. They were subject to seizure of property by the ruling aristocracy and perversion of justice in favour of the rich and powerful. Besides heavy taxation, the peasantry was forcefully conscripted to fight internecine wars.[42]

[38] Ibid.,58.

[39] Maishanu, 'The Jihad and the Formation of the Sokoto Caliphate', 120–1.

[40] Ibid., 120.

[41] Ibid.,122.

[42] Maishanu, 'The Jihad and the Formation of the Sokoto Caliphate', 123

According to John Philips, 'three deepening social contradictions' led to the jihad. Shehu Usman and his followers capitalized on these three contradictions, which provided a fertile ground for revolt upon which the seeds of Islamic revival took roots.[43] The first is a clash between small and local political units versus long-distance trade economies, that is intra-Sudanic trade versus trans-Saharan and trans-Atlantic commerce. The second major contradiction was the conflict between the traditional ruling order based upon pre-Islamic dynasties, which was rooted in non-Islamic myths and rituals and an Islamic society advocated by Usman, in which Muslim scholars legitimated authority and mediated power.[44]

Probably, the third contradiction concerning the enslavement of Muslims is the most poignant. Trans-Saharan and trans-Atlantic slave trades wrought havoc on all aspects of life in the Sub-Saharan region. The slave trade had affected Hausa society profoundly for centuries, but the upsurge of the Atlantic slave trade brought greater violence and unrest. The issue of enslavement became urgent, especially for Muslim scholars, and even more so for the potential victims of slave raids. Indeed, the two competing slave trades, the trans-Atlantic and the trans-Saharan, exacerbated the situation and led to frequent violation of the traditional Islamic exemption regarding the enslavement of Muslims. Most commoners were immediately impacted, and Usman's attacks on the enslavement of Muslims attracted more followers to his preaching tours than any other cause. As time passed, illegal enslavement became a major concern of Usman's teaching, and later would serve as the *casus belli* of the jihad itself.

One of Usman's famous five demands, which he submitted to Sarkin Gobir Bawa in lieu of gifts on the occasion of the Muslim festival, was the release of prisoners. This is often interpreted as a demand for the release of political prisoners, but it is more likely that the Shehu was demanding the release of all freeborn Muslims who had been captured, particularly in Zamfara. Among the prisoners released by Usman's intervention was Prince Abarshi of Zamfara, a prominent Muslim authority of the region.[45]

For the typical supporter of the jihad, these grievances were embodied in the growing arbitrary and despotic rule of the traditional dynasties. Muslims were drafted into their armies to support states that Usman

[43] Philips, 'Causes of the Jihad of Usman dan Fodio', 50

[44] Ibid., 50; see also R.A. Adeleye, *Power and Diplomacy in Northern Nigeria 1804–1906* (New York: Humanities Press, 1971), 5–7.

[45] Philips, 'Causes of the Jihad of Usman dan Fodio', 57.

declared un-Islamic. Also, judges ruled in favour of those who could offer the largest bribes, punished anyone who disrespected them and bestowed upon themselves grandiose titles which have no Islamic ground. These oppressive rulers seem to have been acutely felt in areas where taxation and the administration of justice were wanting.[46]

According to the jihad leaders, the local rulers were guilty of arbitrary punishments and failure to hold trials under the strict rules of procedure and evidence demanded by Islamic law. For example, they replaced the strict, Qur'anic corporal punishment for thieves with fines. Usman criticized the traditional dynasties for claiming the right to rule by heredity and force rather than through consultation. Local rulers imposed unauthorized taxes, such as *kudin gari* and *kudin salla*, a tax on Islamic festival days. They took women without permission and lived with too many wives. The elite ignored the needs of the poor in society while they themselves lived in luxury. Merchants and others involved in commerce and trade across state borders were especially alarmed.[47] It is almost impossible to separate neatly the different causes. The socio-economic and political explanations are intertwined with the ethnic and religious ones.

Ethnic and Religious Cause of the Jihad

Of course, the causes of Islamic revival and reform movements in West Africa from the 1670s until the European colonial conquest in the late nineteenth century are many and complex. Besides the obvious religious reasons, the ethnic component of these movements is often advanced. In the case of Sokoto jihad, Islam gave the Fulani an ideology of social and political cohesion which mobilized them to join the violent reforms. In the case of the Murids in Senegal, there is unmistakable connection between the movement and the Wolof. It is important to note that ethnicity and ethnic identity are complex matters that can easily be essentialized. Adherence to a political and theological cause is often more than ethnic and linguistic. In precolonial West Africa, ethnic, clan, linguistic and regional identity contributed to the success of various jihads. However, the later jihads from the end of the nineteenth to the twentieth centuries were less about ethnic affiliation and more about resistance movements

[46] Murray Last, *The Sokoto Caliphate*, (Longmans: Humanity Press, 1967), xxxi. Philips, 'Causes of the Jihad of Usman dan Fodio', 36 and 53.

[47] Philips, 'Causes of the Jihad of Usman dan Fodio', 54.

against European colonial conquest. Once again, ethnicity and religious motives are integrated into the socio-economic ones.

In Hausaland, the period of wars and turmoil coincided with a rising awareness of Islam among the peasantry. Four categories of people constitute the rural communities that supported the jihad: the settled Fulani scholars, the Fulani herders, the Hausa peasants and the runaway slaves. Usman went on extensive rural tours seeking to convert commoners to Islam and did not visit royal courts until he had a large following. Certainly, the Islamization of Hausa countryside prompted the jihad.

Already by the beginning of the seventeenth century, Muslim scholars in the area started composing various works on Islamic sciences. Islamic learning centres in Kalamburdu, Yandoto, Katsina and Degel emerged before the jihad. A group of scholars held on to the itinerant tradition of Islamic learning, that is to say, moving from one place to another or from one teacher to another. As Islamic awareness increased, scholars became more and more critical of their society's mores. They questioned the existing dispensation with all its iniquity and un-Islamic attitudes. Finally, the growth of slave settlements owned by scholars freed them from patronage and encouraged them to demand the observance of Islamic standards in all aspects of life.[48]

As noted earlier, Usama's followers joined for complex reasons, but the leaders regarded the jihad as fundamentally a religious duty. Those who led the jihad were probably the most educated Muslim intellectuals of their generation. Their conception of a Muslim ideal society was the lynchpin of their philosophy of revolution. For almost all members of West African society, Islamic authority meant scholarship. Usman himself preached that learning was the most important thing for a ruler, and indeed, more important for rulers than for commoners.[49] Ordinary Muslims believed that scholars were the guardians of their written tradition against relapsing and syncretism. Scholars' knowledge gives them the means to communicate across vast distances of space and time. While this does not guarantee their agreement, it does unite them into a self-conscious community with common standards and values. A constant written reference point leads to periodic revival and reform movements

[48] Ibid., 56.

[49] His son, Caliph Bello, would adhere completely to his father's position. The rulers must be the most knowledgeable Muslims in the region. The Fodio family and their entourage were formidable scholars, mystics, and warriors.

motivated by a desire to reach the essence of Islam and prevent unorthodox practices and regressions.[50]

Murray Last aptly notes that 'The war itself was an extension of intensive teaching and preaching.'[51] Certainly, the continued growth of the Muslim community in Hausaland, and the increasing trust in Islamic scholarship as a legitimation of authority at the expense of previous forms of legitimation, facilitated the takeover of existing states in the region and adjacent areas, and even the founding of new states, such as Bauchi and Adamawa.[52] One must admit that it is almost impossible to separate neatly theological and political reasons. They are often combined.

The perennial issue, in Hausaland and elsewhere in the region, was a tendency towards syncretism. Thus, it is not surprising that Islam took on local adaptations, but indigenous beliefs also adopted some Islamic practices. Since there was no impermeable barrier between Islam and other West African religions, Islamic legitimacy affected many non-Muslim traditions. One of the major issues in the jihad was where to draw the line between Islam and other systems of belief and practice. Usman relied on Islamic scholars to solve the problem.

Scholars were held to be the guardians of Islamic tradition against relapsing into syncretism. Their knowledge gave them the means to communicate across vast distances of space and time. Though it did unite them into a self-conscious community with common standards and values, it did not guarantee theological agreement. The Qur'an and Sunna, as written reference points, allow episodic revival and reform movements motivated by a desire to reach the kernel of Islam and keep at bay all forms of syncretism and regressions that obscure the tradition.

The *jihad* was not only a revolt of Muslims against their rulers but also a fight among Muslims. Not only ordinary observant Muslims were divided, but even scholars found themselves on both sides of the violent disputes. Yandoto, the venerable and famous scholarly community where Usman's ancestor Muhammad Sa'ad and the famous al-Bakri had studied, was destroyed by the forces of the *jihad*.[53] No revival or reform movement can prevent chaos within.

[50] Philips, 'Causes of the Jihad of Usman dan Fodio', 22. See Jacques Goody, *The Interface Between the Written and the Oral* (Cambridge: Cambridge University Press, 1987), 133–38;

[51] Murray Last, 'Reform in West Africa: The Jihad Movements of the 19th Century', *History of West Africa*, ed. J. F. A. Ajavi and M. Crowder (London: Longman, 1974), vol. 2, 1. See also Philips, 'Causes of the Jihad of Usman dan Fodio', 21.

[52] Philips, 'Causes of the Jihad of Usman dan Fodio', 21.

[53] Ibid., 24.

This was the result of a long-standing clash between Islam and other systems of belief, which led to heated and acrimonious debates over who was a faithful Muslim. Probably, a majority in the area would consider themselves Muslims. Nonetheless, many of them still engaged in traditional cults and practices which were important to them. The ancestral ceremonies common in the courts of the rulers gave legitimacy to ancient dynasties. The disputes between local forms of legitimation versus Islamic traditions permeated the violent debates between the jihad leaders and their opponents. The former would even utilize the concept of mahdism[54] to boost their position.

In times of unrest and turmoil, the belief that the end of the world would come shortly and that the return of the *Mahdi* (a promised messianic figure) was imminent filled the consciousness of many Muslims. Certainly, such a state of mind played a role in making many Hausa and Fulani ready to fight and die for the cause of Islam. The spread of Mahdism and Sufism predisposed society to welcome an Islamic revival. Indeed, the spread of the Qadiriyya order of Sufis increased the enthusiasm of supporters and added communal organization to their efforts. While the specific impact of the organization as distinct from the general role of Sufism in providing legitimacy to an Islamic scholar who aspired to political leadership may have been exaggerated, there can be no doubt that the Shaykh's Fulfulde poem 'Qadiriyya' was one of the most important pieces of propaganda for the jihad.[55] The tropes of the end of times and the rise of a God-sent leader to restore pristine Islam were a major incentive for supporting the violent jihad.

The Triumph of the Sokoto Caliphate

In 1774, at the age of 20, Usman started his teaching and preaching career. Itinerant preaching went hand in hand with a deepening of his studies of various Islamic sciences. The Shehu's preaching extended far and wide as he journeyed from his own town Degel, in the state of Gobir, to remoter places. His tours took him to the neighbouring states of Kebbi

[54] The myth of the imminent return of the Madhi played a significant role in many Muslim communities throughout the centuries. The Almohad with Ibn Tumart (d. 1130), Muhamad Ahmad (d. 1885), proclaimed himself a Mahdi in Sudan and fought against British colonial invasion.

[55] Abdullah ibn Muhammad, *Tazyin al –Waraqat*, ed. and trans. by Mervyn Hiskett (Ibadan: Ibadan University Press, 1963), p.14. See also Philips, 'Causes of the Jihad of Usman dan Fodio', 28.

and Zamfara and even farther across the river Niger to Illo. At the beginning, he limited his teaching and preaching to the commoners (peasantry, farmers, cattle herders, blacksmiths and weavers) and those who cared to attend his meetings. Thus, for 30 years, he spoke in a confident manner to ordinary people, converted many and stirred others towards orthodox Islamic practices.

However, as his followers and disciples grew larger and larger, he found it necessary to include the ruling classes in his target audience. He visited the local ruler, Sarkin Gobir Bawa, and explained his ideas of orthodox Islam and asked him to observe the sunnah and to establish justice in his land. From there on, Usman took the opportunity to preach freely to the entire community without hindrance. His brother Abd Allah ibn Dan Fodio, remarks, 'the Shehu was enabled thereby to summon (people) to religion, because it came about that those who did not fear God, feared to deny his order because of his connection with the Sultan'.[56]

Usman's increasing influence and the growth of his community alarmed Gobir authorities. During his term, Sarkin Gobir Nafata tried to contain the conflict and adhere to some of the demands for reform. His successor, Sarkin Gobir Yunfa, however, adopted a different course of action. After multiple incidents, the Shehu was ordered to leave Degel, taking with him only his family. He refused to leave his people behind. In 1804, the Shehu and his entire community evacuated Degel to Gudu with their most valuable possessions. This move was considered a Hijra, or migration, which is reminiscent of the Prophet's move from Mecca to Medina in 622. The Hijra was a very significant event for the entire jihad movement. Usman believed that events in his own life mirrored the ones in the life of the Prophet of Islam. His poem '*Munasaba*' and subsequent historians, notably Asma'u, underlined the point.[57]

This emblematic forced migration seemed inevitable. For a certain time, Usman concluded that the clashes between his community and the ruling elites would escalate. He was already laying the ground to prepare his followers for such a situation. He urged his community to arm themselves for self-defence. In Usman's *Masa'il al-Mahimmah* five demands

[56] bid.,86. See Maishanu, 'The Jihad and the Formation of the Sokoto Caliphate', 124.

[57] 'Uthman ibn Fudi, *Bayan Wujub al-Hijra 'ala 'l-'Ibad*, ed. and trans. F. H. el-Masri (Khartoum: Khartoum University Press, and O.U.P., 1978), 143–44. Maishanu, 'The Jihad and the Formation of the Sokoto Caliphate', 126–7; and Philips, 'Causes of the Jihad of Usman dan Fodio', 31–32

were made: (1) the foundation of Islam is the application of Shari'a laws; (2) it is incumbent upon Muslims to follow an Imam or a Caliph; (3) the Hijra or migration from a land of unbelief to the land of Islam is obligatory; (4) those who support unbelievers are themselves to be considered unbelievers; (5) jihad against unbelievers and apostates is obligatory.[58] For the ruler of Gobir, these five points constituted a *casus belli*.

Since his *hijra* to Gudu, the tension between Sarkin Gobir Yunfa and Usman Dan Fodio's community (known as the *jama'a*) intensified. Once Usman was appointed the commander of the faithful, the jama'a considered itself independent from the authorities of Alkalawa and Gobir, the regional sites of power. Muhammad Bello and Abdullah Danfodio were appointed commanders of the army. As Boyd and Mack remark that the Usman dan Fodio did not enjoy vigorous health and was not a warrior. He stayed at the centre of the community with women, children, aged, sick and wounded, but always near the scenes of action, well within the danger zone. In these war zones, there was no place to hide, no food depots to visit and no arsenal from which to obtain weapons.[59] Indeed, many battles were fought and lost with substantial casualties. Muhamad Bello and his uncle Abdullah dan Fodio sustained a considerable loss of men, women and children. Boyd summarizes the hardship endured by Usman's community:

> The women, often hungry and weak from the effects of fatigue and ill health traversed huge distances in the rear of the army. When they could they prepared flour from the whole grain of millet and guinea corn and blended onions, peppers and tamarind for the sauce. Meat and fish, eggs and butter were rare luxuries, medicines unobtainable, their skins cracked because of the lack of oil, water and firewood were hard to obtain. No man or woman with the Shehu on that journey had an easy time. Many were killed or died of disease while others were injured or struggled to master their fears.[60]

Since the hijra of 1804, the fortunes of the community went through cycles of victory and losses. However, after Usman's formal declaration of jihad in *Wathiqat ahl al-Sudan* (the Confidence of the people of Sudan) and the decisive victory at Tafkin Kwato, there was an increase of support for the reform movement. The jihad extended to all the major cities. From

[58] Maishanu, 'The Jihad and the Formation of the Sokoto Caliphate', 126–7.
[59] 'The Essential Nana Asma'u,' in *Collected Works*, ed. and trans. Boyd and Mack, 4.
[60] Ibid.

1805 on, many cities fell, such as Birnin Kebbi, Katsina, Daura and Kano. Finally, in 1808, Alkalawa was taken and Sarkin Gobir Yunfa was killed in battle. The various Hausa states gradually became an Emirate, paying allegiance to Sokoto, the new capital of the Caliphate.

Conclusion

Sufi masters are concerned with devotion, asceticism and spiritual leadership in their communities. Their main responsibility is to guide their disciples on the path of spiritual progress. Even in the case of Sufi masters who acted as generals commanding armies, their political involvement was often rooted in a revolt against socio-political injustice, western colonial invasion or Islamic reformist agenda. They saw themselves as those who order what is good and forbid what is wrong and who observe God's limits (Q. 9: 111–2). The case of Usman dan Fodio is striking. Once the armed jihad was successful, he withdrew from political leadership to become the uncontested spiritual leader of the Caliphate. He did not regard the use of violence as a permanent state of affairs.

Further Reading

Reuven Firestone, *Jihad: The Origins of Holy War in Islam* (Oxford: Oxford University Press, 1999)

David Cook, *Understanding Jihad*, 2nd ed., (Oakland: University of California Press,. 2015)

Christian Décobert, "Ascetisme et Jihad" *Mélanges de l'University Saint-Joseph*, vol. LXII, 2000, 253–283

Maher Charif, "Le martyre et le dijah dans la pensée Islamique moderne" *Mélanges de l'University Saint-Joseph*, vol. LXII, 381–397.

Benjamin C. Brower, The Amir 'Abd l-Qadir and the 'Good war' in Algeria, 1832–1847, *Studia Islamic* 106 (2011), 169–195.

CHAPTER 11

The Predicament of the *Sant-Sipahi* (Saint-Soldier): Sanctioned Violence and Martyrdom in the Sikh Tradition

James M. Hegarty

Introduction

I remember being in a *Gurdwara* with my wife for the *gurpurb* (the anniversary of the birth) of Guru Gobind Singhji some years ago. It was a wonderful event that was full of music and speeches. After a particularly impressive *kīrtan* (devotional song), in which a young boy had played his *tablā* with such vigour that the walls themselves seemed to vibrate, a very young girl, no more than seven or eight, in a dark blue sari, took to the

Positionality: I write as a philologist and historian of Indian religious traditions. I am committed to deepening our understanding of the role of violence in the history of ideas and the relationship of this history to social realities. I am committed to challenging and reducing the use of violence in the name of religion or any other identity construction.

J. M. Hegarty (✉)
History, Archaeology and Religion, Cardiff University, Cardiff, UK
e-mail: hegartyj@cardiff.ac.uk

M. Power, H. Paynter (eds.), *Violence and Peace in Sacred Texts*,
https://doi.org/10.1007/978-3-031-17804-7_11

stage. She proceeded, against a PowerPoint backdrop of gory full-colour illustrations, to enumerate the grisly deaths of some of the martyrs of the Sikh tradition. Throughout this speech, as the slides flicked past, she used the pronoun 'we'. She said: 'We were tortured; we were sawn in half; we were burnt on an iron plate; we were bricked-up alive…' From the perspective of an outsider to the Sikh tradition, this list of horrible final moments, narrated by a young child—using the first-person plural pronoun—was both powerful and incongruous. Of course, it is not necessarily incongruous at all, for a religious tradition, such as that of the Sikhs, within which the idea of martyrdom is of critical importance.

Martyrdom, for the most part, requires that a given martyr is the *victim* of violence (though a death can be self-willed and self-caused, such as through a hunger strike); the martyr's death must, however, be directly caused by their commitment to the values of their faith. For the Sikh, *shahīd*, or martyrdom, is not restricted to death in battle; it requires only the giving up of one's life for the tenets of the Sikh tradition.

There is also an understanding in many religious traditions—and the Sikh tradition is certainly one of these—that the *perpetration* of violence in a just cause—even unto death and consequent martyrdom—is acceptable or, indeed, to be valorised. I will refer to this, alongside martyrdom, as *religiously sanctioned violence*. Both the notions of the Sikh as martyr, often as a victim of violence, and the Sikh as, on occasion, an agent of religiously sanctioned violence, have been central to the development of the tradition over the centuries succeeding the original teachings of Guru Nānak.

My titular *sant-sipahi*, or saint-soldier, is, of course, an abstraction. They are the Sikhs called upon to be, potentially, either the victim or the perpetrator of violence, or both. There is both complementarity and tension between the role of *sant* and the role of *sipahi* in Sikh thought, and we will observe this, albeit briefly, across five centuries of Sikh history.

'Sikh Tradition', of course, is also only a label. Contemporary Sikhs are more likely to refer to themselves as adherents of *Sikhi*. This way of expressing Sikh religious identity, as much as the basic meaning of the word Sikh, from the Sanskrit *śiṣya*, which means, in English, 'a student', foregrounds the very practical and 'applied' orientation of the tradition. Another key self-description is that of *gurmat*, which often refers to the Sikh Religion in toto, and refers to the teachings of the Gurus, as they are preserved in the *gurbāṇī*, the poetry and song of the Gurus. A Sikh, ideally, personifies and embodies the ideal represented by the great Gurus of the tradition, beginning with Guru Nānak, as also their teachings, as preserved in their poetic writings. The follower of *gurmat*, immersed in the *gurbāṇī*, strives to be a *gursikh*, a (true) student of the Guru. One should also bear in mind the broader connotations of the word Guru in Sikh tradition, as it encompasses the authoritative religious text, the *Guru Granth Sāhib,* as well as the specific teacher in the lineage of Guru Nānak, and the very idea of God, who is sometimes described as the ultimate Guru. To follow *gurmat*, in the light of the *gurbāṇi*, and to be a *gursikh*, is, above all, to submit to, and reflect, God's order, or *hukam,* and the power of the divine name, or *nām*. As Guru Nānak's *japji*, the text recited by observant Sikhs every day, says:

> At the ambrosial hour of fragrant dawn meditate on the grandeur of the one true Name. Past actions determine the nature of our birth, but grace alone reveals the door to liberation.[1]

The word 'tradition' should be taken to be, in this paper, a very practical term. Donald Kingsbury's much-quoted definition of tradition as 'a set of solutions for which we have forgotten the problems' captures very concisely, if somewhat irreverently, my orientation to this much-used, and much-abused, term.[2] To understand *Sikhi* and the place of martyrdom and sanctioned violence within it, one has to understand the problems to which Sikh communities, taken together, were responding to. In terms of doctrine, liturgy and day-to-day experience, there are deep continuities for the follower of *sikhi,* as well as departures, which are sometimes more or less well marked, as we shall see.

The present paper proceeds through an analysis of the place of martyrdom and sanctioned violence in Sikh literature and wider media from the period of the inception of the tradition to the present day. Such an ambitious timeframe leads inevitably to selection, compression and omission. My argument is a simple one, Sikhs' concepts of martyrdom and sanctioned violence adapt and change to the circumstances of the tradition, but they do so in ways that reflect continuities in the tradition's commitment to devotion, self-sacrifice and the celebration of divine order.

[1] Hew McLeod, ed. and trans., *Textual Sources for the Study of Sikhism* (Chicago: University of Chicago Press, 1984), 87

[2] Donald Kingsbury, Donald, *Geta* (London: Panther Books, 1984), 63.

The *Guru Granth Sāhib*

This commitment finds its first and most enduring expression in the *Guru Granth Sāhib*, the canonical text of Sikh tradition. It was compiled by Guru Arjan (1564–1606), the fifth Guru. The work has 1430 *angs* (pages), in a standardised pagination, and 5984 *shabads* (verse compositions). Each *shabad* is set to a specific melodic mode, or *rāg*. The text consists of the poetic works of six of the Sikh Gurus, namely: Gurus Nānak, Aṅgad, Amar Das, Ram Das, Arjan and Tegh Bahadur (the latter added by Guru Gobind Singh). It also contains the poetry of several non-Sikhs, whose work was considered to be consonant with that of the Gurus (for a history of the development and constitution of the *Guru Granth Sahīb* see Pashaura Singh's monograph on this topic).[3]

The *Guru Granth Sāhib is* not a text that offers a clear doctrine of martyrdom or of religiously sanctioned violence. What we do find is a strong sense of the importance of self-sacrifice, in which self-discipline and devotion are combined in equal measure. Self-sacrifice is of considerable importance to early Sikh tradition. It is enshrined very clearly in the *Guru Granth Sāhib* and has a long and deep history in South Asian religious thought more broadly. One of the most visceral and celebrated of the images of self-sacrifice in the *Guru Granth Sāhib* is that of the devotee offering their own head (at GGS p.421 v.8.18):

> O Nanak, offering his head, one is emancipated, and honored in the Court of the Lord.[4]

This verse has been seen as foundational for subsequent more clearly articulated ideas of martyrdom and sanctioned violence (such as we shall find in later texts that I take up below). The most famous verse in the *Guru Granth Sāhib* that is recurrently related by Sikhs to the concept of martyrdom is as follows:

[3] Singh, Pashaura, *The Guru Granth Sahib: Canon, Meaning and Authority* (New Delhi: Oxford University Press, 2000).

[4] All references and translations from the *Guru Granth Sāhib* are drawn from *SriGranth.Org* a searchable bilingual online e-text of the GGS in its standard pagination. http://www.srigranth.org/servlet/gurbani.gurbani, accessed 22 October 2021.

> If you desire to play this game of love with Me,then step onto My Path with your head in hand.When you place your feet on this Path,give Me your head, and do not pay any attention to public opinion.[5]

To this may also be added a further famous verse, which commences:

> Death would not be called bad, O people, if one knew how to truly die.
> Serve your Almighty Lord and Master, and your path in the world hereafter will be easy.
> Take this easy path, and you shall obtain the fruits of your rewards, and receive honor in the world hereafter.
> Go there with your offering, and you shall merge in the True Lord; your honor shall be confirmed.
> You shall obtain a place in the Mansion of the Lord Master's Presence; being pleasing to Him, you shall enjoy the pleasures of His Love.
> Death would not be called bad, O people, if one knew how to truly die.
> The death of brave heroes is blessed, if it is approved by God.[6]

The role of these verses in subsequent conceptions of sanctioned violence and martyrdom is not open to question; after all, the final line of the material quoted above, 'The death of brave heroes is blessed, if it is approved by God.' is the dedication on the statue of Udam Singh on the Gandhi Gate in Amritsar.[7] Udam Singh assassinated a former British lieutenant governor of the Punjab, Michael O'Dwyer, for his part in the infamous Jallianwala Bagh massacre. We cannot of course, on the basis of subsequent understandings of the *Guru Granth Sāhib,* know what was precisely in the minds of its authors and early audiences. We can say that the text, while being by no means a work of historical commentary, certainly demonstrates an awareness of political context and the challenges of military conflict. Perhaps the most famous verse of this type is:

> Bringing the marriage party of sin, Babar has invaded from Kābul, demanding our land as his wedding gift, O Lalo.
> Modesty and righteousness both have vanished, and falsehood struts around like a leader, O Lalo.[8]

[5] *GGS* p.1412 v.20.
[6] *GGS* p. 579–80 v.2–3.
[7] Louis Fenech, *Martyrdom in the Sikh Tradition: Playing the 'Game of Love'* (New Delhi: Oxford University Press, 2000), 122.
[8] GGS p. 722 v. 1.

Here, Mughal incursion (Babar or Babur is the first Mughal to conquer northern India) is the cause of social decline. In later hagiographies of Guru Nānak, these events are rooted in the religious behaviours of the people of South Asia.[9] In the verses that I have thus far selected, we find the *concept* of self-sacrifice and the *context* of military conflict and consequent social instability very clearly stated. This instability is also cosmographically enshrined in the *Guru Granth Sāhib* by means of its adoption, and adaptation, of the Hindu notion of the *Kali Yuga*, which is the final and most debauched age of humankind in a cosmological schema of four ages (a schema that entered Hindu thought from around the beginning of the Common Era). The emphasis on the *Kali Yuga* runs through the *entire Guru Granth Sāhib* and is reflected in the compositions of not just Guru Nānak but also the other Sikh Gurus, as well as non-Sikh *bhagats*, who contributed to the *Guru Granth Sāhib*, such as the well-known medieval poet-saints Kabīr and Ravidās. This makes it very clear that the idea of the *Kali Yuga* was a preoccupation of both the Sikhs and medieval South Asian religious movements more broadly.

I have argued elsewhere, in relation to a much earlier Hindu text, the *Mahābhārata*, that the idea of periods of cosmic time that are intrinsically unstable is an important means of constituting what I refer to as 'modernity' in South Asian religious texts; by this, I refer to a deep sense of contemporariness combined with a programme to address the particular challenges of the present.[10] Invoking the *Kali Yuga* is one of the strongest signals that a religious text in South Asia can send that it intends to address the *problems of the present*. The brutish *Kali Yuga* offers unique opportunities for religious self-expression (including, in particular, that of self-sacrifice). The very difficulty of the times makes religious 'short cuts' possible, which would not be available in more stable and pious ages. Indeed, Guru Nānak, in the B40 *Janam Sākhī*, an illustrated manuscript that offers a narrative of the life of the founding Guru, tells us of meetings between both the Mughal emperor Babur and the personified form of the

[9] For an extended discussion of this passage in the *Janam Sākhī* literature see my "Hagiography, religious identity and historical imagination in Eighteenth Century Punjab: exploring Sikh narratives of the life of Guru Nānak." In *Rewriting Holiness: Reconfiguring Vitae, Re-signifying Cults*, ed. Madeleine Gray (London: King's College London Medieval Studies, Boydell and Brewer, 2017).

[10] See James Hegarty, *Religion, Narrative and Public Imagination in South Asia: Past and Place in the Sanskrit Mahābhārata*, (Abingdon: Routledge 2012).

Kali Yuga itself.[11] In the latter encounter, Nānak makes clear that he is offering the most appropriate mode of religious self-expression in the final age of humankind; his is the dispensation of 'song and story' (*kirtan* and *kathā*) in a world of hope and fear (*aṣa aṃdeṣa*). Indeed, the *Guru Granth Sahīb* itself says:

> Understand, that whoever sings the Kirtan of God's Praises, has performed all religious rituals.[12]

In the *Guru Granth Sāhib*, there is often an almost millenarian intensity to some of its statements regarding the Kali Yuga:

> The Dark Age of Kali Yuga is the knife, and the kings are butchers; righteousness has sprouted wings and flown away.
>
> In this dark night of falsehood, the moon of Truth is not visible anywhere.[13]

This kaliyugic context is brought together very clearly with the notion of self-sacrifice time and again:

> I am a sacrifice, my soul is a sacrifice, to those who chant the Nām, in this Dark Age of Kali Yuga...
>
> One who is imbued with the Lord's Love is slandered – this is what I have seen in this Dark Age of Kali Yuga...
>
> In this Dark Age of Kali Yuga, only the Nām, the Name of the Lord, shall be of any real use to you...
>
> The Guru's arrow has pierced the hard core of this Dark Age of Kali Yuga, and the state of enlightenment has dawned.[14]

Cosmic and social instability are also brought together explicitly in the *Guru Granth Sāhib*:

> Those who act like tyrants are accepted and approved – recognize that this is the sign of the Dark Age of Kali Yuga...
>
> Chant the Praises of the Lord; Kali Yuga has come.

[11] See Hegarty, "Hagiography, Religious Identity and Historical Imagination..."

[12] GGS p. 902 v. 2.

[13] GGS p. 145 v. 1.

[14] GGS p. 130 v. 1/p.229 v.6/p. 254 v. 20/p. 332 v. 2.

> The justice of the previous three ages is gone. One obtains virtue, only if the Lord bestows it.
> In this turbulent age of Kali Yuga, Muslim law decides the cases, and the blue-robed Qazi is the judge.
> The Guru's Bani has taken the place of Brahma's Veda, and the singing of the Lord's Praises are good deeds.[15]

These three things, namely, self-sacrifice, social instability due to military conflict and the march of cosmic time, will help to configure the succeeding literatures of Sikh Tradition. The *Kali Yuga* becomes the period within which the unique spiritual opportunities of the teachings of Guru Nānak are made available. It will be this later literature that brings these things into a much more explicit relationship with the possibility of, and need for, martyrdom and sanctioned violence on the part of faithful Sikhs.

The *Dasam Granth*

The *Guru Granth Sāhib* is set against a backdrop of military incursion and cosmic decline. It proclaims beautifully and very forcefully the power of devotion and self-surrender to the divine name and, consequently, the power of self-sacrifice to that end. It is not a literature of this-worldly victory, or martyrdom, or religiously-sanctioned violence. The vicissitudes of the contemporary world of Guru Nānak, and the other authors included in the *Guru Granth Sāhib*, are, instead, the jumping-off point for a new religious dispensation that is uniquely suited to the age; ideas of social change, or political self-determination, are not central, indeed hardly even peripheral, to the text; the trappings of such institutions as caste may indeed be set aside before the Ultimate, but the emphasis is very firmly placed on God and not on a casteless society; vain rituals, lip service to that which one does not believe, greed for the goods of life, all of these things are dross and less than dross in the magisterial vision of the *Guru Granth Sāhib*, which demands the cultivation of a wholly consistent love of God that is embodied in thought and deed. The *Japji* itself states:

> If one were to live through all four yugas or even ten times their span; if one were to be famed throughout the world, acknowledged as leader by all; if

[15] GGS p. 902 v. 1 and p. 903 v. 4.

> one were to earn an exalted name and a glory which covered the earth, yet would it all be futile and wasted without the blessing of God.[16]

This is the voice of a tradition that stands still at some distance from the centres of power; in religious texts, the frequency and clarity of such judgements on political authority tend to be inversely proportional to the level of temporal power being wielded. A good deal of the literature that follows the *Guru Granth Sāhib* departs from this model, however. It reflects a tradition consolidating and expanding in various ways; this is a tradition that must come to terms with temporal power, precisely because it is beginning to exercise it. As the number and diversity of Sikhs increase, the institutional and infrastructural framework of the tradition becomes more elaborate and as the sources of revenue diversify, the tradition must also come to terms with violence and the consequences of conflict (especially the consequences of navigating a relationship with state authorities that are superior in might and resource). It is also the case that, as has been true of almost all religious movements of which we are aware, as the Sikh movement grows and becomes more internally differentiated, and regionally powerful, there is internal friction and, indeed, on occasion, open conflict amongst its members.

The *Dasam Granth*, or 'Tenth Book', is a work that is traditionally attributed to the tenth and final guru, Guru Gobind Singh. It reflects a rather different set of problems that were facing the Sikh Tradition and, unsurprisingly, it offers a rather different set of solutions. It is a compilation of materials which are hagiographic, biographic and cosmo-historical in their focus. The authorship and date of most sections of the book are contested by Sikh and non-Sikh scholars.

By the time of the period of Guru Gobind Singh's leadership of the Sikhs, the relationship between the Mughal authorities and the Sikhs had considerably worsened. It was in this context that Guru Gobind Singh founded the Khalsa (traditionally on the 30th of March 1699), a new movement within a movement, which emphasised loyalty to Guru Gobind Singh and was marked by an initiation rite and five markers of identity and belonging, which were to become the most well-known symbols of the Sikh Tradition as a whole. These are, of course, the 'five K's', which are: the long hair and beard or *kesh*, with the former dressed in a turban; the *kaṅgha* or comb worn in the hair and used to maintain it; the *kara*, which

[16] McLeod, *Textual Sources*, 87

is the iron bracelet; the *kachera*, which is the short underwear; and finally, the *kirpan* or dagger, which is to be carried by all those that have passed through Khalsa initiation. It is in the context of this new development in Sikh piety that the *Dasam Granth* takes shape and it is one that brings with it some marked changes in the prominence given to martyrdom and sanctioned violence.

The *chandi charitra* of the *Dasam Granth*, which is an introductory prayer, is reflective of a movement from a discourse of spiritual self-sacrifice and victory, to one that is more earthly, and warlike, in its orientation:

> Strengthen me, O Lord, that I shrink not from righteous deeds. That freed from the fear of my enemies, I may fight with faith and win. The wisdom which I crave is the grace to sing your praises. When this life's allotted course has run may I meet my death in battle.[17]

This text neatly captures a very clear emphasis on both religiously sanctioned violence ('to fight with faith') and martyrdom ('to die in battle'). A yearning for the grace to sing the praise of God still sits at the heart of the verse, but the setting is one that is much more robustly agonistic.

It is the dramatic account of the life of Guru Gobind Singh, the *vichitar nātak*, which forms part of the *Dasam Granth*, that expands very richly upon that which we find in summary in the *chandi charitra*. This fourteen-canto work provides a narrative of the development of the Sikh Panth or community that is very much focused on the specifics of the caste history of the *Khatris* and the *Sodhi* and *Bedi* lineages within this caste group, as they pertain to the Gurus and Guru Gobind Singh himself. These are explicitly warrior lineages. It moves us from cosmic time to traditional history and locates Guru Gobind Singh's guruship in the context of a divine mission distinct from that of Guru Nānak. The opening invocation of this text is itself interesting and in marked contrast to the *Japji* of Guru Nānak:

> Reverently I salute the sword with affection and devotion.
>
> Grant, I pray, your divine assistance that this book may be brought to completion.
>
> Thee I invoke, All-conquering Sword, Destroyer of Evil, Ornament of the brave. Powerful your arm and radiant your glory, your splendour as dazzling as the brightness of the sun.

[17] McLeod, *Textual Sources*, 55

> Joy of the devout and Scourge of the wicked, Vanquisher of sin, I seek your protection.
>
> Hail to the world's Creator and Sustainer, my invincible Protector the Sword.[18]

The militarism of the *vichitar nātak* is pronounced. God himself is said to take up bow, arrow and sword. The paradox of the infinite compassion and militancy of God is captured in the following verse:

> With the battle fiercely joined. He fights with deadly skill. Treasure of kindness and mercy, giver of eternal grace.[19]

The *vichitar nātak* also seeks to squarely place Guru Gobind Singh in the world of the Sanskrit epics of the *Rāmāyaṇa* and *Mahābhārata*. The tendency of those exercising temporal power to integrate their lineage with, or to compare their history, qualities and achievements to, epic characters is not a new one in South Asian history. The epigraphic record of early South Asia furnishes us with numerous examples of this sort of activity.[20] The *vichitar nātak* connects *khatri* lineages to the sons of Lord Rāma himself, the central protagonist of the *Rāmāyaṇa*. Indeed, later in the poem, Guru Gobind Singh completes strict austerities where they had been previously performed by the Pāṇḍava King, who is the central protagonist of the other great Sanskrit epic, the *Mahābhārata*. In canto 8, we find a series of verses dedicated to the success of Guru Gobind Singh in a specific battle, described in a distinctly epic mode:

> When the arrow struck me it roused me to anger. Seizing the bow I returned the fire, loosing a hail of arrows.
>
> The enemy turned and ran as the arrows showered upon them. Taking aim I shot again, despatching another of their number.
>
> Hari Chand [a noted opponent of Guru Gobind Singh] was slain as his soldiers struggled to escape. So too the ruler of Kotlehar, his life cut short in battle.

[18] McLeod, *Textual Sources*, 58

[19] McLeod, *Textual Sources*, 89

[20] See Hegarty *Religion, Narrative and Public Imagination* for details of this tendency in early South Asia.

> And so they fled from the field of battle, running in fear of their lives. Victory was mine, the battle won, the enemy crushed by the grace of the Lord.[21]

This is an example of what I have described elsewhere as the *domestication* of myth; the epic context as well as an epic genealogy are mobilised to provide a setting for a localised and much smaller-scale theatre of activity. Guru Gobind Singh remains the purveyor of devotional wisdom appropriate to the *Kali Yuga*, but he is also a temporal ruler, who offers peace, not only in the ultimate sense, but also 'in our time':

> Thus did a lengthy period pass, the pious sustained and the evil destroyed. The wicked were slain, rendered limb from limb, dying like dogs the death they deserved.[22]

Another well-known and much-celebrated part of the Dasam Granth is the *Zafarnama*, which reflects the cultural and literary diversity of late sixteenth- and very early seventeenth-century India. Guru Gobind Singh writes his poem against the backdrop of Mughal aggressions against Sikhs in Anandpur, which saw the fall of the Khalsa headquarters there in the December of 1704. The *Zafarnama* stands as perhaps the most elegant letters of complaint ever written. It offers sustained criticism of the Mughal emperor Aurangzeb's dealings with the Sikhs, but while certainly sententious, it is also conciliatory. The poem is written in Persian and in a heroic metre in the style of Firdausi's classic epic, the *Shahnama*. In a way quite different to the direct integration of the mytho-history of the *Rāmāyaṇa* and *Mahābhārata*, by means of genealogy and parallelism, in the *Zafarnama*, Guru Gobind Singh uses the language of power of the Mughal court to express his misgivings. In all cases, however, the different epic resonances underscore an agenda of both spiritual and temporal leadership. This is clear in the closing of the *Zafarnama* and its expression of the working of God's favour:

> See how fate's faithless cycles turn
> Over this world and all it holds.
> Use not your strength to harm the weak
> Nor chisel at your promises.

[21] McLeod, *Textual Sources*, 62 (my brackets)
[22] McLeod, *Textual Sources*, 63

However many troops they lead,
No foe harms him whom God befriends.
Nor will a thousand arts allow
A foe to harm one hair of his.[23]

Guru Gobind Singh returns, in the final verses of the *Zafarnama*, to a position much closer to that of the *Guru Granth Sāhib*. He uses the Persianate epic mode *ironically* and in so doing expresses, in marked contrast to the *Vichitar Nāṭak*, whose epic trappings are Sanskritic and much more triumphalist, the limitations of worldly ambitions in contrast to the limitless power of God.

Popular Sikh Histories and Codes of Conduct of the Eighteenth Century

I have focused on two authoritative texts within Sikh tradition, the *Guru Granth Sāhib* and the *Dasam Granth*. These are internally heterogeneous works, but my argument was that the *Dasam Granth* builds on the foundation of self-sacrifice and the deep emphasis on the consistency of thought and action that sits at the heart of the *Guru Granth Sāhib*, in such a way as to yoke this much more forcefully to the need for religiously sanctioned violence and, when required, martyrdom. What has often been interpreted as a discontinuity, in which the serene Guru Nānak is strongly contrasted to the militant Guru Gobind Singh, is not seen as such within much of Sikh tradition and for good reason; there is a continuity, albeit one configured by the historical experience of the Sikh tradition. This historical experience is, of course, a matter of fact and of interpretation, the latter being more persuasive and important than the former in the shaping of attitudes and values over time.

For the follower of *Sikhi*, the ultimate goal is the complete embodiment of the values of the tradition; this is something more often commonly associated with the more ascetic and renunciatory religious traditions of South Asia (in this context, Gavin Flood calls it 'the performance of the memory of tradition').[24] However, in Sikh tradition, this

[23] Christopher Shackle and Singh Mandair, Arvind-pal, 2005, *Teachings of the Sikh Gurus: Selections from the Sikh Scriptures* (London: Routledge, 2005): 144

[24] See Gavin Flood, *The Ascetic Self: Subjectivity, Memory and Tradition* (Cambridge: Cambridge University Press, 2010): 2.

goal is for all Sikhs, the vast majority of whom are active in the world of day-to-day exchange; that is to say, the goal is to be a *gursikh* living in accordance with *gurmat* and the divine *hukam*. The critical thing to bear in mind is that the nature of that embodiment will change as the tradition adapts to new circumstances; this is precisely what we have observed in the context of Mughal rule and a deepening antagonism between Sikh and Mughal authorities; heroism (which, as we saw, was epically configured in a Sanskritic mode and epically undermined in a Persianate one) and a commitment to direct action against aggressors became more prominent and, consequently, self-sacrifice became more agonistically defined. The more internal values of the tradition, namely the meditation on the divine *Nām*, the name of God, did not disappear, far from it, but they became more and more associated with the militant embodiment of tradition enshrined in the *Dasam Granth* and the works that came after it, at least for those that pursued this line of thought and practice. Religious subjectivities within Sikh tradition were increasingly, though not universally, associated with the possibility of, and necessity for, martyrdom and sanctioned violence. Michael Nijhawan, in his excellent *Dhadhi Darbar: Religion Violence and the Performance of Sikh History*, identifies what he sees as an aesthetic opposition in Sikh traditions:

> One of the distinctive features of Sikh religious practice is the variation between meditative-mystical and heroic-passionate aesthetics, which in their mutual relationship lend themselves differently to processes of political and social resignification.[25]

Nijahawan's variation comes close to fusion on occasion, as we have seen, only for these two aesthetic *foci* to move apart once again.

Turning to specific sources that are likely to immediately post-date the *Dasam Granth*, these fall into two classes: the *Gur-bīlās*, which are hagiographic popular histories, and the *Rahit-nāma*, which are codes of conduct. The *Gur-bīlās* literature offers us the best insights into the development of Sikh understandings of martyrdom and sanctioned violence after the period of the *Dasam Granth* and through the eighteenth century. The *vichitar nātak*—which forms part of the *Dasam Granth*—is itself an early example of this genre (though its precise date is a matter of

[25] Michael Nijhawan, *Dhadi Darbar: Religion, Violence and the Performance of Sikh History* (New Delhi: Oxford University Press, 2006): 39.

scholarly debate).[26] The *Gur-bīlās* literature is not extensive in this period (or perhaps better a limited amount has survived to us). The genre includes, among others, the early eighteenth-century *Srī Gur-sobhā* by Sainapati (1711 CE), which is a work that glorifies the early Khalsa. It states, '[A Sikh's] fortunes were complete by laying down one's life (*prāṇ dīe hui*) as a Khalsa', to which it adds 'When the poet sings of battle all the warriors are filled with joy.'[27] It also includes *Gur-bīlās Pātśāhī*, which is attributed to Koer Singh (mid-eighteenth century). This text also strongly extols the virtue and power of the Khalsa. It provides an account of the life of Guru Gobind Singh and the martyrdom, amongst others, of the Guru's faithful companion and noted scholar, Bhai Mani Singh. There is no doubt that it is in this literature that the *sant-sipahi* becomes prominent. However, it is important to keep in mind that we are reading the early literature of the Khalsa here; it is not at all clear that these rich literary evocations of the heroism, devotion and power of the Khalsa were a direct reflection of the facts 'on the ground'. Indeed, there is considerable evidence of a diversity of views and indeed a diversity of forms of Sikh identity in this period. What we are seeing is the construction of an ideal.

We also find, in this period, the early *Rahit Nāma* literature, which, as manuals of preferred Sikh conduct, gives a more 'practical' and 'applied' perspective on Sikh life. The majority of these also reflect the concerns of the Khalsa, though it is important to note that the Khalsa was not internally homogeneous, as these texts make clear (for details see McLeod:2003). One does not find the heroic pyrotechnics of the *Gur-bīlās* literature in the *Rahit*. The meditative-mystical and heroic-passionate aesthetics are nevertheless in evidence and are taken to be characteristic of the *sant-sipahi*. The *Nasīhat-nāmā* (also known as the *Tanakhāh-Nāmā*) is an early example of a *Rahit* dating to 1718–1719 CE. It says:

> A Sikh of the Khalsa remains absorbed in the divine Name and always repeats it... A Khalsa breaks free from that which binds him. A Khalsa is exalted to kingly rank...
>
> ...Never go unarmed. A Khalsa always carries weapons. A Khalsa never turns his back when fighting. A Khalsa destroys those who oppress [others]. A Khalsa knows how to ride a spirited steed. A Khalsa is always fighting battles...

[26] See Fenech. *Martyrdom in the Sikh Tradition*: 124

[27] Cited and Translated by Fenech. *Martyrdom in the Sikh Tradition*: 127

> Do not listen to anyone who defames the Guru. Kill him. Never abandon the Guru and follow another.[28]

We also find in the same text considerable hostility to Muslims:

> Do not accept a Turk as your master. Do not salute a Turk. Avoid meat cooked by Turks. A Khalsa (Sikh) fights against Muslims. A Khalsa (Sikh) slays Muslims.[29]

The *Prahilād Rāi* (or *Prahilād Singh*) *Rahit-nāmā* is less explicit in its focus on the Khalsa and enmity toward Muslims (though it does say, 'Have not faith in a Turk'). It reflects a more mundane and domestically settled context, although it dates to a similar period. It seems to speak to a constituency larger than that of the Khalsa. This is true also of another *Rahit* of the period, the *Sākhī Rahit Kī,* which emphasises the daily duties of all Sikhs (and probably dates to the 1730s). Finally, the *Chaupā Singh Rahit-Nāmā* is the least 'Khalsa-normative' of the Rahit literature of this period. It seems to offer a more syncretic and inclusive vision of Sikh tradition.[30] Dating to 1765, it presages a number of key debates concerning Sikh identity and the place of the Khalsa in Sikh traditions. All in all, the *Rahit* offers us a more mundane theatre of activity, in which violence is a possibility, indeed, a norm, and opposition to Islam is becoming more prominent. However, the eighteenth-century literature offers very limited evidence of a consolidated approach to either martyrdom or sanctioned violence. At most, we see some vigorous early presentations of the Khalsa as a vector of a Sikh identity. It will be in the succeeding centuries that martyrdom and religiously sanctioned violence become more and more intimately associated with the Khalsa. This period will also see the Khalsa increasingly come to stand for the Sikh tradition in toto.

[28] Hew McLeod, *Sikhs of the Khalsa: A History of the Khalsa Rahit* (New Delhi: Oxford University Press, 2003), 85–86

[29] McLeod, *Sikhs of the Khalsa*, 86 (my brackets)

[30] This encompasses propitiation of the Goddess Durgā and laudatory references to a specific sub-caste of Brahmins, the Chhibbar Brahmanas. See McLeod, *Sikhs of the Khalsa*, 95

Nineteenth and Early Twentieth Century Sources

If Mughal power and the internal expansion, and diversification, of the Sikh tradition were the key stimuli for the growing emphasis on martyrdom and sanctioned violence in the seventeenth and eighteenth centuries, then British power was the key factor for the nineteenth and twentieth centuries in Sikh history. It is important to note that the Sikh heartlands of the Punjab were not conquered by the British until 1849, which means that British influence on the Sikhs before this time was more limited than for other religious constituencies.

One critical vector of British influence was via the Armed Forces. From 1846 onwards (with the raising of the 14th King George's Own Ferozepore Sikhs), Sikhs began to join the forces of the British East India Company in growing numbers. By 1922, six Sikh regiments were merged to form the 11th Sikh Regiment, which would, after Indian Independence, become The Sikh Regiment of the Indian Army. The record of service of the Sikhs in the British and Indian armed forces is thus both a long-standing and distinguished one. One of the contributory factors for the development of the special relationship between the Sikhs and the colonial and post-colonial armed forces is the constellation of ideas known as 'martial race theory'. After the Indian Rebellion of 1857, the British elaborated ideas of there being more and less 'martial races' in South Asia.[31] This idea was developed to exclude, or reduce the influence of, some communities who were particularly associated with the rebellion in the colonial army (Streets: 2004), such as Bengali Hindus, for example. It suggested that some communities in South Asia, for example those self-same Bengalis, were not as well-suited to military activity as others, for example Sikhs or Gurkhas (as well as Pathans, Garwhals, Afridis, Dogras and others). This was said to be due to a combination of cultural and environmental factors. Regions less associated with agitation for independence and the critique of colonial authority but who had put up a stiff resistance to British incursion seemed, rather conveniently, to top the list of 'martial races'. We shall see that the association of the Sikhs with the colonial military forces was one that led to a deepening sense of the Sikhs as a heroic-passionate rather than a mystical-mediative tradition.

[31] See Heather Streets, *Martial Races: The Military, Race and Masculinity in British Imperial Culture, 1857–1914*, (Manchester: Manchester University Press: 2004).

If a special relationship between Sikhs and the colonial army, and in particular the idea of Sikhs as a 'martial race', was important in the development of Sikh understandings of martyrdom and sanctioned violence in this period, then another important, and related, development was religious reform stimulated by colonial critique. The former was a form of laudatory racism (with a heavy dose of 'boy's own' gender discourse); the latter was an outgrowth of missionary critique, as it played out in the context of grass-root and elite social and political reform movements (encompassing movements for gender and caste 'uplift', for example). It was also stimulated by the *realpolitik* of British divide-and-rule policies, which frequently pitted the interests of one community or group against another in colonial South Asia. The Sikhs were no exception in this regard.

Against this backdrop, what can be said with confidence is that the steady trickle of references to martyrdom and righteous battle in eighteenth-century sources, in the context of the growth and development of the Khalsa, becomes a torrent. Martyrdom and armed struggle, perhaps unsurprisingly in the context of institutionalised racism and complex forms of oppression (both subtle and gross), are reflected in a stream of hagiographies and popular histories that increasingly emphasise the capacity for, and necessity of—often violent—self-sacrifice as a form of legitimate religious expression in Sikh Tradition.

Louis Fenech, in his *Martyrdom in the Sikh Tradition*, offers a rich analysis of how one Khalsa reform movement developed the concept of the martyr, or *śahīd*, in this regard. This reform movement, known as the Tat Khalsa, was reacting both to the discourse of 'martial races' and a perceived need to 'cleanse' Sikh tradition of its more popular, syncretic, 'Hinduised' trappings, such as Brahmin-dependency, Goddess worship and, indeed, the worship of demi-gods and non-Sikh *sants* and *pirs*. This need was originally stimulated by missionary criticisms of 'Brahmin mummery', but latterly also by the application of concepts of religion that emphasised the need for distinct and determinate religious practices and boundaries (ideas that informed colonial census-taking activities). The inconsistency of Hindu and Sikh practices were bemoaned. Islam, very much the other of Sikh tradition in the eighteenth century, was succeeded by a pressure and desire to differentiate Sikh and Hindu practices. A prominent example of response to this form of criticism is that of the Tat Khalsa intellectual, Bhai Vir Singh. In 1914, Vir Singh took up, edited and republished a prominent History of the Sikh tradition, namely Ratan Singh Bhangu's 1841 epic *Gur-panth Prakāś* ('*The History of the Guru's*

Panth'). In Vir Singh's reworking of this text, his *Prāchīn Panth Prakāś* (*'The Former History of the Panth'*), 'undesirable' religious practices and social realities are expunged. These include: Goddess worship; Sikhs in poverty; references to Sikhs rioting; and references to Sikhs committing theft. All these things are removed from the edited account. Indeed, Vir Singh denies they were ever even in the original in some instances.[32] Martyrdom is also similarly 'edited'; where it is described as stimulated by devotion to the Goddess Devī, for example it is reframed as martyrdom for the Sikh community or *Panth*. Vir Singh also pays particular attention to one specific martyr, Taru Singh. Taru Singh is notable because his martyrdom was stimulated by a refusal to submit to having his hair, his sacred *keś*, shorn. This commitment to a sacred identity marker of the Khalsa is of particular significance to the editor for obvious reasons. Fenech suggests:

> Our authors do more than simply narrate historical events. It seems that they desire their readers to actually participate in history by exhorting them to mimic the characteristics personified by the martyrs on whom the text elaborates.[33]

It is worth noting that the focus on a distinctively and uniquely Sikh act of martyrdom serves a 'particularising' agenda. It is part of a larger pattern of the replacement of religious *foci* that are more syncretic in origin with those that are more specifically Sikh. Vir Singh and the Tat Khalsa are much less concerned with the persistence of the popular veneration of Sikh martyrs, for example than with Goddess worship amongst Sikhs. In this regard, the Sikh *shahīd* sits at the nexus of the imputed 'martial qualities' of the tradition and the construction of a significant past that is evermore focused on its distinctive, and particularly its non-Hindu, qualities. The Martyr in Vir Singh's work more broadly performs 'new memories' of tradition in this regard; they were built on the old ones, which dated to a different context of conflict and struggle, but they were dependent on a new context, in which theories of race and the distinctive and clearly demarcated nature of nations and religions was increasingly prominent. It is, however, important to make clear the fact that these shifts in emphasis, while reflecting some real changes in the understanding of Sikh tradition, were not experienced as discontinuous by most Sikhs at the time. The

32 Fenech, *Martyrdom in the Sikh Tradition*, 190.
33 Fenech, *Martyrdom in the Sikh Tradition*, 194.

experience of continuity in the succession of Sikh Gurus is wonderfully well expressed in a popular early twentieth-century English-language account of the lives and deeds of the Sikh Gurus, *the Book of the Ten Masters*, by Puran Singh. Singh writes:

> Gobind Singh is Guru Nanak; but he rides a splendid steed, arms himself with a quiver full of arrows and a mighty bow, has a sword hanging in his belt and a hawk perched on his hand and eyes that sparkle with joy and valour of the soul. His heart is gay because of his uncontainable joy.[34]

Puran Singh's work also provides a much more inclusive vision of the Sikh tradition, which includes eloquent '*śahīdi*' sentiments, which explicitly evoke the religious ideal of the *sant-sipahi* or saint-soldier:

> It was this Amritam [initiation] that changed the docile, poor, fearful disciples into the leonine men of the new Khalsa: Saint-soldiers; who were taught to salute the God and the Master with a naked sword swung high in air… Arms were thenceforward the symbol of a disciple's fervour of soul.[35]

Gobind Singh, in Singh's account, says, to his five faithful disciples:

> I go forward and die for others. With my blood, I will buy them, in this world of trade and money-getting, a moral and physical relief. I covet no more but to die naming Him, with His song on my lips and his Nectar flowing out of my mind; fixed on the one purpose, to die for others and to save them from misery! I therefore pray I may die, not in solitude, but in the battlefield ; and not for my glory, but for the glory of the Song that is deathless.[36]

It seems then that even in the context of a new imperial overlord and in the throes of religious reform, there is both consolidation and further popularising of the ideal of the *śahīd* and of the possibility of religiously-sanctioned violence. This passage also elegantly combines the mediative-mystical with the heroic-passionate aesthetics that we have recurrently observed (following Nijhawan). The internet and Bollywood have done

[34] Puran Singh, *The Book of the Ten Masters* (London: Selwyn and Blount Ltd., 1926), 103.
[35] Singh, *Ten Masters*, 103 (my brackets).
[36] Singh, *Ten Masters*, 108

nothing to change this, but they have expanded and recontextualised aspects of it. I will now briefly turn to these contemporary sources.

Sikhiwiki

Sikhiwiki is a one-stop reference resource for Sikhs and non-Sikhs alike. Founded in February of 2005, it describes itself as a 'free Sikh Encyclopaedia and learning tool'. It has had just under five million views since its inception. Its entries are checked, but, as with all such platforms, vary with the views and preferences of its authors (within the boundaries of propriety).

It is worth considering *Sikhiwiki's* entry on martyrdom in extenso, for it presents a very clear statement of a popular Sikh approach to religious violence with just cause:

> ...In a whole-life religion, where the spiritual perception is that God is Love, and Destroyer of the evil, martyrdom is an essential institution. For, life is a game of love; and in helping and protecting the weak from oppression, confrontation with the unjust and tyrants, as explained by the Sixth Master himself to Sant Ramdas of Maharashtra, becomes a religious responsibility, in the discharge of which martyrdom of the religious man or seeker sometimes becomes inevitable. It is, therefore, no accident of history that Guru Arjun was the first prophet in the religious history of India to be a martyr of faith. Nor is it an accident that Guru Tegh Bahadur and the Tenth Master sacrificed their all for the cause of truth or religion.
>
> Similarly, it is no accident that for over a hundred years, the Gurus kept an army and struggled with the oppressive Empire involving the loss of life of thousands of Sikhs who are considered, as in the case of Islam, another whole-life religion, martyrs. Secondly, the Sikh Gurus have demonstrated that not only is martyrdom a religious and essential institution, but it is also the most potent method of education and training a people for making sacrifices for the cause of righteousness, love and truth. This is amply proved by the capacity of the Sikhs to make maximum sacrifices for the cause of religion and man. Thus, the prominence of this institution in Sikhism not only shows its whole-life or character; but also clearly distinguishes it from dichotomous, quietist or pacifist systems where this institution is conspicuous by its absence. Hence, the institution of martyrdom in Sikhism, on the one hand, forms its fundamental feature, and, on the other hand, proves its class and character.[37]

[37] https://www.sikhiwiki.org/index.php/Martyrdom_in_Sikhism, accessed 22 October 2021.

As we know, the idea of 'the game of love' is an old one in Sikh tradition and finds expression in the *Guru Granth Sāhib* itself. Here it is connected to a construction of the history of the Sikh Gurus that places emphasis on the fact of the martyrdom of the fifth, ninth and tenth masters of the tradition. The conflict with the Mughals is referenced but with an effort to separate this respectfully from Islam as a religious tradition, which is described as another 'whole life religion' with its own concept of martyrdom. Not just the institution of martyrdom, but the holding of arms is also enjoined and anchored in the activities of the Gurus themselves. In closing, the passage offers what is almost a monothetic definition of Sikhism based on martyrdom. A monothetic definition is one that is based on the identification of one, distinctive, characteristic that uniquely distinguishes a given concept or thing from all others. Here, the 'institution of martyrdom' is that distinguishing feature for the Sikh tradition. It is also worth noting that, in this entry, 'dichotomous, quietist or pacifist systems' are starkly contrasted to the activist nature of the Sikh tradition, which serves 'righteousness, love and truth' in the 'cause of religion and man'. That is to say, Sikh martyrdom encompasses both religious and social goals. Now, the systems that are the subject of this contrast are likely to be those that enjoin *ahimṣa* or 'non-harm', which is the complete abjuration of violence in any and all forms, including that of the butchery of animals. This idea is one that is most prominently associated with Hindu and Jain traditions in South Asia. It is also conceivable, given the emphasis on 'quietism', that some more monastic (including Jain) or 'sannyasic' traditions are being tilted at here (a *sannyasin* is, in ideal-typical terms, a renunciant, who has performed their own funeral rites and stepped away completely from social connections in order to pursue final release from rebirth or *mokṣa*; it is an estate that is particularly associated with Hindu tradition). Finally, the word 'dichotomous', which would otherwise be a curious and difficult to interpret usage, may refer to renunciatory traditions *within Sikh Tradition*, such as those of the Udāsis, who have had a difficult relationship with mainstream, Khalsa, authorities since the late nineteenth century.[38]

The *Sikhiwiki* entry provides, then, a fascinating capstone to our enquiries thus far; it constitutes a sophisticated statement of the utter centrality of the idea of *śahīd*, and the necessity for not just self-sacrifice, but also

[38] See Harjot Oberoi, *The Construction of Religious Boundaries: Culture, Identity and Diversity in Sikh Tradition* (Chicago: University of Chicago Press DATE?)

sanctioned violence, in the mainstream of modern Sikh thought. These ideas are rooted here in both the *Guru Granth Sāhib*, that is to say, in 'the game of love' and on historical experience and a desire for clear boundaries between Sikh ideology and that of Hindus and Jains (admittedly not directly referred to here). We also see, in all likelihood, an effort to distinguish Sikh from other South Asian religious traditions, such as those of the Hindus and Jains, while holding out an olive branch to another 'whole life religion', namely Islam (reflecting the movement towards Islam and away from Hinduism that commences in the nineteenth century). A recent Bollywood retelling of one of the most famous tales of colonial-era Sikh martyrdom builds on all that we have thus far explored, but does so in a way that reflects very contemporary pressures and concerns.

A Modern Bollywood Interpretation of the *Sikh Śahīd*: Kesari

One of the most colourful and compelling demonstrations of the continuing association of Sikh traditions with the idea of martyrdom and the necessity for violence in defence of faith (and nation) is that of the recent Bollywood blockbuster, *Kesari*.

Kesari, or 'Saffron' (more on this colour below), written and directed by Anurag Singh and starring Akshay Kumar, was the fastest grossing Bollywood film of 2019; with the tag line, 'the bravest battle ever fought', the film takes up the events of the battle of Saragarhi, which was a 'last-stand' battle fought on the 12th of September 1897, between the forces of the British Raj—represented by a wholly Sikh force of just 21 men—and Afghan Tribesmen.[39] Saragarhi was a fortified communication post located between the larger forts of Lockhart and Gulistan, which were originally built for the Sikh emperor, Maharaja Ranjit Singh, as part of his consolidation of his Western borders in the early nineteenth century. The 21 Sikh soldiers of the signalling detachment of Saragarhi fought to the last man against some 10–12,000 Afghan soldiers. The battle is commemorated on its anniversary by Sikh military personnel, as also by some civilians.

In its Bollywood retelling, the entire plotline hinges on the incapacity for a Sikh not to intervene in an issue of social justice. This is made clear

[39] *Kesari*, 2019 [Film], Anurag Singh dir. Dharma Productions/Cape of Good Films, Azure Entertainment and Zee Studios: India.

from the film's opening scene onwards. The scene offers a non-too-flattering depiction of Afghan Muslim tribespeople. In it, we see a 'Mullah' at the head of a baying mob of armed men chasing a lone woman. The Mullah remonstrates with the woman in question recalling her to her husband. She refuses to comply with his wishes. Uttering the Bismillāh (6: 08), he calls forth the husband, who prepares to behead his wife. Despite being ordered not to act by his British commanding officer, the ranking Sikh officer, and the film's hero, Havildar Ishar Singh, intervenes. Before he does this, he closes his eyes and calls upon his Guru and his honour with the words, '*wahe Guru, laaj rakhe*' (6:50). This is a paraphrase of a verse from the *Guru Granth Sāhib*,[40] which is a popular Sikh hymn. Straightening his turban (an act that is accompanied by a burst of sub-bass), he leaps forth and, as he descends from a ridge, lethally shoots the husband, who is about to behead his wife. His lone attack on a large mob of Afghans foreshadows the conflict to come. It is also the source of the lasting enmity between the Mullah and Ishar Singh, which plays out in the Mullah's machinations to destroy him and his unit. The sacred, words of both Mullah and Sikh are also offset, with the words of the Sikh proving true, and the intentions of the Mullah, being frustrated.

The other stimulus for the extraordinary to-the-last-man defence at the heart of the film is that Ishar Singh is called 'a slave' by a British army officer, who then goes on to suggest that the subordination of the peoples of India is due to their being 'something rotten in the land' that 'breeds cowardice' (22:09–22:50); the acts of self-sacrifice in Kesari are taken to be a supreme act, in this regard, of self-determination and bravery; a powerful expression of religious and social agency and the ultimate rejection of imperial hegemony. Throughout the film, this is made most clear in the use of the *Jaikara* (lit. 'the maker of victory'—a Sikh war cry), '*bole so nihal … sat sri Akal*'. It is heard at critical moments in the film again and again. It is translated in the film as, 'One shall be forever blessed, who says, God is the ultimate truth!' Its signal use (at 1:18:45–121:22) is when Ishar Singh offers a speech to the assembled men of his unit that explicitly rebuts the words of the British officer. For this speech, Ishar Singh has donned a saffron turban. He rejects the discourse of slavery and cowardice and states that saffron is the colour of sacrifice (by which he, contextually at least, is referring very much to violent self-sacrifice). At the culmination of his speech, he states that he will not fight for money, or the British, nor

[40] GGS p. 821 v. 2.

for himself; he will fight for the martyrs (*śahīdi*), for his community and for his Guru. It is at this moment that one of his subordinates utters the *jaikara* and everyone joins in and repeats the cry a further three times. These are also the words uttered in one of the film's more arresting closing moments, in which the youngest Sikh soldier in the unit, who is only 19, self-immolates and then—using his own flaming body as a light—detonates a bag of gunpowder that he seizes from one of the Afghan tribal leaders (2:23:01-). The *jaikara* is then taken up by the Sikh soldiers assembled at a fort at some distance from Saragarhi in an act of defiance and of respect for their fellow Sikhs (2:24:28).

As well as the *jaikara*, turbans, saffron or otherwise, are important in *Kesari*. The attempt to remove the turban of a Sikh, as an act of humiliation, the very thing that Vir Singh was so concerned with in his editing of the martyrdom of Taru Singh a century ago, is also a matter of profound concern in this film. The attempt to remove Ishar Singh's turban is part of the opening scene, in which, when he is threatened with this humiliation, his brother Sikhs intervene to help him. It also runs through the film as a humiliation promised by the less noble of the Afghan opponents. In a final act of respect, the Afghan tribal leader promises that none of the turbans of the dead Sikhs will be molested in any way (here, the Afghan is very much presented as a fellow representative of a 'martial race').

Sikh agency is also connected, in Kesari, to the idea of the modern independent Indian nation state; the sovereign and warlike Sikh becomes a model of the ideal citizen, who is willing to take up arms on the basis of religious and social values that are distinctive but which are part of an encompassing 'saffron' mosaic. The values of self-sacrifice and violent opposition are presented as integral to creating the conditions for the democratic, independent India that will succeed the despotic British Empire. That this is dangerous ground in a modern context is obvious to any and all modern South Asian audiences; this is because parts of the Sikh community have been locked, for decades, in a struggle for the foundation of an independent Sikh state, Khalistan. This separatist quest has resulted in violence and political killings. The struggle came to international notoriety when it led to the shelling of the Golden Temple by the Indian Army, as part of Operation Bluestar in 1984 and in the subsequent, and consequent, assassination of the Indian Prime Minister, Indira Gandhi, by her Sikh bodyguards in the same year. *Kesari* attempts to yoke Sikh understandings of martyrdom to loyalty to modern India; indeed, the land of

India is powerfully invoked, and martyrdom rendered *territorial*, in the closing song of the film (2:24:30–2:27:59). The last intonation of the *jaikara* in the film, in fact, commences the closing song, which states:

> Do not mourn O Motherland
> For you I'd bear a hundred blows
> May your glory stay intact,
> Whether I live or die.
> My Land, my beloved,
> Your love runs in my veins.
> With every drop of my blood,
> I will ensure your colour never fades,
> to become one with your soil, and blossom as a garden,
> that's all my heart desires;
> to wash away in your rivers, soaring across your fields,
> that's all my heart desires.

The final refrain of this song is 'Colour me Saffron', which is a reference to the auspicious colour of Ishar Singh's turban, of course, but it is the colour also much used by Hindu Yogis and Mahants and, perhaps, most tellingly, a colour beloved of modern Hindu nationalists, who argue for a religiously inflected, Hinduised, vision of India (conceived of in religious and ethnic rather than territorial terms). It seems that martyrdom, which was used in the nineteenth and early twentieth centuries to delineate a distinctive Sikh tradition, is now being mobilised in ways that bring it more into the Hindu nationalist mainstream. It is tellingly done so in the context of *opposition to Muslim* forces; Islam and Muslim communities in India are more and more presented as the 'other' in contemporary Hinducentric political and cultural discourse. The film closes with footage of the memorial to the historic Sikh martyrs of Saragarhi in situ, as also images of two Gurdwaras, one in Amritsar and one in Ferozepur, which were founded in their memory. This movement, to the memorials of the historic martyrs, is a powerful one; it moves us from the internal universe of the film to the external world of lived and 'factual' historical experience. *Kesari* celebrates a distinct Sikh achievement while somehow integrating it, and Sikh conceptions of martyrdom and sanctioned violence, into a popular—nationalist—history of the antecedent qualities and dispositions that made for the founding of the Indian nation state. The saffron-turbaned *sant-sipahi* remains distinctively a Sikh *śahīd* but fights, in the imaginative universe of *Kesari*, for *bhārat māta*, mother India.

Conclusion

It is by now clear that martyrdom and religiously sanctioned violence are of critical importance within Sikh tradition. As ideas and realities, they have been important in and of themselves as some of the most tangible signals of self-sacrifice and faith commitment for Sikhs throughout the history of the tradition. They have also been used, for over five centuries, in sources both by or about Sikhs, to articulate what is distinctive about Sikhs as a religious community. On the mediative-mystical foundation of the *Guru Granth Sāhib* was built a heroic-passionate aesthetic, configured by wider literatures and widely shared cosmo-historical understandings, such as the idea of the Kali Yuga. The idea of self-sacrifice and sanctioned violence in the cause of the spiritual and material concerns of the day has been used time and again to reengage core Sikh ideas with changing social realities and pressures. From the Mughals, via the British, to the Modern Indian State, ideas of martyrdom and sanctioned violence are repeatedly used to test and to creatively integrate core Sikh values and self-understandings with an ever-changing 'modernity'. Religious violence and the idea of religious violence have, in Sikh tradition, been a critical stimulus for reflection and structured change across a vast variety of media and social contexts. While it is important to note that its uses in theory far exceed its uses in practice, it is equally important that reflection and critical commentary on the dangers of such discourse in the context of heightened communal tensions in, and beyond, South Asia should continue.

Abbreviations

GGS *Guru Granth Sāhib* (followed by page and verse number)

Further Reading

Michael Nijhawan, *Dhadi Darbar: Religion, Violence and the Performance of Sikh History* (New Delhi: Oxford University Press, 2006)

Louis Fenech, *Martyrdom in the Sikh Tradition: Playing the 'Game of Love'* (New Delhi: Oxford University Press, 2000)

Harjot Oberoi, *The Construction of Religious Boundaries: Culture, Identity and Diversity in Sikh Tradition* (Chicago: University of Chicago Press, 1994)

CHAPTER 12

Experiences with Violence: Studying Sacred Text in Interreligious Dialogue

Alisha Pomazon

The relationship between violence and peace in the scriptures of various religious traditions attests to the lived experience of human peoples across the globe. The tension that exists between traditions of peace and traditions of violence within sacred texts themselves not only results in a multitude of different interpretations of the texts but also, and more importantly, shows how these different traditions use and understand this relationship in regard to worldly actions. Further, traditions of peace and violence are intertwined within sacred texts and often illustrate the confusion that comes with the pressing need to act and respond to real-life situations. Thus, the connection between lived experience and sacred text is multi-directional. Just as sacred text reflects real-life concerns, so too do people seek to replicate sacred text, and just as one draws from sacred text, one also reads into it. This multi-directionality of sacred texts means that the various processes that makes reading sacred text interesting, inspiring, and life-giving can also make reading sacred text dangerous, especially for

A. Pomazon (✉)
Religion and Culture, St. Thomas More College, University of Saskatchewan, Saskatoon, SK, Canada
e-mail: apomazon@stmcollege.ca

M. Power, H. Paynter (eds.), *Violence and Peace in Sacred Texts*,
https://doi.org/10.1007/978-3-031-17804-7_12

those who are already vulnerable. Moreover, this multi-directionality means that how one reads sacred text becomes vitally important, as how one reads sacred text literally can be the difference between life and death for oneself and others.

Practitioners of interreligious dialogue are deeply drawn to dialogue precisely because of the matters of life and death that are crucial to them. For instance, the International Council of Christians and Jews (ICCJ) formed its mission around its response to the Shoah, World War II, and antisemitism in general. ICCJ emphasizes how Jewish-Christian organizations can counter prejudice and 'the misuse of religion for national and political domination'[1] because of their commitments to human rights and its affirmation to remain loyal to individual faith commitments. As such, theological debate and text study are essential because they provide the forum for expressing how one's faith is connected to action and for reflecting on how religious traditions respond and contribute to issues of war and discrimination. Moreover, when linked to theories of interreligious dialogue, as Randi Rashkover argues, text study provides participants with the opportunity 'to materially and bodily participate' in divine nearness.[2] Thus, studying sacred text in interfaith dialogue gives participants space to confront issues of violence and seek peace by learning about each other's sacred texts and assertions about worldly action. In this chapter, then, I will draw on my own experiences of text study in interreligious dialogue, including Scriptural Reasoning, to analyze the principles and hermeneutics of dialogue that contribute to peacebuilding in interreligious relations. In doing so, I will pay particular attention to the processes of text interpretation that focus on the various examples of religious violence and scriptural study that are found within this volume.

But first, I would like to tell you a story about the most influential moment of my life. Now, certain moments burn such a place in your memory that the minutes that immediately precede and follow blur. You remember these blurred moments, but you only remember them as blurred. And yet, those blurred flashes form more of your memory because they form your impression of the entire situation. At least, this is

[1] 'About Us', International Council of Christians and Jews 'About Us', http://iccj.org/About-us.2.0.html, accessed November 18, 2019.

[2] Randi Rashkover, 'The Semiotics of Embodiment: Radical Orthodoxy and Jewish-Christian Relations', *Journal for Cultural and Religious Theory,* 2002, vol. 3, no. 3, paragraph 24, https://jcrt.org/archives/03.3/rashkover.shtml, accessed June 13, 2022.

how I 'remember' the blurred moments in which I became invested in interreligious dialogue.

I was a newly minted religious studies major, with an interest in biblical studies and Modern Jewish Thought, just having switched my major from pre-journalism, and in my Jesus of Nazareth class. The topic for the day was Jesus in Islam and we had a Muslim guest speaker. I remember being curious and excited, and by the end of speaker's presentation, I was blown away, engaged, bursting with questions. I wanted to speak to our guest, to thank our guest for his presentation and for opening my mind, and to ask all of my questions (or at least, as many as I could!). However, things went sideways quickly. As the question period opened, one student stood up, pointed her finger at our guest, took a step towards him, and screamed, 'What do you know about my Jesus?'

Her scream is still crystal clear in my memory, as is the fear on his face, because that moment has been seared within me. What followed is blurred (probably because of my shock), but what I remember is that our professor, Donald Bolen, stood up and firmly defused the situation. I have no actual memory of what he said, but my impression stays with me.

So, what do I remember? What was my impression? I 'remember' learning about what it means to respect a member of a religious community speaking about its beliefs and practices. I 'remember' our professor's enthusiasm for what our guest speaker was sharing with us. Most of all, I 'remember' the grace of our professor in the face of that student's violent outburst and as he stood up to protect our guest speaker and defuse the situation.

What I did not understand then was that our guest speaker's look of fear was not just related to what was happening with one student. The context of violence that allowed her to stand up and scream at a speaker in class was something that I had not experience before, and therefore, I had no idea of how much his fear was a response to the history of violence directed against Muslims. I still do not know because I have never spoken with him about this matter as I never saw him again. However, looking back, as I tell this story to you, it is his fear that is the clearest part of my memory, and it was my response to his fear that serves as the catalyst for my work as a scholar and my work in interreligious dialogue. I thought: 'never again will I let that happen in my presence.' I wish I can say that was true, mostly because that would mean that interfaith violence would never happen, but it does, and I have learned that while I cannot prevent violence, I can respond to it, mediate it, and defuse it as much as possible.

Of course, at the source of this classroom conflict were 'competing claims' for truth. Who has the 'right' to claim or say something in any given situation tells us about who has the authority to adjudicate the truth and to ultimately control it. The multiple claims for truth that were competing in my classroom that day were also multifaceted: The White Canadian Christian Female Student against the Brown Foreign Muslim Male Guest-Speaker, all under the 'control' of the White Christian Priest Canadian Male Professor, all in the view of the predominantly White Christian Canadian student majority, a group that I was a member of as a White Catholic Woman. While I am aware that not everyone in the student majority was as affected as I was by that moment, we all were shocked, alarmed, and some not a little angry. As we filed out of the class that day, more than one of us stopped to thank our guest speaker, and more stopped than normally would. When it was my turn to thank our guest speaker, what I remember the most was the relief in his eyes.

At that time, I only knew that I had found my purpose and I worked steadily towards grad school. As I reflect back on how my studies moved forward and how my work unfolded, another time proved memorable in my shaping. During the first year of my PhD in Religious Studies, the theory/methodology class that all of us new to this grad school had to take together was 'Religion and Violence'. At that time, I remember most of us did not quite know how to approach the class because, as a whole, we were students of many different traditions (Judaism, Christianity, Islam, Japanese Religions, Hindu Traditions, and Buddhism). Also, we studied many different time periods (Early Judaism, Classical Hinduism, Christian Patristics, New Japanese Religions, and Contemporary Europe) and already had our own sub-disciplines (Anthropology, Philosophy, Theology, Literature, and Ritual Studies), with myself a student of Modern Jewish Thought. Of course, what that meant was that we began the semester as strangers, with our own academic biases, and were, frankly, not just a little competitive. What was also clear was that none of us were happy because the format of the class meant that none of us were 'comfortable'. We quickly learned that navigating these 'feelings' was precisely the point of the class. We were being taught how to be open to the moment at hand and how to participate in material and styles of knowledge that were not our own or of our choosing. Moreover, the subject matter of the class itself, 'Religion and Violence', was difficult to deal with, as we went through analyses of violence in multiple traditions and through multiple methodologies with both shock and horror.

Unsurprisingly, looking back, most of the class members began to meet the night before our seminar at one of the local pubs. I do not think that we meant to create a 'class before class', but that is essentially what we did. In getting to know each other through the class, we realized that the conversations that the class started needed to be continued. Also, since we were all paranoid over the need 'to sound smart' in class (our seminar assignment was to make two verbal points during each seminar), we would go over the material beforehand and work through issues that we were thinking about. So, did we learn how to co-operate and how to think in community? Yes, we did. Did we learn how to deal with our differences? Yes, we did. Did we learn about the evolving nature of knowledge and harsh competitive structures because invariably someone else would take or bring up one of our points the next day in class, meaning that we also had to think fast in order to respond? Definitely, sometimes with delight and sometimes with anger. However, did that stop us from sharing our innermost thoughts about how the material connected with our studies and with our lives? No, and in fact, our little 'class before class' attracted other grad students in the program into our conversation. Later, once our professor learned what we had done during the semester, he laughed and said, 'Well, that explains a few things', and then told me he wished he could have been a part of our pub conversations. Of course, we would never have been able to have those pub conversations if he would have been there because we needed to learn how to become our own community without him (or 'the authority' that he had over our studies).

Learning through the meeting and clashing of opinions, topics, experiences, traditions, and methods during both parts of 'Religion and Violence' not only bonded my class but also shaped the way I thought about Religious Studies as a whole. I still use two of the texts that I read during the class as part of my own teaching twenty years after I took that class. These texts, *Texts of Terror: Literary-Feminist Readings of Biblical Narratives*[3] by Phyllis Trible and *The Scapegoat*[4] by René Girard, play a vital role in my class 'Monsters and Mischief-Makers' as they help us navigate the literary, linguistic, theological, and anthropological underpinnings of ideas of morality, 'sacred' violence, and the creation of the monstrous 'other' in sacred texts and religious practices.

[3] Phyllis Trible, *Texts of Terror: Literary-Feminist Readings of Biblical Narratives* (Minneapolis, MN: Fortress Press, 1984).

[4] René Girard, *The Scapegoat* (Baltimore, MD: John Hopkins University Press, 1989).

Girard, for instance, focuses on how victims of violence are physically represented in myths (or sacred stories) of persecution,[5] which then leads him to theorize that real acts of violence in 'historical persecutions are the result of degraded superstitions'.[6] The connection between real persecution and sacred persecution then becomes very real for Girard because sacred texts provide one with a record of real persecutions while also providing one with a logic that continues the cycle of persecution. As Girard asserts, once one is caught up in the persecutor's standpoint, one 'adopts the representation of persecution that feeds the violence and is fed in return'.[7] The cycle later becomes salvific because the victim of violence, known as the scapegoat, 'indicates both the innocence of the victims,[8] the collective polarization in opposition to them, and the collective end result of that polarization',[9] which is the purging of violence from the collective, or salvation and the creation of the transcendent, or sacred, itself.[10] However, for us, what becomes interesting in Girard's argument is that the stories of these persecutions hide their mechanisms of persecution,[11] and because of their form as sacred text, they hold more power than historical accounts.[12] Thus, for Girard, it is our job to analyze the texts to find out what was hidden in them, which, of course, is also known as the task of the reader in hermeneutics.

The connection between sacred stories and their readers was the basis for Trible's investigation of four biblical narratives in *Texts of Terror*. These stories, the narratives belonging to Hagar, Tamar, the Unnamed Woman of Judges 19, and the Daughter of Jephthah, are among the most harrowing of the biblical text, as they involve abuse, rape, murder, and human sacrifice. Like Girard, we can also see that she asks about the hidden mechanisms of sacred texts. However, unlike Girard, Trible does not focus on theory, but on the tellings of the stories themselves, asserting: 'If terror

[5] Girard, *The Scapegoat*, 35.

[6] Ibid., 37.

[7] Ibid., 39.

[8] In Girard's argument, the innocence of the victim is not acknowledged by the collective but can only be seen in retrospect once the victim's status of the sacred scapegoat is celebrated. Interestingly, I think that we must question Girard in this regard because this argument assumes the innocence of the victim for the charges but does not explain how the collective justified the charges leveled against the victim to itself.

[9] Girard, *The Scapegoat*, 39.

[10] Ibid., 44.

[11] Ibid., 40.

[12] Ibid., 41.

dominates the study, theory does not.... Story-telling is sufficient unto itself.'[13] Trible explains her reasoning by arguing: 'Stories are the style and substance of life. They fashion and fill existence.... Storytelling is a trinitarian act that unites writer, text, and reader in a collage of understanding. Though distinguishable and unequal, the three participants are inseparable and interdependent. Truly, "in the tale, in the telling, we are all one blood".'[14] For Trible, how one experiences the stories is the salient point in all interpretations of sacred text. Thus, part of her task as an interpreter is to 'tell sad stories'.[15] Clearly, Trible's method of close reading the biblical text through linguistic studies of the text is meant to teach her readers how to read as much as teaching the content of these stories themselves.

Two other points from Trible's 'On Telling Sad Stories' are necessary to consider here, and both are with regard to her claim that readers need to 'perceive the Bible as a mirror'.[16] The first point concerns reading text in community and the search for societal change. She asserts: 'If art imitates life, scripture likewise reflects it in both holiness and horror. Reflections themselves neither mandate nor manufacture change; yet by enabling insight, they may inspire repentance. In other words, sad stories may yield new beginnings.'[17] With this point, Trible calls our attention to the needs of a community while reading sacred texts. That is, she helps readers with the fundamentally important need to bring the text into communal spaces for healing. For example, in her chapter on the unnamed woman of Judges 19, Trible asserts that all of the different types of violence enacted upon this woman represent all of the different types of violence enacted upon women in our society. Thus, in reading this story, 'we can recognize the contemporaneity of the story' and to 'take to heart this ancient story, then, is to confess present reality'.[18] However, for Trible, people must go beyond mere reflection in order to act because the call to 'never again' allow violence entails repentance: 'Beyond confession we must take counsel to say, "Never again." Yet this counsel is itself ineffectual unless we direct our hearts to that most uncompromising of all bibli-

[13] Trible, *Texts of Terror*, xiii.

[14] Ibid., n1. Here Trible cites Ursula K. LeGuin, 'It Was a Dark and Stormy Night; or, Why Are We Huddling about the Campfire?' in *On Narrative*, ed. W.J.T. Mitchell (Chicago: University of Chicago Press, 1981), 195.

[15] Ibid., 1.

[16] Ibid., 2.

[17] Ibid., 2.

[18] Ibid., 87.

cal commands, speaking the word not to others but to ourselves: Repent. Repent.'[19] Her call for repentance in this communal regard connects with the second point, which is about the individual reader. The command to repent, always marked by its status as an imperative verb in the second person, is made to an individual, to the 'you', whether one stands alone or is part of a crowd. Trible's point is again clear to the readers: it is you, as an individual, as a member of a community, who needs to experience these stories, your response needs to be personal, your actions must reflect what you have learned in the process, and your identity will be fundamentally changed through these encounters.[20]

In Girard and Trible's work, we see the argument that sacred texts command one to read for oneself. That is, they argue that readers must always experience the text for themselves, as individuals. However, we also see that readers always bring their entire social, historical, political, and religious contexts with them in their readings as these contexts shape who these readers are as individuals, their reasons for engaging with sacred texts, their methods for reading these texts, and their hopes and needs in doing so. Thus, through Girard's points about theory and Trible's points about practical applications, we can better understand how individual and communal elements both work together and against each other in analyses of violence within sacred texts. With these ideas in mind, let us now turn to what we have learned through the course of this book.

The Role and Toll of Violence in Sacred Text

Let's begin with Alan Mittleman, who starts his chapter 'Interpreting Biblical Violence' with a visceral image of violence at the beginning of the biblical narrative. His intent is to make us aware of the inherent cosmic and human violence within the creation texts of Genesis 1–3 by drawing

[19] Ibid., 87.

[20] Fittingly, Trible had already laid the groundwork for this process in *On Telling Sad Stories* as she asks her readers to use the story of Jacob at Jabbok as a guide for their own foray through the texts. This story, found in Genesis 32:22–32, tells us about Jacob's nighttime struggle with a being sent by the divine. After the struggle, Jacob emerges victorious and is blessed but is forever changed, marked both in body and in name. He may be alive, but he now limps and his name has been changed to Israel. Thus, here Trible argues that encounters with violence and terror fundamentally change our identity, as Jacob's new name, Israel (which has historically been translated as 'struggles with God', attests to, cf. Trible, *Texts of Terror*, 4.

our attention to the conflicts, punishments, and later fratricide in Genesis 4, that form the very foundation of the biblical text as a whole. Indeed, he argues, the 'Bible does not minimize or sugarcoat violence. It mirrors—it may even amplify—the violence that infects the human world'.[21] For Mittleman, the significance of this mirrored and amplified violence leads the Bible's readers to not only confront its violence but, in doing so, also 'confront ourselves'[22] by looking at our actions, our ideas, and our justifications about life, humanity, and divinity in general, and specifically, within the Jewish tradition(s). Mittleman asserts that there remains something especially disturbing about biblical violence[23] because the connection between violence and holiness, or sanctioned violence, in the Bible makes its readers pause, be discomfited, critique one's ideas or beliefs,[24] and invites us 'into a conversation about what can be justified and what cannot'.[25]

What is significant here is that Mittleman connects the agency of the actors in the biblical text to the agency of the rabbinic interpreters, and by extension, to any reader of the text. Mittleman's chapter thus takes seriously the humanity of the actors in the text and the actors interpreting the text in ways that legitimate a reader's participation in the text while also acting in the world accordingly. This process of interpretation and participation thus allows the biblical text to stand as the pole star of a 'decent society' in which 'people have dignity and standing, and where the humiliation and the denigration of others is condemned'[26] and serves as a reminder that these 'intergenerational conversations' are necessary as people continually engage with scripture and its interpretation precisely because they find it relevant.[27]

Ali Hammoud's chapter 'Interpretations of Qur'ānic Violence in Shīʿī Islam' focuses on the general topic of the significance of scripture and scriptural hermeneutics within the lives of religious adherents as well. He begins: 'A sacred text is a source of guidance, beauty and spiritual nourishment—a text that directly addresses the heart and soul of the reader.'[28] He

[21] Mittleman, 'Interpreting Biblical Violence,' 54.
[22] Ibid., 54.
[23] Ibid., 54.
[24] Ibid., 55.
[25] Ibid., 59.
[26] Ibid., 72.
[27] Ibid., 72.
[28] Hammoud, 'Interpretations of Qur'ānic Violence in Shīʿī Islam,' 165.

also asserts that a sacred text 'goes beyond merely influencing the believer's actions; rather, it formulates their entire worldview and directs their practical affairs to attain true felicity'.[29] With these statements, Hammoud also sets the stakes of scriptural hermeneutics within Islam and within the framework of this book as a whole as he analyzes the scriptural hermeneutics of the Iranian Shi'ia scholars *Ṭabāṭabā'ī* (1903–1981) and *Muṭahharī's* (1919–1979) work on the concept of jihad in the Qur'ān. In doing so, Hammoud describes the tension between the historical context of scripture and one's own historical realities, and then further how that tension is negotiated with regard to what one's desires for the future are. That is, he points to how people use scripture to shape their present worldviews and their future goals. For instance, in showing us that we must look at the exegete's methodology as well as the intellectual and social mileu in which the exegete lives,[30] Hammoud argues that one must be careful to distinguish the motivations for engaging in the question with one's methodology for doing so. Here Hammoud makes us pay attention to the interplay between the scholar, the scholar's work, and one's own context by describing the connection between present and past scholarly debates about jihad, as historical events lead 'traditional concepts [being] appropriated to suit modern conventions'.[31] Thus, Hammound asks us to look at the work of those in authority in order to ascertain how their work can be used in one's own. Furthermore, Hammoud's chapter itself illustrates the struggle to do what is right with regard to the traditions themselves as there is a clear parallel here between striving to be true to the tradition while striving to do what is good or just within one's own historical setting, and between the care and attention that is given to past interpretations and one's own participation in connecting sacred texts to present realities.

In her chapter 'Roman Catholic Teachings on Violence and Peace: The Credible Re-enactment of the Kingdom', Maria Power argues that theories of Just Peace are central to Catholic Social Teachings on structural violence. For her, Just Peace is both a response to structural violence and a re-statement of Catholic identity that takes into account the evolution of Catholic teachings on peace, violence, scripture, and tradition. She asserts that Roman Catholic teachings on peace and violence since Vatican II thus

[29] Ibid., 165.
[30] Ibid., 169.
[31] Ibid., 175.

require an understanding about the use of scripture and tradition as the foundation for action[32] because active responses to violence stem directly from evolving ideas of Catholic identity and its transmission.[33] As such, Power notes that Roman Catholic responses to violence and its corresponding teachings about peace are not merely theoretical but focused on real-world problems. These teachings on peace, then, are 'ever relevant' for Roman Catholics because all 'members of the Church have a role to play in the interpretation of scripture'[34] as the 'teaching manifest in scripture is viewed as evolving over time and therefore has to be reinterpreted for each new age'.[35] Power thus pays particular attention to and critiques the teachings concerning 'the responsibility to protect'[36] because they may become the means of potential harm for all, not just those who are responsible for the violence. Moreover, Power argues that this harm is not only physical but also causes moral damage and violates overall quests for justice, quoting Cardinal Cahal Daly to prove her point: 'The worst consequences of violence, however, have been moral and spiritual... Human life is now cheaper and more expendable than an armalite rifle.'[37] Thus, Catholic teachings on Just Peace, as Power explains, show us that any type of violence that prevents human life from flourishing and damages human life in any capacity is actually a repudiation of scriptural teachings and the point of the incarnation within Christian thinking.

The responsibility to protect, alongside ideas of divine incarnation, also plays a vital role in Simon Brodbeck's chapter 'Violence and Peace in the Mahābhārata and Rāmāyana'. Here he argues that both texts narrate epic wars and the connections between violence, ritual, and power.[38] Brodbeck describes the violence as acting on two planes at once—the cosmic/divine and the earthly/human. According to his analysis of these two texts, divine violence is juxtaposed to human violence, and while the first is necessary within the larger narrative, the second only comes about because the

[32] Power, 'Roman Catholic Teachings on Violence and Peace: The Credible Re-enactment of the Kingdom,' 145.

[33] Ibid., 145.

[34] Ibid., 146.

[35] Ibid., 147.

[36] Ibid., 149–150.

[37] Ibid., 152.

[38] Brodbeck, 'Violence and Peace in the Mahābhārata and Rāmāyana,' 11.

human responsibility to protect others has been abrogated. Thus, while both epics tell stories of the successes of divine incarnations during battles, Brodbeck argues that these texts teach that violence is acceptable only inasmuch as it is divinely guided for a divine purpose because of the toll war takes on human life;[39] humans who act with violence may 'win the war', but deeply suffer in multiple ways (politically, socially, personally) if action is not divinely guided. Brodbeck points out that the Mahābhārata and Rāmāyana present systems in which responses to past violence becomes a part of each text's message. However, he notes that the Mahābhārata has a different understanding of violence than does the Rāmāyana. The Mahābhārata's King Janamejaya is able to avoid suffering because he does not want to perpetuate the violence of the past, while Rāma's suffering increases throughout the Rāmāyana when divine purpose no longer guides Rāma's actions. Thus, Brodbeck shows us that how survivors cope after war becomes part of the text's message about how violence affects society as a whole, which allows him to conclude that the texts themselves also 'implicitly critique the very theology that they present'.[40]

If Brodbeck shows us how responses to violence work within and throughout sacred texts, Ankur Barua shows us how outside violence affects views of sacred texts themselves. In 'Spectres of Violence and Landscapes of Peace: Imagining the Religious Other in Patterns of Hindu Modernity', Barua argues that 'conceptual archetypes from Sanskrit texts were instrumentalised to configure antagonistic attitudes towards socio-religious outsiders'[41] during India's colonization by Britain. Barua's analysis draws on two main interrelated academic concepts. First, like Brodbeck, Barua describes the connections between sacred cosmology and worldly action, noting how modern scholarship focuses on 'the interweaving between sacred cosmology and socio-political organization in religiously-motivated violence'.[42] Second, Barua's arguments show us how religious violence is used in shaping collective identities, and how these identities thus reflect ideas about of fractured identities, or 'us' versus 'them' identities in general. Furthermore, he notes that Hindu vs. Muslim identities in India are identities that are acutely problematized by the entry of a third

[39] Ibid., 17.

[40] Ibid., 28.

[41] Barua, 'Spectres of Violence and Landscapes of Peace: Imagining the Religious Other in Patterns of Hindu Modernity,' 30.

[42] Ibid., 49.

party, here the British, that seeks to bring 'order' to a fractured society. Barua explains that the British sought to bring order by creating a law code based on sacred texts, but since this third party did not understand the already multivalent identities in these texts, the 'order' enforced only further fractured society and effectively changed the way Hindu groups interpreted their sacred texts as a result.[43] The two examples that Barua uses, the hypermasculinized violence elevated in the Vedas and the diametrically opposed Ahimsa movement by Gandhi, further show that nationalized religious identity, as constructed as a response to external factors, only exacerbates the tension between communities that are already struggling for their 'place' in the political and economic societies. Thus, the main point that we see in Barua's chapter is that when identity is constructed from outside of the tradition or text, the external imposes a different interpretation onto a tradition and a text in ways that forces that community to re-evaluate the textual tradition and the ideas within it, both elevating past textual traditions to support ideas about current political/social/economic contexts (here the Vedas) and expanding core teachings to include new worldly and cosmological realities (here Gandhi's teachings of dharma and ahimsa).

In 'Buddhism and the Dilemma of Whether to Use Violence in Defence of a Way of Peace', Peter Harvey examines foundational Buddhist teachings in both Theravāda and Mahāyāna traditions to discuss the use of violence within nationalist movements and for the protection of Buddhism itself.[44] In doing so, Harvey investigates direct teachings of the Buddha in the Pali Canon and then reflects on how Buddhist leaders follow these teachings while acting in the world. Throughout Harvey's analysis, we can see that Buddhist teachings on and responses to violence reflect the tension between a vision of an ideal existence and a desire to act quickly to protect Buddhism. Essentially, Harvey shows us that responses to violence and its uses depend on whether or not a response takes into account short-term or long-term goals.[45] At the same time, the multiplicity of responses demonstrates Buddhist understandings of human action. For instance, one of Buddha's five ethical precepts to avoid intentionally killing a sentient being is connected to Buddha's key value of non-anger because if

[43] Ibid., 38–39.

[44] Harvey, 'Buddhism and the Dilemma of Whether to Use Violence in Defence of a Way of Peace.'

[45] Ibid., 96.

one practices non-anger, one would be able to avoid killing a sentient being, since killing is often the result of anger. Harvey asserts that Buddhist texts, in this example, the *Dhammapada*, gives a 'realistic assessment… of the negative mental states and tendencies that exist in the human mind, so that fully living up to such ideas is recognized as being a long-term project'.[46] Thus, Buddhist texts teach how one can nurture values and act ethically. Accordingly, Harvey examines how a Buddhist leader moves towards ideal forms of action by both seeing the consequences of violent action and incorporating Buddhist teachings into one's political actions. However, as Harvey points out, one of the major problems here is when defending Buddhism itself brings about violent action.[47] Thus, in terms of Harvey's work in this chapter, we can see that Buddhist teachings and responses to violence show both the necessity for action but the need to mediate that action by paying attention to the consequence of the action and the results on society and people themselves.[48]

Minib Dallh also looks at the connections between violence, political action, and religious reform within the context of 'Islamic revival, renewal and reform in 19th century West Africa'[49] in 'Sacralized Violence in Sufism'. Dallh's analysis begins with a detailed linguistic and historical examination of the term 'jihad' throughout several centuries but focuses mainly on the usage of jihad in Sufi teachings. Essentially, he defines jihad as a struggle or a striving for something in the face of something else.[50] Within the chapter, he asserts that this struggle can be spiritual,[51] for the sake of God,[52] and against those who do not support Islam.[53] Thus, through his investigation of the term, he notes that the term itself is polyvalent and changes in understandings of the term reflect changes in several political, religious, and historical contexts. More specifically, he shows us that the context itself shapes how jihad is understood as a whole by looking at how the martial jihad of Usman dan Fodio founded the Sokoto Caliphate. Fodio's jihad, which was based on 'people's dissatisfaction with

[46] Ibid., 96.
[47] Ibid., 97–98.
[48] Ibid., 117.
[49] Dallh, 'Sacralized Violence in Sufism,' 188.
[50] Ibid., 190.
[51] Ibid., 192.
[52] Ibid., 190.
[53] Ibid., 205.

the local Muslim rulers and their allies',[54] also was 'the result of a long-standing clash between Islam and other systems of belief, which led to heated and acrimonious debates over who was a faithful Muslim'.[55] What we can see in Dallh's analysis is that what is often at stake in jihad is the question of authority and legitimacy of political and religious rule. Therefore, for us, the significance of this chapter lies in its highlighting of the place of religious scholarship in the context of societal violence. Dallh asserts that religious scholars have knowledge that 'gives them the means to communicate across vast distances of space and time'.[56] Thus, when these scholars point out the discrepancies between religious teachings and political practices, especially those that harm others, they give people the grounds on which to fight against their injustices, while also showing that violence is contingent, not permanent, within the overall understanding of jihad in Sufism.[57]

While Dallh investigates the external forces at work in legal and political responses to violence within sacred text, Laliv Clenman analyzes the internal forces at play in 'A Hermeneutic of Violence in Jewish Legal Sources: The Case of the Kippah'.[58] In this chapter, Clenman argues that rabbinic tradition appears to innovate violence when it is not (biblically) mandated in order to assert that the threat of violence in religious legal texts is 'an inherent, necessary and even desirable characteristic' of those texts.[59] She uses the Kippah punishment, a punishment deemed suitable for violent acts that may not be tried according to normal means of due process, to show us that normal means of legal processes do not cover all crimes. Thus, the community needs forms of protection against crimes not covered in the biblical traditions in order to stop inaction.[60] Clenman points out that the rabbis make this violent innovation in order to keep peace, not to enact violence itself, in situations that do not have precedent action, and thus, in 'the face of the unknowable and the insoluble, this violence keeps the peace'.[61] The punishment of the Kippah cell is therefore a

[54] Ibid., 198.
[55] Ibid., 205.
[56] Ibid., 203.
[57] Ibid., 208.
[58] Clenman, 'A Hermeneutic of Violence in Jewish Legal Sources: The Case of the Kippah,' 74.
[59] Ibid., 75.
[60] Ibid., 87.
[61] Ibid., 88.

violence that 'eliminates an irresolvable legal problem'[62] and acts as 'harm-reduction' for the whole community,[63] limiting the violence of the perpetuators of the crimes at hand. Interestingly, Clenman also asserts that both 'Talmuds, using different methodologies, ultimately dismiss or constrain the violence of the *kippah* punishment'[64] because they are clearly uncomfortable with violence as a whole, and especially because of their view that this type of violence is a human action that can be seen as 'in the excess of and in absence of a divine punishment'.[65] However, Clenman does not want to dismiss this aspect of rabbinic legal tradition because this punishment was devised to protect the community as whole, and through 'its violence, the law keeps [the community's] peace'[66] by eliminating greater and more threatening forms of violence that could tear the community's identity apart from the inside.

The connection between idea, ideal, and identity forms the basis of James Hegarty's argument in 'The Predicament of the *Sant-Sipahi* (Saint-Soldier): Sanctioned Violence and Martyrdom in the Sikh Tradition'. According to Hegarty, two points are central here. First, a 'Sikh, ideally, personifies and embodies the ideal represented by the great Gurus of the tradition, beginning with Guru Nānak, [and] also their teachings, as preserved in their poetic writings'.[67] In this point, Hegarty establishes the connection between the Gurus and their actions, the sacred texts, and contemporary Sikhs. To practice the tradition, then, one must learn how to apply its values to one's own life;[68] and so, a Sikh should seek to embody the Gurus' values by following in their literal or historical footsteps,[69] especially the value of active engagement in political and social life through self-sacrifice. As Hegarty asserts, for the Sikh, 'the idea of martyrdom is of critical importance'[70] because it entails one's commitment to ideas of social change and political self-determination that are found in sacred texts. Moreover, Hegarty argues that 'Sikh concepts of martyrdom and

[62] Ibid., 87.
[63] Ibid., 88.
[64] Ibid., 93.
[65] Ibid., 91.
[66] Ibid., 93.
[67] Hegarty, 'The Predicament of the *Sant-Sipahi* (Saint-Soldier): Sanctioned Violence and Martyrdom in the Sikh Tradition,' 210–211.
[68] Ibid., 211.
[69] Ibid., 222.
[70] Ibid., 210.

sanctioned violence adapt and change to the circumstances of the tradition, but they do so in ways that reflect continuities in the tradition's commitment to devotion, self-sacrifice and the celebration of divine order'.[71] Accordingly, the sacred texts continually connect self-sacrifice to devotion to the divine.[72] However, Hegarty also asserts that the idea of religiously sanctioned violence develops throughout the history of the tradition, and as the community comes to terms with the violence that it was subjected to by the Mughal and British Empires[73] and through its own internal struggles.[74] Most importantly, though, Hegarty's points show us that the ideals and ideas of the Sikh tradition are always focused on one's present,[75] and as such, religiously sanctioned violence becomes 'a critical stimulus for reflection and structured change across a vast variety of media and social contexts',[76] even as its use 'in theory far exceed[s] its use in practice'.[77]

Helen Paynter's chapter 'Apologists and Appropriators: Protestant Christian Reckoning with Biblical Violence' clearly delineates the types of violence that appear in the Christian Bible in order to answer the question 'how is the violence of the text to be reconciled with the conventional Christian view of God as all-loving?'[78] In asking this question, Paynter quickly shows us that the Christian view of God as all-loving is often in tension with how God is portrayed in the biblical text. More specifically, we can see in her question that what is at stake in descriptions of violence in the biblical text is how Christian understandings of the 'being' of God are often at odds with the 'actions' of God. The problem that results from this tension is theological in nature, as Christians are to model themselves according to the actions of God since humans were created in the image of God. Thus, how God and the actions of God are understood have significant relevance for Christian action in the world. Paynter points out, however, that many Christians have become (or always were) distinctly uncomfortable with the violence in the text, seeking to create a state of 'shalom', while minimizing, justifying, or historicizing away various types

[71] Ibid., 211.
[72] Ibid., 213.
[73] Ibid., 225.
[74] Ibid., 217.
[75] Ibid., 214.
[76] Ibid., 235.
[77] Ibid., 235.
[78] Paynter, 'Apologists and Appropriators: Protestant Christian Reckoning with Biblical Violence,' 119.

of violence. On a practical level, however, the biblical text has also been used as a justification for contemporary violence, because one is to do as the Bible commands, and if God commanded it, it must be good.[79] Here Paynter's analysis becomes relevant for us more broadly as she shows us how many Christians have historically critiqued the correlation between 'goodness' and 'commandment'. When we look at the violence that is commanded during the Conquest of Canaan as Paynter does, Christians are called to question justifications of violence because their worldly actions need to be in line with their major values.[80] Thus, Paynter's work illustrates how complicated the process of moral and textual alignment is for religious traditions, since Christians continually question the relevance of the biblical text as a model for their actions precisely because of their desire to create peace and critique historical and textual violence.

Interestingly, the individual chapters in this volume seem to shy away from defining 'violence' itself. Instead, the contributors are clearly not interested in essentializing violence in regard to sacred text, focusing rather on individual moments or traditions of violence. The reason for this, I think, is because any one definition of violence would not allow for the type of deep analysis of the texts and traditions in which they wish to engage. Moreover, one definition of violence would counteract many of the arguments that we see in this text overall. For instance, we can see three main threads running through the course of this volume: the ideas of connection, participation, and agency. That is, people who read sacred text need to connect to it, participate in interpreting it, and be allowed the agency to act with it. To define 'violence' in one way with regard to the multiple texts, multiple traditions, and multiple means of participating and acting with these texts and traditions would be to undermine these interconnected multiplicities and the ideas, ideals, and identities that are contingent upon them.

What, then, do these chapters help us understand about violence and its relation to sacred texts? The first point that comes to mind is that a sacred text's role in creating, sustaining, and critiquing an individual's and a community's worldview can be evaluated in terms of the individual's and community's response to violence because these responses are directly related to the desires, needs, and problems of these communities and individuals, and the critiques and evolution of ideas that adherents bring to the texts.

[79] Ibid., 128.
[80] Ibid., 140.

The chapters by Power, Brodbeck, Harvey, and Paynter are especially helpful in understanding this point. Second, the concepts of conversation and participation are vital to our topic because they show how individuals and communities look to sacred text to help them respond to violence in the past, present, and future contexts. Many of the contributors focus on the relevance of the place of sacred text in the lives of a tradition's adherents, most notably, Mittleman, Hammoud, Barua, and Dallh, in terms of the of the conversation, or relationship, that is formed between the reader and the text in this regard. The third point is how the sacred text is the basis of identity and thus becomes the foundation for innovation in dealing with aspects of violence, ideas that we found in Hegarty and Clenman. Finally, the major point that we saw throughout the volume is that there is a significant toll that is taken on all who either engage in, or are victim of, violence. No matter the context, divine/cosmic violence, human violence, protective/defensive violence, all types of violence affect the victims and the perpetrators, and all change as a result. How one judges these changes and effects is also a major factor in understanding this relationship, however, this is also a frustrating point because judgement is dependent on all the factors mentioned. Therefore, the main point that we can take away here is that the relationship between violence and sacred text itself continues to evolve and change.

Interreligious Dialogue and Violence

In August 1947, the International Council of Christians and Jews met in Seelisberg, Switzerland, to combat antisemitism and 'any form of hate movement [that] constitutes a menace, not only to the group against which it is immediately directed, but to the community as a whole, and [that is] a violation of the fundamental ethical principles of the Judaeo-Christian tradition upon which so much of all that [is] best in our western civilization depends'.[81] This emergency conference, as it was called then, was clearly a response to the atrocities of World War II. The Seelisberg Conference, as it is called now, became the foundation on which Jewish-Christian Relations in the western world was built for three main reasons. The first was that this conference was attended by sixty-five people from nineteen countries, thus establishing the international reach of the coun-

[81] ICCJ, *Reports and Recommendations of the Emergency Conference on Anti-Semitism*, (Seelisberg, 1947), 2.

cil's work, as most of the delegates were chosen precisely because of their abilities to influence decision-making processes. The second reason was that the conference delegates themselves were vitally moved by the conference not only because of the common goals of their work but also because of the fellowship that was created.[82] Finally, the most significant reason is because the Commission on 'The Task of the Churches' wrote a list of ten points about educating Christians on Judaism, commonly known as The Ten Points of Seelisberg, based on the work of Jewish historian Jules Isaac, a member of the Commission, which did indeed become foundational for Christian education on Judaism. These points, aimed at dismantling hateful and harmful Christian prejudices against Jews and Judaism, particularly Point 7,[83] focused on how Christian scripture had been weaponized against Jews and called for Christians to relook at its scriptural traditions in light of the violence that had been done to Jews and Judaism because of these past interpretations of the source material.

The 'return to scripture', or the movement of *Ressourcement*, which had already been operating in French Jewish-Catholic learning circles since the 1920's, also provided the intellectual grounding for this Commission, and then later for the work of the Roman Catholic's Second

[82] '[I]t was an interesting and moving experience to see the way in which, as the Conference proceeded, the common concern for the combating of a particularly dangerous form of hatred and intolerance, and the sense of a common task in seeking to promote, through educational means, a new spirit of understanding and co-operation between all [humans] of good-will who look for the establishment of a true and lasting peace, had the effect of binding the members together into a living fellowship.... It [may] take a very considerable time to carry into effect many of the recommendations set out... But the value and the success of the Conference are not to be asserted in those terms only. That it met at all is a fact of far-reaching significance. That its members learned to know and to respect each other as they did, is an achievement of which the value cannot be overestimated' (ICCJ, *Reports and Recommendations*, 6).

[83] 'Avoid presenting the Passion in such a way as to bring the odium of the killing of Jesus upon Jews alone. In fact, it was not all the Jews who demanded the death of Jesus. It is not the Jews alone who are responsible, for the Cross which saves us all reveals that it is for the sins of us that all that Christ died. Remind all Christian parents and teachers of the grave responsibility which they assume, particularly when they present the Passion story in a crude manner. By so doing they run the risk of implanting an aversion in the conscious of sub-conscious minds of their children or hearers, intentionally or unintentionally. Psychologically speaking, in the case of simple minds, moved by a passionate love and compassion for the crucified Saviour, the horror which they feel quite naturally towards the persecutors of Jesus will easily be turned into an undiscriminating hatred of the Jews of all times, including those of our own day' (ICCJ, *Reports and Recommendations*, 15).

Vatican Council on Jewish-Christian relations, which culminated in *Nostra Aetate*. As Celia Deutsch asserts, the movement sought 'to mine the past to renew a vision of the Church in relation to the contemporary world' by turning to history and to Jewish sources in order to respond to the needs of its community.[84] Jules Isaac, influenced by the ideas of the movement, would then use his studies on Christian Scripture as a way 'to gain a new perspective on modern issues',[85] leading to his groundbreaking work on Christian antisemitism in *Jesus and Israel: A Call for Necessary Corrections on Christian Teachings on the Jews* (1948). Moreover, Deutch points out, the personal relationships developed within the movement became a primary source of inspiration for its members. As people of different faiths and backgrounds came into contact with one another, they became influenced not only by the ways in which people responded to their scriptural traditions but also by the struggles and threats that the communities faced in everyday life,[86] leading members of the diverse group to later participate in the development of both the ICCJ and *Nostra Aetate*.

It is here, at the juncture of *Ressourcement*, the history of the ICCJ, the influence of *Nostra Aetate*, French Jewish-Catholic Dialogue, and the study of antisemitism in Christianity, that I find myself placed. While my academic work focuses mainly on Jewish responses to antisemitism in the academy, especially through the work of Hermann Cohen in the late eighteenth and early nineteenth centuries in Germany, my interest in Interreligious Dialogue actually began with my fascination with the writings of the German Jew Franz Rosenzweig as an undergraduate and I wrote my MA Thesis on Rosenzweig and Salvation Theories in the context of Jewish-Catholic Relations. As part of this work, I was introduced to the French Catholic order of the Congregation of Our Lady of Sion (more commonly known as the Sisters of Sion), an order that focuses on fostering Jewish-Christian Relations. Serendipitously, my academic appointment at the University of Saskatchewan in Saskatoon brought me right to the doorstep of the order as Saskatoon is the home of many sisters who were and are active in local and international levels of interreligious relations. During a workshop that I led on Jewish-Christian Reconciliation

[84] Celia Deutsch, 'Journey to Dialogue: Sisters of Our Lady of Sion and the Writing of Nostra Aetate,' *Studies in Christian-Jewish Relations,* 2016, vol. 11, no. 1, 1–36, 15.

[85] Cf. Richard Francis Crane and Brenna Moore, 'Cracks in the Theology of Contempt: The French Roots of Nostra Aetate,' *Studies in Christian-Jewish Relations,* 2013, vol. 8, no, 1, 1–28, 14.

[86] Deutsch, 'Journey to Dialogue,' 16.

for the Prairie Centre for Ecumenism in 2013, I met Sr. Donna Purdy, a Sister of Sion, who not only became a dear friend and mentor but who, along with Sr. Kay McDonald, later invited me to become associated with the order and become a member of the Roman Catholic Diocese of Saskatoon's Interfaith Commission, which she was serving on as Chair at that time. As fate would have it, Donald Bolen, the Roman Catholic Bishop of Saskatoon (2010–2016, now Archbishop of Regina), a member of the Pontifical Council for Promoting Christian Unity, and my Jesus of Nazareth professor, had previously invited me to begin work with him on creating a Scriptural Reasoning group in Saskatoon as both he and I were drawn to the process of Scriptural Reasoning, and I had participated in several Scriptural Reasoning groups since being introduced to the process in 2005. Unfortunately, we were unable to create a Scriptural Reasoning group as envisioned by Bishop Bolen. However, through my work with the Sisters of Sion and my interlapping relationships with other academic, religious, interreligious, and multifaith groups in Saskatoon, the practice of interreligious dialogue soon became central to my life. In 2017, I was appointed to the Congregational Jewish-Christian Development Team of the Sisters of Sion, and as part of our work, I was able to attend my first annual ICCJ meeting in 2018 in Budapest, Hungary.

My relationship with interreligious dialogue, which had begun as a fledgling academic interest, has thus become deeply ingrained into my personal life and religious journey. My interest and later participation in interreligious dialogue, which began as a way to combine my academic interests into a cohesive project (Modern Jewish Thought, Biblical Studies, and the way people interact with the world around them), became the means by which I learned about and developed my own religious identity as a Catholic woman strongly devoted to social justice issues. Thus, what has been my guiding research question—how do people enact what they 'believe'?—also guides my life's activities. Overall, my interest in interreligious dialogue stems from a deep desire to understand how and why people participate in worldly activities through using the values that they hold most dear. In regard to the work contained in this volume, I have come to a deeper understanding and appreciation of *why* people participate in interreligious dialogue. To explain how the contributors have expanded my theoretical and spiritual horizons, I seek to use their work as a lens through which I will look at two mainstays of my experience with interreligious work: Scriptural Reasoning and The Congregation of Our Lady of Sion.

Scriptural Reasoning, as an interreligious practice, 'names a method for studying Scriptures across the borders of any tradition'.[87] Peter Ochs, one of the co-founders of Scriptural Reasoning, explains that the purpose behind creating Scriptural Reasoning was two-fold: 'One of our goals was to find better methods for teaching religions by way of the study of Scripture and for teaching Scripture in a way that was enriched by both academic and traditional forms of commentary. Another goal was to find methods for peaceful encounter across religious traditions.'[88] The focus of the program, then, is to bring people of different faiths together, usually, but not limited to, Christianity, Judaism, and Islam, not only to discuss their individual and shared scriptural traditions but also to form interreligious friendships. As a practice, Scriptural Reasoning has become part of many peacebuilding endeavors worldwide as groups seek to use it as a way to mediate interreligious conflict.[89] Generally speaking, the process of Scriptural Reasoning begins by gathering together members of multiple religious traditions, who then focus on a common theme or communal issue by looking at short passages drawn from the different scriptural traditions that relate. Ideally, participants 'meet in small groups and one at a time, each passage of scripture is read out loud to the rest of the group. Others may never have come across it before so they give an "introduction," explaining a little of its context in the scripture and its importance in the faith tradition'.[90] After this small introduction and led by a facilitator, 'participants then discuss the passages one at a time—they may begin by asking questions to help them understand it better, or share a reflection or something that particularly strikes them as they hear it. In this way, an open and interactive discussion begins and the participants are able to reflect together on the possible meanings of the text'.[91]

Randi Rashkover, the scholar who introduced me to Scriptural Reasoning, explains how multiple traditions studying sacred texts together can create real change in the world in her article 'The Semiotics of Embodiment'. According to Rashkover, who focuses here on Jewish-Christian relations, studying differing views on sacred text and ideas about

[87] Peter Ochs, *Religion Without Violence: The Practice and Philosophy of Scriptural Reasoning* (Eugene, OR: Cascade Books, 2019), 1.

[88] Ibid., 1.

[89] Ibid., 1.

[90] 'What is Scriptural Reasoning?' Scriptural Reasoning, http://www.scripturalreasoning.org/what-is-scriptural-reasoning.html, accessed 8 May 2022.

[91] Ibid.

incarnation, which are based on the basic tenets of *ressourcement*, can foster Jewish-Christian relations by giving both sides of this dialogue access to each side's fundamental understandings of their own identities. So, why and how does studying sacred text together foster Jewish-Christian relations? Rashkover asserts that studying text together allows Jews and Christians to appreciate the commonalities in their exegetical practices, eliminates misconceptions about the other, and allows people to come 'together to embark on the important work of celebrating the work of God's creative Word within the material world'.[92] As is often argued within the field of interreligious dialogue, finding a way to read scripture together not only involves mutually enriching dialogue with and the accepting of the other but more importantly, finding oneself in the other,[93] as we have seen earlier in this chapter through the work of Jules Isaac and can see in the many testimonials of members of Scriptural Reasoning.[94] Accordingly, comparing modes of one tradition's scriptural study with that of another during interreligious scriptural study can lead either to, or begin with, one side finding itself in the other. Thus, as the basis of her argument, Rashkover points out that looking at the scriptural hermeneutics of other traditions allows one insight not only into others but also into one's own tradition. Therefore, she seeks to 'highlight the eucharistic character of rabbinic hermeneutics and the rabbinic character of Christian hermeneutics'[95] in Jewish and Christian scriptural practices to show how Jews can find themselves in Christian texts and how Christians can find themselves in Jewish texts.

When relating interreligious dialogue back to the idea of real-world change, Rashkover's work, along with the description of Scriptural Reasonings' process, is helpful here because, as she and they note, when we come to the text, we are bringing with us the 'things' that matter to us. That is, our embodied self (with links to the divine through both the Torah in Judaism and through the incarnation of Jesus for Christians) has desires and needs that must be met. When we take those needs to sacred texts, readings of which have changed over time (as we have seen through

[92] Rashkover, 'The Semiotics of Embodiment,' paragraph 33.

[93] Cf. Leonard Swidler, 'The Dialogue Decalogue: Ground Rules for Interreligious Dialogue,' *Inter-Religio*, 1984, vol. 5. 30–33; Mary C. Boys, *Has God Only One Blessing?: Judaism as a Source of Christian Self-Understanding* (New York, NY: Paulist Press, 2000).

[94] 'Testimonials,' Scriptural Reasoning, http://www.scripturalreasoning.org/testimonials.html, accessed 8 May 2022.

[95] Rashkover, 'The Semiotics of Embodiment,' paragraph 1.

the work of the contributors of this volume, mostly in the work of Mittleman, Hammoud, and Barua on text as well as Power and Brodbeck on incarnation), people feel empowered to act in their own contexts because they can take part in the process of re-creation through the idea of incarnation.[96] If we take this idea of incarnation seriously, our embodiment is a gift, and as Rashkover asserts, the desires and the materiality of our existence can be 're-situated amidst plentitude and grace and merges with gratitude, worship and joy'.[97] Thus, the relationship that exists and changes between the community, sacred text, and the leaders/authorities/scholars of the community becomes ever more important as the community as a whole is called to renew itself (as we saw in Clenman, Paynter, Hegarty, Harvey, and Dallh).

The transformative powers of interreligious dialogue come from confronting deep questions of human existence, which most often come from experiences of deep suffering. Thus, we delve into the hard texts because they are the texts that speak to us the most. Jill Jacobs, a Jewish rabbi who focuses on using sacred text in social justice work, explains that when groups in conflict look at sacred texts, these texts can cut through stalemates, and even if members of a group disagree, 'each has become more sympathetic to the other side and better able to see the nuance of the debate. Instead of vilifying the other, the two now can have a conversation about their differences'.[98] Moreover, sacred texts 'do contain significant wisdom about human nature, strategies for human relations, and descriptions of how a more ideal world might function'.[99] Being open to what a text has to say to us means that we might be able to see how past communities have dealt with problems. As Jacobs also notes, even if one generation solves a problem, the possibility always remains that that same problem can 'resurface in another generation',[100] therefore going 'back to the sources' provides present answers. Confronting real-world issues is thus an integral part of interreligious dialogue because it not only helps with the problems themselves but also because through building relationships, a wider support network becomes available to all participants, and

[96] Rashkover, 'The Semiotics of Embodiment,' paragraph 14.

[97] Ibid.

[98] Jill Jacobs, *Where Justice Dwells: A Hands-On Guide to Doing Social Justice in Your Community* (Woodstock, VT: Jewish Lights Publishing, 2011), 148–9.

[99] Ibid., 149.

[100] Jill Jacobs, *There Shall Be No Needy: Pursuing Social Justice through Jewish Law and Tradition* (Woodstock, Vermont: Jewish Lights Publishing, 2009), 16.

the relationships built can have a profound effect on all participants involved.

The transformations that result from interfaith interactions can be seen in the history of the Congregation of Our Lady of Sion. Theodore Ratisbonne, a Jewish convert to Catholicism, founded the Congregation of the Sisters of Our Lady of Sion in France in 1843. He founded the Congregation in part due to his belief that God's love for the Jewish people as shown in scripture needed to be enacted in the Christian world.[101] As the Sisters of Sion's understanding of their own mission and vocation changed through their interactions with Jewish people, especially during the Shoah as they participated in French Resistance movements by sheltering Jewish people, later during their behind-the-scenes participation in the passing of *Nostra Aetate*, and through their work at Ein Kerem in Israel, they rewrote their Congregation's Constitution, which was passed in 1984. The changes the Congregation went through shifted their original emphasis from educating Jewish children to undertaking their own education on Judaism. For instance, they emphasized that their work and teaching required a strong foundation on Judaism that could only be achieved by investing in their own education,[102] an awareness of which had already been present much earlier.[103] In educating themselves about Judaism and the Jewish people, the Sisters of Sion were clearly influenced by the *ressourcement* movement of the 1920's and 1930's that sought to find answers within the sources of the Church.[104] Thus, their mindfulness of the need for further education grew even more, and they called for lectures, publications, dialogue groups, and international encounters between Jews and Christians.

The education that the Sisters of Sion undertook, along with their interest in *Nostra Aetate*, allowed them to bring new words to their changing understanding of their identity. In building on their experience, their mission and work fundamentally changed how they, and the Church, saw themselves in relation to other world religions, and Judaism in particular. The rewriting of their Constitution, for instance, expressed 'a

[101] Congregation of Our Lady of Sion. *Constitution and Norms of Application* (Printed privately, 1984), 2. Hereafter noted as Constitution.

[102] Charlotte Klein, 'From Conversion to Dialogue—the Sisters of Sion and the Jews: a Paradigm of Catholic-Jewish Relations?' *Journal of Ecumenical Studies*, 1981, vol. 18, no. 3, 388–400, 395.

[103] Deutsch, 'Journey to Dialogue,' 19.

[104] Ibid., 15.

self-understanding radically different from their 1874 version' of their Constitution.[105] At the same time, their work on *Nostra Aetate* illustrates the real-world implications of interreligious dialogue. The Sisters of Sion, then, not only hoped to increase their knowledge and relationships with the Jewish people because this was their mission but also for the benefit of the entire Catholic church.[106] As the education that they undertook as part of their congregational mission allowed them to learn more about contemporary Judaism, so too did it allow them to bring a renewed knowledge of the Jewish beginnings of Christianity in liturgy, scripture, and theology. Together, their knowledge of Judaism, along with their relationships with Jewish people, drove the Sisters of Sion to become highly trained in biblical and theological scholarship on Judaism. This knowledge, in turn, propelled them to become involved with the promulgation of *Nostra Aetate*. Cardinal Augustin Bea, for instance, confirmed the Sisters of Sion's mission and vocation when he spoke to the Congregation on November 13, 1965: 'The Declaration [*Nostra Aetate*] is a program for the future, a program for all, but above all for you, Sisters of Our Lady of Sion. Now your task is given to you by the Church herself.'[107] As a result of their knowledge and mission, then, the Sisters of Sion were asked to take charge of implementing aspects of *Nostra Aetate* 4 and founded SIDIC (Service Internationale de Documentation Judéo-Chrétienne/ International Service for Jewish-Christian Documentation) in order to do so.[108] Their work on Jewish-Christian relations, then, has become a major part of the Congregation's identity, and these changes to their identity were enabled through their continued education on sacred texts and their attention to the implications of real-world interactions.

Conclusion

The contributors to this book have taught us some fundamentally important lessons on the connections between sacred text, traditions of textual interpretation, history, and contexts of violence. The contributors have demonstrated for us that flexibility is key to taking these topics seriously,

[105] Boys, *Has God Only One Blessing?*, 21.

[106] Our Lady of Sion, Constitution, 1; Klein, 'From Conversion to Dialogue,' 389.

[107] Congregation of Our Lady of Sion, 'History,' (Printed privately, 1984), 12.

[108] For a detailed history of Sisters of Sion's involvement in the writing and history of *Nostra Aetate*, cf. Deutsch, 'Journey to Dialogue,' 4–8.

as their work, grounded in the traditions themselves, illustrates how viewing these traditions from multiple vantage points allows religious adherents their own ways to enter into the discussions on religion and violence. More importantly, the contributors show us how we are constantly drawn to violence because it is in the structure of our experience, whether cosmological, historical, political, social, or scriptural. There is a danger in thinking that we only have one structure available to us in thinking about these problems, and here is where the flexibility of the contributors' work is most illuminating, as there is always more than one answer. And this is where peace comes in: Peace is the 'out' of the cycle, the ability to do something different, the ability to change, and the ability to take responsibility for past actions in order to heal.

Index[1]

A
Abraham, 53, 62, 129
Abrogation, 169, 170, 177, 180–181, 184
Ad Dharm, 47
Advice, 25, 27, 97, 101, 102, 121, 172
Africa
  Africans, 197
  sub-Saharan, 5, 194, 195, 197, 201
  West, 188, 194–197, 202–204, 250
Ahiṃsā, 22, 23, 35, 36, 44, 230
Ai, 137
Alī, 167
All-India Hindu Mahasabha, 41
All-India Muslim League, 40
Amalek/ites, 49, 53, 67, 69, 69n39, 70, 126
Ammonites, 126, 127
Ancestors, 12, 16, 25–27, 103, 204
Anger, 26, 57, 59, 66, 96, 102, 109, 219, 241, 250
Animal, 11–13, 23, 35, 36, 41, 50, 57, 58, 67, 79n15, 105, 109, 111, 121, 230
Antisemitism, 238, 255, 257
Arahat, 104, 105, 107
Arjuna, 17, 19, 21–24, 28, 32, 36, 45
Arthaśāstra, 14, 15
Arya Samaj, 40, 41, 47
Aśoka/Ashoka, 22, 100, 104
Aśvamedha, 35
Atraharsis Epic, 120
Attachment to views, 97
Avatāra, 18, 33
Ayodhya, 48

B
Babylonian Talmud, 74, 75, 79n14, 82n27, 89–91
Bavli, 75, 78n13, 86, 86n38, 89–92, 91n50, 91n51, 92n53

[1] Note: Page numbers followed by 'n' refer to notes.

M. Power, H. Paynter (eds.), *Violence and Peace in Sacred Texts*,
https://doi.org/10.1007/978-3-031-17804-7

Beit Din (Jewish Rabbinical Court), 79–82, 84, 85, 88–92
Benedict XVI, 161
Ben-Menahem, Haninah, 90, 91n50
Berkowitz, Beth, 76, 77, 77n10, 80n20, 84, 93
Bhagavadgītā/Bhagavad gītā, 9n1, 16, 19, 21, 22, 28, 31, 32, 36, 44, 45, 113
Bhai Vir Singh, 226
Bhīma, 23
Biblical, law, 63, 90, 91n50
Bodhisattva, 101–103, 109, 111, 113
Bollywood, 228, 231–234
Boon, 18
Brahman, 10, 34
Brahmin, 10–12, 16, 32–34, 37, 110, 111, 224n30
Buddha-nature, 113, 114
Buddhism, 4, 22, 95–117, 240, 249, 250

C
Cain and Abel, 54
Cakravartin, 99, 113
Caliph, 168, 203n49, 207
Caliphate, 5, 194, 208
Canaan, conquest of, 70, 124, 126–140, 254
Canaanites, 49, 56, 66–71, 67n32, 128, 129, 135, 138
Canonical, 6, 193, 212
Catholic social teaching, 5, 144, 145, 149, 157–160, 161n77, 246
Cattle/cows, 13, 16, 41, 43, 87, 206
Chastity, 12, 13, 23
Chatterjee, Bankim Chandra, 40
Chatterjee, Tarinicharan, 38
China, 95, 96, 113, 114
Christian Realism, 147–150
Christocentric hermeneutic, 131
Class (social), 14
Colonial/ization, 3, 30, 35–39, 48, 50, 106, 108, 126, 188, 194, 195, 202, 203, 205n54, 208, 225, 226
Communalisation, 108
Comparative hermeneutical approaches, 3
Compassion, 71, 96, 109, 161, 219, 256n83
Compulsion, 88, 171, 178, 182, 183
Conciliation, 20
Congregation of Our Lady of Sion (Sisters of Sion), 257, 258, 262
Cover, Robert, 76–78, 84, 88, 93, 94

D
Dasam Granth, 6, 216–222
Death penalty, 58, 60, 61, 75, 77, 80n20, 83
Dehumanising/dehumanisation, 13
Deification, 12
Dei Verbum, 147
Delusion, 96
Demons, 18, 33, 43, 48
Deuteronomy, book of, 56, 68, 69, 71, 128
Development (economic), 159
Devotion/devotional, 28, 208, 211, 212, 216, 218, 220, 223, 227, 253
Dhammapada, 96, 250
Dharma, 4, 19, 22, 31–37, 42, 44
Dharma/Dhamma, 17, 100, 102, 111–113, 116, 249
Dharmaśāstra, 11, 14
Dicing, 20, 23
Dissention, 14
Divine law, 62
Divine plan/divine context, 19, 23, 27
Divino Afflante Spiritu, 146

Doubt, 56n10, 65, 97, 107, 205, 223
Draupadī, 19, 20, 23
Due process, legal, 81, 251
Duryodhana, 20, 22, 24
Duṭṭhagāmaṇī, 104–108, 107n50

E
Earth, 17, 19, 20, 28, 33, 72, 120, 122, 129, 168, 171, 183, 217
Eastern Buddhism, 96
Eden, 120
Emirate, 200, 208
Enlightenment, 38, 64, 215
Equanimity, 97
Eschatological battle, 133
Ethics, 35, 55, 72, 100, 102, 104, 107, 122, 139, 190
Ethnic, 71, 98, 103, 107n50, 108, 198–205, 234
Euthyphro problem, 71
Evangelii Gaudium, 161n77
Exile, 17, 18, 20

F
Fenech, Louis, 226, 227
Fire, 11, 12, 25, 26, 61, 124, 135, 219
'Five K's,' 217
Flood, 121
Francis, 143, 149, 155, 161n77, 161n81
Fratelli Tutti, 144n1, 149, 149n32, 161n81
Fratricide, 54, 245

G
Gandhi, Mahatma, 35, 36, 43–46, 249
Gaudium et Spes, 154n53, 155, 160
Gender, 10, 12, 13, 27, 32, 35, 120, 121, 226
Generosity/giving, 11, 71, 96, 97, 147
Genesis, 54, 56, 89, 120, 121, 123, 134, 244, 244n20, 245
Genocide, 53, 67, 70, 129
Gift/s, 11, 14, 20, 201, 213, 261
Girard, René, 241, 242, 242n8, 244
God-sanctioned, 188
Godse, N.V., 46
Golwalkar, M.S., 44, 46
Government, 11, 37, 39, 40, 46, 103, 108, 114, 116, 122, 181
Governor-General Ellenborough, 50
Greed, 45, 96, 97, 216
Gur-bīlās literature, 222, 223
Guru Gobind Singh, 209, 212, 217–221, 223, 228
Guru Granth Sāhib (GGS), 6, 211–217, 221, 230–232, 235
Guru Nānak, 210, 211, 214, 214n9, 216, 218, 221, 228, 252

H
Hadith/hadīth, 169, 170, 192, 193
Halakhah (Jewish law, religious), 76
Halhed, N.B., 37
Hanbali, 192
Harivaṃśa, 17
Hastings, Warren, 37
Hate/hatred, 42, 45, 96, 97, 99, 255, 256n82, 256n83
Hausaland, 194, 197, 200, 203, 204
Heaven, 12, 80, 87, 91, 91n51, 104, 105
Hedgewar, K.B., 44
Hell, 110, 111
Ḥerem, 67, 68, 69n37, 69n38, 70, 71, 134, 134n70, 137, 138

Hindrances, five, 97
Hindu/Hinduism, 3, 9, 10, 22, 29–51, 100, 103, 112, 113, 214, 225, 226, 230, 231, 234, 248, 249
Hindutva, 46, 50
Horse sacrifice, 17, 25, 27
Household/householder, 11, 32
Human flourishing, 120, 152, 153, 155, 156, 160
Humans/humanity, 4, 5, 13, 17–21, 27, 28, 33, 35, 36, 40, 44, 45, 48, 51, 54, 57, 61–63, 64n26, 66–69, 71, 79n15, 86, 87, 89–92, 91n51, 96, 105, 107, 113, 117, 120, 122, 123, 124n37, 130, 131, 133, 145n5, 150–154, 156–160, 161n77, 166, 177, 178, 181–184, 190, 237, 238, 242, 244, 245, 247–250, 252, 253, 255, 256n82, 261
Ḥusayn, 5, 168
Husband, 20, 125, 125n42, 232

I

Icchantika, 110–112
Idolatrous city, 56
Idolatry, 61, 62, 69n38, 71, 128
Imam, 5, 167–169, 175, 185, 207
Imāmāh, 167, 168
Imam shafa'i, 191
Incarnation, 33, 34, 155, 162, 247, 248, 260, 261
Indian Army, 225, 233
Indian National Congress, 40
Indra, 13, 17, 19, 25, 26
International Council of Christians and Jews (ICCJ), 238, 255, 257, 258
Interpretation, rabbinic, 55, 58n15
Interreligious dialogue, 237–264
Isaac, Jules, 256, 257, 260
Isaiah, book of, 81, 81n24, 122
Islam
  Islamic, 5, 43, 50, 168, 169, 175, 177, 188, 189, 191, 193–198, 201–206, 208, 250
  Islamization, 203
Israel, ancient nation of, 126
Israel, Land of, 69, 69n38
Itihāsa, 18

J

Jackson, Bernard, 77, 77n11, 78, 78n13, 80, 83, 84, 86, 87n40, 88, 88n44, 90n49, 91n50
Jacobs, Jill, 261
Jainism, 22
Janamejaya, 16, 17, 23–28, 248
Janam Sākhī literature, 214, 214n9
Japan, 96, 99, 112, 114, 116, 143, 151
Jātakas, 101, 103
Jesus Christ, 121n17, 131–133, 138
Jewish-Christian relations, 255–257, 260, 263
Jihad/jihād
  armed, 5, 188–190, 194, 195, 197, 208
  defensive, 167, 174, 175, 177, 179
  greater, 188, 192–193
  lesser, 188, 192–193
  martial, 188, 189, 191, 250
  offensive, 167, 174, 175, 177, 179, 183–185
  spiritual, 188
Jōdo-shin, 116
John XXIII, 151, 155n55, 158, 161
John Paul II, 149n32, 152, 153
Joshua, 70, 71, 124, 126–128, 134–138, 135n73, 140
Judaism, rabbinic, 64, 74, 74n2
Jurisgenesis, 76, 84, 93

Jus ad Bellum, 147–150
Jus in Bello, 150–153
Justice, procedural, 56, 61
Justice, substantive, 61
Justification for war, 15, 19
Just Peace, 5, 144, 146, 154–162, 246, 247
Just War, 5, 147–150, 153–155, 162

K

Kali Yuga, 33, 214–216, 220, 235
Kanem-Borno, 198
Karet, 4, 55, 56, 58n15, 60, 65, 70, 74–79, 74n2, 75n3, 77n10, 77n11, 79n17, 80n18, 80n20, 82, 84, 89–93, 91n50, 92n53, 92n54, 245, 251, 252, 260
Karma/karmic, 98–100, 105, 109–111
Karṇa, 22, 24
Kathir ibn, 192
Kauravas, 16, 17
Kauṭilya, 14, 15
Kāvya, 18
Kesari, film, 231–234
Khalsa, 217, 218, 220, 223, 224, 226–228, 230
Kingdom of God, 123, 148, 155, 158, 160
King/kingship, 11, 13–18, 20–24, 26–28, 30, 33, 48, 64, 99–102, 104, 105, 107, 108, 110, 122, 139
  See also Monarchical
Kippah (rabbinic prison cell), 4, 74–94, 251, 252
Kṛṣṇa, 16–19, 21, 23, 24, 28, 32, 36, 50
Kṣatriya/kshatriya, 10, 11, 14, 15, 17, 21–23, 32
Kumārila, 35
Kurukṣetra, 16, 17, 19, 21–25, 27

L

Levite's concubine, 53–54
Leviticus, book of, 120
Liturgy, 11, 211, 263
Lotus Sūtra, 116
Loving kindness, 96
Luke, gospel of, 161

M

Mahābhārata/Mahā-bharata, 3, 9–28, 31, 38, 46, 100, 214, 219, 220, 247, 248
Mahā-parinirvāṇa Sūtra, 110–116
Mahāvaṃsa, 103–109
Mahāyāna, 96, 109–113, 116, 117, 249
Mahmud of Ghazni, 42, 50
Maimonides, Moses, 55n7, 57–59, 61–65, 63n23, 64n26, 69n38, 70, 79n14
Mamluk, 192
Manu, 11
Manu-smṛti, 100
Māra, 112
Marabout, 195, 196
Marcion, 131, 131n60, 132
Martial race, 225, 226, 233
Martyr/Martyrdom, 5, 6, 168, 190, 191, 209–235, 252
Masculinity, 13, 14, 27, 46
Mather, Cotton, 126–127
Meccan, 170–172, 191
Mendelssohn, Moses, 64–66
Merneptah Stela, 134
Messenger/envoy, 15
Military, 13, 49, 69, 102, 115, 151, 152, 168, 184, 188n3, 192, 193, 197, 198, 213, 214, 216, 225, 231
Mindfulness/mindful, 96, 97, 262
Mishna, 74, 74n2, 75, 77–80, 80n18, 80n20, 82, 82n27, 82n28, 85, 86, 87n41, 89, 90, 91n51, 93
Mleccha, 32–34, 42

Modernity, 29–51, 63, 66, 214, 235
Monarchical, 10
See also King/kingship
Mongol, 192
Moonje, B.S., 41
Moral injury, 152, 152n42
Morley-Minto Reforms, 39
Moses, 59–62, 124
Mountbatten, Lord, 45
Mughal Empire, 253
Muhammad, 167–169, 171–173, 176, 178, 184, 185, 191, 192
Mukerji, U.N., 39
Murderer, 4, 58n15, 78, 81n21, 82, 82n28, 84–90, 89n47, 90n49, 91n50, 123
Murderer, serial, 82, 83, 88
Muslim, 29–44, 46–48, 50, 51, 103, 126, 166, 168, 170–172, 176–179, 184, 189n7, 191–194, 196, 197n32, 198–201, 203–205, 203n49, 205n54, 207, 216, 224, 234, 239, 248, 251
Muṭahharī, Murtaḍa, 170, 175, 179–183, 246
Myth/mythology/mythological, 2, 11, 19, 20, 27, 28, 32, 54, 120, 201, 205n54, 220, 242

N
Nachmanides, Moses, 57–59, 69n38
Naskh, 169, 170
Nationalism, 4, 31, 38, 108, 109, 117
Negotiation, 14, 109
New Jerusalem, 123
Nichiren, 116
Nijhawan, Michael, 222, 228
Noachide Laws, 57, 58
Nomos, legal, 84, 85, 87
Non-violence, 46, 100, 109, 122, 124
Northern Buddhism, 96
Nostra Aetate, 257, 262, 263

O
Ochs, Peter, 259
Offender, 60, 80, 82, 83, 89, 93
Origen of Alexandria, 127
Orthodox/orthodoxy, 3, 10, 194, 196, 198, 206
Orthopraxis, 193
Overpopulation, 19

P
Pacem in Terris, 161
Pacifism, 153–154, 166, 187
Palestine, 134
Palestinian Talmud, 89
Pali Canon, 95, 103, 112–113, 249
Pāṇḍavas, 16, 17, 20, 22, 24
Paul, the apostle, 122
Paul VI, 155, 158, 162
Persecution, 190, 242
Pharisaic, 87n40
Philosophy/philosophical, 3, 11, 12, 64, 96, 130, 169, 203, 240
Political, 2, 5, 23, 30, 31, 38–40, 49, 50, 63, 65, 69, 98, 99, 106, 108, 109, 114, 148, 149, 155, 168, 175, 187, 191, 194–197, 194n23, 200–202, 204, 205, 208, 213, 216, 217, 222, 233, 234, 238, 244, 249–252, 264
Polyphony, 136
Polyvalent, 188–193, 250
Pratap, Maharana, 44
Precepts, five ethical, 96, 249
Priest, 10, 13, 25, 32–34, 80, 91n51, 111, 116
Priest, Jewish (Cohanim), 10, 13, 25, 32–34, 80, 80n19, 80n20, 91n51, 111, 116

Prisoners of war, 139
Protection, 20, 41, 115, 117, 219, 249, 251
Proverbs, book of, 121
Punishment
  belly exploding, 81, 82
  capital, 53, 60, 65, 75, 77, 77n11, 80, 82–85, 87, 88n44, 89, 90
  force-feeding, 81, 82
  Kippah (imprisonment), 75, 76, 78n13, 79–88, 90–94, 251, 252
  lashes (rabbinic), 82
  measure-for-measure (Talion), 85, 86
  non-standard, 80, 84
  starvation, 75, 79, 80
Purāṇas, 31, 33, 34

Q

Qadiri, 188, 194
Qur'ānic, 165–186, 190, 245
Quran/Qur'ān, 166, 167, 169–174, 176, 179, 180, 185, 186, 190–192, 246

R

Rahab, 138
Rahit Nāma literature, 223
Rāhula, Walpola, 106, 107
Rāma, 17–21, 23–27, 43, 48, 50, 219, 248
Rāmāyaṇa, 3, 9–28, 31, 43, 219, 220, 247, 248
Rām-līlā, 42, 43
Rape, 53, 56, 59, 125, 152, 242
Rashi, 56, 60, 92n54
Rashkover, Randi, 238, 259–261
Rashtriya Svayamsevak Sangh (RSS), 44
Rāvaṇa, 16, 18–20, 23, 25–27, 43
Rebirth, 34, 98, 105, 111, 230
Recidivist, 4, 82, 83, 85–88, 91–93, 92n54
Redemptive trajectories, 139
Reform, 71, 188, 194–199, 202–204, 206, 207, 226, 228, 250
Refuser (of rabbinic legal warnings), 4, 82n28, 85–87
Religious law, Jewish, 76
Religious Studies, 239–241
Reputation, 27, 101
Responsibility to protect, 145, 149, 247, 248
Ressourcement, 256, 257, 260, 262
Revelation, book of, 123
Revival, 188, 194–199, 201–205, 250
Ṛgveda, 13
Rhetoric, battle of Ancient Near East, 135
Righteous war, 15
  See also Just War
Rite/ritual, 10, 11, 13, 16, 21, 23, 25, 31, 33, 36, 47, 48, 80, 80n19, 116, 165, 217, 230
Rome, empire of, 123
Rules of conduct, 15

S

Sabbath, violation of, 59–62, 65
Sacrifice/sacrificial, 11–13, 17, 21, 23, 25, 27, 31, 34, 35, 41, 43, 50, 64n26, 67, 71, 215, 229, 232, 242
Sālehī-Najafābādī, Ne'matollāh, 175, 183–185
Śaṃkara, 34, 35

Samurai, 115
Sanctioned violence, 5–6, 209–235, 245, 252, 253
Saṅgha, 108, 113
Sanskrit, 9–11, 13, 30, 32, 33, 37, 42, 102, 210, 219, 248
Sant-sipahi, 209–235, 252
Savarkar, V.D., 42, 43, 46
Schlissel, Yishai, 75n3
Scriptural Reasoning, 6, 238, 258–260
Second Vatican Council, 144, 147, 151, 155, 162, 256–257
Self/non-Self, 3, 31, 34, 35, 42, 45, 50, 68, 113, 167, 189, 193, 260
Self-sacrifice, 123, 211, 212, 214–216, 218, 221, 222, 226, 230, 232, 233, 235, 252, 253
Senegambia, 196, 197
Sermon on the Mount, 5, 122, 160
Sexual violence, 124–126
Shāfiʿī, 185
Shalom, 120–123, 253
Shaykh, 198, 205
Shehu, 198, 199, 201, 205–207
Shi'a/shi'i/Shīʿī, 5, 165–186, 245, 246
Shīʿīsm, 167–169
Shingon, 116
Shivaji, 44
Shoah, 238, 262
Shōgun, 115, 116
Sikhi, 210, 211, 221
Sikhiwiki, 229–231
Sin, 25, 60, 61, 67, 68, 107, 107n50, 108, 159n74, 213, 219, 256n83
Singh, Puran, 228
Sīrah, 169, 170
Sītā, 17–20, 23, 25–27
Skill in means/skilful means, 109, 115
Slander, 111, 112
Slave trade, 195–197, 201
Snakes, 16, 24–27, 86
Southern Buddhism, 95
Spinoza, Benedict, 63–65
Sri Lanka, 95, 101, 103–109
State, 14, 31, 33, 35, 40, 44, 46, 63–65, 68, 80, 80n19, 86, 93, 95–97, 103, 106, 114, 115, 128, 134, 144, 149, 150, 159, 161n77, 171, 177–180, 182, 183, 192, 197, 198, 200–202, 204, 205, 208, 215–217, 223, 232–234, 250, 253
Storytelling, 243
Subjects (of king), 25–27, 34, 59, 75, 81, 87, 87n40, 91, 91n51, 92n54, 100, 103, 126, 131, 138, 140, 144, 148, 156n58, 159, 176, 200, 230, 240
Suffering, 17–19, 21–24, 34, 45, 97, 98, 109, 125, 153, 248, 261
Sufi, 5, 50, 187–190, 193, 195, 196, 198, 205, 208, 250
Sufism, 5, 187–208, 250, 251
Sui generis argument, 128–130
Sunnah, 191, 206
Sunni/Sunnī, 167, 168, 185, 193, 198
Swami Dayananda, 40
Sword, 7, 56–58, 115, 122, 127, 137, 170, 177, 179–181, 189, 190, 192, 218, 219, 228
Symbolic, 85, 196

T

Ṭabāṭabāʾī, 173, 175–178, 182, 184, 246
Tafsīr, 168, 175
Taint/stain, 20
Takṣaka, 24

Talion, law of, 55
Tannaitic (rabbinic), 74n2, 75, 77, 78, 78n13, 84, 85, 88–91, 88n44, 91n50, 91n51, 93
Targum, 90n49
Tat Khalsa, 226, 227
Teaching, 4, 5, 17, 18, 44, 46, 63, 75, 90, 91n51, 100, 104, 105, 107, 110, 112–114, 121, 127, 144–148, 150, 151, 153–155, 157–160, 162, 168, 185, 201, 204–206, 210, 211, 216, 241, 243, 246, 247, 249–252, 259, 262
Tendai, 114–117
Ten Points of Seelisberg, 256
Textual interpretation, 263
Theology, 5, 28, 31, 34, 131n60, 146, 167–169, 248, 263
Theomachy, 54
Theravāda, 95, 101, 103–109, 249
Tiantai, 114
Tolerance, 6, 49, 103, 109
Torah, 55, 62, 63, 64n26, 66, 72, 86, 89, 260
Tosefta, 74, 74n2, 75, 80n18, 81, 82, 82n28, 83n29, 84–87, 89, 92n54, 93
Tradition, 2, 3, 5, 6, 10, 14, 35, 37, 40, 55, 59, 60, 69n39, 70, 72, 74–76, 75n3, 78, 78n13, 80n18, 80n20, 83, 84, 88, 96, 134, 145–150, 160, 162, 166, 168, 169, 171, 183, 188, 191, 193, 203–205, 209–235, 237, 238, 240, 241, 245–247, 249, 251–257, 259, 260, 263, 264
Trible, Phyllis, 241–244, 244n20
Tughluq, Muhammad bin, 33

U
Udam Singh, 213
Unwholesome/unskilful, 96, 97
Upaniṣads, 31, 34, 35
Upāya-kauśalya Sūtra, 109–110
Usman dan Fodio, 5, 188, 194, 196–198, 197n32, 198n33, 203n49, 207, 208, 250

V
Vajrayāna, 96
Vālmīki, 10, 17, 18, 20, 21
Veda/Vedas/Vedic, 11–13, 31–35, 37, 38, 40–42, 47, 216, 249
Vengeance, 24, 59, 121, 122
Vigilante killing, 88
Violence, legal, 76–78
Violence towards women, 26
Viṣṇu, 17–19, 25, 28, 33, 34
Vyāsa, 10, 19, 28

W
War, commanded, 53, 68, 69
War, discretionary, 68
War, holy, 39, 51, 66, 66n30, 68, 70, 133, 166, 196
Warrior-knight, 115
Warrior monks, 114
War/warfare, 4, 9, 14–24, 22n45, 27, 33, 43, 46, 49, 54, 66n30, 67n32, 68–70, 69n38, 98–103, 107–109, 113, 124, 127, 129, 133, 134, 139, 140, 145, 147–156, 154n53, 161, 167, 168, 170, 171, 173–181, 183, 184, 188, 190, 191, 193, 196, 197, 199, 200, 203, 204, 207, 232, 238, 247, 248

Wife, 12, 17, 18, 23–27, 56, 101, 125, 209, 232
Wisdom, 40, 66, 97, 98, 121, 122, 150, 172, 218, 220, 261
Witnesses, 4, 6, 31, 60, 81–83, 82n28, 85–87, 88n44, 89, 90n49, 91n50, 93, 119, 136, 144, 145, 169
Witnesses, to murder, 83, 85, 86, 88n44
Witnessing, 18, 82, 87n40, 88, 91n50

Y

Yerushalmi, 75, 89, 90, 90n49, 91n50
Yoga/yogic, 24, 27, 35
Yudhiṣṭhira, 17, 18, 21–24, 27

Z

Zafarnama, 220, 221
Zealot, Jewish (*qanaim*), 79, 79n17, 80, 80n18, 80n20, 91, 93
Zen, 115

CPSIA information can be obtained
at www.ICGtesting.com
Printed in the USA
LVHW081327050323
740957LV00007B/1109

9 783031 178030